SH
EIGHT

The eighteenth century has long been acknowledged as a pivotal period in Shakespeare's reception, transforming a playwright requiring 'improvement' into a national poet whose every word was sacred. Scholars have examined the contribution of performances, adaptations, criticism and editing to this process of transformation, but the crucial role of fiction remains overlooked. *Shakespeare and the Eighteenth-Century Novel* reveals for the first time the prevalence, and the importance, of fictional characters' direct quotations from Shakespeare. Quoting characters ascribe emotional and moral authority to Shakespeare, redeploy his theatricality and mock banal uses of his words; by shaping in this way what is considered valuable about Shakespeare, the novel accrues new cultural authority of its own. Shakespeare underwrites, and is underwritten by, the eighteenth-century novel, and this book reveals the lasting implications for both their reputations.

KATE RUMBOLD is a Lecturer in English Literature at the University of Birmingham. She has published widely on the quotation and reception of Shakespeare, with particular focus on the eighteenth century, and is the co-author, with Kate McLuskie, of *Cultural Value in Twenty-First-Century England: The Case of Shakespeare* (2014).

SHAKESPEARE AND THE EIGHTEENTH-CENTURY NOVEL

Cultures of Quotation from Samuel Richardson to Jane Austen

KATE RUMBOLD

CAMBRIDGE
UNIVERSITY PRESS

CAMBRIDGE
UNIVERSITY PRESS

University Printing House, Cambridge CB2 8BS, United Kingdom

One Liberty Plaza, 20th Floor, New York, NY 10006, USA

477 Williamstown Road, Port Melbourne, VIC 3207, Australia

314-321, 3rd Floor, Plot 3, Splendor Forum, Jasola District Centre, New Delhi - 110025, India

79 Anson Road, #06-04/06, Singapore 079906

Cambridge University Press is part of the University of Cambridge.

It furthers the University's mission by disseminating knowledge in the pursuit of education, learning and research at the highest international levels of excellence.

www.cambridge.org
Information on this title: www.cambridge.org/9781107584891

First published 2016
First paperback edition 2018

A catalogue record for this publication is available from the British Library

Library of Congress Cataloging in Publication data
Rumbold, Kate Louise, 1978– author.
Shakespeare and the eighteenth-century novel : cultures of quotation from Samuel Richardson to Jane Austen / Kate Rumbold.
pages cm
Includes bibliographical references and index.
ISBN 978-1-107-13240-5 (Hardback : alk. paper) –
ISBN 978-1-107-58489-1 (Paperback : alk. paper)
1. Shakespeare, William, 1564–1616–Influence. 2. Shakespeare, William, 1564–1616–In literature. 3. English fiction–18th century–History and criticism. I. Title.
PR2976.R86 2015
822.3′3–dc23 2015023284

ISBN 978-1-107-13240-5 Hardback
ISBN 978-1-107-58489-1 Paperback

For my parents, and in memory of
Rose Frances Adlington

Contents

Illustrations

Acknowledgements

This book has its origins in a doctoral thesis at the University of Oxford, where I was fortunate to be supervised by Abigail Williams. Her generous and astute advice continues to inspire me. My thesis also benefited greatly in its early stages from the input of Emma Smith, Lucy Newlyn and Katharine Turner. The insightful comments of my examiners, Michael Dobson and Fiona Stafford, marked the first step in the transformation of my thesis into the book it is today.

My work has subsequently been enriched by my colleagues, mentors, friends and students at the University of Birmingham. At the Shakespeare Institute, Tara Hamling, Jaq Bessell and Kathryn Prince were a constant source of inspiration and cheer, and Kate McLuskie encouraged me to pursue this project alongside my post-doctoral duties. I have the early meetings of the Restoration and Eighteenth Century cluster in the Department of English to thank for years of friendship, mentorship and support from Hugh Adlington, Tom Lockwood, Anne McDermott, Sebastian Mitchell, Valerie Rumbold and Gillian Wright. I would like to thank the College of Arts and Law for the semester of study leave in 2013 that helped me to complete this project, and Ewan Fernie, Andrzej Gasiorek, Susan Hunston, Helen Laville and Michael Toolan for their guidance. I am deeply grateful for the friendship and compassion of all these colleagues, and Fiona Gilyead, Islam Issa, Rex Ferguson, Suganthi John, Luke Kennard, Dan Moore, Sophia Robertshaw, Will Sharpe, Karen Simecek, Erin Sullivan and Emily Wingfield.

My thanks to the staff of the Bodleian Library; the British Library; the National Art Library, London; the Houghton Library, Harvard University (especially Susan Halpert); the Folger Shakespeare Library and the Library of Congress, Washington DC; Columbia University Library and the New York Public Library, New York; the Cadbury Research Library, Birmingham (especially Martin Killeen) and the Shakespeare Institute Library. My visit to the Houghton Library was made possible by a Maxwell-Meyerstein Research Grant from the English Faculty, Oxford, and by the kind hospitality of Katie Ross and family; to the Folger Shakespeare Library, by a short-term fellowship, and the help of Carol Brobeck; and to Columbia University, by a visiting scholarship and the support of Jean Howard. I am grateful for a Universitas 21 fellowship to McGill University, Montreal, and the privilege of extended discussion there with Peter Sabor and Paul Yachnin.

I am grateful to the Bodleian, the British Library, the Folger and the Cadbury Research Library for permission to reproduce the images that appear in this book. 'Serena Reading' was acquired by George Romney's patron Lord Thurlow in the eighteenth century and has remained in his family ever since. I am especially grateful to Simon Cowley for permission to reproduce this beautiful image on the jacket.

I presented papers that would become part of this book at Britgrad, the Oxford English Graduate Conference, and at the conferences of the British Shakespeare Association, the Shakespeare Association of America, the British Society for Eighteenth-Century Studies, and the Canadian Society for Eighteenth-Century Studies, as well as the Ohio Valley Shakespeare Conference and the '1759' conference, Belfast. I was invited to present work at the Restoration to Reform seminar, Oxford, the English Graduate seminar, UCL, the Shakespeare Club, Stratford and the Université Paul Valéry Montpellier III, and I am grateful to my hosts, especially Helen Hackett and Nathalie Vienne-Guerrin, and to all those attending, for helping me to develop the project. Earlier versions of parts of this book have appeared in the journals *Borrowers and Lenders* and *Literature Compass* and in the essay collection *Reading 1759*, and I am grateful to the editors for permission to revisit that material here. I am grateful, too, to all those who have read drafts along the way, especially Tom Keymer, Julie Maxwell, Beth Palmer, Fiona Ritchie and Peter Sabor. In particular, I would like to thank Sally Baggott for scrutinising my draft manuscript and championing my work.

It has been a privilege and a pleasure to work with Linda Bree at Cambridge University Press. I am grateful for the kind assistance of Anna Bond, Ezhilmaran Sugumaran and Emma Collison, and for the excellent suggestions of my two anonymous readers at the press.

Over the years, my work has benefited from the generous collegiality of many scholars of Shakespeare, his reception, the early modern period and the eighteenth century, including Paula Backscheider, Linda Bree, Christie Carson, Geoff Day, Christy Desmet, Brean Hammond, Andy Kesson, Peter Kirwan, Elizabeth Kraft, Doug Lanier, Jean-Christophe Mayer, Jim

McLaverty, Kevin Petersen, Daniel Pollack-Pelzner, Clive Probyn, Shaun Regan, Christopher Ricks, Adam Rounce, Katherine Rowe, Marcus Walsh and Rene Weis. Special thanks to Alice Eardley, Alexandra Harris, Johanna Harris, Kathryn Holland, Beth Palmer, Elizabeth Scott-Baumann and Gillian Woods for wonderful inspiration and support.

For years of treasured friendship and unwavering support, I am thankful to Helen Brothwell, David and Danna Cuin, Helen Fina, Helen Forrest, Rob George, Emily Holden, Liz Sawyer, Bronwen Merner, Dawn Miller, Sarah Parkinson, Alice Welham, Danny Westgate and Nicky Yeeles. I appreciate more than ever friends in Seagrave: Gail Adams, Karen Bevans, Lyn Brown, John and Jan Dean, Sandy Lewis, Mary Thompson and Angela Wells.

Thanks to my family, including Sarah, Nick, Lauren, Bruce and Kim Tucker, Helena Dawes, Mike Kaiser, Michael and Judith Adlington, Rod, Anna, Toby, Lily and Monty Adlington, and newest honorary family members Jan-Michael Thomas and Alice McKenna, for their love and kindness.

I am most thankful for my beloved parents, Joanna and Ken Rumbold, and sister, Gemma Rumbold, and for their love, support, humour and encouragement. I am proud to be part of Team Rumbold, and grateful that many parts of this book were written at the kitchen table, fuelled by tea and the best company.

This book is dedicated to my parents, and to the memory of my daughter, Rose Frances Adlington. Rose graced our days in the final stages of writing this book, and she has enriched our lives in ways that we couldn't have imagined, not least by opening our eyes to the overwhelming love and support of colleagues, family and friends old and new. For helping me to appreciate all of this and for giving me courage, my deepest thanks are reserved for Hugh: strongest and dearest of companions, bringer of love and happiness, and toughest and best reader of the whole book.

CHAPTER 1

Introduction

> What a mind must *Shakespear* have possessed! what amazing powers! what divine illuminations!—I am astonished every time I think of him and cannot give utterance to the big idea I have of him—the best compliment we can pay our immortal bard must be in his own words,
>
> The poet's eye in a fine phrensy rolling
> Doth glance from heav'n to earth, from earth to heav'n,
> And as imagination bodies forth
> The form of things unknown, the poet's pen
> Turns them to shape, and gives to airy nothing
> A local habitation and a name.[1]

So says Mr Melville, a character 'of good sense, as well as an excellent scholar', to the eponymous hero of *The Amours and Adventures of Charles Careless* (1764), when he finds the latter 'reading one of *Shakespear*'s plays'.[2] For Robert Gale Noyes, author of the only previous book-length study of Shakespeare in eighteenth-century fiction (1953), Melville's observation supports the wider 'thesis that Shakespeare was virtually beyond criticism' at this point in the eighteenth century.[3] Examining 750 novels published between 1740 and 1780 for mentions of Shakespeare, Noyes assembles a 'testimony' about 'the drama, the stage, and Shakespeare', and credits the novel with doing a 'fundamentally sound job of reporting' Shakespeare's praise.[4] As his title, *The Thespian Mirror*, suggests, Noyes concludes that the novel reflects growing admiration for the playwright in the eighteenth century.

The words 'testimony' and 'reporting', like the '*Mirror*' of Noyes' title, are, however, signs of an earlier critical moment: as J. P. Hunter has noted, 'verbs such as "reflect," "mirror," "portray," and "picture," and their noun equivalents' have been supplanted as critical terms in recent years by the less passive concept of 'representation'.[5] For all his vivid examples, Noyes' 'mirror' metaphor threatens to relegate novel writers to the status of 'a recorder or photographic mechanism for preservation rather than the active agent *within* history as well as a scribe of it'.[6] Noyes sets out to consider the novels as a neglected 'body of criticism', but concludes only that they 'add jewels to Shakespeare's diadem of praise', passively echoing, rather than actively contributing to, Shakespeare's status.[7]

It is, however, in articulating the novel's reflective role that Noyes gestures to what it is, as this book argues, that the novel actually *does* do for Shakespeare:

> Almost every opinion they [the novelists] held can easily be duplicated in the non-fictional criticism, academic or journalistic, of their times. But to say this is not to admit that study of their Shakespearean passages is without value, for their testimony adds to the sum total of what is already known, and their lively presentation affords much pleasure. Their manner, indeed, rather than their critical ideas, is important, for here, virtually, we have criticism in action. Their expression of opinions about Shakespeare is livelier, more dramatic, more humorous, more emotional, and hence more readable, than that of their soberer contemporaries.[8]

Noyes suggests that, while the novels are largely derivative in their attitudes to Shakespeare, 'their manner' is more important than their 'ideas'. For him, the novelists' lively, dramatic, humorous, emotional and readable treatment of Shakespeare makes received critical ideas accessible to a wide audience.

By contrast, I argue that the novelists' lively, dramatic, humorous and emotional handling of Shakespeare's words is not a mere conduit of received ideas: it *constructs* Shakespeare's value in the eighteenth century. His words are not merely admired by numerous characters – from educated 'scholars' like Mr Melville in *Charles Careless* to fashionable men and women – but *applied* to their 'emotional' situations. In the process, these words accrue new authority. Shakespeare's theatricality is absorbed into, and legitimated by, the characterisation techniques of prose fiction; through the 'humorous' misquotation of Shakespeare by aspiring individuals, novels instil in their readers a new literary judgement. The novels help to *make* Shakespeare 'a living issue, worth arguing and fighting over'.[9] Noyes tends to record commentary on Shakespeare rather than quotations, but it is quotation – and, in particular, quotation by character – that is crucial to establishing Shakespeare's status. Performances and editions of Shakespeare's plays would contribute to his growing reputation in this century; and the extracts of his words in anthologies and periodicals would familiarise readers with his speeches,[10] but novels in particular will help to construct Shakespeare not just as an 'immortal bard', but, as Melville says, as '*our* immortal bard', through snippets of 'his own words'.

Shakespeare's 'own words' are a major presence in the eighteenth-century novel, and novelists punctuate their pages with direct quotation. Other English authors such as John Milton, John Dryden, Thomas Otway, Abraham Cowley, Nathaniel Lee, Nicholas Rowe and more besides are also quoted in fiction; and the classics, the Bible and other proverbs and sayings feature frequently too. But all of these sources pale into insignificance next to Shakespeare: first, for his ubiquity; second, for the range of characters who invoke him; and third, for the warmth with which they do so. Overt quotation by characters is especially abundant in the work of mid-century novelists such as Samuel Richardson, Henry Fielding, Sarah Fielding and Laurence Sterne (who collectively quote Shakespeare nearly 200 times in their fiction alone), as well as many lesser-known or anonymous authors. This formal practice, in which an indented or italicised quotation briefly interrupts the flow of the narrative, can appear a stylistic oddity: a sign of a discrete period in literary history between the 1740s and 1760s when everyone invoked Shakespeare. This distinctive kind of intertextuality, however, would boost the cultural status of Shakespeare and the novel, and influence significantly the narrative techniques of later fiction.

Shakespeare and the novel: all rise?

It would be easy to assume that cultural status was all Shakespeare's to bestow. At mid-century, novels 'remained a dubiously respectable form, perhaps partly because women wrote and read so many of them'.[11] By the time Samuel Richardson's *Pamela* was published in November 1740, eliciting both critique and praise and unleashing 'a market-led multiplication of lowbrow print',[12] the 'immortal Shakespeare' had become a staple of the London stage, his complete works celebrated in at least three eighteenth-century editions, and his person shortly to be represented in a marble statue in Poet's Corner, Westminster Abbey, erected '124 years after [his] death by public esteem'.[13] Shakespeare's promotion to the status of England's national poet was well underway – a process, as major accounts of this period attest, achieved by the appropriation of Shakespeare's plays to new political and cultural interests, as a side-effect of a project to further national interests in foreign wars, and by the gradual promotion of his every line as sacred.[14] By quoting Shakespeare (as *Pamela* does once, and subsequent novels do on numerous occasions), mid-century prose fiction appears to align itself with a vernacular literary tradition, and to borrow the authority of this august literary figure.

Yet 'Shakespeare' at mid-century was not a securely legitimating name, even after the theatrical vogue for 'improving' his plays through adaptation had been replaced with textual reverence. Samuel Johnson's Preface to his edition of Shakespeare still censured the playwright for his 'loosely formed' plots, his disregard for 'time or place', his fondness for the 'quibble' and the 'conceit', and, above all, for his apparent ability to 'write without any moral purpose': a failure of writerly duty that even the 'barbarity of his age' could not excuse.[15] Recent critics have begun to ask 'What did Shakespeare do to the eighteenth century?' as well as 'What did the eighteenth century do to Shakespeare?', drawing attention not merely to one-way acts of appropriation in which Shakespeare is manipulated for new political and cultural ends, but to a dialogic relationship between borrower and borrowed.[16] This book, however, reveals 'Shakespeare' to be not just a coherent author who 'gradually penetrated' eighteenth-century culture and came to 'dominate' it,[17] or who 'scripted' modern ideas about human nature,[18] but a complex figure shaped by the literary forms in which he appeared – forms which in turn benefited from his presence. In the eighteenth century, amidst multiple ways of encountering his work, Shakespeare and the eighteenth-century novel mutually construct each other as morally and emotionally valuable, and help to establish each other as dominant cultural forms.

The fortunes of Shakespeare and the novel are closely entwined, yet the novel remains absent, or briefly touched upon, in major accounts of Shakespeare's eighteenth-century promotion, which often focus on performances, adaptations, actors, complete works editions and playtexts. For Michael Dobson, Shakespeare's appearances in the novel are more the sign of his increasing domestication than the engine of it.[19] Two separate 'rise' narratives describe the cultural fortunes of Shakespeare and the novel, respectively. The notion of the 'rise of the novel' was given its most definitive expression by Ian Watt, who attributed the genre's emergence to the rise of the middle classes, and its 'formal realism' to growing interest in the personal experience of the individual. This compelling thesis has been repeatedly challenged. It has been exposed as a retrospective construction that reflects the values of the late-eighteenth and nineteenth century (Defoe, Richardson, Henry Fielding, Smollett and Sterne all posthumously profiting from the nineteenth century's interest in realism, for example).[20] Twentieth- and twenty-first-century criticism has rediscovered work by women; pre-Richardsonian publications; Gothic fiction; late-century sentimental and political novels previously passed over en route to Jane Austen; and, more recently, 'it'-narratives and experimental fiction that seem far from the private experience of the individual. The very idea of a 'rise' has been challenged by feminist critics who argue that 'Literature is not progressive';[21] and by others who lament the 'pernicious influence of evolutionary views of the novel'.[22] The story of the novel's rise – 'a fictional narrative – a kind of novel about the novel'[23] – is in fact a continual redefinition of the boundaries of what constitutes valuable prose fiction, by which process the realist novel came to seem defining.

The story of the eighteenth-century 'rise' of Shakespeare has been more readily accepted. This is despite the strong resemblance between the terms that underpin that rise – the emergence of the bourgeois middle-class, for example, or of 'patriarchal family, constitutionalism, economic individualism, nationalism'[24] – and those employed in Watt's account of the rise of the novel. In the narrative of Shakespeare's reception, it is anti-French nationalism, growing reverence for the English literary past and the rejection of neoclassical rules of drama that served to elevate him from a 'provincial playwright' in need of improvement at the beginning of the century to a sacred demi-god near its end. Critics often talk as if Shakespeare's rise was natural, and unstoppable. Its most extreme manifestation, 'bardolatry', is said to have a 'genesis' and a 'growth', and to have 'steadily . . . increased' during the century.[25] The 'seed of Bardolatry' that 'took root at the beginning of the eighteenth century' was 'in full flower' or 'full-blown' by its close.[26] Shakespeare 'rose through the ranks of poets' in a steady 'accession to pre-eminence', taking 'progressive steps' on his 'journey'.[27]

The eighteenth-century careers of Shakespeare and prose fiction can appear not only separate, but mutually opposed. In *Shakespear Illustrated*, novelist and critic Charlotte Lennox compared Shakespeare's work to *the Novels and Histories on Which his Plays are Founded*, and found it wanting. Next to the superior 'Probability' of his prose sources, the unnatural 'Contrivance' of his dramatic plots seemed a backwards step.[28] In Lennox's eyes, 'Shakespeare antiquates the novel and makes it romance'.[29] By contrast, Samuel Johnson, posing as '*The* AUTHOR' in the dedication to Lennox's study, demoted the novel in order to give credit to Shakespeare: 'a very small Part of the Reputation of this mighty Genius depends upon the naked Plot, or Story of his Plays'.[30] The eighteenth-century growth in the status of Shakespeare and of prose fiction, as I argue in this book, however, represents neither a parallel process of inexorable 'rise', nor a century-long struggle for cultural dominance. The presence of Shakespeare's words in the novel promotes the value of both the dramatist and the genre of prose fiction.

Acts of quotation

Shakespeare appears in the mid-century novel chiefly through direct quotation, most often delivered by character. The overt quotation of Shakespeare and other authors begins in earnest in the work of Samuel Richardson and is repeated, adapted and adjusted in later texts. Quotations in Richardson's epistolary fiction are revealing of character: the rakish Robert Lovelace writes to his confidant, John Belford, that 'these lines of Shakespeare came into my head:/ *Thy heart is big. Get thee apart, and weep!*'.[31] Henry Fielding's narrator muses on human behaviour: 'why, in any Case, will we, as *Shakespear* phrases it, "put the World in our own Person?"'.[32] Sarah Fielding's most virtuous characters make sense of the world through Shakespeare, reasoning 'if *Shakespear* is right in saying, that man is a player, hypocrisy must then begin at home' (while her least virtuous fruitlessly compare their dilemmas with those of Shakespeare's characters);[33] and passersby in Laurence Sterne's fiction cannot help but declaim 'Alas, poor YORICK!' aloud.[34]

Until now, though, critics discussing Shakespeare's presence in the eighteenth-century novel have tended to overlook, or even disparage, such instances of overt quotation, in favour of more subtle forms of allusion. As one critic says of Henry Fielding's classical references, 'his practice of relying on allusions requires a thorough understanding of the authors he cites, since he is not just repeating their words but is summarizing their ideas'.[35] Just as humanist Renaissance education trained its students not simply to quote, but to rework, classical, rhetorical and Biblical material in new and compelling ways, regarding loose or free quotation as a sign of understanding and appreciation rather than careless unconcern,[36] modern criticism often implicitly, and sometimes explicitly, treats allusion as a marker of greater authorial knowledge and skill. For many critics, allusion connotes the strong author described by Harold Bloom, forcefully wrestling with, rather than weakly emulating, his literary predecessors.[37]

Others have treated overt quotation in, for example, *Clarissa* and *Tristram Shandy* as the outward sign of an extended parallel with, say, *Hamlet* or *Lear*. Such an approach can lead to contortions, as when in *Clarissa* a single direct quotation, beginning '*Ay, but to die, and go we know not where*',[38] and a couple of possible echoes of *Measure for Measure*, are taken as evidence of a larger 'skeleton of allusion' to that play. Such a claim is difficult to defend in a vast, quotation-filled novel: even if Clarissa 'echoes' Isabella, has 'traces' of Juliet, is 'like' Ophelia and 'has parallels' with Desdemona, she cannot live out all their fates.[39]

To treat a quotation as the tip of an iceberg is often to defend the author from the charge that their quotations are just 'embellishments'.[40] One critic, keen to prove that Henry Fielding does more than 'merely quote lines from Shakespeare's plays' in *Tom Jones*, distinguishes between quotations that 'merely interrupt or ornament' the text, and those allusions and analogues that have a sustained, thematic resonance with the original.[41] It has been argued that 'the most effective appropriations of earlier works into later writing are usually those that invoke the full force of a passage's original context'.[42] True as this often may be, this approach can imply that free-floating quotations are devoid of meaning: empty signifiers cut off from their original speaker. Others defend quotations by demonstrating their structural significance: Herman Meyer denied that quotations offer the 'momentary delight' of 'raisins in the cake', and argued instead for their integral narrative function, such as contributing to the 'finely balanced harmony of contrasts' in *Don Quixote*.[43]

Alternatively, quotations are sometimes regarded as outward emanations of the texts that inhabit the author's mind. Henry Fielding is said to have 'had *Macbeth* in mind' in a certain passage in *Tom Jones*, while the Shakespearean echoes in *Tristram Shandy* have been regarded as evidence of Laurence Sterne's 'delight'[44] in Shakespeare's plays: *Hamlet* was 'never far from his mind', and 'may even have colored his view of life'.[45] Such an approach can sometimes figure the author as the passive recipient, by osmosis, of cultural influences that include Shakespeare. This resonates with Julia Kristeva's notion of intertextuality as a textual 'mosaic of quotations' and cultural signs.[46] Kristeva's sense of the associations that words bring with them from previous discourses outweighs their deliberate invocation by a decision-making author; she seems to 'evade human subjects in favour of the more abstract terms, text and textuality'.[47] Likewise, Roland Barthes's assertion that the text is a 'tissue of past citations', and that 'any text is an intertext', reinforces his declaration of 'the death of the author'.[48] These important approaches to intertextuality cannot quite account for the deliberate presence of direct quotations, nor, more importantly, for their delivery by fictional characters.

For all their insights, then, existing approaches to intertextuality in fiction often inadvertently dismiss the most significant form of literary reference in the eighteenth-century novel. From Pamela Andrews to Emma Woodhouse, numerous characters quote Shakespeare overtly. When they do so, what is most significant is not the original context of the borrowed words, but the act of quotation itself. The attitudes that characters strike when quoting Shakespeare – earnest or histrionic, admiring or showing off, thoughtfully reworking or casually recycling – evoke the numerous ways in which Shakespeare might be encountered in this period. Characters attend and discuss the theatre, read Shakespeare in their libraries, collect quotations in their commonplace books and hear him invoked in polite conversation. But when they quote 'as I read in a book last night', or 'with a theatrical air', the quotation's real source is often less important than the provenance that character chooses to present.

The central method of this book is to scrutinise these acts of quotation, and the acute judgements that other characters, and, by extension, readers, make about them, in order to trace precisely how characters confer value upon particular lines, and on Shakespeare; how they navigate Shakespeare's theatricality; and how they determine what constitutes proper engagement with his words. Stefan Morawski defines a quotation as a 'semantic portion designed to perform a certain function in a new and extraneous semantic structure of a higher order',[49] and the function of quotations in the mid-century novel is neither primarily decorative, nor structural: it is a sophisticated tool for characterisation. Studies that have previously noted the connection between quotation and characterisation have tended to see characters illuminated from the outside, for example, through the mock-heroic discrepancy in stature between Shakespeare's tragic heroes and Fielding's lowliest characters, as described by the narrator: between 'the sincerity of Othello and the hypocrisy of Square and Mrs Wilkins'.[50] But quotation's most important contribution to characterisation, this book shows, is to be found in the repeated acts of self-presentation by characters themselves.

Shakespeare says well

The promotion of Shakespeare is almost a side-effect of quotation by character. Quotations in mid-century fiction have three major effects, collectively and cumulatively, on the perceived status of Shakespeare in the eighteenth century and beyond. First, by repeated application of his words to the personal situations of novelistic characters, novelists help to construct 'Shakespeare' as a figure of emotional and moral authority on whom individuals can draw. Second, while they demonstrate Shakespeare's theatricality in the histrionic outbursts of some of their characters, novelists also rehabilitate it by aligning Shakespeare's dramatic skill with the emerging representational mode of the novel. Third, novelists draw comic attention to the increasing banality of quoting Shakespeare in polite company, and, in doing so, train their readers in new modes of literary quotation and conversation.

These three chief effects are the subjects of Chapters 3, 4 and 5 respectively. First, Chapter 2 places quotation by fictional character in the context of emerging literary and cultural practices of quotation. In the past, increasingly ubiquitous sources like Shakespeare have been difficult to categorise: Sterne's modern editors list Shakespeare not as one of the 'sources' for *Tristram Shandy*, but as a figure who is quoted 'liberally' in the novel, 'as we would expect', because his plays, like the Bible and the *Book of Common Prayer*, were part of 'the entire literature available to the age'.[51] This book draws attention to the practical ways in which such figures became part of that literary milieu, not only through complete works editions and performances, but also through anthologies, periodicals and the sociable exchanges of polite conversation. Chapter 2 builds on important studies that have explored the pre-history of the novel in popular print culture, asking for the first time what the pieces of Shakespeare that circulated in those forms brought with them into the novel, and how the novel transformed them.

Chapter 3 shows how quotations in mid-century fiction construct Shakespeare as a knowing figure of emotional and moral authority. In a period when Shakespeare was, to adapt a term used by Dobson (see Chapter 3, pp. 52–3), 'embodied', or given human form – in statuary, in stage characters who professed to be him, and in actors who professed special knowledge of him – the novel goes further to create a compelling image of Shakespeare the author. Fictional characters not only frequently quote Shakespeare, but treat the words of his dramatic characters as the playwright's own wise insights. They introduce quotations with admiration:

> Shakespeare says well. . .[52]
>
> saying in the words of their admired *Shakespear*. . .[53]

and connect Shakespeare's words with the situations in which they find themselves:

> Nor will there be any fear of taking them when they are in any act that has *the relish of salvation in it*, as Shakespeare says—so that my revenge, if they perish in the flames I shall light up, will be complete as to them.[54]
>
> 'Faith,' cries *Booth*, 'it was an odd Dream—and not so easily to be accounted for, as that you had formerly of my Marriage; for as *Shakespear* says, *Dreams denote a foregone Conclusion*.'[55]

> he had (as *Shakespear* terms it)
>
> *———with jealousy infected*
> *The sweetness of affiance,———*
>
> and in its stead introduced into my mind anxious doubts and gloomy suspicions.[56]

These approving quotations often attribute the insight or 'moral sentiment' to the figure of Shakespeare. They exhibit for the reader a direct relationship with 'our beloved Shakespeare', whose beneficent observations are 'applicable to many Motions of the human Mind'.[57] The aptness of the quotation – or, indeed, its complete inappropriateness – in turn confirms how well Shakespeare's sentiments are fitted to his own characters. Quotation enacts, and reenergises, the critical truism of Shakespeare's knowledge of human nature. Characters confirm in practice the truth of his observations and, by their own experience, turn fragments of Shakespeare's plays into precepts.

The eighteenth-century novel does not, however, entirely transform Shakespeare into a wise, gentlemanly authority figure, better fitted for the library than for the stage. Shakespeare's eighteenth-century reception is sometimes summarised as a relocation from 'stage to page', but Chapter 4 shows that, rather than simply suppressing Shakespeare's theatricality, the novelists exploit it. Shakespeare's potentially dubious association with the stage contributes to the characterisation of dangerous figures such as Richardson's Lovelace, who noisily declaim his words ('Thou wilt say I rave. And so I do!' (p. 146)). Yet even the most virtuous character, including Lovelace's seeming moral opposite, Clarissa, is touched, when they quote, by the pejorative associations of performance: are they acting? The act of quotation exaggerates the inherent self-dramatisation of the mid-century fictional character. Dramatic quotation resonates with eighteenth-century discussions of character in terms not of 'individualities and inner lives' but of surfaces and social relations; and with an 'understanding of the self' represented by the 'masquerade'.[58] It reveals the porous boundaries between dramatic and novelistic characterisation.

At the same time, the novel rehabilitates Shakespeare's theatricality by celebrating its capacity, in the right hands, to represent life truthfully. The actor David Garrick is named repeatedly in fiction of the period: *Tom Jones*' Partridge confidently declares after seeing him perform the role of Hamlet, 'why I could act as well as he myself. I am sure if I had seen a Ghost, I should have looked in the very same Manner, and done just as he did'.[59] Novelists connect the naturalistic style of acting for which

Garrick was celebrated with the true-to-nature modes of representation that the mid-century novel promotes in itself. Hamlet's advice to the players that they 'o'erstep not the modesty of Nature' is upheld as a guide not only for theatre practitioners but also for writers of fiction: it may, as Sarah Fielding suggests, 'if the Writer pleases, be most Part of it adopted also by him for his own Advantage'.[60] Shakespeare's theatricality remains, however, a disruptive force:

> Angels and ministers of grace defend us! cried my father
>
> A discourse devoutly to be wished for!
>
> Alas, poor Yorick! cried I, what art thou doing here?[61]

Such exclamatory quotations throw the characters in Laurence Sterne's fiction into the postures of the stage, and challenge Shakespeare's categorisation as an extract-dispensing moral authority. As Chapter 4 reveals, though, the novel's quotation practices ultimately move Shakespeare beyond the physical constraints of both theatre and book and into the realm of the imagination.

Third, the novelists draw satirical attention to the emerging practice of quoting Shakespeare's words in polite society. Chapter 5 shows how novelists criticise, and ultimately contribute to, this fashion: at best, a marker of Shakespeare's newfound status, and at worst, a display of desperate social compulsion. Sarah Fielding's Ophelia reports with scepticism the Marchioness's declaration that she, '*too full of the Milk of human Kindness*', pitied Ophelia for her impending destitution ('I was little disposed to believe the Marchioness was so very full of the *Milk of human Kindness* as she pretended'), and exposes the woman's Shakespeare quotation as self-flattering affectation.[62] This Shakespearean phrase, and others, from 'patience on a monument' to 'trifles light as air', are already conversational currency, readily appropriated by those who wish to be seen to quote Shakespeare (*Sir Charles Grandison* has 'owing to his obsequious love for you; and to the *milkiness of his nature*, as Shakespeare calls it'[63]). The repetition of well-worn bits of Shakespeare might seem to diminish their meaning. Chapter 5 shows, however, that novelists exploit the associations they have accrued in circulation. In turn, novels add layers of meaning, lastingly associating Shakespearean phrases with the new social situations to which they are applied in fiction.

Characters are highly responsive to one another's fashionable quotations. The variations on 'milk of human kindness' are reported with disdain by Ophelia and Harriet Byron, respectively. Other misguided attempts at quotation variously elicit a sigh of regret (at 'quotations misunderstood also and misapply'd'[64]), silence or a change of subject. Through characters' reactions, the novelists train their readers to distinguish poor acts of quotation from more fitting kinds of admiration. Yet what constitutes an appropriate response to Shakespeare is not a fixed standard. The phenomenon of 'banal Shakespeare' does not trail behind Shakespeare's canonisation as national poet by several decades, but is an integral part of that process. Meyer descries the 'banalization' of 'classic writers' such as Goethe, Schiller and Lessing, of whom quotation is a 'conspicuous characteristic of bourgeois culture'.[65] The banalisation of Shakespeare, however, is not an after-effect of, but an important contributor to, the playwright's 'classic' status. By pointing out the inadequacies of so many attempts to admire Shakespeare, the novelists suggest that he is worthy of more, and elevate him to a transcendent status.

The three central chapters of the book, then, reveal how the novel ascribes moral and emotional authority to Shakespeare, and enacts for readers his applicability to their personal situations. The novel does not suppress the arresting theatricality of his words, but rather unites drama and fiction in their capacity to represent truthfully human life. By pointing to laughably poor appropriations of Shakespeare's words, the novel helps to codify what constitutes fitting admiration. It at once makes Shakespeare's words accessible to all readers, and places him out of their reach – a double manoeuvre echoed in the deifying celebrations of that 'immortal' 'demi-god' Shakespeare at the Stratford Jubilee of 1769.[66] Novelists both contribute to Shakespeare's establishment as a wise 'national poet', and exploit the ambiguity of what it means to quote his words; they shape, by selective quotation, what will be valued about Shakespeare for years to come.

The final two chapters of this book reveal the persistence of these mid-century quotation practices in late-eighteenth- and early-nineteenth-century fiction. At first sight, the overt quotations by character of the mid-century novel seem to disappear, to be replaced with new modes of intertextuality. But as the case studies of Chapters 6 and 7 show, the influence of these earlier quotation practices is still very much present. In Ann Radcliffe's Gothic fiction, explored in Chapter 6, quotations from Shakespeare most frequently appear as chapter epigraphs, rather than words spoken by her characters.

> Can such things be,
> And overcome us like a summer's cloud,
> Without our special wonder?
>
> MACBETH[67]

Yet while these formal quotations seem the property of Radcliffe's narrator, setting the tone for seemingly supernatural occurrences, they often dramatise the thoughts and fears of her characters. Radcliffe's formal Shakespearean epigraphs represent at once the omniscient view of the narrator, and the partial, anxious perspective of the character, capturing their worries and delusions even when they cannot articulate them themselves. Radcliffe's quotations contribute to the impression of complex interiority, letting characters' unfounded fears linger in the text long after the narrator has dismissed their imagined supernatural causes.

The book ends with a close study of an author who, though she only infrequently quotes Shakespeare, often echoes the mid-century novelists in her approach. Jane Austen has Emma Woodhouse borrow (then contradict) Shakespeare's authoritative insight that 'the course of true love never did run smooth'.[68] She draws attention to Shakespeare's still-dangerous theatricality in head-turning domestic performances by Henry Crawford and John Willoughby; and she delights in the comic opportunities afforded by Shakespeare's banality, or, in the words of Edmund Bertram, the fact that 'we all talk Shakespeare'.[69] Chapter 7 reveals that Austen's relationship with Shakespeare is mediated by the mid-century novel. Her handful of direct quotations invokes not just Shakespeare, but earlier quoting characters such as Clarissa and Lovelace. The influence of the mid-century novel is felt not just in Austen's glancing references to Shakespeare: the blurring of the perspectives of character and narrator that quotation permits is, this book argues, an important potential contributor to Austen's narrative technique. While some have argued that Austen's free indirect discourse is an innovation inspired directly by Shakespeare's soliloquies, Chapter 7 shows that 'the prose Shakespeare' might derive this technique, at least in part, from the practice of quoting Shakespeare in earlier fiction.

Novel benefits

What does this mean for the novel? As all the following chapters show, the ways in which the novelists promote 'Shakespeare' also serve to promote the value of prose fiction. When fictional characters apply Shakespeare's words to their situations, and remark on how 'finely' or 'nobly', and with what 'peculiar aptness of expression', Shakespeare captures a particular emotional state, they are, in turn, celebrating their own skilful characterisation. By admiring Shakespeare's insight, the novelists emphasise the value of their own genre as an accurate representation of human emotions and behaviours. This is only enhanced by an awareness of characters' capacity for self-dramatisation, and while novelists might initially seem to reject outright the more histrionic aspects of Shakespeare's theatricality, they actually exploit it to enrich their characterisation. Novels assume the status of guides as they alert their readers to the social positioning that takes place around literature. This is not, however, a one-way didacticism, as in the morally oriented criticism of the 1960s, in which novels direct an impressionable audience. Instead, novels train their readers in active judgement and discernment: Sarah Fielding urges readers to read 'with the Attention which is necessary to digest, and extract Utility from Writings', rather than 'skimming over the Surface of Authors, with the view only of filling up a Chasm of Time, which is not so fortunate as to be engaged to some more entertaining Amusement'.[70] Novelists urge their readers to consider the complex question of what it means to quote Shakespeare, and take the credit for the insight that they gain.

The novels examined in this book are not uniform in their approach to Shakespeare. Their fiction constitutes a patchwork of practices that are echoed and adapted to new ends in each new text. Yet while the disparate novelists considered might not regard themselves as engaged in exactly the same 'general enterprise' (as McKillop sees it, to raise the value of their genre)[71], the image of 'Shakespeare' that they cumulatively construct, and the ways of engaging with his work that they demonstrate for their readers, have a lasting influence on the status of both Shakespeare and prose fiction. Many of the novels discussed in this book would be considered canonical: their frequent quotations are enlisted in their realistic explorations of character, nature and social foibles. Because their handling of Shakespeare has received most attention to date, they are also the best place in which to begin to challenge critical assumptions about the playwright's role in fiction. Yet as the opening example from *Charles Careless* suggests, the practice of invoking Shakespeare became increasingly widespread as the century continued:

> as Shakespeare says, I had rather hear a kitten cry, mew, than be plagued with such skimble scamble stuff.[72]
>
> It were rejoined the earl, as our Shakespear says, it were indeed a consummation devoutly to be wished.[73]
>
> Let us then hold the *murrour* up to nature, as Shakespeare says, and make the wicked tremble.—I am by birth a North country Englishman[74]

In these far less familiar works, as in more canonical texts, Shakespeare's emerging wisdom is invoked seriously, playfully and with an awareness of its social currency. The practice of quotation by character extends far into the eighteenth century, and beyond.[75] This book points to its ongoing effects on Shakespeare's reputation, and suggests the exciting scope for continued scholarly investigation into the mutually beneficial relationship between Shakespeare and fiction in this and the centuries that followed.

CHAPTER 2

Quotation culture

> Quote seldom, and let it be, at least,
> Some Fact that's prov'd, or Thought that's well exprest.[1]

Flashy quotations, according to Benjamin Stillingfleet, are anathema to sociability. In his 1737 poem, *An Essay on Conversation*, he advised readers to talk with modesty and restraint, and to 'seem judicious more than learn'd'. In this brief couplet, Stillingfleet offers us a rare, explicit guide to the emerging rules of quotation in the eighteenth century. When Stillingfleet's poem was published, the vernacular literature of previous centuries was increasingly being celebrated alongside the classics of Latin and Greek. The question of what it meant to quote English literature, however, was only just beginning to be explored. In this chapter, I argue that the literary references of the mid-century novel are best understood as part of a developing practice of vernacular quotation: a social, intellectual and cultural practice represented in, and, in turn, influenced by, prose fiction.

This chapter asks what it would mean for certain characters (rather than their authors) to quote another's words at this point. I first explain the phenomenon of quotation by character, and show how it differs from other modes of intertextuality. I then explore in turn the sources that might have informed the quotation practices of these fictional characters, including printed plays, anthologies, the spiritual autobiography, periodicals, performances and polite conversation. All of these sources (with the exception of spiritual autobiography) contributed to the growing reputation of Shakespeare, influencing audiences of various sizes according to their price and accessibility. The novel, though, plays a unique role in shaping Shakespeare's posthumous identity, constructing him through selective quotation as a figure not just of cultural but of moral and emotional authority.

Quotation by character

If 'no form is more "intertextual" than the novel', and quotation, misquotation and allusion have characterised prose fiction over its two-thousand-year history,[2] then no kind of intertextual reference is more formal or frequent than the direct quotations of the mid-eighteenth-century novel. These quotations remain as visible to a twenty-first-century reader as to their original audience. In *Sir Charles Grandison*, Clementina's borrowed exclamation of surprise is clearly visible even after it has been reported in Sir Charles' letter to Dr B., copied by Dr B. to Harriet Byron, and finally transcribed in a letter from Harriet to Lucy:

> Good God! said she.—Then in English breaking out into that line of Hamlet, which she had taken great notice of, when we read that play together—
>
> *Angels, and ministers of grace, defend us*!
>
> She left her mother, and stept gently towards me, looking earnestly with her face held out, as if she were doubtful whether it were I, or not.[3] (see Fig. 1)

Quotation is just as overt in the racy prose of John Cleland's *Memoirs of a Woman of Pleasure* (1748–9):

> . . . the brute-machine, driven like a whirlwind, made all smoak again, and wedging its way up, to the utmost extremity, left her in point of penetration nothing either to fear, or to desire, and now,
>
> *"Gorg'd with the dearest morsel of the earth"*
> Shakespear.
>
> *Louisa* lay, pleas'd to the heart, pleas'd to her utmost capacity of being so, with every fibre in those parts, stretch'd almost to breaking, on a rack of joy, whilst the instrument of all this overfulness, search'd her senses with its sweet excess . . .[4] (see Fig. 2)

In these two rather different texts, and many more besides, borrowed fragments of literature are clearly presented on the page with italicisation, indentation or framing white space. They are frequently attributed to their author, sometimes with admiration; and their applicability to their new situation remarked upon. Even if the reader does not recognise the source, they can be in no doubt that they are in the presence of a quotation.

The presence of such overtly visible quotation immediately distinguishes the mid-century novel from its predecessors and successors. Formal

I aroſe. I was unable to bear this affecting ſcene— She ſaw me.

Good God! ſaid ſhe.—Then in Engliſh breaking out into that line of Hamlet, which ſhe had taken great notice of, when we read that play together—

Angels, and miniſters of grace, defend us!

She left her mother, and ſtept gently towards me, looking earneſtly with her face held out, as if ſhe were doubtful whether it were I, or not.

I ſnatched her hand, and preſſed it with my lips— O madam!—Deareſt Lady!—I could ſay no more.

Figure 1 Samuel Richardson, *The History of Sir Charles Grandison*, 2nd edn, 6 vols. (London, 1753-4), iii. 118

enjoy'd her pain: and ſoon now, by dint of an enrag'd enforcement, the brute-machine, driven like a whirlwind, made all ſmoak again, and wedging its way up, to the utmoſt extremity, left her in point of penetration nothing either to fear, or to deſire, and now,

" *Gorg'd with the deareſt morſel of the*
" *earth.*" Shakeſpear.

Louiſa lay, pleas'd to the heart, pleas'd to her utmoſt capacity of being ſo, with every fibre in thoſe parts, ſtretch'd almoſt to breaking

Figure 2 John Cleland, *Memoirs of a Woman of Pleasure*, 2 vols. (London, 1748-9), ii. 194

quotation is not a defining characteristic of late seventeenth-century prose fiction. The nearest relation to quotation in Aphra Behn's epistolary work, *Love-Letters between a Noble-Man and his Sister* (1684), for example, is the allusive exclamation in one of Silvia's letters to Philander, 'but oh like *Cowley*'s Lute, my Soul will sound to nothing but Love!'.[5] Despite the constant, conversational presence of the first-person narrator in works such as Daniel Defoe's *Moll Flanders* and Jonathan Swift's *Gulliver's Travels*, early eighteenth-century prose fiction also lacks much formal quotation. Robinson Crusoe might begin his spiritual conversion with a 'biblical lottery' of opening the Bible at any page and 'depending on providence to choose a relevant passage', but his succour in distress is not generally literary.[6] A single poetic couplet apiece makes the narrators of Defoe's *The Farther Adventures of Robinson Crusoe* (1719), *Moll Flanders* (1722) and *Roxana* (1724) his most prolific quoters; and only Moll's, beginning 'according to my Lord *Rochester* . . .', resembles the mode in which characters in subsequent fiction will habitually address their sources.[7] Similarly, while Swift's Gulliver reports, in italics, the alien words he hears and learns to understand,[8] he gives only one formal literary quotation: two untranslated, unattributed lines from Virgil's *Aeneid* that he introduces as a 'Maxim' that 'I imposed on myself' about truth-telling in travel writing. He undermines his quotation with the admission that 'I know very well, how little Reputation is to be got by Writings which require neither Genius nor Learning, nor indeed any other Talent, except a good Memory, or an exact *Journal*'.[9] A tentative practice at the beginning of the century, quotation will be commonplace by the middle decades. Fragments once used to marvel at the unusual will be quoted to reflect on day-to-day experience, in ordinary speech and letters.

The quotations in the mid-century novel, delivered predominantly by fictional characters, are also distinct from the forms of intertextuality that characterise late eighteenth- and early nineteenth-century fiction. Ann Radcliffe, Matthew Lewis and Walter Scott make frequent use of the literary epigraph, or chapter motto. Such quotation is also indented, surrounded by white space and prominently displayed, yet its placement makes it, in Gérard Genette's term, 'paratextual': where mid-century quotations are fully incorporated into speeches and letters, quotations in the Gothic novel operate at the edges of chapters and texts, and are often thought to provide a 'sense of indirect backing' for the author, even if, as later chapters reveal, they can represent the perspective of fictional characters.[10]

It is ironic that, for all its visibility, quotation in mid-century fiction often eludes critical analysis. As mentioned in Chapter 1, direct quotation is sometimes overlooked in favour of more subtle, and seemingly more sophisticated, allusion. The most straightforward direct quotation can test the limits of the language of 'intertextuality'. This critical discourse focuses chiefly on two objects of study: the author (the 'influences' they experience, and the habits of 'allusion' and 'reworking' they perform in their work) and the text (as in Kristeva's notion of the textual 'mosaic' of borrowed words). Yet the figures that do most of the quoting in the mid-century novel fit neither of these categories. What does it mean for Walter Shandy, rather than Laurence Sterne, to quote from *Hamlet*? For Robert Lovelace, rather than Samuel Richardson, to rant in the words of Shakespeare, Dryden and Otway? For Tom Jones, rather than Henry Fielding, to rhapsodise in the words of Milton? These characters are not literary authors, nor part of a poetic lineage, yet are more deliberate in their quotations than the 'textual mosaic' notion permits. They are 'ephebe' to no literary precursor, and have no 'poetic father' wilfully to misread in order to prove their own literary originality.[11]

Instead, characters quote for a variety of reasons, some gaining social and cultural advantage by it, and some losing it. Characters are self-conscious about their quoting abilities, and acutely attentive to others' facility with borrowed words. Speaking of the heroine of Richardson's *Clarissa*, Lovelace declares that 'I can quote a text as well as she', while Sterne's *Tristram Shandy* laments Uncle Toby's lack of 'skill ... in the fragments'.[12] Characters respond judgementally to others' quotations. Sarah Fielding and Jane Collier point out in a footnote that quotations 'put in the mouth of' their least savoury characters show up the poor reading and moral laxity of the speakers, and do not reflect badly on the authors of either *The Cry* or of the quoted texts. They emphasise that quotation by character is not just a displacement of novelists' anxieties about their literary borrowings, but a deliberate function of character, to be judged in this case with revulsion by both heroine and reader.[13]

The quotations that occur in fictional conversations and correspondences are not merely fragments of printed text. Novelists translate contemporary practices of quotation into the speech habits and epistolary styles of their characters. In the context of the novelists' self-conscious experimentation with print, including Richardson's influential 'innovations in the printing of direct dialogue and recounted speech',[14] graphic conventions such as italics, underlining and exclamatory punctuation can lend emphasis and, by extension, the impression of the cadences of speech, to printed quotations. As in the italic presentation of Clementina's quotation, they create what James McLaverty has described in the context of

Pope's poetry as a typography that 'compensates for the absence of voice',[15] and operate on the boundaries of print and speech.

Cultures of quotation

Julie Sanders has observed that 'authors who allude to or quote Shakespeare have the greatest chance of their reading audience both registering the allusion and being able to see a writer's critical movement beyond the mere act of quotation or recitation'.[16] While this might be true of twentieth-century fiction, because of Shakespeare's by-then established status, the same cannot necessarily be said of the eighteenth-century novel. Before Shakespeare achieved the status of 'national poet', and when multiple conflicting editions and adaptations of his plays existed, the novel reader's primary task was not so much to recognise the precise context of the borrowed lines, as to respond to the act of quotation itself. The reader, trained to read and respond to fragments in anthologies, on the stage, in editions, in periodicals and in polite speech, would pay attention to the delivery of these borrowed phrases, and, along with other characters who hear the quotation, readily interpret their significance.

The early- to mid-eighteenth century saw a major re-valuation of older literary writing in English. As Jonathan Brody Kramnick observes, 'For literary critics of the late seventeenth and early eighteenth century, writers like Spenser and Shakespeare were rather uncouth. Far from classics, writers from the early ages of English society were imperfect versions of their modern progeny.' The narrative, constructed by eighteenth-century writers and critics, of improvement up to the present day, would be replaced by one of decline. By the middle of the century, 'modern culture seemed beleaguered by the book trade, literacy, and rationality. In contrast, the past shone with value and achievement'.[17] The smoothly turned, polite phrases of contemporary poets, upheld for echoing the patterned precision of the classics, would eventually lose favour, and the difficult, barbed language of an earlier age – namely, Shakespeare's – would become, in a complex process of promotion, increasingly venerated. Where 'the Good *Shakespear* himself' had once been marginalised in Edward Bysshe's *Art of English Poetry* because, like other 'Ancient' writers, such 'as *Chaucer*, *Spencer*, and others', 'the Garb in which they are Cloath'd, tho' then Alamode, is now become so out of Fashion, that the Readers of our Age have no Ear for them',[18] his presence would grow in subsequent editions of the handbook, and in culture more widely.

What did it mean to admire and quote in conversation these newly valued 'classic' texts of English literature? The social rules for quoting the ancient classics are much more apparent. In *Tom Jones*, Miss Abigail, taking Partridge's Latin quotation to be 'some affront', huffily tells him that 'You may be a Gentleman, Sir; but you don't show yourself as one to talk *Latin* to a Woman'.[19] In his *Miscellanies*, Henry Fielding also counsels polite reserve through the example of an imaginary character:

> Wisely different is the amiable Conduct of *Sophronus*; who, though he exceeds the former in Knowledge, can submit to discourse on the most trivial Matters, rather than introduce such as his Company are utter Strangers to. He can talk of Fashions and Diversions among the Ladies; nay, can even condescend to Horses and Dogs with Country Gentlemen. This Gentleman, who is equal to dispute on the highest and abstrusest Points, can likewise talk on a Fan, or a Horse-Race; nor had ever any one, who was not himself a Man of Learning, the least Reason to conceive the vast Knowledge of *Sophronus*, unless from the Report of others.[20]

Those who would appear polite should match their conversation to the company and resist parading their superior learning, especially if ladies are present.

But if vernacular literature is accessible to all, and not just to classically educated men, how does it change the emerging rules of quotation? Lord Chesterfield advised his son that 'classical' English authors like Milton, Dryden, Pope and Swift are 'frequently alluded to by, and are often the subjects of conversations of, the best companies. . . . It is not pedantic to quote and allude to them, which it would be with regard to the ancients'.[21] Yet some of the charges of inappropriate display of learning carry over into vernacular literature: 'Pedantry' is no longer confined to those obsessively conversant in the classics, but can now 'put on e'ery Shape', 'No matter of what Kind the Subject be;/ From Laws of Nations down to Laws of Dress'.[22] Others are self-conscious about showing that they have spent their time in leisure entertainments such as the theatre. In the middle of the century, the practice of quoting Shakespeare and other English authors could represent a display of knowledge, or the mindless recitation of remembered snatches of drama; an ideal of polite conversation, or its worst contortions. Open to women, children and the relatively untutored, as well as to cultured men, vernacular quotation could engage all parts of a company, but also foster unhealthy competition.

The emerging practices of vernacular quotation, and their associated values, are important resources for the mid-century novel. Critics have thoroughly documented the genre's non-fictional sources, from journalism to spiritual autobiography, and examined the influence of these prose forms on narrative representation in fiction. Only rarely noted, however, is the influence of the habits of *quotation* practised in these contexts. Other important influences on the novel, from the literary anthology to polite conversation, have been less extensively examined, but their quotation practices are equally significant. By drawing attention to these precursor texts, this chapter does not simply expand the range of potential sources for the novel, but historicises its acts of quotation and suggests their significance for contemporary readers. Novelists respond to, and in turn, inform, an emerging culture of quotation.

Editions

It would be natural to ascribe the growth of Shakespearean quotation in the novel to the publication of a series of eighteenth-century editions of his complete works.[23] Nicholas Rowe's 1709 edition (with its entrances and exits, act and scene divisions and lists of dramatis personae) was supplanted by Alexander Pope's of 1723–5 (with its greater aesthetic concern with Shakespeare's beauties and faults). In its turn, Pope's reliance on taste as an editorial tool was challenged by Lewis Theobald's scholarly method: he set out, in *Shakespeare Restored* (1726) and *The Works of Shakespeare* (1733), to 'restore' Shakespeare's texts from their documentary origins. These were followed by Thomas Hanmer's Oxford edition of 1743–4, much maligned for its poorly signalled and sometimes ill-founded emendations, and William Warburton's edition of 1747. The sense that each new edition supplanted its predecessor was cultivated in part by Jacob Tonson, the publisher of the majority of these editions, who used notions of 'obsolescence and novelty' to market his product to a fashionable audience.[24] The novelists studied in this book were well aware of editors and their work: Henry Fielding collected at least three editions of Shakespeare (as well as 'Jonson, Beaumont and Fletcher, Shirley, Wycherley, Otway, Dryden, Southerne, Congreve, Farquhar, Steele, Thomson, and several others'[25]) and subscribed to Theobald's 1734 edition.[26] The narrator of *Tom Jones* (1749) ventures that 'perhaps, thou may'st be as learned in Human Nature as *Shakespear* himself was, and, perhaps, thou may'st be no wiser than some of his Editors' (ii. 523).

Might an eighteenth-century fictional character be inspired by an edition to quote Shakespeare? These publications are said to have established a Shakespeare 'for home reading',[27] but it is debatable exactly how many homes could have afforded this luxury. Rowe's edition, priced at the 'substantial sum' of 30 shillings, cost the equivalent of the weekly salary of the

Drury Lane prompter.[28] Tonson viewed Shakespeare 'as a premium product, saleable as a luxury rather than a popular item', and subsequently offered Pope's six-volume edition at 'a staggering six guineas (126 shillings) per set'.[29] After Shakespeare entered the public domain in 1731, Robert Walker sold single plays for a third of Tonson's price of a shilling, making Shakespeare affordable to a popular audience. But Tonson and other '"proprietors" used their deeper pockets to print huge editions of 10,000 copies of each play and to sell them at below cost at predatory prices' – and then raised their original prices even higher. Over the century, 'the minimum price of access to Shakespeare's printed works became ever more expensive and readerships ever more limited';[30] it was not until after the end of perpetual copyright in 1774 that Shakespeare would again become widely affordable in print.

While all of these editions promoted Shakespeare, only Pope and Warburton's editions drew attention to particular lines in a way that might actively encourage quotation. In Pope's edition, 'suspected Passages' which are 'excessively bad' are 'degraded to the bottom of the page', and

> Some of the most shining passages are distinguished by comma's [*sic*] in the margin; and where the beauty lay not in particulars but in the whole, a star is prefix'd to the scene. This seems to me a shorter and less ostentatious method of performing the better half of Criticism (namely the pointing out an Author's excellencies) than to fill a whole paper with citations of fine passages, with *general Applauses*, or *empty Exclamations* at the tail of them.[31]

These markings signalled that some lines deserved particular attention, and, perhaps, repetition (see Fig. 3). Thanks to the prohibitive cost of Pope's edition, his choice of 'beauties' is more likely to have influenced contemporary quotation practices via William Dodd, who used Pope's index as the basis of his more affordable two-volume duodecimo collection of extracts, *The Beauties of Shakespear* (1752), discussed in the next part of the chapter.[32]

What the novelists do appear to take from the editions is a sense of the mutability of Shakespeare's text. Early eighteenth-century conjectural emendations of Shakespeare resulted in multiple versions of his playtexts. Even as Shakespeare's language was increasingly regarded as 'sacred', the novelists themselves were working within a more fluid conception of Shakespeare's wording:

> *Who steals my Gold steals Trash; 'tis something, nothing;*
> *'Twas mine, 'tis his, and hath been Slave to Thousands:*
> *But he who filches from me my good Name,*
> *Robs me of that* WHICH NOT ENRICHES HIM,
> BUT MAKES ME POOR INDEED.[33]

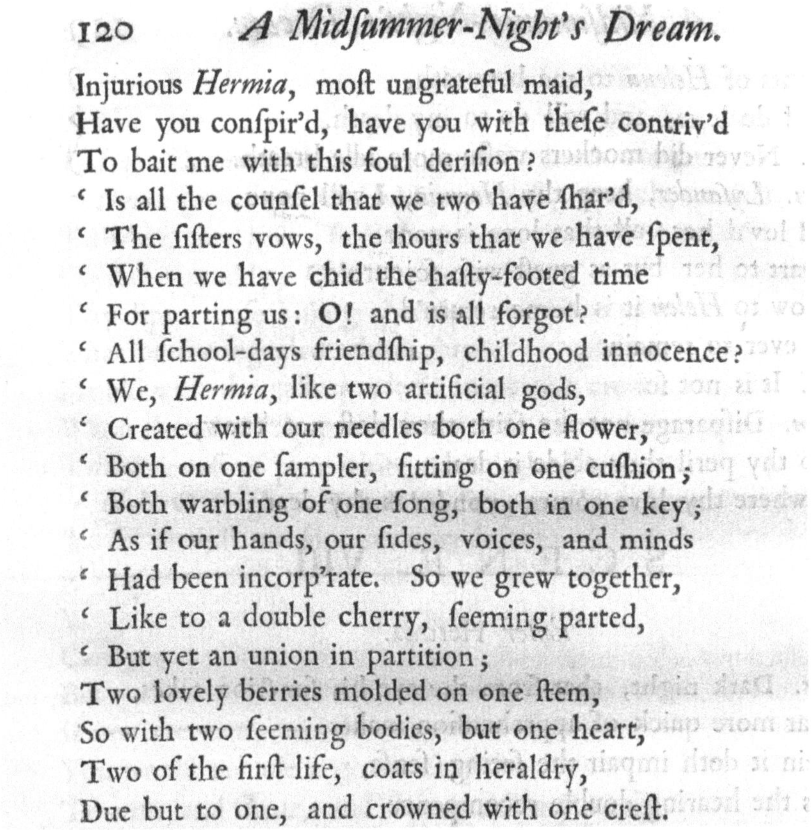
120 *A Midſummer-Night's Dream.*

Injurious *Hermia*, moſt ungrateful maid,
Have you conſpir'd, have you with theſe contriv'd
To bait me with this foul deriſion?
' Is all the counſel that we two have ſhar'd,
' The ſiſters vows, the hours that we have ſpent,
' When we have chid the haſty-footed time
' For parting us: O! and is all forgot?
' All ſchool-days friendſhip, childhood innocence?
' We, *Hermia*, like two artificial gods,
' Created with our needles both one flower,
' Both on one ſampler, ſitting on one cuſhion;
' Both warbling of one ſong, both in one key;
' As if our hands, our ſides, voices, and minds
' Had been incorp'rate. So we grew together,
' Like to a double cherry, ſeeming parted,
' But yet an union in partition;
Two lovely berries molded on one ſtem,
So with two ſeeming bodies, but one heart,
Two of the firſt life, coats in heraldry,
Due but to one, and crowned with one creſt.

Figure 3 William Shakespeare, *The Works of Shakespear. In Six Volumes. Collated and Corrected by the Former Editions, by Mr. Pope* (London, 1725), i. 120

Fielding's narrator in *Tom Jones* is noisy, spluttering and, if we judge by contemporary editions, inaccurate in his quotation from *Othello*. Pope, who marks these lines as a beauty, offers slightly different wording and punctuation: '*Who* steals my purse', 'Robs me of *that, which*', and '*And* makes me poor indeed' (italics added).[34] Theobald has heavier punctuation: ''tis his;' 'thousands;', 'But he,', and, like Pope, 'Robs me of That,' and 'And', rather than 'But', 'makes me'.[35] Theobald's note suggests that there are 'Several Passages in the Classics' that might have given Shakespeare this hint. Fielding's borrowing might be not a failed transcription but a quotation that playfully echoes the practice of emendation. To focus exclusively on the influence of the editions, though, is to underestimate the novelists' creative use of other intermediary sources, several of which are discussed in the rest of this chapter.

Quotation books

The quotation book or miscellany is one of the most obvious influences on the handling of quotation in the mid-century novel. It promotes the admiration of fragments of literature, and, with its abstract headings or 'topics' such as 'Love', 'Jealousy' or 'Grief', facilitates their application to new settings. These printed texts would proliferate after the end of perpetual copyright,[36] but even the relatively limited array of collections that circulated before this time bore an important set of associations that are adopted by the novel.

The practice of quoting English literature in the eighteenth century was informed by earlier attitudes to knowledge. As Ann Moss has shown, 'Commonplace-books were the principal support system of humanist pedagogy', and these forms, most popular in the Renaissance, had classical origins: 'It is in Latin, and not in vernacular languages . . . that the history of commonplaces is embedded'.[37] These classical models were increasingly used and adapted in Britain and Europe. A number of collections of extracts published around the turn of the seventeenth century institutionalised in English literature the practice of prizing the choice flowers – the best expressions and the most useful knowledge – from one's reading and arranging one's extracts for ready reuse.[38]

For all the persistence of the formal qualities of quotation, however, their function changed drastically between the seventeenth and eighteenth centuries. In this time, as Margreta de Grazia has observed, quotation marks were transformed from signs of a 'commonplace', or common land where all might freely graze, to symbols of the private property of an individual author.[39] Extracts that once promoted reuse by readers now demanded reverence. Early printed anthologies sometimes included mention of authors' names: Robert Allot's *Englands Parnassus*, for example, suffixes each extract with an abbreviated attribution such as '*Ed. Spencer.*', '*M. Drayton.*' and '*W. Shakespeare.*'. Allot's purpose is not so much to promote reverence as to signal that 'the choysest flowers of our modern poets' (or 'our English poets' on the running header) were well represented in the collection; authors play a secondary role to the 'descriptions of bewties, personages, castles, pallaces, mountaines, groues, seas, springs, riuers, &c.' promised in his subtitle.[40]

In the eighteenth century, however, authors' names came to signal ownership. In the early century, popular miscellanies still conflated pieces from different authors without attribution, exploiting and perpetuating the 'popular repertoire of songs, poems, and textual snippets which were floating free of authors and which could be used in a vast range of different ways', on the principle that 'anonymity was the default mode' of transmission.[41] As Edward Bysshe proclaims in the second edition of *The Art of English Poetry*, however, 'That the Reader may judge of every Passage with due Deference for each Author, he will find their Names at the End of the last Line . . .'. [42] Shakespeare emerges in this century as a named author with excellent expressions all of his own, subject of a devoted section, 'Shakespeareana', in Charles Gildon's *Complete Art of Poetry*; and of a whole book of extracts (the first vernacular author to be treated in this way) in Dodd's *The Beauties of Shakespear*. Quotation books reflect the gathering force of the 'proprietary understanding of authorship'[43] during the century.

What made an extract valuable also changed in this time. Seventeenth-century collections prized the well-expressed but familiar idea, often as a model for writers. The 'Shakespeare' that appears in collections such as *Englands Parnassus* and *Bel-védere* (both 1600) is unfamiliar to a modern reader: he not only trails behind Edmund Spenser, Michael Drayton and other of his contemporaries in number of appearances, but is chiefly represented by his then popular narrative poems, *Venus and Adonis* and *The Rape of Lucrece*. When quotations do come from his plays, such as *Romeo and Juliet* and *Richard II*, it is primarily from their most sententious parts. Compilers such as Allot appear less interested in the romantic expressions of the central love story of *Romeo and Juliet*, and more concerned to reproduce Friar Lawrence's 'sage advice' to 'love moderately', or Romeo's 'glib Petrarchan clichés on the pains of loving Rosaline', such as 'Love is a smoke made with the fume of sighs . . . a madness most discreet' – lines, that, out of context, become 'genuine warnings on the "madness" and "chaos" that love can bring' (see Fig. 4).[44] By the mid-eighteenth century, usefulness was not the primary selection criterion of *The Beauties of Shakespear*: Dodd set out to collect the 'finest passages of the finest author' for their aesthetic value. The guarantee of their quality lay in Longinus' definition of the sublime, a kind of writing which

> . . . is grand and lofty, which the more we consider, the greater ideas we conceive of it; whose force we cannot possibly withstand; which immediately sinks deep, and makes such impression on the mind as cannot easily be worn out or effaced: in a word, you may pronounce that sublime, beautiful, and genuine, which always pleases and takes equally with all sorts of men.[45]

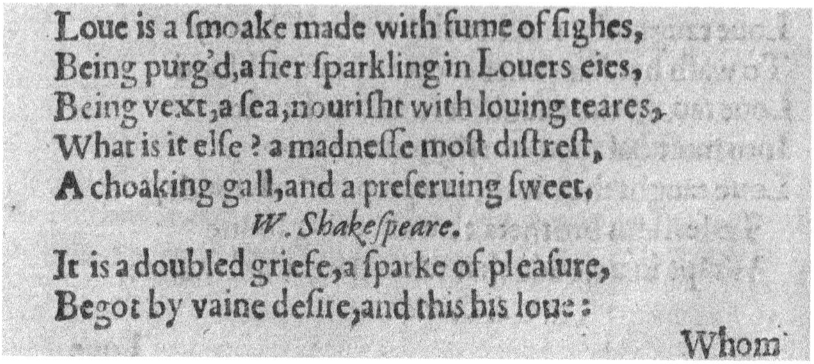
Loue is a ſmoake made with fume of ſighes,
Being purg'd,a fier ſparkling in Louers eies,
Being vext,a ſea,nouriſht with louing teares,
What is it elſe ? a madneſſe moſt diſtreſt,
A choaking gall,and a preſeruing ſweet,
W. Shakeſpeare.
It is a doubled griefe,a ſparke of pleaſure,
Begot by vaine deſire,and this his loue :
Whom

Figure 4 Robert Allot, *Englands Parnassus* (London, 1600), p. 173

Dodd's readers would, he hoped, be moved irresistibly by the supremely striking nature, rather than the aptly expressed sentiment, of his selections from Shakespeare (see Fig. 5).

The perceived purpose of these extracts of literature also changed significantly. In the sixteenth and seventeenth centuries in particular, fragments of literature were raw material for new work. As Ann Moss observes of students of that period, 'when they came to construct compositions of their own, they were encouraged to use their commonplace-books as a resource, culling from them quotations, examples, and other illustrative material, as well as replicating the categories of thought enshrined in the commonplace-heads'.[46] These extracts were the building blocks of literary invention, and Renaissance students were trained to 'view all literature as a system of interchangeable fragments, and to view the process of composition as centered on intertextuality rather than imitation'.[47] Compiling and collecting – whether reassembling quotations into new observations, or binding together books according to taste, as in Jeffrey Todd Knight's recent study – 'came to have an important structural impact on the production of Renaissance literature', fostering the idea that the literary work was 'flexible and contingent', and that writing was a work of 'repurposing and recontextualization'.[48] Without our modern sense of authorial ownership, the material forms of sixteenth- and seventeenth-century texts, and contemporary educational practice, actively encouraged the gathering, compiling and reworking of fragments.

In the course of the eighteenth century, the borrowing of words and phrases from earlier literature – words strictly belonging to another

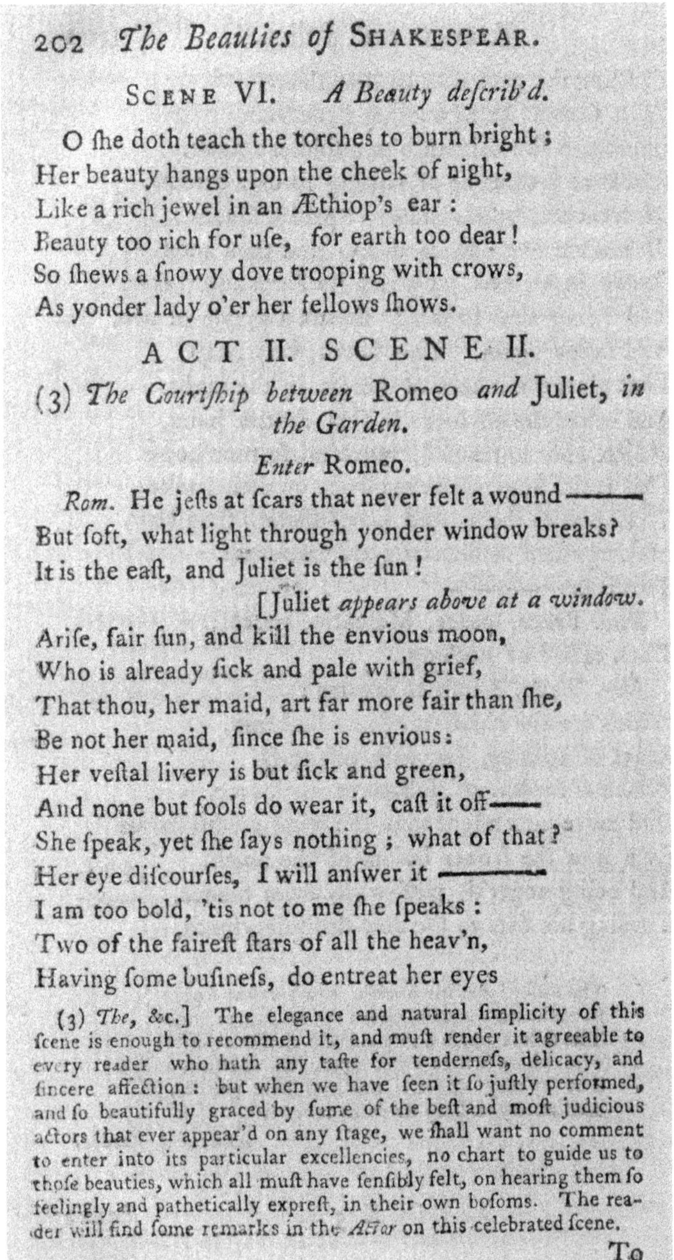

202 *The Beauties of* SHAKESPEAR.

SCENE VI. *A Beauty deſcrib'd.*

O ſhe doth teach the torches to burn bright;
Her beauty hangs upon the cheek of night,
Like a rich jewel in an Æthiop's ear:
Beauty too rich for uſe, for earth too dear!
So ſhews a ſnowy dove trooping with crows,
As yonder lady o'er her fellows ſhows.

ACT II. SCENE II.

(3) *The Courtſhip between* Romeo *and* Juliet, *in the Garden.*

Enter Romeo.

Rom. He jeſts at ſcars that never felt a wound——
But ſoft, what light through yonder window breaks?
It is the eaſt, and Juliet is the ſun!
[Juliet *appears above at a window.*
Ariſe, fair ſun, and kill the envious moon,
Who is already ſick and pale with grief,
That thou, her maid, art far more fair than ſhe,
Be not her maid, ſince ſhe is envious:
Her veſtal livery is but ſick and green,
And none but fools do wear it, caſt it off——
She ſpeak, yet ſhe ſays nothing; what of that?
Her eye diſcourſes, I will anſwer it——
I am too bold, 'tis not to me ſhe ſpeaks:
Two of the faireſt ſtars of all the heav'n,
Having ſome buſineſs, do entreat her eyes

(3) *The, &c.*] The elegance and natural ſimplicity of this ſcene is enough to recommend it, and muſt render it agreeable to every reader who hath any taſte for tenderneſs, delicacy, and ſincere affection: but when we have ſeen it ſo juſtly performed, and ſo beautifully graced by ſome of the beſt and moſt judicious actors that ever appear'd on any ſtage, we ſhall want no comment to enter into its particular excellencies, no chart to guide us to thoſe beauties, which all muſt have ſenſibly felt, on hearing them ſo feelingly and pathetically expreſt, in their own boſoms. The reader will find ſome remarks in the *Actor* on this celebrated ſcene.

To

Figure 5 William Dodd, *The Beauties of Shakespear*, 2 vols. (London, 1752), ii. 202

author – accrued negative connotations. Writing publicly to 'the Author of Sir Charles Grandison', Edward Young counsels his friend:

> let not great Examples, or Authorities, browbeat thy Reason into too great a diffidence of thyself: Thyself so reverence as to prefer the native growth of thy own mind to the richest import from abroad; such borrowed riches make us poor.[49]

When Young promotes the 'native growth' of the author's mind over the deceiving glitter of 'borrowed riches', he not only encourages a friend to have confidence in himself, but also articulates current thinking about the value of originality over the derivativeness of imitation. '*Originals* are the fairest Flowers: *Imitations* are of quicker growth, but fainter bloom'; the former are 'great Benefactors; they extend the Republic of Letters', while the latter are only 'Duplicates of what we had, possibly much better, before'; and we read imitation with the 'languor' of one who 'listens to a twice-told tale', but 'throng' around the 'perfect stranger' of an original as if to learn 'news from a foreign land'.[50] Young's celebration of originality, couched in terms of novelty and news, has another purpose: to justify Richardson's relatively uneducated 'original genius' by framing him in the same terms as Shakespeare, 'a Star of the first magnitude', who, like other 'Genii', has 'much reliance' on his 'own native powers'.[51] The hint of Englishness in 'native powers' and 'native growth' also promotes the vernacular tradition, legitimating both Richardson's, and Shakespeare's, relative lack of classical training.

The reception of Bysshe's *Art of English Poetry* is a telling indicator of the changing status of 'borrowed riches' in new literary creation. In this handbook for aspiring poets, Bysshe included 'Rules for Making Verses' and a collection of quotations from English literature. The excerpts displayed exemplary poetic figures, on the principle that we can 'better judge by a piece of Painting, how beautifully Colours may be dispos'd, than by seeing the same several Colours scatter'd without design on a Table'.[52] Bysshe's handbook went through multiple editions, but was increasingly disparaged. When the would-be poet Dabler in Frances Burney's play *The Witlings* composes ghastly verse, Bysshe is his trusty aide: 'Let's see,—sad, bad, Lad, Dad,—curse it, there's never a Rhyme will do!—Where's the art of poetry?—, here,—now we shall have it; (*reads*) Add,—hold, that will do at once'.[53] In the twentieth century, Bysshe was regarded as the 'sort of book' to which poets might have referred only in 'dire distress' – though Samuel Richardson, Henry Fielding, Samuel Johnson and Horace Walpole all owned a copy.[54]

By the mid-eighteenth century, then, quotation books encouraged readers to admire excerpts of English literature for their beauty and expressiveness, to treat them as the revered property of an admired author and, rather than silently recycling them, to acknowledge their reuse. These transformations were not, however, clear cut. Dodd's mid-century collection has mixed priorities: 'beauty' is a central selection criterion, but many of the headings are hangovers from the commonplace tradition of collecting useful knowledge, and sententious pieces like Friar Lawrence's advice about too-hasty passion, or Romeo's stilted Petrarchan devotion, appear under '*Violent Delights, not lasting*' and '*LOVE*'.[55] At the same time, Dodd's collection, organised by play and act, evokes the dramatic performance of Shakespeare's plays: 'Scene VIII. *Enter Ghost and* Hamlet'.[56] Dodd is sure that all readers will find something to admire amidst its 'trifling love tales', 'sober *saws* of morality' and 'home-felt observations of experience'.[57] The diverse selection criteria stem partly from Dodd's idiosyncrasies as a compiler, but also testify to a persistent ambiguity in the purpose and value of quotation, and what it meant to deploy it.

The presentation of overt quotations in the mid-century novel often resembles that of the quotation book. Josua Poole's *The English Parnassus* (1600) laid out his quotations under alphabetical headings ('Fruit, Fruitfull, Frown', etc.), each one indented and separated from the surrounding extracts by white space. Allot's *Englands Parnassus* also used headings, adding abbreviated references to the author in the margin. Letter-writing fictional characters often echo this layout and style of attribution. In the first edition of *Clarissa*, Lovelace quotes *The Tempest*:

> *—Full many a lady*
> *I've ey'd with best regard; and many a time*
> *Th'harmony of their tongues hath into bondage*
> *Brought my too diligent ear. For* several *virtues*
> *Have I lik'd* several *women. Never any*
> *With so full soul, but some defect in her*
> *Did quarrel with the noblest grace she ow'd*
> *And put it to the* foil. *But* SHE!—*OH* SHE!
> *So perfect and so peerless is created,*
> *Of ev'ry creature's best.—*[58]

Lovelace writes these lines in a spontaneous fit of passion, having encountered the unattainable Clarissa; the emphatic switch from Ferdinand's intimate, first-person 'you, oh you', to Lovelace's clamorous, third-person 'SHE!—*OH* SHE!' only confirms his distance from her. When, however, in the second edition of *Clarissa*, the lines are newly

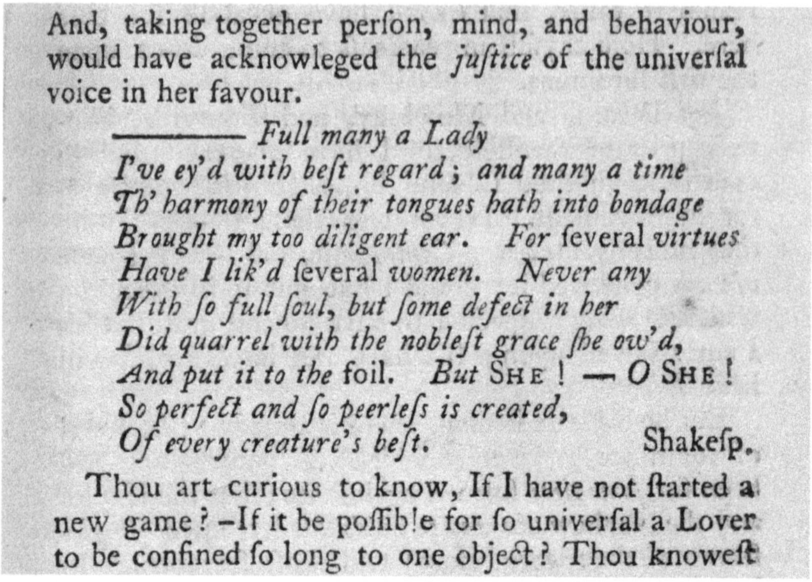

And, taking together perſon, mind, and behaviour, would have acknowleged the *juſtice* of the univerſal voice in her favour.

——— Full many a Lady
I've ey'd with beſt regard; and many a time
Th' harmony of their tongues hath into bondage
Brought my too diligent ear. For ſeveral *virtues*
Have I lik'd ſeveral *women. Never any*
With ſo full ſoul, but ſome defect in her
Did quarrel with the nobleſt grace ſhe ow'd,
And put it to the foil. *But* SHE ! — *O* SHE !
So perfect and ſo peerleſs is created,
Of every creature's beſt. Shakeſp.

Thou art curious to know, If I have not ſtarted a new game? –If it be poſſible for ſo univerſal a Lover to be confined ſo long to one object? Thou knoweſt

Figure 6 Samuel Richardson, *Clarissa. Or, the History of a Young Lady* . . . 2nd edn, 7 vols. (London, 1749), i. 203

suffixed with the abbreviation 'Shakesp.',[59] the quotation even more clearly recalls the formal conventions of the anthology (see Fig. 6). Many of Richardson's second-edition adjustments to *Clarissa* are designed to underscore Lovelace's moral dubiousness, and to reinforce the novel's moral. This attribution suggests that Lovelace's sincere feelings are borrowed from a written source. It also hints at the intermediary genre where he might have found, and copied, the lines he now so passionately exclaims.

Richardson has long been accused of relying on Bysshe's *Art of English Poetry*, since many of the quotations in *Clarissa* seem to hail from that source, including those extracts from Dryden that are mistakenly ascribed by both Bysshe and Richardson to Shakespeare. Richardson became a printer's apprentice when rendered financially unable to go to university, and has been negatively compared to Henry Fielding for his relative lack of formal education. Critics have used Richardson's quotations to gauge his learning. On one hand, Michael E. Connaughton argues for a 'dependence' on Bysshe born of limited reading and therefore an ignorance of the context of his quotations.[60] On the other, Jocelyn Harris argues for Richardson's knowledge and wide reading by proving that his quotations and allusions are well contextualised, organic and connected; she brushes off the charge of reliance on Bysshe.[61] More recently, Leah Price has helpfully suggested that this critical impasse might be resolved, not by denying Richardson's use of Bysshe, but by treating the popular handbook as a valid source and context in its own right.[62]

The present study goes even further than Price to suggest that Richardson's borrowings from Bysshe, particularly after *Pamela*, are not covert, thinly-disguised thefts from the commonplace tradition – nor evidence that he '"pretends" to read most of the writers he quotes'[63] – but deliberate, with the aim of enriching his characterisation. Lovelace is supposedly a figure of literary prowess: at university, he was 'always noted for his vivacity and courage; and no less, it seems, for the swift and surprising progress he made in all parts of literature: For diligence in his studies, in the hours of study, he had hardly his equal' (p. 49). For all his apparent 'diligence', though, it is Lovelace whose quotations most often visually resemble anthology extracts and, more frequently than those of any other character, are to be found in Bysshe (the example from *The Tempest*, unusually, is not). His impassioned quotation from *Measure for Measure* on the terrors of death, beginning '*Ay, but to die*' (p. 1148), can be found in Bysshe under the heading 'DEATH'.[64] His cry of 'Perdition catch my soul, but I do love her' (p. 146) appears under 'LOVE'.[65] He might have turned to 'PATIENCE' to find adapted lines from *Macbeth* ('Come what come may') that flattered his persistence (p. 571); and to 'REVENGE' to borrow the words '*the relish of salvation in it*' (p. 1184).[66] Bysshe's titles represent the places in which such an ill-intending character might have browsed. Richardson denounces in his correspondence this age of 'dictionary and index-learning', in which people are willing to settle for only a 'smattering' of knowledge,[67] and Lovelace's friend Belford laments their dubiously second-hand knowledge. He and Lovelace had always admired the style and simplicity of biblical passages, but only when they 'by way of quotation in the works of other authors, popped upon us' (p. 1125); they 'only skim the surface' in their reading (p. 1131). The charge of dependence and derivativeness should not fall at Richardson's door, but at Lovelace's.

Would Lovelace's dependence on Bysshe be more excusable in another character who lacked his education? While quotation might be a kind of public display well suited to aristocratic male discourse, the dependence it can connote is not: as Oliver Goldsmith observes in his preface to *The Beauties of Poesy*, 'Compilations of this kind are chiefly designed for such as either want leisure, skill, or fortune, to choose for themselves;

for persons whose professions turn them to different pursuits, or who, not yet arrived at sufficient maturity, require a guide to direct their application'.[68] Might reliance on a printed anthology be more acceptable in a woman, for whom reading unchaperoned the entire works of certain authors might be a morally dubious activity? Clarissa's Shakespeare quotations are not drawn from Bysshe, even if some of her quotations from other authors can be found there, and the single example that does appear in his handbook – 'I could a tale unfold', a scrap of *Hamlet* that she scribbles in deep distress (p. 893) – is listed in Bysshe under the unrelated category of 'ASTONISHMENT'. Clarissa's first Shakespeare quotation resembles a piece of commonplace wisdom, but is not to be found in Bysshe.[69] Lovelace, by contrast, can quote the bawdy Matthew Prior unaided, but relies on Bysshe for quotations from the man he calls 'our English pride and glory' (p. 1148). Lovelace and Clarissa's Shakespeare quotations help to polarise them, not through a simplistic distinction between one who reads whole plays and one who reads only extracts (after all, Clarissa may have found these lines extracted in other texts; see p. 53), but through their contrasting attention: she the intelligent reader who responds thoughtfully to her borrowings; he the flamboyant speech-maker casually dependent on his quotation book to supply his rhetorical flights.

Spiritual autobiography

If the anthology corralled excerpts and hinted at the abstract situations of 'Love' or 'Rage' to which they might apply, another genre showed readers more explicitly how to incorporate quotations into their own personal narrative. 'Spiritual autobiography', as it is retrospectively termed, best epitomised by John Bunyan's *Pilgrim's Progress* (1678) and by his autobiographical tale of imprisonment, *Grace Abounding to the Chief of Sinners* (1666), has been identified by some critics as a precursor of eighteenth-century narrative fiction. The genre, with its focus on the individual's personal narrative of spiritual growth, steeped in the details of their 'utterly mundane activities', has a demonstrable influence on, for example, Defoe's *Robinson Crusoe*.[70] The trope of struggles overcome in a spiritual journey recurs in later fiction, even when that fiction deals with less overtly dangerous trials than shipwreck, starvation or abject loneliness. Beyond these narrative similarities, there is also a striking resemblance between the way they and the mid-eighteenth-century novel quote prior texts.

The personal narratives of spiritual autobiography or 'life writing' include frequent quotations from the Bible. Lady Anne Clifford's autobiographical 'Summarie of the Records & a true memoriall of the Life of mee' (1652–3), incorporated into the final volume of the *Great Books of Record*, uses numerous passages from Scripture 'to attest to the providential workings of God in her life, which enabled her to overcome her enemies'; while Grace Mildmay's (1552–1620) life story – one of the earliest existing autobiographies by an English woman, 'grafts her readings of scriptures onto her every topic', incorporating Scriptural references in almost every margin.[71] One author of her own life gives even more significance to the lines she quotes.[72] In the 1674 *Narrative of the Persecutions of Agnes Beaumont*, a young Bedfordshire girl calls on the Bible when her reputation is under attack. She has defied her father and ridden on the back of John Bunyan's horse to attend his prayer meeting in Gamlinghay. The social implications are serious:

> So on Wednesday morning, the next day after the fair, when my poor father lay by the walls, came somebody in and told me what a report there was of me at Baldocke Fair. But that scripture bore me up, 'Blessed are ye when men shall revile you, and say all manner of evil of you falsely, for my name sake.'[73]

At the very moment Agnes hears this gossipy 'report . . . of me', she calls to mind Jesus' words from the gospel of Matthew for support. Her quotation has a double narrative function: it repeats the words that apparently came to mind at that instant, and it retrospectively dramatises her past-tense story of persecution.

Agnes has no doubt that this Scriptural quotation is relevant to her personally, nor that she is worthy of its succour: her text is grounded, as her modern editor observes, in the 'Calvinist doctrines of the personal calling by God to the saint – whether male or female, slave or free', and the attendant need for 'public testimony' (p. 2), and comes with the confidence of predestination. The 'ye' in 'Blessed are ye' speaks to Agnes as an individual as well as one of a community of believers. Her quotations appear to bypass their written, biblical source and come to her directly from God.

The directness of God's words, however, can feel both supportive and oppressive. When Agnes capitulates to her father's commands and promises not to go to any more meetings,

> so soon as I got within the door, that dreadful scripture came upon my mind, 'They that deny me before men, them will I deny before my father and the angels that are in heaven'; and that word, 'He that forsaketh not

> father and mother and all that he hath, is not worthy of me.' 'Oh,' thought I, 'what will become of me now? What have I done this night?' (p. 58)

God's words crowd upon Agnes in her mingled righteousness and regret. Defying her father because of her beliefs, she experiences the problematic tension between 'freedom of worship' and lack of freedom at home (p. 6). Later, after her father has been buried, and Agnes cleared of accusations of involvement in his sudden death, God's words come to sustain her. As she prepares to go into Biglesworth to show her innocence, 'The Lord was wonderful good to my soul, that morning: that scripture ran mightily through my mind as I was going to the market'. The phrase beginning 'Blessed are ye, when men shall revile you' returns to her, but now with a more positive final clause: 'rejoice and be exceeding glad, for great is your reward in heaven'. It is accompanied by the confident statement that 'As many as are incensed against thee shall be ashamed.' This rush of scriptural assurance leaves Agnes 'very comfortable in my soul' (pp. 82–3).

Whether they chastise or uphold her, these Biblical quotations appear to come to Agnes involuntarily. From one perspective, this is a sign of sincerity: Agnes' facility with Scriptural quotation has been regarded as 'proof' of piety, a demonstration of the 'wedding of God's Word to one's heart and mind' (p. 14, note). From another perspective, these quotations could be read as part of Agnes' deliberate self-presentation: vital ingredients in her performance of piety. In this embattled narrative of slander and trial overcome, it is not so much Agnes' virtue as her virtuous *reputation* that is at stake, and quotation could be a deliberate act of 'brazen self-vindication' (p. 13, note) as much as a sign of salvation. Molekamp captures the sceptical reaction that Beaumont's assurances of involuntary quotation can trigger: 'the biblical text which Beaumont claims "came" to her...'; 'citing passages that were *apparently* bestowed upon her in a prophetic manner' (italics added; pp. 68–9). Consciously or unconsciously, Beaumont's phrase 'came upon my mind' is an attempt to play down the possibility of pretence.

This compelling mixture of modesty and confidence, of performance and piety, is reminiscent of another Bedfordshire servant. Richardson's *Pamela* – like his subsequent novel, *Clarissa* – features numerous biblical quotations, Pamela's typically from the Psalms and Clarissa's from the Book of Job. Beaumont's manuscript was not printed until the 1760s, but is a vivid, if extreme, example of a genre available to Richardson and his readers. Pamela, like Agnes, deploys quotations to prove her piety to her parents. Recalling how she had heard

Mr. B. say to Mrs Jewkes that Pamela might be thawed by kindness and love rather than fear, Pamela writes:

> Is he not a wicked sad Man for this?—To be sure, I blush while I write it. But I trust, that that God, who has deliver'd me from the Paw of the Lion and the Bear; that is, his and Mrs. *Jewkes*'s Violences; will also deliver me from this *Philistine*, myself, and my own Infirmities, that I may not defy the Commands of the Living God!—
>
> But, as I was saying, this Expression coming into my Thoughts, I was of Opinion, I could not be too much on my Guard, at all times; more especially when he took such Liberties. . .[74]

Pamela, in her indignant outburst, adapts I Samuel 17: 36–7.[75] Like Agnes, she speaks as if the words came to her directly and involuntarily: 'this Expression coming into my Thoughts'. She also demonstrates faith in God's personal attention in her trials: 'I trust that that God, who has deliver'd me . . . will also deliver me. . .'. Like Agnes', though, Pamela's quotations can breed scepticism. Richardson prints in the second edition a letter from an 'anonymous Gentleman' who declares 'That if the sacred Name were seldomer repeated, it would be better; for that the Wise Man's Advice is, *Be not righteous over-much*'.[76] Other characters also hint at the possibility of Pamela's pretence. Mr B. calls her an 'artful young Baggage' and 'a subtle artful Gypsey'. When Mrs Jervis assures him that Pamela's prudent behaviour has won her nothing but respect, he exclaims 'that's her Art' (p. 26); he later declares 'let such Fellows as *Williams* be taken in by her artful Wiles; I know her now, and see that she is for any Fool's Turn, that will be caught by her' (p. 168).

The moral ambiguities of biblical quotation persist in Pamela's literary references. When Mr B., his true nature rapidly emerging from behind the persona of kindly master, tries to pull Pamela on to his knee for a kiss, Pamela's shock occasions the very first quotation in the novel. She summons a line not from the Bible, but from *Hamlet*:

> O how I was terrify'd! I said, like as I had read in a Book a Night or two before, Angels, and Saints, and all the Host of Heaven, defend me! (p. 29)[77]

Pamela's cry of terror sounds like a naïve misquotation of *Hamlet*. In fact, she transforms Hamlet's cry at the sight of the ghost of his father – 'Angels and ministers of grace defend us!' – into the raw materials for her own spiritual autobiography. She expands 'angels and ministers of grace' into a pious triplet of divine protection: 'Angels', 'Saints' and 'all the Host of Heaven'. When she turns Hamlet's first person 'defend us!' from the first person plural into the first person singular 'defend me!', she invokes God's personal protection, just as she elsewhere calls to God to 'deliver me'. Pamela's quotation, like Agnes', is both a record of the words that occurred to her at that moment and a crucial part of her retrospective account of herself.

Quotation allows for the possibility of pretence in both Pamela and Agnes. Pamela's pious approach sanctions her borrowing from *Hamlet*, but also gives a sense of her precociousness and concern for how she appears to others. Richardson's novel appears to adapt from spiritual autobiography the simultaneously virtuous and self-dramatising qualities of quotation. Pamela is a self-conscious reader of romance, too, and this plea for protection also dovetails with the romance tropes of 'journey, struggle, and heroic triumph' that critics find in early modern life writing.[78] Pamela's borrowings from Shakespeare and other sources are not simply literary allusions, but self-conscious acts of quotation: an extension of a practice of biblical borrowing considered more appropriate for women, for whom few positive role models for classical quotation exist.

Periodicals

If editions provided novels with the wording of Shakespeare quotations, and anthologies the practice, then spiritual autobiography appears to exhibit for the novel the act of quotation by character in prose. Another, more consistently masculine, model for quotation by character is to be found in the early eighteenth-century periodical. Critics have connected the novelty and immediacy of the periodical with the eighteenth-century novel;[79] and credited the 'missionary work' of Richard Steele and Joseph Addison, and the growing presence of references to Shakespeare in periodicals in the first half of the century, with the public's increased knowledge of his plays.[80] To date, however, the two phenomena have not been connected. The periodical essay's handling of the words of Shakespeare and other authors is an important influence on the mid-century novel's mode of intertextuality.

Quotations in the periodical can be at once conversational and epistolary. The journalistic persona of 'Isaac Bickerstaff', who ostensibly penned the *Tatler* articles of Steele and Addison, quotes Shakespeare, seemingly as he comes to mind, in communications with friends and readers. In a Christmas Eve number, Bickerstaff describes how, yesterday, in the still of a dark night, he pondered on 'the proper Employment of a thinking Being', and the 'Perfections' towards which such a being should aspire.[81] Since 'My Mind is of such a particular Cast, that the Falling of a

Shower of Rain, or the Whistling of Wind, at such a Time, is apt to fill my Thoughts with something awful and solemn', he is susceptible to the night-time sounds of the street:

> I was in this Disposition when our Bellman began his Midnight Homily (which he has been repeating to us every Winter Night these Twenty Years) with the usual Exordium.
>
> *Oh! mortal Man, thou that art born in Sin!*
>
> Sentiments of this Nature, which are in themselves just and reasonable, however debased by the Circumstances that accompany them, do not fail to produce their natural Effect in a Mind that is not perverted and depraved by wrong Notions of Gallantry, Politeness, and Ridicule. (ii. 169)

By this point, the reader already has a strong sense of the moral compass of Bickerstaff's essay. Bickerstaff idealises the virtuous mind, unfettered by the fashionable traits of 'Gallantry, Politeness, and Ridicule'. In his pensive mood, the words of a certain playwright occur to him:

> The Temper which I now found my self in, as well as the Time of the Year, put me in Mind of those Lines in *Shakespeare*, wherein, according to his agreeable Wildness of Imagination, he has wrought a Country Tradition into a beautiful Piece of Poetry. In the Tragedy of *Hamlet*, where the Ghost vanishes upon the Cock's Crowing, he takes Occasion to mention its Crowing all Hours of the Night about *Christmas* Time, and to insinuate a Kind of religious Veneration for that Season.
>
> *It faded on the Crowing of the Cock.*
> *Some say, That ever 'gainst that Season comes*
> *Wherein our Saviour's Birth is celebrated,*
> *The Bird of Dawning singeth all Night long;*
> *And then, they say, no Spirit dares walk abroad:*
> *The Nights are wholesom, then no Planets strike,*
> *No Fairy takes, no Witch has Power to charm,*
> *So hallowed, and so gracious is the Time.*
>
> This admirable Author, as well as the best and greatest Men of all Ages, and of all Nations, seems to have had his Mind throughly seasoned with Religion, as is evident by many Passages in his Plays, that would not be suffered by a modern Audience; and are therefore certain Instances that the Age he lived in had a much greater Sense of Virtue than the present. (ii. 169–70)

Shakespeare's words occur to Bickerstaff in a highly individualised setting: on a certain night before Christmas, in a certain frame of mind, hearing the cries of the watchman (who had greeted him with a '*Good morrow,*

Mr. Bickerstaff' (ii. 168)) and of the bellman from his home in Sheer-Lane, on the edge of the city of London, on Saturday, December 24, 1709. Yet in the course of his reflection, Bickerstaff reorientates the quotation from the personal to the public. He warmly observes that 'This admirable Author' has a religious sensibility that 'would not be suffered by a modern Audience', and is of an age that had 'a much greater Sense of Virtue than the present' (ii. 169–70). This leads Bickerstaff to reflect critically for the remainder of the article on the arrogant or misguided irreligiosity of Free-Thinkers and atheists. (This private/public manoeuvre is familiar in *The Tatler*: elsewhere, lines from *Richard III* 'threw me into a deep Contemplation. I began to reflect upon the different Ends of good and bad Kings. . .' (ii. 67).)

Bickerstaff makes a case for the greater virtue of Shakespeare's age, suggesting that a modern audience would reject the religious tincture of his works out of lack of understanding. He laments the contemporary taste for the polished and the modern over the rejected writings of Shakespeare's age. Yet Shakespeare, at this point in the century, is not just a writer of undervalued poetry, but one of a number of cultural attractions, and promoting Shakespeare as Steele does is part of a wider moral project to combat the 'Degeneracy of our Understanding' (i. 39) threatened by the new frivolous stage entertainments that favoured 'Dress and Sound' (i. 19) over language. Bickerstaff's quotation suggests that Shakespeare's 'Wildness of Imagination' has a truthfulness that overshadows the artificial show of the contemporary theatrical scene; his 'just representation of human life' (i. 258) is capable of improving an audience.

Bickerstaff does not just promote the admiration of Shakespeare. He also promotes a particular way of talking about the author in polite conversation. It has been noted that the periodicals set out to improve 'town talk' for a non-classical readership (*The Spectator* apparently 'set a fashion' for Milton);[82] and that '*The Spectator*'s interweaving of aesthetic discussion with broadly topical matters represented for Jürgen Habermas the dual project of widening the scope of literary culture and refining the taste of the new reading public'.[83] Both *The Spectator* and *The Tatler* also demonstrate the conversational act of literary quotation in a way that anticipates the quotation by character of the eighteenth-century novel. In form and visual appearance, periodical and novel quotations have striking similarities. Despite the restrictions of the advertisement-crammed, folio half-sheet format, Bickerstaff's quotations are still generously framed with white space, and, in the 1710 collected duodecimo reprint, italicised (see Fig. 7). They visually resemble are returned to Duſt as well as he, and that there is no Difference in the Grave between the imaginary and the real Monarch. This made me ſay of human Life it ſelf with *Mackbeth :*

To Morrow, to Morrow, and to Morrow,
Creeps in a ſtealing Pace from Day to Day,
To the laſt Moment of recorded Time !
And all our Yeſterdays have lighted Fools
To their Eternal Night ! Out, out, ſhort Candle !
Life's but a Walking Shadow, a poor Player,
That ſtruts and frets his Hour upon the Stage,
And then is heard no more.

The Mention I have here made of Mr. *Betterton*, for whom I had, as long as I have known any Thing, a very great Eſteem and Gratitude for the Pleaſure he gave me, can do him no good, but it may poſſibly be of Service to the unhappy Woman he has left behind him, to have it known, That this great Tragedian was never in a Scene half ſo moving as the Circumſtances of his Affairs created at his Departure. His Wife, after the Cohabitation of Forty Years in the ſtricteſt Amity, has long pined away with a Senſe of his Decay as well in his Perſon as his little Fortune, and in Proportion to that, ſhe has her ſelf decay'd both in her Health and her Reaſon. Her Husband's Death, added to her Age and Infirmities, would certainly have determined her Life, but that the Greatneſs of her Diſtreſs has been her Relief, by a preſent Depravation of her Senſes. This Abſence of Reaſon is her beſt Defence againſt Age, Sorrow, Poverty, and Sickneſs. I dwell upon this Account ſo diſtinctly, in Obedience to a certain great Spirit, who hides her Name, and has by Letter applied to me to recommend to her ſome Object of Compaſſion, from whom ſhe may be concealed.

This, I think, is a proper Occaſion for exerting ſuch heroick Generoſity; and as there is an ingenuous Shame in thoſe who have known better Fortune to be reduced to receive Obligations, as well as a becoming Pain in the truly Generous to receive Thanks in this Caſe, both thoſe Delicacies are preſerved ; for the Perſon obliged is as incapable of knowing her Benefactreſs, as her Benefactreſs is unwilling to be known by her.

Errata *in the laſt :* Col. 1. Lin. 17. *inſtead of* the Liberal Science, *read* the only Liberal Science; *for* telle, *read* tell.

ADVERTISEMENT.

Whereas it has been ſignified to the Cenſor, *That under the Pretence that he has encouraged the* Moving Picture, *and particularly admired the* Walking Statue, *ſome Perſons within the Liberties of* Weſtminſter *have vended Walking Pictures, inſomuch that the ſaid Pictures have within few Days after Sales by Auction returned to the Habitation of their firſt Proprietors ; that Matter has been narrowly looked into, and Orders are given to* Pacolet *to take Notice of all who are concerned in ſuch Frauds, with Directions to draw their Pictures, that they may be hanged* in Effigie, in Terrorem *of all Auctions for the future.*

N. B. *All poſſible Care is taken to prevent falſe Purchaſers at the Sale mentioned in the following Advertiſement.*

A Small Parcel of excellent Pictures, lately brought from beyond Sea, of Nicholas and Gaſpar Pouſſin, Luca Jordano, Claude Lorain, Franceſco Bologneſe, Franceſco Mola, Brouwer, Teniers, Wouwerman, Berchem, and other celebrated Maſters, will be ſold by Auction on Monday the 8th Inſtant, at Mr. Breſſans at the Two Flower Pots, the Houſe next beyond the Stables in Somerſet-houſe-yard ; where Catalogues may be had, and the Pictures view'd Three Days before the Sale.

Advertiſements.

TO ſatisfy Gentlemen and Ladies who it is that would impoſe, in Relation to thoſe Men and Women's Gowns, to be ſold at the Olive-Tree and Still at Charing-Croſs ; advertiz'd againſt in the Poſt-Man, with Invitation to Ludgate-Hill : If they pleaſe to enquire at any Shop on the ſaid Hill, they may be ſatisfied that there is not a Quarter of the Choice as there is in the Room at Charing-Croſs ; nor can they afford ſo good Pennyworths, becauſe upon Examination, theſe will be truly found to be the Goods of Perſons that failed.

THE Sale of Looking-Glaſſes by Auction at the Engine Looking-Glaſs Warehouſe in Beauford-Buildings in the Strand, which was put off to the latter End of April, is now fixed for Tueſday the 9th Inſtant, without fail ; where Attendance will be daily given, and Catalogues delivered out every Day till the Day of Sale, the Trade being left off, and the Houſe to be lett, and no more of the Engine-Work to be had after this Sale. Note : Moſt of the Glaſſes that were unfitted by Reaſon of the Time of the firſt Sale being prolonged, are now fitted up in curious Frames of ſeveral Sorts. This will be the fineſt Shew of great Glaſs, Tea-Tables, China-Wares, Fans, Indian Screens, and ſeveral other Rarities, that was ever ſhewn in England. They may be viewed every Day till the Time of Sale.

*** This Day is publiſh'd, Bibliotheca Anatomica, Medica, &c. containing a Deſcription of the ſeveral Parts of the Body : Each done by ſome One or more Eminent Phyſician or Chirurgeon ; with their Diſeaſes and Cures. Illuſtrated with ſeveral Hundred Figures, done by the beſt Artiſts, and from the trueſt Deſigns, as appears by the Names to each Figure. This Sixth for April, contains Kerkeringius of the Generation of the Bones in the Fœtus, with Two large Plates, repreſenting the Bones of the 5th, 6th, 7th, 8th, and 9th Months, very near as big as the Life : Dom. Gagliard, Phyſician at Rome, his Anatomy of the Bones, &c. Printed by J. Nutt in the Savoy ; and ſold by J. Morphew near Stationers-Hall. Where may be had the preceding Months. Alſo, Atlas Geographus for March, and compleat Sets of them.

*** The Peerage of England, or an Hiſtorical and Genealogical Account of the preſent Nobility. Containing, the Deſcent, Original, Creations, and moſt remarkable Actions of them, and their reſpective Anceſtors. Alſo the chief Titles of Honour and Preferment they now enjoy : With their Marriages and Iſſue, continued down to the Year 1709. and the Paternal Coats of Arms of each Family in Blazon. Collected as well from our beſt Hiſtorians, publick Records, and other ſufficient Authorities, as from the perſonal Informations of moſt of the Nobility. To which is prefix'd, An Introduction of the preſent Royal Family of Great Britain, traced thro' its ſeveral Branches down to this Time, and terminating with the Proteſtant Succeſſion as ſettled by Act of Parliament. Printed for Abel Roper and Arthur Collins at the Black Boy in Fleetſtreet. Price 6 s. N. B. There's a ſmall Number printed on a large fine Paper. Price bound 10 s.

A Gentleman would purchaſe a Place for Life, about 150 l. or 200 l. per Annum, within the Bills of Mortality, leaving Particulars in Writing with Mr. Charles Mac Culloch, at the Wheat Sheaf againſt Tom's Coffee-houſe in Ruſſel-ſtreet, Covent-Garden, they will be further treated with about the ſame.

THIS Chryſtal Coſmetick, approved of by the Worthy Dr. Paul Chamberline, viz. cures all red Faces, takes off all Morphew, Pimples, and Freckles, cleanſing and adorning the Face and Hands of both Sexes in a very beautiful Manner. Price of the largeſt Bottle 6 s. the leſſer 3 s. Sold at Mr. Allcroft's by Exchange-alley, Cornhil ; Mr. Jackſon's, the Corner of Wood-ſtreet, Cheapſide ; the Comb under St. Dunſtan's Church, Fleetſtreet ; Mrs. Brecknock's, the upper End of St. James's-ſtreet, Piccadilly. Note, to prevent Counterfeits, each ſingle Bottle with Directions, is tied and ſealed with this Coat of Arms, a Frett, with a Lion Rampant in a Canton.

THE Royal Beautifier ; or the greateſt Coſmetick in the World : Which even to a Miracle fortifies the Skin againſt Wind and Sun, and makes ſuch as are pale and wan, look freſh and lively, and have a charming Countenance. It certainly takes away Freckles, Spots, Pimples, Scurf, Morphew, and Sun-burning ; and miraculouſly makes the Complexion plump, freſh, ſmooth, and delicately fair, even to Admiration. It having met with great Applauſe, as appears by the daily Reſort of People from all Parts of the Town to fetch it, there being more than Ten Dozen diſpoſed of within theſe Fourteen Days. To prevent Counterfeits it is only ſold at Lemery's Head at Charing-Croſs, at 2 s. 6 d. per Pot, with Directions at large.

☞ An Incomparable Beautifying Cream for the Face, Neck and Hands, takes away all Freckles, Spots, Pimples, Wrinkles, Roughneſs, Scurf, Morphew, Yellowneſs, Sun-burning, renders the Skin admirably Clear, Fair, and Beautiful, has an excellent pretty Scent ; is very ſafe and harmleſs, and vaſtly tranſcends all other Things ; for it truly nouriſhes the Skin, making it inſtantly look Plump, Freſh, Smooth, and Delicately Fair, though before Wrinkled and Diſcolour'd. Sold only at Mr. Lawrence's, Toyſhop at the Griffin the Corner of the Poultry near Cheapſide, at 2 s. 6 d. a Gally-pot, with Directions. Beware of Counterfeits under other Names.

Sold by *John Morphew* near *Stationers-Hall* ; where *Advertiſements* are taken in.

Figure 7 *The Tatler*. By Isaac Bickerstaff Esq., 2 vols. (London, 1709-[1711]), (Tuesday, May 2nd to Thursday, May 4th 1710)

the classical mottoes that headed many of Bickerstaff's essays ('*Procul O! Procul este Profani!* Virg.' (ii. 168) in the Christmas Eve number).

Novel quotations, like those in the periodical, are introduced in terms of individual reflection. Bickerstaff's quotations, he tells the reader, occurred to him at a particular moment, and triggered immediate reflection: they are, for him, a mental and emotional resource as well as a function of his prose. His sombre religiosity is at least as morally instructive as the quotation itself. Narrators and characters in novels eagerly adopt this reflective mode of quotation: '*Shakespear*', muses the narrator of *Tom Jones*, 'hath nobly touched this Vice, when he says that. . .'.[84] Portia, in *The Cry*, co-opts Shakespeare into her assertion that:

> Mercy must be felt, description hath no force to reach it: for (as *Shakespear* says)
>
> *It droppeth as the gentle dew from heaven*
> *Upon the place beneath: it is twice blest;*
> *It blesseth him that gives, and him that takes.*[85]

Both these individuals, whether engaging conversationally with the imaginary reader, or combatively with the 'the Cry', quote Shakespeare, like Bickerstaff, for the purposes of moral reflection.

Yet the novel also adapts the periodical's mode of quotation to new ends. It frequently resists Bickerstaff's reflective turn to the public and the political, and applies Shakespeare's words instead to the individual's own emotional situation.

> What's the matter with me!—Whence this dew-drop!—a tear!—as I hope to be saved, it is a tear, Jack!—Very ready, methinks!—only on reciting!—But her lively image was before me, in the very attitude she spoke these words—and indeed at the *time* she spoke them, these lines of Shakespeare came into my head:
>
> *Thy heart is big. Get thee apart, and weep!*
> *Passion, I see, is catching:–For my eyes,*
> *Seeing those beads of sorrow stand in thine,*
> *Begin to water—*
>
> I withdrew, and wrote to the captain to the following effect— (p. 709)

Like Bickerstaff's quotation, Lovelace's Shakespeare (albeit a piece of *Julius Caesar* already reshaped by Bysshe) 'came into my head' 'at the *time*' he spoke with Clarissa, and also furnishes his letter to Belford: it evokes his immediate response and fuels his later, emotional reflection. Unlike Bickerstaff's quotation, it remains at the level of his personal interests.

Performance

Two final important influences on novel quotations are not written, but spoken. Some of *The Tatler*'s quotations are triggered by the contemporary stage. Bickerstaff reflects, for example, on the performance in *Hamlet* of the late actor Thomas Betterton (who died in 1710):

> the soliloquy, where he began the celebrated Sentence of, *To be, or not to be*; the Expostulations where he explains with his Mother in her Closet, the noble Ardor after seeing his Father's Ghost, and his generous Distress for the Death of *Ophelia*; are each of them *Circumstances* which dwell strongly upon the Minds of the Audience, and would certainly affect their Behaviour on any parallel Occasions in their own Lives. (i. 493)

Bickerstaff's memories are anchored in moments of theatrical intensity: the definite articles in 'the soliloquy', 'the Expostulations' and 'the noble Ardor' imply that these are especially memorable scenes or 'celebrated Sentences'. The theatrical culture in which Bickerstaff participates was focussed on 'points': 'climactic' moments 'in a speech, role, or situation', often underlined by 'gesture' or 'vocal inflection', which, thus emphasised, had a special ability to command the audience's attention.[86] Harriet Byron in *Sir Charles Grandison* compares the applause she and Sir Charles receive for their skilful dancing with that given by audiences to 'some well-performed part, or fine sentiment, in a play' (ii. 346), suggesting that points received special technical emphasis from the actors who delivered them, and were eagerly awaited by an appraising audience. Quotation, or the singling out of particular lines as a focus for dramatic judgement, seems a natural offshoot of this practice.

'Points' culture has two important manifestations in the novel. First, it incites all kinds of fictional character to repeat fine speeches in declamatory tones. In *A Sentimental Journey*, Sterne describes how a performance of Euripides' *Andromeda* in Abdera, 'the vilest and most profligate town in all Thrace', captured the hearts of its hearers:

> of all the passages which delighted them, nothing operated more upon their imaginations, than the tender strokes of nature which the poet had wrought up in that pathetic speech of Perseus,
>
> *O Cupid, prince of God and men*, &c.
>
> Every man almost spoke pure iambics the next day, and talk'd of nothing but Perseus his pathetic address—'O Cupid! prince of God and men'—in every street of Abdera, in every house—'O Cupid! Cupid!'—in every mouth, like the natural notes of some sweet melody which drops from it

> whether it will or no—nothing but 'Cupid! Cupid! prince of God and men'—The fire caught—and the whole city, like the heart of one man, open'd itself to Love.[87]

The audience feels compelled to repeat this beautiful line, and the effects are transformative: 'the golden age return'd' to Abdera. More ordinarily, however, stage-struck quoters can sound like annoying show-offs. An excited Miss Stevens, in William Dodd's little-known novel, *The Sisters*, goads her companions to come to the playhouse as quickly as possible to secure a spot in the pit before Garrick speaks:

> Lord, Mr. *Jaison*, 'tis *Romeo* and *Juliet* to night. Had you never any inclination to act? I do think now, if you would do *Romeo*, I could do *Juliet* vastly well.
>
> *Give me my* Romeo, *ye gods; and when he's dead—*
>
> Stay, stay, how is it? something about stars and cutting—
>
> *I'll cut him out in little* tiddy *stars,*
> *And he shall make the face of heaven so* vastly *fine,*
> *The birds shall sing, and think it is* not *day.*
>
> Don't you think there's a good deal of Miss *Bellamy*'s manner in that now?[88]

Inspired to act, but lacking the talent or memory to do so, Miss Stevens staggers her way through one of Juliet's famous speeches, a wannabe George Anne Bellamy to Garrick's Romeo. She falls wretchedly short of Bellamy's 'point', filling the gaps with her own habitual exaggerations of 'tiddy' and 'vastly', and adding 'birds shall sing', perhaps a confused memory of another speech ('It was the nightingale, and not the lark,/ That pierced the fear-full hollow of thine ear' [III. 5. 1–3]). If points inspire mindless repetition, they also, in a second important effect, invite judgement, training hearers to appraise their delivery. Miss Stevens' quotation is met with mockery: 'Though their Spirits were very low, neither *Caroline* nor Mr. *Jaison* could refrain laughing at the girl's giddy lightness and impertinence' when she interrupts their private conversation.[89]

What does it mean for novel characters to quote from the stage? The answer to this question is shaped in part by what it means for them to attend the theatre. Richardson's anti-theatricality was class-inflected: he declared in *The Apprentice's Vade Mecum* (1733) that 'under proper Regulations, the *Stage* may be made subservient to excellent Purposes, and be an useful Second to the *Pulpit* itself' . . . 'But for a young *Tradesman* himself, much more an *Apprentice*, to make this a favourite Diversion, and to *haunt* or frequently go to a Play-house, who can bestow his Time much more to the Advantage of his Business, which 'tis probable will suffer by it, it must be allowed to be of very pernicious Consequence in several Respects'.[90] These 'Respects' included the fact that 'all our modern Plays are calculated for Persons in *upper* Life', and that the instruction they contained would go over the heads of lowly spectators; the 'Loss of Time and Expence of Money'; the temptation of 'lewd Women', the audience's capacity to be made 'Dupes and Fools of the Hero', the 'Depravity' of contemporary plays; and their propensity to 'detach' the mind of the spectator 'from his Business'.[91] Richardson's implied distinction between the credulous apprentice who attends the theatre once and comes away spouting '*Scraps of a Play*',[92] and the upper-class gentleman for whom an opinion of current performances is almost a requirement, suggests that quoting from the theatre will mean something rather different in his novels for Pamela and Lovelace.

Pamela herself echoes Richardson's ambiguity about the stage when she avers, in the second volume of the novel *Pamela in her Exalted Condition*, that 'I think the Stage, by proper Regulations, might be made a profitable Amusement' in cases 'where Instruction is kept in View all the Way; and Vice is punished, and Virtue rewarded'; but that 'I think there is hardly one Play I have seen or read hitherto, but has too much of Love in it'.[93] When the young Pamela prefaces her only Shakespeare quotation with the words 'as I read in a book the other night', it allows for the possibility that she is over-reaching her servant status by dipping into grand books of her lady's possession (something that Ian Watt thinks that servants, unlike other working-class people, had the daylight leisure time to be able to do[94]); or reading at night with a candle and concerted effort. To stress that she came across the phrase 'in a book' can also minimise its theatricality in a way more appropriate for a young servant girl. When Pamela marries Mr B., arrives in 'high' life and is propelled to the 'new World' of London (p. 303), she mitigates her initially reluctant theatrical excursions by agreeing to Lady Davers' request to write about them, and by stressing that she has 'read as well as seen' them (p. 341).

If Pamela has indeed read *Hamlet*, then she quite soon forgets about it, because in *Pamela in her Exalted Condition* she is bemused by Lord Jackey's laughing reference to '*A palpable Hit*', and surmises that it must be a phrase from 'some Character in a Play' (p. 117).[95] It might be that Pamela never read beyond Act I of *Hamlet* to Osric's cry in Act V, but it might also mean that Richardson was not in complete control of Pamela's quotations. *Pamela in her Exalted Condition* was a reluctant, rushed continuation to his successful first novel, and he appears to borrow heavily from Bysshe to supply its quotations. Doody suggests that Richardson first discovered in his failed sequel the ingenious idea of referring to stage dramas: 'decorative' here, Doody maintains they became important thematic elements of Richardson's subsequent novels.[96] This present study suggests that Richardson discovered the idea of using Bysshe as a convenient source of quotations, but subsequently developed the practice, not of extended structural or *thematic* allusion, but of creating character by hinting at the places where people find their quotations.

Polite conversation

A final source for the novel's mode of quotation is found in the mid-eighteenth-century conventions of polite conversation. Polite conversation is an ideal that connotes the grace and generosity of the highest forms of social interaction; it is also a dubious behaviour that compels one to say what people want to hear, rather than what one really thinks, at the risk of being trivial, insincere and hypocritical.[97] Pamela observes in her final *Exalted* letter that '*true Politeness* . . . is but another word for *Virtue* and *Honour*', a meaning that implicitly contrasts mere social polish (p. 599); while Henry Fielding distinguishes not between performance and sincerity, but between two kinds of social performance, negative and positive: self-serving 'Affectation', which, like a 'Farcical Actor on the Stage', 'always over-acts her Part', and the beneficial sincerity which, like the 'judicious and just Actor', represents the 'truest and finest Strokes of Nature'.[98]

Literary and theatrical topics were co-opted into polite conversation, fuelled by the print and performance sources mentioned earlier. When the eponymous hero of *The Vicar of Wakefield* and his family meet 'two young ladies richly drest, whom he [the Squire] introduced as women of very great distinction and fashion from town', his daughters' heads are turned by their conversation:

> The two ladies threw my girls quite into the shade; for they would talk of nothing but high life, and high lived company; with other fashionable topics, such as pictures, taste, Shakespear, and the musical glasses.[99]

'Shakespear' and other modish theatrical entertainments, such as 'the musical glasses', are grouped as 'fashionable topics' on which to discourse. The innocent vicar is initially impressed, attributing their casual profanities to their 'tip-top quality breeding' ("Tis true they once or twice mortified us sensibly by slipping out an oath; but that appeared to me as the surest symptom of their distinction. . .').[100] His daughters are inspired to emulation: their pride in their appearance is reawakened, and 'all my long and painful lectures upon temperance, simplicity, and contentment, were entirely disregarded'.[101] Their unpolished neighbours, 'The poor Miss Flamboroughs, their former gay companions, were cast off as mean acquaintance', and

> the whole conversation ran upon high life and high lived company, with pictures, taste, Shakespear, and the musical glasses.[102]

In this word-for-word repetition of the polite speech habits of the fine women, the narrator hints that Olivia and Sophia Primrose parrot, as if by rote, the conversational clichés they have heard, with no further knowledge of the town they still hope to visit. It comes as almost no surprise that the delightfully named Lady Blarney and Miss Carolina Wilelmina Amelia Skeggs, who offer to promote Olivia and Sophia to new heights of sophistication through a 'single winter in town', are 'abandoned women of the town' masquerading as '*ladies of great distinction*' in order to deceive.[103]

Judged in this light, the act of quoting literature and drama in company, whether in the drawing room or the coffee house, could seem the height of refinement, a dangerous performance, or, more mundanely, a pedestrian retailing of other people's wit.[104] To use quotation to aid communication, improve understanding and contribute through dialogue to mutual enjoyment of literature's beauties is one thing; to turn a play into a tedious monologue to show off one's acting ambitions is quite another.[105] In Eliza Haywood's 1725 *The Tea-Table*, the irritating 'Lord Critick', a 'Titled *Coxcomb*', interrupts the conversation with great 'Impertinence', and 'teiz'd' the company with 'ridiculous Remarks on the Scenery, the Plot, the Diction' of a new play he has seen in rehearsal (finally breaking off, to the assembled company's relief, only to compliment a new influx of ladies). While some assume his '*Quality* gave a Sanction to his *Judgment*', he is firmly contrasted with the wise worthies who resume their conversation after he has left.[106] For them, by contrast, drama can furnish morally instructive conversation: 'So truly has a late celebrated *Poet* made JANE SHORE complain on this Occasion, that methinks it shou'd be a Warning to the whole Sex'.[107] It will become commonplace in fiction to criticise characters who quote literature merely to display their scraps of knowledge, name-dropping what they have seen at the theatre in the same breath that they talk about their new clothes.

When characters quote, then, they might be flaunting their learning, aspiring to politeness, murmuring words of comfort, or spouting from the theatre. Quotation might suggest leisured laziness or industrious self-education, brashness or modesty, the mindless recycling of literary wit and wisdom or the genuine admiration of a poetic 'beauty'. A theatrical quotation could represent an emotional response to moving lines, a souvenir from a fashionable excursion, or an excuse for histrionic affectation; sincerity or pretence; borrowed words or 'real' feeling. These ambiguities, generated by an array of contemporary quotation practices, and inflected by the gender, class and education of the speaker, make quotation an effective tool for nuanced characterisation. Shakespeare, at once a figure of stage and book, praise and censure, sincerity and performance, encapsulates and exaggerates these contradictions. The *declared* source of a character's quotation – whether book, stage or a scrap overheard in conversation – will become a crucial part of their self-presentation. Eighteenth-century novelists knew that, thanks to the prominence of the century's rich cultures of quotation, they had an audience ready to judge the significance of every act of quotation.

The sources named in this chapter – performances, editions, anthologies, periodicals, polite conversation – all contributed to the growing reputation of Shakespeare in the eighteenth century, helping to confirm the impression that the playwright was a central part of cultural life. But among these cultural forms, the novel has a perhaps unique impact on Shakespeare. The anthology, a relatively inexpensive form, extracted Shakespeare's plays under abstract headings that suggested their applicability. The novel, by contrast, showed quotations *applied* to the specific situations of fictional characters. Where periodical personae such as Isaac Bickerstaff applied Shakespeare's words to new situations, a much larger and more diverse array of fictional characters, including men and women of all stations, tested and proved the aptness of Shakespeare's insight into all manner of emotional circumstances, and called on him personally as a guide. Editions and performances (whether in the theatre or in private, amateur form) encouraged people to admire his works, but, while they familiarised readers and audiences with great speeches, these remained, inevitably, in character; the novel, by selective quotation, ascribes the words not to their speakers but to 'Shakespeare'. Novels were not necessarily more accessible than these other cultural forms.[108] Printing was still expensive, 'literacy rates grew only slowly, and novel reading and writing remained the preserve of the relatively wealthy'. But circulating libraries 'sowed the seeds of a more democratized relationship between the British people and fiction' and 'Serial and extract publication in newspapers, magazines, anthologies, and chapbooks also expanded access to affordable fiction'.[109] Thanks to the proliferating forms in which people could encounter prose fiction, and to its influence on other writers, the distinctive effects of its quotation practices on the perceived value and authority of Shakespeare's words would be felt for many years to come.

CHAPTER 3

Shakespeare's novel authority

On Wednesday, April 12th, 'Your unhappy CLARISSA HARLOWE' writes to Anna Howe to 'pursue my melancholy story' (pp. 398, 387). Tricked into Robert Lovelace's chariot and carried unwillingly to St Albans, she is forced to reside with him as his 'sister' to preserve her reputation (p. 388). Now that she is in his grasp, Lovelace is full of vows and compliments, but Clarissa is weary of his 'extravagant volubility'. She tells Anna:

> True respect, true value, I think, lies not in words: words *cannot* express it. The silent awe, the humble, the doubting eye, and even the hesitating voice, better show it by much, than, as Shakespeare says,
>
> —*The rattling tongue*
> *Of saucy and audacious eloquence.* (p. 397)

Clarissa quotes Theseus' words from the final act of *A Midsummer Night's Dream*, when he chooses for the nuptial evening's entertainment what the rude mechanicals proudly call '"A tedious brief scene of young Pyramus / And his love Thisbe"'.[1] Philostrate tries to discourage him:[2] the performers are 'Hard-handed men that work in Athens', and their attempts at tragedy laughable. But Theseus is insistent: 'I will hear that play'. He assures his new wife that he has seen 'great clerks', poised with prepared speeches, struck dumb by his arrival, but has extracted from their stuttering words as much sense of their loyal duty as if they had been articulate (v. 1. 72, 82, 93–103). Confiding in her friend, Clarissa gives new, private purpose to Duke Theseus' public point about the expressiveness of awkward silence. For him, diffidence is a virtue in a subject; for her, it is a virtue in a lover.

Clarissa takes Shakespeare for her authority in matters of the heart, deploying the words 'as Shakespeare says', and, in the second edition of the novel, 'as our beloved Shakespeare says', to clinch her argument.[3] It is, however, when Richardson's characters most appear to borrow Shakespeare's authority that they actually confer it upon him. Clarissa imagines

'Shakespeare' as a wise figure on whom she can call directly for advice and comfort. She applies his words to a new emotional situation, and she tests them against her own experience, the prefix 'as Shakespeare says' implicitly pronouncing them to be justly observed. Far from borrowing a ready-made piece of wisdom, this fictional character actively transforms a detached phrase of Shakespeare's into what Richardson would call a 'moral sentiment', with lasting effect.

It is often said that Shakespeare became an 'author' in the eighteenth century, constructed as the sole possessor of his work by the emergence of copyright and a new emphasis on the 'individual subject'.[4] Less frequently observed is the process by which he became, at the same time, an 'authority' – a word that shares with 'author' a common Latin etymology in 'auctoritas'.[5] Marcus Walsh suggests that contemporary editing practice was shaped by the fact that 'for the eighteenth-century public, and for eighteenth-century editors, Shakespeare was, like Milton, a figure of *auctoritas* and quasi-sacred status', but it is important to note that Shakespeare's 'auctoritas' was under construction.[6] Among the more enduring definitions of 'authority' in the *OED*, two seem precisely to capture the kinds of status that Shakespeare achieves in the eighteenth century. The first definition could refer to Shakespeare's growing literary influence on subsequent writers: 'Power to influence the opinions of others, esp. because of one's recognized knowledge or scholarship; authoritative opinion; acknowledged expertise'.[7] It is with this sense of literary and artistic authority in mind that Fiona Ritchie and Peter Sabor observe that Shakespeare exerted 'a profound influence on a variety of authors' in the eighteenth century.[8] The second, however, invokes a different domain: 'Power to influence the conduct and actions of others; personal or practical influence'.[9] It is with this more 'personal or practical' sense of authority in mind that Elizabeth Griffith writes in *The Morality of Shakespeare's Drama Illustrated* that she wishes to 'expound the document of the moralist': to bring to the fore Shakespeare's moral advice.[10] Eighteenth-century novels, as this chapter shows, help significantly to establish in Shakespeare the impression of this second kind of authority. Novels grant Shakespeare influence over the behaviour of fictional characters and, by extension, readers, and, via repeated acts of quotation, invest him with an enduring emotional and moral authority.

Earlier studies of Shakespeare and 'authority' have explored how his plays represented, examined and contested the official forms of power that shaped early modern England and early modern performance.[11] A political perspective persists in the study of Shakespeare's reception – or how the author acquired authority of his own – in subsequent centuries. For Dobson, in the late seventeenth and early eighteenth century 'Shakespeare the Author, just as much as his *oeuvre*, becomes the centre of a struggle for the right to speak for the core of the national culture',[12] and he observes a number of competing, politically motivated cultural appropriations that invest authority in Shakespeare's name in order to legitimate their cause. In this chapter, I argue that, alongside high political borrowings, novelists confer on Shakespeare the ability to speak knowledgeably in the domain of the human emotions. This is not to say that Shakespeare has a ready-made moral value that props up prose fiction: rather, it is to argue that novelists ascribe that value to Shakespeare through the quotation of his words by characters in novels.

So far, so Richardson, one might say, but the practice of investing Shakespeare's words with moral significance – whether earnestly, as in Richardson's case, or more casually or inadvertently, as in others – is widespread in fiction. Focussing in particular on the work of Richardson, Henry Fielding and Sarah Fielding, I trace in this chapter the processes by which novelists variously, but collectively, ascribe emotional and moral authority to Shakespeare. First, I examine how novelistic characters construct a fully-realised image of Shakespeare – or 'embody' him – as a knowing, insightful author, by treating his dramatic characters' words as his own insightful utterances. Texts from *Clarissa* to *David Simple* demonstrate for the reader a direct relationship with a benignly advisory figure. Second, I show that, when characters such as Sarah Fielding's hold Shakespeare's phrases up against new situations, they affirm the 'great propriety and judgment' of his observations. 'Propriety' in this context does not refer necessarily to 'conformity to accepted standards of behaviour or morals',[13] but to 'Accuracy; justness':[14] 'appropriateness to circumstances or conditions; suitability, aptness, fitness; conformity with what is required by a rule, principle, etc.; rightness, correctness, accuracy'.[15] Quoting characters invite readers to assess the fit between Shakespeare's words, their own circumstances and those of Shakespeare's dramatis personae. In so doing, they confirm, sometimes by contrast, how 'finely expressed' are Shakespeare's ideas, and how aptly fitted his characters' speeches are to certain human situations; they approve, as if measuring by novelistic standards, his skill in characterisation.

Finally, I argue that it is ultimately the experiences of novel characters, corroborated by the sympathetic judgement of the reader (who is trained by the novelists to assess, as in Adam Smith's model of sympathy, whether a person's situation justifies their behaviour), that confirm Shakespeare's insight. In place of a vaguer contemporary admiration for Shakespeare's extraordinary knowledge of human nature, quoting characters grant specific phrases the force of moral truths. They reverse the critical truism that, in the eighteenth century, knowledge based on precepts and known authorities gave way to knowledge based on personal experience. In the eighteenth-century novel, sayings from Shakespeare are tested against characters' and readers' experiences, and when proved to be true, accrue the force of precepts.

It is not just Shakespeare who gains authority by this means: the process mutually promotes the cultural status of Shakespeare and the novel. All of the novelists discussed in this chapter are admired (albeit by one another) for their astute knowledge of human nature; by making Shakespeare a benchmark of apt emotional expressions, they celebrate their own ability to craft characters that are 'true pictures of Nature'. At the same time, novels exhibit a growing sense that what constitutes 'human nature' is not stable, but is rather an aggregation of individual experiences. Through their myriad quoting characters, they offer themselves, and Shakespeare, as new kinds of authority: not stores of old wisdom and precepts, but rich human examples able to respond knowingly and insightfully to the complexities of modern experience.

'As Shakespeare says': embodying the author

The eighteenth-century novel 'embodies' 'Shakespeare' as a sage author figure with wise insights to impart. The notion of Shakespeare's eighteenth-century embodiment is borrowed from Michael Dobson, who identifies the processes by which the playwright was given physical form in other, less directly literary media: in the marble statue of Shakespeare in Poets' Corner, Westminster Abbey, erected in 1741, and in the human figure of the actor, David Garrick.[16] These physical manifestations of 'Shakespeare' built on new biographies, complete works and even appearances of the playwright as a ghostly character on stage and in essays. They conferred certain qualities upon Shakespeare: Dobson borrows the words of J. G. of Stratford to describe the bookish figure in the Westminster Abbey as 'Noble, awe-inspiring, venerable, and intensely serious'.[17] The statue was 'conceived by its sponsors as an affirmation of the national poet's resistance to ministerial corruption, but variously treated by contemporaries as a monument to Jacobite nostalgia, to female patronage, and to the supremacy of the study over the theatre'.[18] Each of these interest groups made Shakespeare an author in their own image.

Alongside these public, physical incarnations of 'Shakespeare', there is another, less overtly political, story to be told about the literary and textual processes that 'embodied' Shakespeare as an author figure, to rather different ends. The quotation hastily and inaccurately added to the blank scroll to which the Westminster Abbey statue of Shakespeare meaningfully points,[19] nonetheless showed how phrases spoken by characters in Shakespeare's plays could be presented as the author's own observations about the passage of time, and the inevitable dissolution of 'The Cloud cupt Tow'rs,/ The Gorgeous Palaces,/ The Great Globe itself'. The mid-century novel, with its numerous invocations of Shakespeare's wisdom, lends Shakespeare authority on an at once larger and more domestic scale. The novel, by repeated quotation, renders 'Shakespeare' a morally valuable 'author function': a proper name that is not just 'indicative' of a certain person, but a 'description' of their qualities and associations – at the very historical moment when 'who wrote it and when and how becomes important to the status and value of the work'.[20] Perhaps the novel's most significant contribution is to construct Shakespeare as a *personal* authority on whom all kinds of individuals can call.

It is easy to underestimate the transformational effect of novel quotation on Shakespeare's status. Clarissa's quotation above has the appearance of a sententious observation simply lifted from the commonplace tradition. Between the first publication of Theseus' speech in *A Midsummer Night's Dream* in 1600 and of Clarissa's letter in *Clarissa* in 1748 lie several intermediary acts of quotation that had already given this speech wider significance. In the early eighteenth century, the author of a letter to *The Spectator* in praise of the modest lawyer turns to 'the Sentiments the greatest among the Ancients of different Ages entertain'd upon this Virtue', and quotes '. . .*In the Modesty of fearful Duty / I read as much as from the ratling Tongue / Of sawcy and audacious Eloquence*. . .' in order to 'advance the Merit of Modesty'.[21] Later, in a book of literary extracts, *The British Muse* (1738), this passage is included under the heading 'SILENCE':

> Out of this silence yet I pick'd a welcome:
> And in the modesty of fearful duty
> I read as much, as from the rattling tongue
> Of sawcy and audacious eloquence.[22]

This '*Collection of Thoughts Moral, Natural, and Sublime, of our English Poets: Who Flourished in the Sixteenth and Seventeenth Centuries*' quotes Theseus as part of its project to illustrate chronologically, and under abstract headings, the '*gradual Improvements of our Poetry and Language*'.

While these earlier extractors had celebrated Shakespeare's lines as usefully expressive or descriptive, Clarissa invests them for the first time with moral authority. It is her surrounding prose that turns a sliver of *A Midsummer Night's Dream* into a maxim. She anticipates the quotation with her own rhetorical triplet of 'awe', 'eye' and 'voice'; and, with the hinging comparative 'better ... than', creates a resounding contrast between 'true affection' and 'saucy and audacious eloquence'. She also makes Theseus' statement more emphatic. Theseus could see duty '*as much*' – that is, equally well – in awkward silence as in 'rattling' eloquence. Clarissa, by contrast, declares that such awkward actions '*better* show it by much' (italics added). She thus turns a one-and-a-half-line fragment into a forceful observation by 'Shakespeare'. So successful is she in doing so that the observation (if not Shakespeare's words themselves), would be excerpted in the collection of 'Moral and Instructive SENTIMENTS' appended to the third edition of *Clarissa*. Richardson categorises the words 'Silent awe, the humble, doubting eye, and even the hesitating voice, are the natural indications of true and respectful Love' as one of those pieces 'interspersed throughout the Work, as may be presumed to be of general Use and Service'.[23] Shakespeare's phrase, implicitly present in Clarissa's adapted maxim, has accrued, via her quotation, the value of a 'moral sentiment'.

The authority with which Clarissa invests this quotation is not only moral but emotional. She redirects lines about the appropriate way for a clerk to address a duke to discuss the appropriate manner in which a male suitor might address a woman, and in 'Moral and Instructive SENTIMENTS' the lines appear under the heading not of 'Silence', nor of 'Modesty', but of 'Love'. Theseus concludes, of course, that 'Love, therefore, and tongue-tied simplicity/ In least speak most, to my capacity', but the new context of the novel has shaped the quotation into a truth about not dutiful but romantic love. It is possible that Clarissa's personal and emotional use of the phrase influenced its later anthologisation. In the years following *Clarissa*'s publication, it appeared in any number of collections of Shakespearean extracts. It was included in a longer speech under the heading 'Modest Duty always acceptable' in Dodd's *Beauties of Shakespear*; admired as part of a 'beautiful passage' in Elizabeth Griffith's *The Morality of Shakespeare's Drama Illustrated* (1777); and catalogued under 'EMBARRASSMENT' in George Kearsley's *The Beauties of Shakespeare* (1783).[24]

It is almost certain that later fiction institutionalised Clarissa's application of the words to romantic love. In the anonymous novel, *Chit-Chat*

(1755), the phrase is a measure of the ideal suitor: Charlotte's nervous admirer, 'the young academician' Welford, is not 'accustomed to gallantry', but

> Charlotte was wise enough to read more in 'the modesty of fearful duty' than in 'the rattling tongue of saucy and audacious eloquence'...

As she knew Welford was 'lately come from the university', she proffered subjects on which she 'supposed he could show himself to advantage': the 'state of poetry' and 'rising geniuses'.[25] In Clara Reeve's epistolary *School for Widows* (1791), Rachel Strictland (in the same letter to fellow widow Frances Darnford in which she relates how she deftly fended off a marriage proposal) quotes these lines of 'SHAKESPEARE' to describe the 'sincere' and 'eloquent' gratitude of the silent and tearful Mr and Mrs Elton when she proposes to employ their son George as a tutor to the youths in her care.[26] Where anthologies and essays made the lines more abstractly applicable, Clarissa's quotation demonstrates their emotional application, particularly by women, in domestic settings.

Most influentially of all, Clarissa's quotation exhibits a one-on-one relationship with the knowing figure of 'Shakespeare'. She transforms the quotation from a neat expression of a widely accepted idea into a unique piece of Shakespeare's own wisdom. She is not the first to attribute the lines to Shakespeare rather than to Theseus: the *British Muse* followed the quotation with the words 'Shakespeare, in his *Midsummer Night's Dream*', and *The Spectator* says that '*Shakespear* also has express'd himself in the same favourable Strains of Modesty'.[27] Clarissa, however, attributes the lines to Shakespeare with greater emotional intensity, partly because of the confiding way in which she writes to Anna, and partly because of the personal nature of her predicament, far from friends and with her reputation in jeopardy. The strength of her emotional connection with the author is increased in the second edition of *Clarissa* when 'as Shakespeare says' becomes 'as our beloved Shakespeare says'. Even if 'our beloved' was a fussy addition by Richardson, anxious to play down any sense of unfeminine excess in Clarissa's solitary reading and to present it instead as a safely communal act,[28] it only further emphasises that Shakespeare is a source from which both of these young women draw comfort and inspiration – and suggests that many more might follow their lead.

This direct, emotional relationship with the figure of 'Shakespeare' is shared by many characters in mid-century fiction, including in Richardson's other novels. Quoted by Pamela alone in Richardson's first novel, Shakespeare is admired by everyone in his last. Sir Hargrave Pollexfen and Mr Selby might have a penchant for old adages, and the vivacious

Charlotte Grandison for modern drama, but Shakespeare is invoked, often by name, by all manner of characters in *Sir Charles Grandison*, from Sir Charles's shy admirer, Lady Anne, to his cruel father, Thomas Grandison, as well as by the hero and heroine, Sir Charles and Harriet Byron. Shakespeare is by no means the only literary voice to be heard in Richardson's novels: there is just one Shakespeare quotation in each of the two parts of *Pamela*; in the first edition of *Clarissa* he ranks behind the most-quoted author, Dryden, by thirteen quotations to sixteen; and he shares space with, for example, Hargrave's comic verse, Young's poetry, and Handel's music in *Sir Charles Grandison*. In each of these novels, quotations from the Bible outweigh every other source. Yet Shakespeare stands out by far for the warmth with which he is praised by all. Other poets and playwrights receive milder admiration: Clarissa recalls 'those charming lines' of 'Mr. Rowe' (p. 445) and Robert Lovelace invokes 'the gentle Waller' (p. 670); and while Dryden is dubbed Lovelace's 'favourite Bard' (p. 761), the highest praise he receives in the novel is that 'once I thought [he] said well ...' (p. 1473). Shakespeare, by contrast, is upheld as 'our English pride and glory' (p. 1148). By the third edition, when the only other additional epithet is to the 'celebrated' Swift, Shakespeare is both 'beloved' and 'immortal'. Unlike Dryden, Pope, Lee, Rowe and others, Shakespeare's words are never attributed in Richardson's novels to that general fund of poetic excellence, 'the poet says well'. The named figure of 'Shakespeare' 'advises well' and 'says well' more often than any other author, and all kinds of character feel able to apply his words to their personal circumstances.

Collectively, these fictional characters embody Shakespeare as a personal advisor. Rachel Trickett has suggested that Shakespeare represents a 'secular scripture' in Richardson because he is 'referred to in *Clarissa* by every kind of character, with no particular appropriation'.[29] The novel, however, does not simply *represent* Shakespeare's wise benignity; rather, he *becomes* a 'secular scripture' through characters' repeated acts of admiration and quotation. Novel quotations are the agent, not the mirror, of his status. This process continues even when Shakespeare is quoted to pernicious ends. Robert Lovelace, frustrated that Clarissa is 'Refusing to see me, refusing her meals', writes to his confidant John Belford

> But Shakespeare says;
>
> *Come what come may*
> *Patience and time run thro' the roughest day.*
>
> And that shall be my comfort. (p. 571)

Lovelace echoes the immediacy of Clarissa's relationship with 'Shakespeare', calling on Shakespeare, ostensibly benignly enough, for 'comfort'. Yet Lovelace's is a sinister kind of 'comfort': confident of his ability to wait with 'patience' for Clarissa to surrender to his desires, he invokes Shakespeare's authority as a guarantee of his success. While much of this might be bluster, Lovelace's misquotation of Macbeth's 'Time and the hour' (1. 3. 147–8; see Chapter 2, p. 33) only contributes to the sense of wilful corruption.

Lovelace exploits the impression of a direct relationship with Shakespeare to even more chilling effect when he writes to Belford to describe Clarissa's fury after the fire, which she thought was a trick to seduce her. Lovelace withdraws to strengthen himself, and she 'to cool', and he tells Belford that he keeps in mind a piece of Shakespeare's wisdom:

> Shakespeare advises well:
>
> *Oppose not rage, while rage is in its force;*
> *But give it way awhile, and let it waste.*
> *The rising deluge is not stopt with dams;*
> *Those it o'erbears, and drowns the hope of harvest.*
> *But, wisely manag'd, its divided strength*
> *Is sluic'd in channels, and securely drained...* (p. 800)

Lovelace transforms this dramatic speech into matter-of-fact 'advice'. He presents the imperative 'Oppose not rage' as Shakespeare's personal hint about how to overcome Clarissa's resistance. 'Wisely manag'd' suggests his wished-for control of Clarissa; 'divided', 'sluic'd' and 'drain'd' his ominous intentions. By constructing Shakespeare as 'advisor', Lovelace imbues these violent words with uncomfortable authority. He lends the force of axiom to his own personal interests ('the rising deluge is not stopt with dams'), and renews his confidence in the fulfilment of his wishes ('Is ... securely drained'). These are not, in fact, Shakespeare's words, but come from John Dryden's adaptation of *Troilus and Cressida* (1679), courtesy of the intermediary source, Bysshe's *Art of English Poetry*, in which Richardson seems to have Lovelace dabble (see Chapter 2, pp. 33–4). As with 'Patience and time', the way in which Lovelace forces 'Shakespeare' into the role of advisor is only an extreme version of the effort expended to embody 'Shakespeare' as an authority figure in *any* act of quotation.

Embodying Shakespeare is a widespread practice among the characters of mid-century fiction. Portia, one of several virtuous characters with Shakespearean names in Sarah Fielding and Jane Collier's 'dramatic fable',

The Cry, delivers twenty-four of the text's thirty-six Shakespeare quotations as she defends her life's decisions against the jury of untruth, 'the Cry'. She, like Clarissa, treats Shakespeare as an insightful author, advising the Cry not to 'invite into your breasts such evil passions as are, according to *Shakespear* in his *Winter's Tale:—Goads, thorns, nettles, tails of wasps—*'.[30] Indeed, Shakespeare is explicitly embodied in this tale as a moral figure who 'could never be provoked to return such paltry spite' as shown him by Ben Jonson (i. 164). In a twist on the direct relationship with Shakespeare demonstrated by Portia and Clarissa, Richardson's Clementina repeats 'those lines of *your* Shakespeare' (italics added) that Sir Charles Grandison had formerly read to her.[31] Sir Charles is an intermediary who effectively permits the Italian woman only indirect access to this English authority – and who will ultimately reject her in favour of the English, confidently Shakespeare-quoting, Harriet Byron. Male characters, too, invoke a direct relationship: Smollett's Ferdinand Fathom meets a gentleman who talks of those who 'as my friend Shakespear has it, *have seen better days*' and a chevalier paraphrases to Peregrine Pickle some words of 'your admired Shakespear' on bad actors when describing the leading lights of the English stage.[32] Booth, in Henry Fielding's *Amelia*, remarks 'How finely doth *Shakespeare* express it in his *Othello*!'.[33]

Henry Fielding, as this last example suggests, also embodies Shakespeare in his fiction, but his manner of doing so is usually rather different. An emotional adviser in Richardson and Sarah Fielding's novels, Shakespeare appears a more distant authority in Henry Fielding's fiction. Fielding frequently invokes the classics, calling on Homer and Aristotle in the preface to *Joseph Andrews* to gather support for his 'comic-epic-poem-in-prose', and citing numerous authorities in the first chapters of books in *Tom Jones*, parts of the novel often regarded by critics as most closely resembling an authorial voice.[34] Shakespeare appears among these grand, authorial quotations, such as when the narrator, reflecting on the analogy between the world and the stage in Chapter I of Book VII, turns from Thespis, Aristotle and 'the Greeks' to the 'immortal Shakespeare' for corroboration. He is frequently quoted admiringly, often with an accompanying 'as Shakespeare phrases it', and twice with the commendation that his descriptions are 'nobly' deployed.[35] In *Amelia*, the narrator introduces a quotation from *Othello* with the superlative praise that 'the greatest Genius the World hath ever produced, observes in one of his most excellent Plays...' (p. 246). Delivered in this confident narratorial voice, Shakespeare's words are granted a prestige and authority on a par with the classics.

Strikingly, Fielding, unlike his sister, and Richardson, and other mid-century novelists, tends not to put these quotations in the mouths of his characters, especially in his earlier fiction. Of the thirteen Shakespeare quotations in *Tom Jones*, for example, the narrator delivers all but two. The narrator, however, is as idiosyncratic as other quoting characters: his Shakespeare quotations are frequently dashed off, sometimes misquoted and often playful in their typography as Fielding gives the impression of shouting or whispering in casually borrowed words (see Chapter 2, pp. 24–5). Yet just as *Tom Jones* creates a divide between a 'model' narrator who quotes classical authors with dexterity, and characters who try, and fail, to do the same,[36] so Fielding's narrator's relationship with Shakespeare is distinct from that of his characters.

Fielding holds Shakespeare out of his characters' reach. The narrator of *Tom Jones* tantalises unlikely characters with Shakespeare quotations. Miss Bridget, accompanied by the housekeeper, assumes her familiar eavesdropping post and strains to hear her brother Squire Allworthy's conversation with Jenny Jones about a foundling boy discovered in the parish:

> This Hole in her Brother's Study Door, was indeed as well known to Miss *Bridget*, and had been as frequently applied to by her, as the famous Hole in the Wall was by *Thisbe* of old. This served to many good Purposes. For by such Means Miss *Bridget* became often acquainted with her Brother's Inclinations, without giving him the Trouble of repeating them to her. It is true, some Inconveniences attended this Intercourse, and she had sometimes Reason to cry out with *Thisbe*, in *Shakespear*, 'O wicked, wicked Wall!' (i. 55)

Nosy Miss Bridget seems undeserving of the parallel with '*Thisbe*, in *Shakespear*', whose romantic intramural communications with Pyramus are enacted in *A Midsummer Night's Dream*. But the narrator suggests only that Bridget 'had sometimes *Reason* to cry out *with* Thisbe' (italics added); he does not say that she ever actually did, and thus the quotation remains out of her reach. Thisbe's dramatic cry of intense love seems comically incongruous with Bridget's spinsterish hunger for gossip. Yet when a plot twist reveals Bridget to be Tom's mother, this passionate quotation suddenly appears more fitting and Shakespeare gains an impression of narrative prescience over the unfolding of fictional events.

Henry Fielding constructs Shakespeare as a skilful writer with utmost narrative control. Shakespeare represents not Fielding's classical inheritance, but his dramatic training. Fielding praises Shakespeare in his novels, as he did in his plays, as a benchmark of dramatic excellence. The narrator of *Tom Jones* cries 'O, *Shakespear*, had I thy Pen!' (ii. 555) when attempting to describe the face of a stricken servant, and calls on 'Genius' to guide him as it guided 'thy *Shakespear*' (ii. 686). He frequently praises Shakespeare's craft as a playwright:

> For this Reason *Shakespear* hath artfully introduced his *Desdemona* soliciting Favours for *Cassio* of her Husband, as the Means of enflaming not only his Jealousy, but his Rage, to the highest Pitch of Madness. (i. 501)

Fielding's narrator implies that, as a dramatist, he has special insight into the 'Reason' for Shakespeare's artistic decision. He admires Shakespeare not just for his portrayal of human emotions ('Jealousy' and 'Rage'), but for the judgement with which Shakespeare 'artfully introduced' a situation to best dramatic effect: for his judiciousness as a story writer as well as his human insights. It is this combination of attributes, as the next part of the chapter explores, that will underscore Shakespeare's authority.

'Great Propriety and Judgment': Shakespeare's accuracy

When Fielding, in his reference to Desdemona, Cassio and Othello, speaks simultaneously of Shakespeare's understanding of human emotions, and of the dramatic skill with which he deploys that knowledge, it marks a small but crucial shift in Shakespeare's eighteenth-century reception. Shakespeare's knowledge of human nature had been celebrated since the 1623 publication of the First Folio, when, in their prefatory material, John Heminges and Henry Condell said of the playwright that

> as he was a happy imitator of nature, [he] was a most gentle expresser of it. His mind and hand went together, and what he thought he uttered with that easiness that we have scarce received from him a blot in his papers.[37]

For Heminges and Condell, what Shakespeare perceives in Nature flows unmediated on to the page: 'what he thought he uttered'. Their image of Shakespeare as at once a 'happy imitator'[38] and a 'gentle expresser' of nature is intended to be complimentary, recasting Shakespeare's lack of scholarly art as a virtue. Yet the 'easiness' or facility that his fellow actors admire can occlude the craft in Shakespeare's representations of 'nature'. This oddly passive image of Shakespeare recurs through the seventeenth and into the eighteenth century, from Thomas Fuller's observation that 'as *Cornish diamonds* are not polished by any Lapidary, but are pointed and smooth even as they are taken out of the Earth, so *nature* it self was all the *art* which was used upon him';[39] to John Dryden's that he had the 'largest and most comprehensive soul. All the Images of Nature were still present to him, and he drew them not laboriously, but luckily'.[40]

In comparing Shakespeare favourably with more 'laboriously' learned contemporaries such as Ben Jonson, critics often played down Shakespeare's labour or poetic craft in favour of his effortless perception of nature.

By contrast, Fielding's novels construct Shakespeare as a conscious, decision-making author who precisely deploys his knowledge of human nature in his writing. This is not a completely new idea: in the same set of dedicatory materials in which Heminges and Condell stressed Shakespeare's native fluency, Ben Jonson insisted that poetry takes work:

> Yet must I not give nature all; thy art,
> My gentle Shakespeare, must enjoy a part.
> For though the poet's matter nature be,
> His art doth give the fashion; and that he
> Who casts to write a living line must sweat—
> Such as thine are—and strike the second heat
> Upon the muses' anvil, turn the same,
> And himself with it that he thinks to frame;
> Or for the laurel he may gain a scorn,
> For a good poet's made as well as born.[41]

Rather than hand all the credit to Nature, Jonson draws attention to the 'sweat' and 'second heat' of work necessary to transform matter into art and man into poet; he might include himself in his image of 'the poet' who works at the 'anvil', the labourer at his craft. Fielding, however, presents Shakespeare's work as more intellectually elevated. Shakespeare's observations do not naturally emanate from him, nor does he toil over them: he saw emotional situations and then, as Fielding's narrator says, 'nobly described' them for his audience; Shakespeare understands the workings of jealousy and 'for this Reason' arranged his narrative of Othello and Desdemona to greatest effect. Fielding's Shakespeare is neither 'laborious' nor 'lucky', but perceptive and judicious, using his insights into human nature to achieve powerful dramatic effects.

Fielding thus constructs Shakespeare's authority by lending a new sense of precision and skill to Shakespeare's natural ability and 'comprehensive soul'. Every major eighteenth-century editor of Shakespeare's complete works had chorused praise of his insight into human nature: Pope observed that 'he is not so much an Imitator, as an Instrument, of Nature; and 'tis not so just to say that he speaks from her, as that she speaks thro' him', while Warburton observed that, 'widely excelling in the Knowledge of Human Nature, [Shakespeare] hath given to his infinitely varied Pictures of it, such Truth of Design, such Force of Drawing, such Beauty of

Colouring, as was hardly ever equalled by any Writer'. Theobald seems to come closer to Fielding's position when he admires the 'Draughts of Nature' visible in his characters, and the 'Propriety and Justness' with which his ideas are applied to them.[42]

Yet the novelist takes this idea further. Shakespeare's perceived knowledge of the 'hidden operations of human nature' linked him, as Gefen Bar-On Santor has shown, 'in the popular imagination to the achievement of Isaac Newton',[43] and early eighteenth-century editors often disregarded his language in the process of excavating his insights, not venerating 'Shakespeare's expressive faculty as the essence of his genius', but finding instead that his expressions 'often fail to match the greatness of his understanding'.[44] Through frequent narratorial praise, Fielding certainly reinforces, in Theobald's words, the 'Propriety and Justness' of Shakespeare's observations. But through quotation, Fielding shows that Shakespeare's words and phrases are not merely the vehicle, but the source, of his value. For Fielding, unlike Shakespeare's early editors, Shakespeare's worth lay in the exact congruence of insight and word: the playwright's knowledge of human nature is exemplified by his choice of dramatic language. While Jean I. Marsden traces in the early century the changing answer to the question of 'whether the essence of Shakespeare's talent lies in *mimesis* or in *logos*, in representing nature or in language',[45] Fielding's praise and frequent quotation seem to unite the two qualities in one.

Other novelists reinforce this sense of Shakespeare's unusual insight by having characters apply admired words and phrases from Shakespeare's plays to their own lives. Cynthia, in Sarah Fielding's first novel, *David Simple*, for example, says that she only appreciated the perceptiveness of one of Shakespeare's lines when she saw its application in real life:

> I think *Shakespear* has made *Hamlet* give the best Description that can be of them, in that one Line he speaks to *Ophelia*;—*Ye lisp—and ye amble,—and ye nick-name God's Creatures*. An Expression I never understood till I knew the World enough to have met with some of those sort of Women.[46]

From 'I think' to 'the best', Cynthia's statement is carefully appraising. She finally 'understood' the force of Shakespeare's 'Expression' when, long after she read *Hamlet*, she encountered such women in real life and applied Hamlet's observation directly to them. Camilla in the same novel observes that 'the poor unhappy deceived Man stared with Fury, his Eye-Balls rolled, and like *Othello*, he bit his nether Lip with Fury',[47] confirming, by sympathetic contrast between a 'real-life' situation and Shakespeare's depiction of Othello, the skill of his characterisation.

In one sense, then, novels increasingly separate Shakespeare's wise words – 'as Shakespeare phrases it' – from his characters and plays. In another, simultaneous sense, novels make Shakespeare's characters a measure of the accuracy of his insights. Shakespeare had already been praised in the eighteenth century for the naturalness and appropriateness of his characters' speech. Margaret Cavendish, defending Shakespeare from the criticism that his plays 'were made up onely with Clowns, Fools, Watchmen, and the like', had remarked that:

> to Express Properly, Rightly, Usually, and Naturally, a Clown's, or Fool's Humour, Expressions, Phrases, Garbs, Manners, Actions, Words, and Course of Life, is as Witty, Wise, Judicious, Ingenious, and Observing, as to Write and Express the Expressions, Phrases, Garbs, Manners, Actions, Words, and Course of Life, of Kings and Princes.[48]

To draw characters 'Properly, Rightly, Usually, and Naturally', whatever their status, requires acute observation and judicious writing. Yet Cavendish, albeit figuratively, speaks of Shakespeare's characterisation not as a skill, but as the result of shape-shifting: 'so Well he hath Express'd in his Playes all Sorts of Persons, as one would think he *had been Transformed* into every one of those Persons he hath Described' (italics added).[49]

For his editors, Shakespeare's representation of a great diversity of characters provided a basis 'for the discovery and testing of empirically verifiable general laws'.[50] The eighteenth-century novel, by contrast, aligns Shakespeare with its own more detached aspirations to the accurate construction of character:

> The great Master, and the deepest Penetrator into the inmost Recesses of human Nature, in the Instructions which he with such great Propriety and Judgment introduces from the Mouth of *Hamlet* to the Players, may, if the Writer pleases, be most Part of it adopted also by him for his own Advantage.[51]

Sarah Fielding admires Shakespeare for the 'great Propriety and Judgment' with which he makes his characters speak in ways that befit their circumstances. The words given with such 'great Propriety' to Hamlet are his advice to actors to 'o'er-step not the Modesty of Nature' and 'to hold, as it were, the Mirror to Nature'. Well fitted to their original speaker, these words also offer sound advice on the construction of character. For Fielding, accuracy has moral value: she paraphrases Bossu's assertion that Aristotle and Horace both think 'That Poets teach moral Philosophy', and that 'Poets thus excel simple Philosophers' because poetry is 'wholly an Imitation' (i. xv-xvi). In this view, shared by Philip Sidney and other authors that Fielding cites, the value of poetry is in the accuracy of its 'Imitation', and, among authors who imitate nature, Shakespeare is regarded as pre-eminent.

Fielding's quotations test these prefatory claims: through quotation she juxtaposes her own characters with Shakespeare's, comparing the aptness of their words to their respective situations. Early in *The History of the Countess of Dellwyn*, Charlotte Lucum's father, keen to secure her lucrative marriage to the wealthy Lord Dellwyn, coerces her into frequent socialising. Her reluctant forays into polite society, tolerable at first, become all-consuming:

> She was introduced among a Set of Acquaintance, to whose Splendor in Dress she could by no means arrive, and consequently she often
>
> "*Pined in Thought*,"
>
> Like *Viola* in *Shakespeare*'s *Twelfth Night*; But it could not be said, with Propriety, that, like *Viola*,
>
> *She sat, like* Patience, *on a Monument*,
> *Smiling at* Grief.
>
> For, however possible it may be to support disappointed Love with Patience, it is one of the characteristical Marks of disappointed Vanity, to throw the Mind into Perturbation and Impatience. (i. 41)

If the words 'Like *Viola*' that follow the first quotation from *Twelfth Night* briefly extend to Charlotte the hope of identifying with Shakespeare's heroine, the narrator's blunt 'But it could not be said, with Propriety, that, like *Viola*, "*She sat like* Patience, *on a Monument,/ Smiling at* Grief"', shuts down the association. Viola's 'disappointed Love' and Charlotte's 'disappointed Vanity', the former's 'Patience' and the latter's 'Perturbation and Impatience', are opposites; a mock-heroic contrast. That the shallow Charlotte could not be compared 'with Propriety' to the virtuous Viola can suggest, to the modern reader at least, that the distinction between the two women is a moral one.

As mentioned earlier, however, the moral definition of 'propriety' was not dominant in 1759 when *The Countess of Dellwyn* was published. To say that Fielding's Charlotte could not, 'with propriety', be equated with Shakespeare's Viola is not to hold the former up to a fixed ethical standard, but rather to compare the aptness of their sentiments to their circumstances. Viola, who 'pined in thought' in her 'disappointed Love', represents a perfect fit between circumstances and behaviour, while Charlotte, in merely 'disappointed Vanity', behaves in a way that seems deliberately to flout the 'propriety of character'. Fielding, of course, is no less accurate in her own construction of Charlotte, since one of the 'characteristical Marks' of 'disappointed Vanity' might well be histrionic overreaction.

As this example suggests, Shakespeare's insight is not only proven when the quoted words fit their new situation well. Mock-heroic misfits can be just as affirming, and Fielding exploits for comic effect the disjuncture between the behaviour of Shakespeare's characters and her own. Lady Fanny Fashion takes Charlotte under her wing, but her frequent purchases drive her new mentee to jealous distraction. The dazzling new earrings and necklace which Lady Fanny sports for their visit to court have Charlotte retiring early to her apartment professing a headache. But

> No rest was that night to be found: Not *Macbeth*, but
> *Di'monds, had murthered Sleep:*
> Diamonds, as adequate to the Purpose as any Ruffians whatsoever. (i. 46)

In her mock-tragic distress, Charlotte can still see the diamonds when she closes her eyes. The preposterous image of life-threatening jewellery highlights the impropriety, or lack of fittingness, of Charlotte's reaction to this trivial cause, compared with the murderous circumstances, and more appropriate distress, of the lines quoted from *Macbeth*. When she starts 'as if she had seen all the Ghosts in *Richard the Third*; and her Mind, at that time, might be likened to a Theatre, on which the Tragedy of a glittering Cross, and a pair of Diamonds, was acting, with much more Propriety than the envious Critic called *Othello* The Tragedy of the Handkerchief' (i. 46–7), Fielding ironically hints that Charlotte's histrionics even outdo Shakespeare: not one but 'all the Ghosts'; 'much more Propriety'. This irony is sustained: just as when the narrator suggests that 'Lady *Dellwyn* had full as much Reason to call Lady *Fanny* her evil Genius, as ever *Mark Anthony* had to give that Denomination to *Caesar*' (ii. 15–16), the impartial spectator is prompted to laugh at, rather than sympathise with, Charlotte's disproportionate response.

Fielding maintains this mock-tragic disjuncture throughout the novel: the 'not *Macbeth*' construction keeps Charlotte at a distance from Shakespeare. Other characters draw on Shakespeare for intellectual insight and emotional support, but the guilty Countess has no such comfort. She never quotes – or even speaks, for that matter – in this third-person narrative, and the Shakespeare quotations that cluster around her remain beyond her control. When she reflects that she 'was doomed for Life to endure the Company, and even the Fondness, of a Man utterly disagreeable to her', she 'wanted Words to express herself, and was ready to exclaim, with *Hamlet, Oh! horrible, horrible, most horrible!*' (i. 101–2); yet while she might be 'ready' to borrow Hamlet's words, she is not allowed to speak them. She and her companion's 'Minds were too much disturbed by Anxiety to suffer them to say with [Brutus] . . .' (ii. 260) (italics added). The subsequent quotation remains in the narrator's control, leaving the women adrift and uncomforted by 'beloved Shakespeare'.

Shakespeare's characters benefit from these regular contrasts: Charlotte is so unpleasant that they cannot help but appear, by contrast, more admirable. The narrator ends a digression on Hotspur, Cordelia and '*Harry* the Fifth' with an abrupt new sentence, 'But to return to Lady *Dellwyn* . . .' (ii. 31), briskly distinguishing the Countess and her fellow silly women from these grand Shakespearean forbears. When Charlotte later laments her fall into adulterous disgrace, the narrator quotes:

> *I do repent me, as it is an Evil*
> *And take the Shame with Joy*;
>
> are the expressive Words *Shakespeare* put into the Mouth of the penitent *Juliet*. But Lady *Dellwyn*'s Vanity was too predominant to suffer her to feel any thing but Rage and Despair. (ii. 206)

The bald conjunction 'But' is shorthand for the emotional gulf between the Countess's speechless 'Rage and Despair' and the 'expressive Words *Shakespeare* put into the Mouth of' Juliet; and between the two fictional women. Juliet, Hotspur, Cordelia and '*Harry* the Fifth' are primarily celebrated as well-drawn characters, but by repeated contrast with the ill-tempered Countess they also gain a sense of moral superiority. Juliet's 'penitence' sounds exemplary when juxtaposed with Charlotte's 'vanity'. The same is true of Charlotte's motley associates: the supercilious Lady Fanny 'reversed the Picture of the Ghost in *Hamlet*' (ii. 26) and the emotionless 'Lord *Dellwyn* was not like *Othello*' (ii. 114).

The 'Shakespeare' who emerges from these juxtapositions is not only a moral authority, but an actively reproving judge of character. Captain Drumond feels keenly Shakespeare's penetrating vision: scheming to engineer Lord Dellwyn's jealousy, he 'wished such strong Pictures as *Shakespeare* drew of deep Villainy had never been written'. He lives in fear of being exposed by Shakespeare's accurate portrayals of human nature. He has, however, 'no Occasion for being under any Apprehension on this Account', for Dellwyn had 'never condescended to read any thing so trifling as *Shakespeare*'s Plays; and, if he had perused them, there was no manner of Danger that he should know the Characters again in real Life' (ii. 117); he is ignorant of the imitative power of fiction. The Countess also experiences Shakespeare's judgements viscerally. When she reflects that it is her own fault that she must spend her life with the aged, creaking Lord Dellwyn, the truth becomes so 'glaring' that she can 'no longer shut her Eyes close enough' (i. 100) to block it out.

> The more she considered, the more Reason she perceived for Self-condemnation: She had no longer any Relish for her once favourite Amusement of Reading; and mostly disliked those Authors who have penetrated deeply into the intricate Paths of Vanity in the human Mind. (i. 102)

The phrase 'penetrated deeply into the intricate Paths of Vanity' recalls the prefatory description of Shakespeare as the 'deepest Penetrator into the inmost Recesses of human Nature'. The subsequent observation that 'to peruse, with Pleasure, true Pictures of Nature, requires either a clear or a hardened Conscience; which *Shakespeare* has manifested to be his Opinion' (i. 103) confirms the allusion. For those with a guilty conscience, Shakespeare's accurate ability to draw 'true Pictures of Nature' makes him a source of unbearable truths. These crowd upon Charlotte in moments of deepest regret, all the more painfully because she was once an accomplished, sensitive reader, for whom reading philosophy to her father in her childhood engendered in her 'an utter Contempt of all Falsehood' (ii. 38).

Other female authors such as Cavendish had admired the way that Shakespeare 'Peirces the Souls of his Readers with such a True Sense and Feeling thereof, that it forces Tears through their Eyes';[52] and Elizabeth Montagu would later praise his 'discernment and penetration into characters'.[53] Fielding applies to a guilty, fictional protagonist the critical truism of Shakespeare's knowledge of human nature, and ability to see into people, and makes him seem searching and accusatory. Ten years after the publication of Fielding's novel, a 'comic serenata' at the Stratford Jubilee would take this image of Shakespeare to its natural extreme:

> *If he saw ye he knew ye,*
> *Would look thro' and thro' ye,*
> *Thro' skin, and your flesh and your cloaths,*
> *Had you vanity, pride,*
> *Fifty follies beside,*
> *He would see 'em, as plain as your nose:*
> *Tho' sins I have none,*
> *I am glad he is gone,*
> *No maid would live near such a mon.*[54]

For the 'Country Girl' who sings this song, the truism of Shakespeare's penetrating vision is entirely new. She, like Fielding, takes the trope literally: '*If he saw ye he knew ye/ Would look thro' and thro' ye*'. When turned on 'ye', the dramatist's insights sound judgemental, even invasive. Shakespeare, in this ironic song, is a figure of fear, not least because of his rather unnerving x-ray powers: able to see not only 'thro' skin, and your flesh' but also through 'your cloaths', he poses even more of a threat to innocent young maidens.

'Proved the truth of Shakespeare's observation': novel experience

The novel, then, constructs Shakespeare as advisory, insightful, even morally searching. It applies fragments of Shakespeare to the emotional situations of a variety of novelistic characters, and in doing so, confirms the justness of his observations. Where anthologies and commonplace books also extracted and admired fragments, the novel tests their value in action before approving them: as anthologist Dodd says in his little-known novel, *The Sisters* (1754), Lucy 'prov'd the truth of Shakespear's observation'.[55] The final part of this chapter shows how the novel fully establishes Shakespeare's authority by testing his words against the *experience* of characters and readers, in order to 'prove' his insights.

Characters' individual experiences were growing in significance at this point. The Aristotelian certainties of a divine, enduring human nature were being rejected in favour of a more scientific approach to human behaviour, focussed on the individual; David Hume and others had rejected the notion of innate ideas, and proposed that humans only have knowledge of things they experience directly.[56] Mid-eighteenth-century fiction, as Liz Bellamy argues, represented wider literary and cultural tensions between public and private virtue, between moral precept and individual experience and between epic and novel.[57] Richardson's novels 'embody the moral confusion' of the mid-century: *Clarissa* combines an 'experiential narrative structure' with an 'editorial insistence on the exemplary function of character and the preceptial nature of fictional morality'; a tension between 'didacticism' and 'representation'.[58] That fiction substituted 'example' for 'precept' is a story the eighteenth century told of itself: Clara Reeve's *The Progress of Romance* (1785) later saw novels as 'making entertaining stories their *vehicle* to convey to the young and flexible heart, wholsome [*sic*] truths, that it refused to receive under the form of moral precepts and instructions'.[59] Idiosyncratic characters in novels, from Tom

Jones to Tristram Shandy, conveyed 'wholsome truths' to the reader not by moral exposition, but by example.

Anxieties attended this growing focus in literature, culture and society on private experience. Some felt that readers of the novel would miss the moral point, unable, for example, to learn the appropriate lesson simply by following the experiential process by which Tom Jones has virtue inculcated in him by, in Fielding's words, 'Reflexion on his past Follies'.[60] Lady Echlin wrote to Richardson to urge him to make *Clarissa* more straightforwardly moral: the novel 'ought to be perused with very serious attention: and if every reader wou'd properly receive, consider, & regard this lesson, it might help to reform the Licentious, and mend the present age'.[61] As the steady accretion of guiding notes in each successive edition of *Clarissa* suggests, Richardson, too, wanted the reader to pay 'very serious attention' to the text. But where Echlin desired readers to 'receive, Consider, & regard' a clear-cut moral 'lesson', Richardson demanded that his readers engage actively with the complexity of his characters' experiences in order to derive instruction from the text. As Bellamy observes, 'The emphasis on experience implied a degree of interpretative autonomy on the part of the reader which was not to be found within writings based on a code of inflexible moral precepts'.[62] The reader must navigate the contradictory claims to truth of Richardson's Lovelace and Clarissa, and weigh up the value of their competing narratives. Tom Keymer argues that the multi-voiced nature of the epistolary form 'problematises the definable core of meaning' and 'focuses attention instead on the only events to which our access is reliable or direct—the epistolary acts in which the novel's most interested parties create and communicate their various conflicting tales'.[63] Quotations, invoked by characters to construct authority for their beliefs, are intense instances of 'epistolary acts' that require the reader's careful appraisal.

If Richardson's novels exploit the boundaries between precept and experience, so too do his quotations. While Clarissa extracts lines selectively from Shakespeare and applies them thoughtfully to new emotional situations, Lovelace, as discussed in Chapter 2, appears to have turned to Bysshe's handbook of poetry to find lines that, in the guise of comfort and advice, flattered his willpower. Ominously, the advice to 'Oppose not rage' appears in Bysshe on the same page as 'RAPE', suggesting that by casually dipping into a stock of ready-made extracts, Lovelace might have found the lines that defend his motives: '*It is* resistance *that inflames desire*' (p. 609). With his frequent recourse to Bysshe, Lovelace represents the dangers of the fluent recycling of printed commonplace precepts.

By contrast, Clarissa, like an early modern woman compiling a commonplace book of scriptural quotations, carefully reads and extracts valuable information, even if from intermediary sources.[64] Her very first quotation places her opinion and Shakespeare's on different sides of a comparative phrase, saying that silence 'better shows it by much than, as Shakespeare says. . .', rather than, 'as Shakespeare says, better shows it by much . . .', even though the gist of the whole observation derives from him. She does not simply repeat prior wisdom, but develops new insights whose truth is confirmed by her own experience. As discussed in Chapter 2, Lovelace's passionate quotation from *The Tempest*, beginning 'Full many a lady . . .', is newly suffixed in the second edition with the abbreviation 'Shakesp.'. This formulation hails from the margins of early anthologies, but Lovelace contorts the quotation to his own situation by the heavy-handed change of pronouns to 'she', with emphatic, speech-like italics. Lovelace's quotations thus dangerously combine the axiomatic force of old precepts with the persuasive *impression* of his own pained experience. Clarissa's rather old-fashioned but intensely thoughtful commonplacing habits ironically bring her closer to the century's growing fascination with individual experience.[65]

Sarah Fielding's Portia also rejects outright the recycling of precepts. The jury known as 'the Cry' might unthinkingly rally all the sources they know against Portia, thinking that she 'could not dare to hold her own opinion against what they had read in so many different books' (ii. 86), but she, by contrast, refuses to accept Shakespeare's insights unthinkingly. She might refer to 'that grand master of human nature (I need not say I mean *Shakespear*)' (i. 112), but she acknowledges that ''Tis the application alone which gives value to any sort of knowledge' (i. 182), and she only applies Shakespeare's words after careful appraisal: 'if Shakespeare is right in saying. . .'. Whether she cites Shakespearean characters ('I think, as *Desdemona* says. . .' [ii. 194]), situations ('I must, like the grave-digger in *Hamlet*, acknowledge. . .' [ii. 128]), or apposite fragments ('This was indeed the unfolding of a tale that *harrowed up my soul*' [iii. 187]), she proves the insightfulness of Shakespeare's observations by testing them carefully against her own experience. In doing so, characters such as Portia and Clarissa construct what will become influential Shakespearean precepts.

To propose, as this book does, that fragments of Shakespeare's plays, via characters' experiences, become precepts, is to complicate the critical narrative of the eighteenth century, in which precept gives way to private, novelistic experience, after a period of tension in the mid-century novel. For characters, the most valued parts of Shakespeare are not just the pithy, sententious lines celebrated in early seventeenth-century anthologies (see p. 27); by virtue of their continuous application to new emotional situations in eighteenth-century fiction, many of Shakespeare's lines come to resonate with a sense of truth.

The reader's judgement is crucial to the process of turning Shakespeare's words into precepts. All of the novelists discussed in this chapter devote considerable energy to guiding their readers in how to engage productively with their fictional texts. Sarah Fielding offers the most explicit guidance of all, urging the 'judicious Reader' to look beyond the 'incidents' of the story to the 'Moral', and not to read superficially in the way that 'Children see Tragedies', or that the 'Multitude in Holiday-time throng to see Shakespeare's Play of *Harry the Eighth*', mesmerised only by noise and show'.[66] In *The Governess*, a novel for children, Fielding sternly criticises those young readers who might one day thoughtlessly gobble up and mindlessly recite quotations: an older pupil, Jenny, passes on to the inhabitants of a 'little female academy' her mother's advice that 'it was to no manner of Purpose to read ever so many Books, which would only stuff my Brain, without being an Improvement to my Mind'; and their tutor, Mrs Teachum, trains them in the close reading necessary to extract the value from 'all kinds of Writings', even 'Plays'.[67]

Quotations frequently elicit the reader's judgement. The reader is required to arbitrate, for example, in Henry Fielding's *Tom Jones*, when Squire Western's sister upbraids him for meddling in her care of Sophia. Mrs Western 'had lived about the court, and had seen the world', and, confident in her own sophistication, is moved to quote literature:

> —'Your Ignorance, Brother,' returned she, 'as the great *Milton* says, almost subdues my Patience.' (*Footnote: the Reader may perhaps subdue his own Patience if he searches for this in* Milton)—'D—n Milton,' answered the Squire: 'if he had the Impudence to say so to my Face, I'd lend him a Douse, thof he was never so great a Man.' (i. 321)

Squire Western is irritated that his sister has brought a third party into their argument: unaware of quoting convention, he takes 'Your Ignorance . . . as the great *Milton* says' to mean that Milton has insulted him behind his back. He blusters 'D—n Milton', and threatens to curtail the 'great' man's gossiping. But if his ignorance is risible, Mrs Western is little more informed, since, as the narrator hints, her words are nowhere to be found in Milton. Should the reader approve Western's hearty dismissal of her affectation and risk seeming ignorant of 'the great *Milton*' themselves? Or laugh at his ignorance and risk association with the shallow posturing of someone who is 'perfect mistress of manners, customs, ceremonies, and fashions'? There is a political dimension to this question: Squire Western demands of his sister, 'do you think no one hath understanding unless he hath been about at Court', and denounces the 'parcel of Round-heads and Hanover Rats' who occupy that realm. Squire Western and Mrs Western appear to be one of the 'neatly antithetical pairs of characters'[68] in Fielding's work. Reader-response theorist Wolfgang Iser suggests these are a deliberate device to enlist the reader's involvement, requiring them to negotiate between two extremes and find a meaning that resides 'somewhere between or even above the poles' of the 'moral conflict'.[69] Fielding's texts, like many other mid-century novels, make moral appraisal and judgement a continuous requirement of the 'sagacious' reader.

The dispassionate, judgemental gaze that the reader is required to cast over quoting characters is reminiscent of Adam Smith's contemporary model of sympathy. In the same year that Sarah Fielding's *Countess* was published, in a chapter in *The Theory of Moral Sentiments* (1759) entitled 'Of the manner in which we judge of the propriety or impropriety of the affections of other men, by their concord or dissonance with our own', Smith proposed that 'In the suitableness or unsuitableness, in the proportion or disproportion which the affection seems to bear to the cause or object which excites it, consists the propriety or impropriety, the decency or ungracefulness of the consequent action'.[70] According to Smith, the propriety of an emotional response, and its deservingness of sympathy, is measured by its 'suitableness', or fittingness, to the 'cause or object which excites it'. For Smith, the person who determines the propriety of the match is the observer:

> When the original passions of the person principally concerned are in perfect concord with the sympathetic emotions of the speaker, they necessarily appear to this last just and proper, and suitable to their objects; and, on the contrary, when, upon bringing the case home to himself, he finds that they do not coincide with how he feels, they necessarily appear to him unjust and improper, and unsuitable to the causes which excite them. (p. 16)

It is the spectator, then, who assesses how far a situation warrants sympathy in accordance with how they themselves might respond to a similar 'cause or object'. They measure it against their own experience.

Sarah Fielding, like many fellow novelists, encouraged readers to judge the accuracy of characters' behaviour with exactly this scrutiny:

> . . . as the Writer must be thoroughly acquainted with the Bent of the Dispositions of the Miser, the Lover, the Friend, and the Parent, before he can make any of them act with Propriety on this or any other Occasion,

> so must the Reader also have some Degree of Knowledge of them before he can judge truly whether they are represented right or wrong, or distinguish what is natural from the wild Fancies of the Poet's Brain.[71]

For Fielding, the impartial, detached spectatorship and the 'knowledge' of different people and situations that critics can find so demanding in Smith are a reasonable expectation.[72] She requires this impartiality and knowledge of the author, in order to make their characters 'act with Propriety on this or any other Occasion', but she also requires it of the reader, so that they can discern what they read, holding it up against their 'knowledge' to 'distinguish' and 'judge truly' the accuracy of the author's observations. Held up for the reader's appraisal against Viola's more fitting behaviour, for example, Charlotte's reaction seems all the more out of kilter with (to borrow Smith's term) its 'objects'. In turn, the reader confirms and ascribes 'great skill, deep penetration, an accurate observation, and almost perfect knowledge of men' to both Shakespeare and the novelist.[73]

Through repeated acts of quotation, judgement and approval, novels render Shakespeare a repository of emotional expressions, or 'objects', against which others' behaviour can be measured. The words 'like patience on a monument', quoted to illustrate the difference between Charlotte's peevish jealousy and Viola's painful unrequited love, would become, through frequent acts of quotation, a detached trope judged accurately to represent the pining lover. As Chapter 5 will show, an anxious Tom Jones, and a hopelessly adoring Clementina in *Sir Charles Grandison*, are both described (or in Clementina's case, describe themselves) in these words. By the time that a pushy gentleman at an assembly glibly compares the heroine of Frances Burney's *Evelina* (1778) to 'patience on a monument', Viola's words are a well-worn phrase readily available to describe any lady who lacks a dance partner. Shakespeare's line, repeatedly tested against characters' experiences, becomes emotional shorthand for a certain romantic situation, and, in turn, banal.

The notion that Shakespeare accrues authority by repeated reader judgement would resonate with Smith. As he observes in his *Theory*:

> our continual observations upon the conduct of others, insensibly lead us to form to ourselves certain general rules concerning what is fit and proper either to be done or to be avoided (p. 303)

These 'general rules' are not 'a priori principles', but 'inductions from our customary conduct', gradually formed.[74] The 'objects' against which characters' behaviour can be measured are not fixed standards, but accrue authority through repeated acts of judgement. Charlotte Lennox had criticised Shakespeare's plays earlier that decade for their un-novelistic lack of probability (see p. 5). Novels, however, by extracting, quoting and applying Shakespeare's words, detach his observations from their variously improbable plots, and give the impression of their universal applicability. For Lennox, Viola's transvestism 'very much lessens the probability of the story' in *Twelfth Night*; but, in the novel, 'Patience on a monument', detached from the wider plot of the play and linked only to the feeling of Viola's particular speech, becomes a benchmark of human emotion.

Selective quotation, then, is crucial to Shakespeare's authority. Not all of Shakespeare's work is a model of propriety, as Smith himself avers: the playwright's entry in the index to *Rhetoric and Belles Lettres* reads like a roll-call of offences against literary decorum.

> Shakespeare, William: confusion of metaphors, 27; Hamlet's soliloquies parodied, 42; indirect description in King Lear, 60; descriptions more animated than Spenser's, 63; often uses contradictory epithets, 73; grave-diggers break unity of Hamlet, 117; breaks unity of time, 118; of place, 119; vast variety of characters, 122; breaches of decorum and propriety, 122; Othello, 125.[75]

Shakespeare's 'inconceivable variety of characters' makes it 'almost impossible to keep up the decorum and propriety of the pieces'.[76] Novels, however, minimise the effects of Shakespeare's excessive 'variety of characters' by focusing on particular, well-observed lines. Their quotations function as synecdoche, conferring insight and value on all of Shakespeare's utterances by extension. By this halo effect, Shakespeare's works become not just a mixed bundle of disconnected 'practical axioms and domestick wisdom', but a source of 'general and predominant truth'.[77]

Novelists thus influence the more explicitly moral interpretations of Shakespeare that characterise the late eighteenth and nineteenth centuries. The aim of Griffith's *The Morality of Shakespeare's Drama Illustrated* (1775), as mentioned earlier, was not to celebrate the beauties but to 'expound the document of the Moralist'. Though Griffith quotes copiously from editions and criticism in her preface, her system of morality appears to be informed by developments in fiction: she declares that 'Example is better than precept' (p. 526). Where in previous collections 'the precepts are disposed methodically, under separate heads or chapters; as Ambition, Bravery, Constancy, Devotion, and so on to the end of the alphabet', she finds far more 'entertaining, and consequently so well able to answer the *utile dulci*', those works 'where the documents rise out of the action immediately before our eyes, and are constantly varying with the shifting of scenes, persons, and subjects' (p. xiii). Griffith's combination of prose narrative and Shakespearean quotation resembles the mid-century novel, and she knows it is the novelistic twists and turns of emotions and 'scenes' in the 'intire *quicquid agunt homines* of human life' (p. xiii) that will most readily communicate Shakespeare's domestic morality to a reader.

Another book entitled *The Beauties of Shakespeare* (1783), published by George Kearsley, returned to the more preceptial format of headings. It deliberately distinguished itself from Dodd's collection of the same name by stressing its usefulness in 'impressing on the memory of Youth some of the sublimest and most important lessons of Morality and Religion'.[78] Like the novels observed in this chapter, the collection's preface moves subtly from praising Shakespeare for his penetrating observation to framing him as a force for good. He is upheld as an author 'who, with the most subtle penetration, has pierced through the dark developments of the human heart; who has painted the most beautiful scenes of Nature; who has given life and action to Virtue, inculcating the noblest system of morality, and animating mankind to tread those steps which lead to the happiness of individuals, and, in consequence, to the general good of the Community'.[79] Dodd's and Kearsley's selections heavily informed the yet more explicitly helpful nineteenth-century collections of *Aphorisms from Shakespeare* (1812), *Apothegms from Shakespeare* (1850), *Shakespeare's Household Words* (1859) and *Sayings from Shakespeare* (1864), which took advantage of the end of perpetual copyright to reproduce the morally valuable and efficacious insights of Shakespeare for a growing domestic audience.

Eighteenth-century prose fiction, then, contributes significantly to the growing impression of Shakespeare's emotional and moral authority, especially when it prizes intense, individual experience.[80] In a genre concerned with proving its own foundation in truth and nature, Shakespeare is celebrated for his emotional and moral acuity. Shakespeare at once underwrites, and is underwritten by, the novel: the novelists praise Shakespeare's knowledge of human nature, and are praised in turn for theirs. Henry Fielding is celebrated for this quality in the dedication to Francis Coventry's *Pompey the Little*,[81] and himself praises his sister for her '*deep Knowledge of Human Nature*', and the way that the sentiments of her novels were carefully adapted to different characters, observing that '. . .*there are some Touches, which I will venture to say might have done honour to the Pencil of the Immortal* Shakespear *himself*'.[82] Yet all of the novelists examined in this chapter are aware of the instability of essential, enduring qualities of 'human nature' in the eighteenth century. For them, Shakespeare's formal quotations at once recollect the enduring 'truths' of long-held precept and the myriad complexities of individual experience. Shakespeare is both celebrated by the novelists as a voice from the past, and recast as a scientist of the modern age who is alive to fluctuations in individual behaviour; he gains a more responsive authority in the process. The novelists are also aware, as Shakespeare was as a dramatist of disguise, magic and metatheatricality, that seemingly essential qualities of human behaviour can be assumed and performed to 'Conceal me what I am', and just as easily cast off again.

The next chapters of the book will see Shakespeare's acquired moral authority become more fascinatingly complicated. In Chapter 4, I show that, by the middle of the century, the persistent theatricality of Shakespeare's words can still erupt unexpectedly in fiction, despite the calm, authoritative persona he has achieved in the novel. Quoting drama only exaggerates the challenge faced by all feeling characters in the mid-century novel: that they must perform themselves aloud, in letters and conversation, in public and private, to others and to themselves. Even thoughtful, moral characters such as Clarissa must display their virtue to an often suspicious audience of peers and to the reader. Shakespeare's continuing association with the stage will challenge the perceived fixity of older, preceptial forms of knowledge and render 'our beloved', embodied, authoritative 'Shakespeare' a live, and even dangerous, presence when quoted in polite eighteenth-century society.

CHAPTER 4

Theatrical Shakespeare

> He lies buried in a corner of his church-yard, in the parish of——, under a plain marble slabb, which his friend *Eugenius*, by leave of his executors, laid upon his grave, with no more than these three words of inscription serving both for his epitaph and elegy.
>
> Alas, poor YORICK!
>
> Ten times in a day has Yorick's ghost the consolation to hear his monumental inscription read over with such a variety of plaintive tones, as denote a general pity and esteem for him;—a footway crossing the church-yard close by the side of his grave,—not a passenger goes by without stopping to cast a look upon it,—and sighing as he walks on,
>
> Alas, poor YORICK![1]

In the eighteenth century, so the familiar story goes, 'Shakespeare' was transplanted from the theatre to the book. Published in quarto and folio editions in the seventeenth century, Shakespeare's plays took off as a print phenomenon in the eighteenth, appearing in a succession of expensive complete works editions, as well as in cheaper single plays and even in books of quotations.[2] Gary Taylor observes that 'Rowe's Whig edition looked backward to the stage; Pope's Tory edition looked forward to the book,' and that while William Davenant, as 'Cavalier, courtier, playwright, theatre manager, adapter of texts', shaped Restoration Shakespeare, it was the book publisher Jacob Tonson who most heavily influenced his reception in the first half of the eighteenth century.[3] Shakespeare's appearances in print did not stop there. During the 1750s and 60s, many of Shakespeare's characters begin to 'migrate independently into the novel', 'rapidly escaping the stage altogether'.[4]

'Stage to page' is a governing metaphor of Shakespeare's eighteenth-century reception. The catchy phrase, however, can underplay the continuing theatrical presence of Shakespeare in this period. While Shakespeare 'for home reading'[5] grew, his stage life did not, of course, recede. On the contrary, Shakespeare's presence on the London stage increased after the Shakespeare Revival of the 1730s; and adaptations and 'improvements' of his plays steadily gave way to more textually faithful performances. By the middle of the century, a consumer of 'Shakespeare' in the London theatre could not only enjoy a substantial range of tragedies, histories and comedies,[6] but also choose between competing productions of the same play on a given night, with star attractions including Spranger Barry, Charles Macklin, Kitty Clive, Hannah Pritchard, Peg Woffington and David Garrick. If Tonson's editions of Shakespeare were prohibitively expensive – the equivalent in the present day of 'somewhere between £300 and £450' in Rowe's case, and '£1000 and £1500' in Pope's – this vivid, theatrical Shakespeare was accessible to a wider audience.[7]

This chapter argues that Shakespeare's appearance in the eighteenth-century novel does not represent a complete 'escape from the stage'. Novels might detach Shakespeare's words from his plays, and embody the dramatist as a figure of authority, but he remains a figure of the theatre. I argue in this chapter that Shakespeare's theatricality is a vital part of his function in prose fiction. 'Theatricality' describes qualities specifically 'Pertaining to or connected with the theatre or "stage", or with scenic representations',[8] but can also refer more abstractly, and pejoratively, to 'artificial', 'affected' and 'assumed' behaviour.[9] Both these meanings are at work in prose fiction. Characters go to the theatre on numerous occasions: Henry Fielding's Tom Jones and Partridge, Sarah Fielding's Ophelia and Lord Dorchester and Smollett's Tabitha Bramble, among others, all see Shakespeare performed on stage. But even more pervasive in novels are the 'artificial', 'affected' and 'assumed' behaviours that Shakespeare encourages in his admirers.

In the first part of the chapter, I argue that all fictional characters are performers. In novels from *Joseph Andrews* to *Jack Wander*, the obviously 'affected' characters that strut and fret in borrowed lines from Shakespeare are often minor figures, and their histrionics a comic foil for the sincerity and depth of feeling of the central characters. But closer analysis reveals that when protagonists dissociate themselves from such theatrical behaviour, it is often a defensive act. Constantly required to present themselves favourably in letters and in speech, characters such as Pamela and Clarissa are aware that they are just as much performers as the ranting cameo players, and their celebrated sensibility interpretable as a mark either of sincerity or affectation. The novelists might appear to distance their central characters – and their fiction more widely – from the stagey poses struck in the name of Shakespeare, but they are keenly aware that self-dramatisation is at the heart of novelistic character in this period, and that the act of quoting drama only intensifies it.

The novel is not a non-theatrical form. Novelists do not simply distance their fiction from the theatre as an opposite or lesser mode of representation; rather, they celebrate in it the qualities that are most like the novel. When Tom Jones in Fielding's novel takes the hapless schoolmaster Partridge to the theatre to see *Hamlet* performed, Partridge is self-assured, knowingly scoffing that it is 'but a Play', and that 'Ghosts don't appear in such Dresses as that, neither'.[10] But when Garrick's Hamlet sees his father's ghost, Partridge is struck with fear: he 'fell into so violent a Trembling, that his Knees knocked against each other' (ii. 853). For the duration of the ghost's speech, 'he sat with his Eyes fixed partly on the Ghost, and partly on *Hamlet*, and with his Mouth open; the same Passions which succeeded each other in *Hamlet*, succeeding likewise in him' (ii. 854). He insists that it was not the fake ghost that scared him, but Garrick's reaction: 'when I saw the little Man so frightned himself, it was that which took Hold of me' (ii. 854). Yet after the performance, restored to his habitual assurance, Partridge proclaims the man who played the King the best actor, because he 'speaks all his Words distinctly, half as loud again as the other' (ii. 857). Garrick's Hamlet he dismisses out of hand: 'why I could act as well as he myself. I am sure if I had seen a Ghost, I should have looked in the very same Manner, and done just as he did' (ii. 857).

Partridge inadvertently draws attention to an emerging mode of dramatic representation so skilfully naturalistic that it effaces its own art, and that is personified in David Garrick. He admires in the King the bombastic, declamatory acting of the past. By mocking Partridge's misguided theatrical judgements, Fielding aligns his novel with Garrick's realistic representation of human behaviour, and with his celebrated ability to move his audiences, as he did Partridge, through a succession of strong emotional responses. He and other novelists find not only in Shakespeare's psychologically acute writing, but also in its skilful performance by leading contemporary actors, a kind of mimesis that, by its invisibility, seems to offer a 'true picture of nature'. They rehabilitate Shakespeare's theatricality, aligning it with the aspirations of the novel.

But Shakespeare's dramatic speeches will not always submit to this novelisation. As the opening example from Laurence Sterne's *Tristram Shandy* visually confirms, some dramatic phrases refuse to be contained. Quoting lines like 'Alas, poor YORICK' and 'Angels and ministers of grace defend us!' can lead Sterne's characters helplessly into theatrical postures. In the final part of this chapter, a close study of Sterne's work in particular will illuminate the ways in which the most detached fragments of Shakespeare quoted in the novel can still vividly evoke the stage in the mind of the reader, and, by a train of association, bring the theatre and its gestures into the Shandy household, threatening domestic order. This disruptive theatricality is not simply a property of Sterne's experimental fiction, but is evident in prose fiction all along the perceived arc of 'stage to page'. Even the 'antitheatrical'[11] Richardson exploits Shakespeare's persistent theatricality to add shades of ambiguity to the modest quotations of his moral characters.

Thus, as well as celebrating and co-opting Shakespeare's performance as a novelistic form of mimetic representation, novelists embrace Shakespeare's theatricality – with all its power to deceive – in order to enrich their characterisation. Shakespeare is not diminished in the process. Straddling the worlds of the novel and the theatre, the images of Shakespearean performance evoked through quotation will come to exist in a new realm, confined by neither stage nor book: the theatre of the imagination. The novelists' version of Shakespeare's theatricality would thus inform Romantic associations between Shakespeare, creativity and the poetic imagination.

All the men and women merely players

If all characters in the eighteenth-century novel are performers, it does not seem so at first glance: theatricality appears the province of the noisiest declaimers of borrowed lines of drama. In Chapter 3, numerous fictional characters admired Shakespeare's words and drew on them for comfort and guidance, constructing 'our beloved Shakespeare' as an emotional and moral authority. By contrast, this chapter introduces a type of character who engages with Shakespeare not by drawing on his newfound wisdom, but by declaiming his speeches, often to the consternation of other characters. In Herbert Lawrence's novel *The Contemplative Man; or, The History of Christopher Crab, Esq.; of North-Wales* (1771), Mr and Mrs Crab are on their way to Oxford when Mr Crab meets, unbeknownst to him, an actor. This figure paces up and down 'in a very disorderly Manner', then

> without any Signs of Provocation, he flew like a Madman, upon the poor Ostler, who was cleaning some Coach-Harness at the Stable-Door, and seizing him by the Collar with both his Hands, he cried out as loud as his Voice would let him,

> Villain, be sure thou prove my Wife a Whore;
> Be sure of it: Give me the ocular Proof,
> Or by the Worth of mine eternal Soul,
> Thou hadst been better have been born a Dog,
> Than answer my wak'd Wrath.

> When Mr. *Crab* had heard and seen this, he hastened back to the House, saying to himself as he went along, the Devil may part you both for me. And as he came into the Room to Mrs. *Crab* and the Captain, here, says he, we have got a Madman in the Yard: I wish we were well out of this Town. I'm afraid this Fellow will drive in here and do us a Mischief. I'll bolt the Door. Pray, says the Captain, how does the Man behave? Behave! says Mr. *Crab*, why he run like a Fury at the Ostler, and collar'd him; and then he roar'd out, *Villain, be sure thou prove my Wife a Whore*, and such stuff as that. Ha! ha! ha! I'll be hang'd, says the Captain, if this same Madman be not my Friend *James Maccloud*, rehearsing the Part of *Othello*.[12]

Crab innocently leaps to the conclusion that this violent stranger is a dangerous 'Madman' likely to do the company a 'Mischief'. The Captain, with knowing laughter, dismisses his fears. The threat that Crab carefully repeats, '*Villain, be sure thou prove my Wife a Whore*', is, the Captain reveals, already a quotation, and the man speaking the words an actor. Crab has been deceived by an act of dramatic quotation, and is led inadvertently to quote Shakespeare himself.

This violent-sounding actor stands in deliberate, stark contrast to Crab. When the Captain asks Crab 'how does the man behave?', he distinguishes between who the man really is – 'my Friend *James Maccloud*' – and Maccloud's words and actions. Crab, however, echoes the Captain's question with an uncomprehending 'Behave!'. Unlike the Captain, Crab had trustingly equated the man's outward behaviour with his true character, without recognising the possibility of performance. His naïve reaction confirms his sincerity, and the direct connection between what he feels and what he says. A similar confusion arises in *The Adventures of Jack Wander* when Jones tells Jack how he was bemused by an outburst from a fellow drinker:

> I had begun to regale myself with some good liquor, when a tall raw-bone man, who sat opposite reading, suddenly started up, and fixing his eyes on me, exclaimed, I'll hear no more, 'Die prophet in thy speech, for this amongst the rest was I ordained.' Astonished, and terrified at his behaviour, and by no means prepossessed in favour of his appearance, I concluded . . . that he was frantic, and began to deprecate his fury.[13]

Jones is bewildered: like Christopher, he assumes that the speaker is mad, or 'frantic'. 'Astonished, and terrified at his behaviour', he tries to placate the raging man. But the man laughs, begs Jones' pardon and assures him that 'what he had repeated was an extract from a celebrated play; that he was to exhibit the principal character of in the evening'.[14] This hungry-looking figure is an actor who was most likely 'reading' his lines from Shakespeare before launching into this rehearsed speech; Jones' response, by contrast, comes from the heart.

This contrast is reinforced when the former tricks the good-hearted Jones into paying the bill, then takes him to visit his 'theatre, which was a ruinous barn'.[15] Strolling players toured the country performing in barns and inns, and their perceived proximity to poverty and criminality is evident in Smollett's *Humphry Clinker* when Wilson, an actor, is reprimanded for attempting to duel with his beloved's brother: 'The mayor observed that it was great presumption in Wilson, who was a stroller, to proceed to such extremities with a gentleman of family and fortune; and threatened to commit him on the vagrant act'.[16] Likewise, this strolling player in *Jack Wander* tells Jones that 'Our heroine, was a lady's woman, who quitted her mistress's service, to shine in Juliet; she, a wretched creature, however she may subsist: a young actress, though an execrable performer, may live where a man of superior talents would starve; you understand me?'.[17] His heavy hint that this serving-class Juliet had access to an alternative income as a woman of the town lends a moral dimension to the contrast between these minor characters and the novel's virtuous heroines and heroes. Despite all this, Jones becomes an actor himself.

In both *Christopher Crab* and *Jack Wander*, the central characters of Christopher and Jack profit from comparison with these bit-part actors. So does Shakespeare: the play in *Jack Wander* was 'miserably perform'd, yet the beauties of the author were still visible'.[18] Christopher and Jones' terrified responses seem naïve to other characters, but for the reader, such encounters only emphasise the innocence of these characters. This is intensified by dramatic irony: alerted by the layout of the page or the running quotation marks, the reader would realise long before either character that they were in the presence of a quotation. Christopher and Jones are 'archetypal victims' of sensibility: examples of 'the sensitive, benevolent man whose feelings are too exquisite for the acquisitiveness, vulgarity and selfishness of the world',[19] too easily duped into sympathy or terror by hammed-up performances.

Jones and Christopher might be accosted by actors, but novelists and other eighteenth-century commentators reveal contemporary anxieties about the theatrical impulse in all sorts of people. The theatre was seen to distract men and women alike from their trades and occupations, and spouting clubs were popular urban gathering places for 'journeymen and apprentices of barbers, tailors, and other crafts, who, to the grief of their masters and parents, meet once a week to guzzle porter and imitate the speeches of that wicked wight, Garrick who has done more mischief than the king of *Prussia*'.[20] Fuelled by such gatherings, the urge to repeat and perform Garrick's words was evidently diverting young people from their proper 'crafts' and intruding on daily life. The 1762 novel *The Life, Travels, and Adventures of Christopher Wagstaff, Gentleman* describes with distaste those people who attend the theatre 'and are yet made arrant coxcombs thereby. A kind of stage-pedantry almost totally infects their looks, manner, voice, and common conversation. They are actors in real life.'[21] One of these 'actors in real life' cannot help but quote Shakespeare:

> at dinner, he will frequently address himself to a fricassee, or a pudding, in the following terms,
>
> Thou com'st in such a questionable shape
> That I will speak to thee——. . .
>
> If a single string of a fiddle is touched, or a key of a harpsichord, he immediately cries,
>
> If music be the food of love, play on.——. . .
>
> He has frequently disturbed a whole neighbourhood, in the dead of the night, by bellowing thro' the streets,
>
> —— What hoa, Brabantio!
> Look to your house, your daughter, and
> your bags!——. . .
>
> If he takes a jaunt in a post-chaise, his constant exclamation is;——
>
> Gallop apace, ye fiery-footed steeds
> To Phoebus mansion; such a waggoner
> As Phaeton would whip you to the west, *&c.*
>
> Or, if he calls for a horse at an inn, it is in the stile, and with the impetuosity, of King *Richard* in the tragedy:—
>
> A horse, a horse, my kingdom for a horse.
>
> If a lady looks out of a window, as he is passing by,
>
> It is the east, and Juliet is the sun!——. . .[22]

Infected with the theatre, this man's compulsive quotation is triggered by the tiniest verbal or visual association: he 'appears in more characters within the compass of a dozen hours, than *Garrick* himself does in a twelve-month, and of all men living has the best title to that old theatrical motto, *Totus mundus agit Histrionem*'.[23] At worst, the man's ability to put on and put off 'characters' with alacrity is disturbing: how many Joneses and Christopher Crabs might he deceive? At best, it renders him unstable: as well as being more than a little tiresome, he has no 'character' of his own.

For all the emotive phrases they have at their disposal, these 'actors in real life' often have a limited emotional range, repelling their hearers and distressing themselves. In *David Simple*, Cynthia describes to Camilla a woman who stumbled 'accidentally' on Congreve's lines '*If Happiness in Self-Content is plac'd/ The Wise are wretched, and Fools only bless'd*'. She now strides round 'like a Heroine in a *Tragedy*, repeating the forementioned Lines', then sets herself down 'perfectly satisfied with her own *Parts*, because she found she could with *Art* raise an Uneasiness, and Vexation in her own Mind'.[24] In a continuation of the novel, David Simple learns of Selimena, an unhappy wife who 'walks and struts about the Room, repeating, in an audible Voice, all the tragick Strains her Memory can furnish, where Women lament their hard Fate, when some dire Mishap has befallen them'; she self-indulgently performs, and thus extends, her misery.[25]

Such characters often function as warnings against the excesses of feeling, or the negative side of sensibility. In *The Cry*, the repentant Cylinda says that she once considered putting aspics to her veins 'like *Cleopatra*', and declared that 'like *Hamlet*, I could have said,/ *I will fight with* her *on this score,/ Until my eye-lids will no longer wag*—/ —For, *I love* Eustace'.[26] She realises, too late, that she has only ranted in the manner of Shakespeare's characters, rather than extracting their wisdom. Like other self-indulgent readers represented in fiction, she has used books to find her plight echoed in literary language, rather than to gain strength and comfort. As a result, her life has been '(without a metaphor) a tale told by an idiot, and my imagination a strutting player, full of sound and fury signifying nothing'.[27]

These shallow, ranting quoters seem to serve as a foil for the greater depth and integrity – and true sensibility – of the protagonists. As Cylinda says to the virtuous Portia, 'your story is such a contrasting picture to my follies'.[28] In a play, such over-the-top characters would be an effective metatheatrical device:

> Metatheater deepens character in two ways. One is that it seems to cast off theatricality as an inferior or questionable representational mode so that what is being acted is given the status of non-theatrical representation.[29]

In their characters' stagiest quotations, novelists make the same metatheatrical manoeuvre. They place these most casually play-acting characters on the fringes of the action, and disparage as insincere the 'representational mode' of the theatre that they signify, in order to 'deepen' novelistic character, and raise the status of their own 'non-theatrical representation'. Lord Shaftesbury drew a significant distinction when he observed that 'the good Painter must come a little nearer to TRUTH, and take care that his Action be not *theatrical*, or at second hand; but *original*, and drawn from NATURE her-self'.[30] If the 'theatrical' is equated with the derivative and 'second-hand', then novelists see themselves on the other side of this divide, proffering art that is 'drawn from NATURE her-self' – that, like *Pamela*, 'has its Foundation in TRUTH and NATURE'. Through these hyper-theatrical characters, novelists claim for their genre the status of the natural, 'non-theatrical' form and define themselves by what they are not.

But the mid-century novel is not a non-theatrical form: performance is inherent in the genre. The novel might displace excessive theatricality on to its minor figures but, in truth, all its characters must act. T. S. Eliot described the 'theatrical' 'attitude of self-dramatisation' that he found in Othello's final speech, in which the tragic hero, with an eye to posterity, exhorts his hearers to 'Speak of me as I am . . . speak/ Of one who loved not wisely but too well' as a 'universal human weakness', for 'nothing dies harder than the desire to think well of oneself'.[31] Self-dramatisation is a generic condition of the mid-century novel, and the epistolary novel in particular obliges all characters to perform themselves, and their virtue, to one another. Pamela's tears splash on to the page as she writes to her parents after the death of her mistress:

> O how my Eyes run!—Don't wonder to see the Paper so blotted![32]

The messy combination of words and tears seems a mark of sincerity, closing any potential gap between Pamela's feelings and their written expression. But Henry Fielding gleefully exposes that gap again, famously drawing attention in his parody, *Shamela*, to the impossibility of 'writing to the moment':

> —Odsbobs! I hear him just coming in at the Door. You see I write in the present Tense, as Parson *Williams* says. Well, he is in Bed between us, we both shamming a Sleep, he steals his Hand into my Bosom, which I, as if in my Sleep, press close to me with mine, and then pretend to awake'.[33]

Fielding's critique is directed at Richardson, but his parody confirms the potential for performance in fictional characterisation more widely – including Fielding's own.

Quoting drama exaggerates the self-dramatisation that is an essential, even necessary, quality of novelistic character, including those central to the narrative. Harley, the eponymous hero of the *Man of Feeling*, turns to Shakespeare not for a maxim, but to express his pain as, racked with unrequited love for Miss Walton, he is barked at by her lap-dog: '—"The little dogs and all/ Tray, Blanch, and Sweetheart, see they bark at me!"'.[34] When Joseph Andrews' beloved Fanny is abducted, Parson Adams exhorts him to show Christian resignation, but Joseph cannot resist quoting Shakespeare in his anguish:

> They remained some time in silence; and Groans and Sighs issued from them both, at length *Joseph* burst out into the following Soliloquy:
>
> *Yes, I will bear my Sorrows like a Man,*
> *But I must also feel them as a Man.*
> *I cannot but remember such things were,*
> *And were most dear to me—*.[35]

After 'Groans' and 'Sighs', Joseph's 'Soliloquy' from *Macbeth* is the last in a triplet of self-indulgent noises that 'issued from them'. Joseph 'burst out', as if involuntarily, in Macduff's words, but admits to a baffled Adams that these are 'some Lines he had gotten by heart out of a Play'. He perhaps memorised the speech as a fashionable young man in London, when 'his Hair was cut after the newest Fashion, and became his chief Care', 'He applied most of his leisure Hours to Music', and 'was a little too forward in Riots at the Play-Houses and Assemblies'.[36] Jill Campbell suggests that such quotations allow Fielding 'to meditate upon the question of how spontaneous feeling may be framed within the space of convention'.[37] Yet the delivery of a speech which Joseph appears to have committed to memory in full expectation of repeating calls into question the sincerity even of this good-hearted character. He fleetingly resembles the 'arrant coxcomb' mentioned earlier, his quotation the affectation of an 'actor in real life'.

At the very moment he expects to elicit most sympathy, Joseph's Shakespeare quotation tinges his character with over-the-top acting. His quotation lacks 'fittingness' or aptness (see Chapter 3, pp. 64–5), for even Joseph must admit that his predicament is on a different scale to that of the original speaker, Macduff, who learns that his entire family has been murdered. Macduff's emotional speech precedes the manly action of bloody revenge; Joseph's precedes only helpless inaction. Tied 'discoursing back to back' with the Parson, Joseph has no choice but to 'bear' and 'feel' his sorrows until, some time later, a neat piece of *deus ex machina* returns Fanny safely to him, and he is 'delivered from his Captivity'[38] not by his own strength, but by hers. 'I must also feel them as a man', a phrase which might, as in Chapter 3, have been fashioned into valuable emotional guidance from 'Shakespeare', comes out as a sigh of self-pity – and in self-indulgent 'Soliloquy' rather than in dialogue. Ultimately, in the theatre, Macduff has no choice but to speak these words aloud. In the novel, by contrast, it would be entirely possible for the narrator sympathetically to quote Macduff's lines to describe, in the third person, how keenly Joseph felt the loss of his beloved. Instead, Fielding has Joseph quote in the first person: as a result, Joseph risks seeming affected, exaggerated, even insincere.

Shakespeare's theatricality, then, implicates all who quote him, whether they are virtuous Clarissas or ranting Lovelaces. We more readily expect histrionics of Robert Lovelace, who bursts into Richardson's novel in a letter to John Belford that bristles with impassioned theatrical quotations from Sir Robert Howard, Dryden, Otway and Shakespeare. Summarised in the second edition of *Clarissa* as a display of his 'Pride, Revenge, Love, Ambition, or a Desire of Conquest' and his 'early vow to ruin as many of the other Sex, as he can get into his power',[39] the letter follows his snubbing by Clarissa at her family church, and is filled with declarations of frustrated love and pride. One of his first quotations is an outburst borrowed from Shakespeare:

> Thou wilt say I rave. And so I do!
>
> *Perdition catch my soul, but I do love her.*[40]

This short quotation is not attributed to its source (*Othello*, III. 3. 92–3), nor its author. Lovelace quotes for the sheer melodramatic pleasure of the line, regardless of its tragic implications. In the second edition of *Clarissa*, the exclamation mark in the preamble ('do!') is replaced with a colon ('do:'), which makes the quotation an extension of his noisy 'rave'.[41] Lovelace dramatizes himself in a series of postures: here, as the raving lover; next, as a rather Miltonic figure creeping about the paddock and garden walls of Harlowe Place; and, in the rest of the letter, in numerous roles from 'hero of romance' (p. 146) to protagonist of a 'revenge' (p. 147). His letter is a theatre of quotation and he hops between characters self-consciously: 'could'st thou have thought that I . . . could adopt those over-tender lines of Otway?' (p. 144). Of course, Lovelace is writing, not speaking, and his apparently spontaneous rant is carefully spelled out for his reader.

In direct contrast to Lovelace, Clarissa's first Shakespeare quotation is anti-histrionic.[42] With the quotation first examined in Chapter 3 (p. 49), Clarissa calls thoughtfully on his words:

> True respect, true value, I think, lies not in words: Words *cannot* express it. The silent awe, the humble, the doubting eye, and even the hesitating voice, better show it by much, than, as Shakespeare says,

> —*The rattling tongue*
> *Of saucy and audacious eloquence*. (p. 97)

Clarissa's quotation seems to reject Lovelace's noisy, performative literary references. She quotes to support her belief that love is better expressed in diffidence than in 'extravagant volubility', and she shuns Lovelace's loquacious praise, prefacing her quotation with the observation that he is 'too full of professions' and says 'too many fine things of her'.

On the surface, Lovelace and Clarissa represent the difference between book and stage: she makes neat maxims while he snatches soliloquies.[43] Lovelace is a self-congratulating 'Proteus' (p. 1243), revivifying anthology pieces with dramatic verve. Clarissa is 'well read in Shakespeare' (p. 1148), applying dramatic words to domestic contexts. She prefers tragedies to comedies for their 'instruction'; men like Lovelace 'love not any tragedies but those in which they themselves act the parts of tyrants and executioners; and, afraid to trust themselves with serious and solemn reflections, run to comedies, to laugh away the distresses they have occasioned, and to find examples of as immoral men as themselves' (p. 618). Clarissa and Lovelace represent the opposing poles of 'private' and 'public',[44] and of 'novelistic' and 'dramatic',[45] that characterise the novel's central 'double yet separate' correspondence 'between two young ladies of virtue and honour' and 'between two gentlemen of free lives' (p. 35). It has been said of Clarissa that, unlike Lovelace, 'she is not "play-acting" with life, and does not choose a role artificially'.[46] His self-dramatisation seems to be matched by Clarissa's earnest sincerity.

Yet Clarissa is just as much a performer as Lovelace. She might not be '"play-acting" with life', but she is still a self-dramatiser, 'a trait', as critics have noticed, 'that results from too strong a sense of self-importance and from an awareness that the world is always watching her and that she must respond accordingly'.[47] Clarissa's quotations from Shakespeare, however, have not hitherto been considered in this light. Her moralising extract urgently performs, for the benefit of Anna (and, by extension, the benefit of her family, her friends and herself) her imperviousness to Lovelace's charms. Much later, after her rape, when the formal epistolary structures of her writing break down altogether and she writes in scattered quotations, she seems only to pour out feeling rather than to extract morality: '—Oh! you have done an act/ That blots the face and blush of modesty;/ Takes off the rose/ From the fair forehead of an innocent love,/ And makes a blister there!' (p. 893). Even these emotional quotations, however, are not above performance: when she cannot express herself directly, these exclamatory fragments of stage dialogue dramatise her rage and distress. With 'I could a tale unfold—/ Would harrow up thy soul!—' (p. 893) she threatens a dramatic revelation.[48]

It is partly because she is a performer herself that Clarissa is so vehemently disparaging about other characters' theatrical behaviour. Clarissa and Lovelace lodge with a 'widow and her two nieces'. When Clarissa argues with Lovelace about what constitutes an appropriate church in which to worship, the two younger women offer unsolicited comments. Miss Horton admires the couple's 'innocent mirth', and another agrees:

> Very true, joined in Miss Martin. And Shakespeare says well, *That youth is the spring of life, The bloom of gaudy years*; with a theatrical air she spoke it: and for her part, she could not but admire in my spouse, that charming vivacity which so well suited his time of life. (p. 532)

Clarissa scorns the needlessly 'theatrical' air that Miss Martin gives the quotation (a misattribution, via Bysshe, from Dryden), her italics contemptuously evoking the woman's affected, flirtatious delivery. The 'widow', Mrs Sinclair, is, unbeknownst to Clarissa, a brothel-keeper, and Polly Horton, Sally Martin and Dorcas Wykes her associates: Clarissa is right to surmise that Miss Martin is acting here, even if she does not register the woman's larger performance of virtue. But Clarissa is at this very moment acting the part of Lovelace's wife, and earlier tried 'to adjust my countenance before I went down, to an easier air than I had a heart' (p. 530). In the discourse of sensibility, the female body is associated with sincerity,[49] but as Clarissa's sister points out, the body can be manipulated to portray particular emotions. As Lovelace announces in his very first quotation (in this case, from Sir Robert Howard), '*He who seems virtuous does but act a part,/ And shows not his own nature, but his art*' (p. 143). Clarissa's virtue must continually be performed, and her contempt of Miss Martin is a defensive manoeuvre.

Clarissa's modest Shakespeare quotation, then, is part of a sustained performance of virtue that starts from the first page of the novel. Anna Howe, writing in the furore that follows Lovelace's duel with Clarissa's brother, observes that it is inevitable that 'whatever relates to a young lady, whose distinguished merits have made her the public care, should engage everybody's attention' (p. 39). Clarissa is on stage: 'Every eye, in short, is upon you, with the expectation of an example' (p. 40). To play down the possibility that Clarissa is a performer, Anna and Clarissa counter every mention of Clarissa's public role with a statement of her blameless discomfort under scrutiny: 'I know how *it must hurt you* to become the subject of public talk' (p. 39; italics added); 'now push'd into blaze, as we see, *to your regret*' (p. 40; italics added); and in Clarissa's reply, 'I am exceedingly concerned to find, that I am become so much the public talk, as *you* tell me, and as *everybody* tells me, I am' (p. 53). She even professes reluctance to tell her story: Anna, not Clarissa, opens the novel, urging her friend Clarissa to defend herself against false accusations, but Clarissa modestly shies away from self-presentation: 'It is not for a child to seek to clear her own character, or to justify her actions, at the expense of the most revered ones' (p. 52).

For all these manoeuvres that downplay performance, Richardson deliberately retains the thrilling possibility that Clarissa is an actress. He does so by giving voice indirectly to those who most vehemently accuse her of deceit: her family. Anna mentions James Harlowe's 'natural imperiousness and fierce and uncontrollable temper' (p. 39), and Clarissa observes that '. . .my poor sister is not naturally good-humoured' (p. 43); while Clarissa is praised by contrast as 'So steady, so uniform in your conduct' (p. 39). To compare James and Arabella's bad *nature* to Clarissa's exemplary *conduct* raises the question of whether she is really their moral superior, or simply a more skilful performer, better able to keep the family temper under control. Her spiteful siblings intimate the latter. Rejected by Lovelace, Bella jealously observes that Clarissa might 'try to engage such a man; she had patience; she was mistress of persuasion; and indeed, to do the girl justice, had *something* of a person' (p. 45). Instead of modesty and restraint, Bella sees in Clarissa only '*well-acted* indifference' (p. 46) and a superficial show of virtue designed to allure men.

By putting this negative judgement in the mouth of Arabella, reported by Clarissa, Richardson anticipates criticism of Clarissa and displaces it on to an unpleasant character, but ensures that the idea of performance is attendant on Clarissa's character. Richardson's earlier heroine, Pamela, also attracted criticism for her seeming artfulness. Early readers were divided into 'Pamelists and Anti-Pamelists' who respectively defended Pamela as a virginal 'Example for Ladies to follow', or accused her of being a 'hypocritical, crafty Girl, in her Courtship; who understands the Art of bringing a Man to her Lure'.[50] But in *Pamela*, as well as in *Clarissa*, Richardson anticipated this disapproval. As Mark Kinkead-Weekes points out, 'Richardson himself has both dramatised and resolved the possibility of hypocrisy in his heroine.'[51] Jenny Davidson goes further to suggest that 'Pamela does not accidentally fall short of the ideal of sincerity the novel seems to endorse. . .; Richardson presents her . . . as deliberately, even cold-bloodedly adopting arguments to justify deceptive practices within the framework of virtue the novel has constructed'.[52] The possibility of performance in both women lends ambiguity to their characters. When Lady Bradshaigh suggested that Clarissa would be unimpeachable had she not gone to London, Richardson replied that 'I did not want her to be wholly blameless'.[53] Such ambiguity enriches, rather than undermines, Richardson's characterisation: Clarissa and Pamela's quotations suggest at once the morality and the theatricality of their characters.

Novel and theatre

Just as Clarissa initially seems the polar opposite of the flamboyant, performing Lovelace, the novel can appear the opposite of the theatre. Neither opposition, however, is so clear-cut. In the pages of the novel, the theatre might appear a rejected 'other', but it is fascinatingly aligned by the novelists with the priorities of fiction. Ian Watt defined eighteenth-century fiction, epitomised in his eyes by Defoe, Richardson and Fielding, by its unprecedented 'truth to individual experience', and traced its development through the century in the advancing psychological 'formal realism' of its characters.[54] For Watt, 'character' refers to 'the stable elements in the individual's mental and moral constitution', as distinct from 'personality', namely behaviour.[55] More recent studies, however, have historicised eighteenth-century 'character'. They have traced the changing meanings of 'character' in the century, from signifying legible and knowable 'types' of people at its beginning to referring to the most indescribable and unique qualities of the individual by its end;[56] and demonstrated how, in the decades before the end of the century, people saw themselves as capable of switching between identities with the ease and fluidity of attendees at a masquerade.[57]

Important studies of sincerity, hypocrisy and politeness acknowledge the widely understood capacity for people to perform their 'character' in the eighteenth century.[58] Lionel Trilling remarks that 'It is surely no accident that the idea of sincerity, of the own self and the difficulty of knowing and showing it, should have arisen to vex men's minds in the epoch that saw the sudden efflorescence of the theatre.' Sincerity is histrionic, and retrospectively constructed: 'we play the role of being ourselves, we sincerely act the part of the sincere person'.[59] Novelists are acutely aware, for example, that the discourse of politeness can lead both virtuous and immoral characters into socially sanctioned deceptions. In Henry Fielding's *Amelia*, Mrs Bennet declares that 'what the World generally calls Politeness, I term Insincerity'.[60] When Colonel James, expecting to see only his admired Amelia, finds her husband at home, the narrator remarks upon the 'great Joy which he suddenly conveyed into his Countenance at the unexpected Sight of his Friend', which 'is to be attributed to that noble Art which is taught in those excellent Schools called the several Courts of *Europe*' (p. 361). One of those men able to 'put on Friendship with as much Ease as they can a laced Coat' (p. 361), James' social skills mask his worst intentions. But even the most virtuous characters can be gifted social performers: the mild-mannered Amelia herself was 'too polite to shew much Confusion; for though she knew nothing of the Town, she had had a genteel Education, and kept the best Company the Country afforded' (p. 202).

Despite new understanding of the performativity of novelistic character, Watt's contested notions of 'psychological realism' and 'truth to individual experience' are still used, albeit with caveats, to distinguish the novel from the stage. While novels have 'subjects', and interiority, 'character is paramount' in drama. Novelists gave

> the illusion of sincere protagonists to whose inner life readers could have unmediated access. In contrast, ... dramatists emphasized a rhetoric of surfaces, refusing to represent 'subjects' vested with individuality or an active inner life.[61]

Lisa A. Freeman here acknowledges that the novel presents the '*illusion* of sincere protagonists', if not sincerity itself, but she still distinguishes between novel and theatre in binary terms.[62] As the quoting characters discussed so far suggest, however, the apparently consistent 'subjects' of prose fiction are highly conscious of the constructedness of their own and one another's 'characters'. Their conflicting self-presentations constitute a 'rhetoric of surfaces' typically associated with drama.

Performance is central to a novelistic notion of character that is still founded in appearances, gestures and speech. Female novelists influenced by the theatre, for example, 'knew that to act like a lady was, in a sense, to perform a role'; the 'theatrical images and practices' that they consequently incorporated into their fiction 'called into question the ideals of femininity that their novels seem to support'.[63] Yet performance can also be a necessary ingredient for the expression of truthful experience, since 'theatrical frames often enable the articulation of truths and passions that may, under alternate conditions, be otherwise inexpressible'.[64] This latter statement is applicable not only to female dramatists finding self-expression in the theatre, but also to 'truthful' characters in the novel, who, through borrowed words, present themselves as sincere.

While novelists, then, might reject some aspects of the theatre, they align their work with other valuable qualities of the contemporary stage. Fielding's *Essay on the Knowledge of the Characters of Men* describes life as a 'masquerade' of artificial characters, wherein the disguises of the 'Cardinal, the Friar, or the Judge' cannot 'long conceal the Sot, the Gamester, or the Rake'.[65] In Fielding's metaphor of life as stage, however, the theatre is not the opposite of sincerity:

> the Generality of Mankind mistake the Affectation for the Reality: for as Affectation always over-acts her Part, it fares with her as with a Farcical Actor on the Stage, whose monstrous over-done Grimaces are sure to catch the Applause of an insensible Audience; while the truest and finest Strokes of Nature, represented by a judicious and just Actor, pass unobserved and disregarded.[66]

Fielding does not simply associate 'Affectation' with the stage, and sincerity with the absence of the stage. Instead, he likens both good and bad characters to actors: the affected man to the 'farcical actor' (like the King that Partridge admires, above) and the unaffected man to the 'judicious and just Actor' (like Garrick's naturalistic Hamlet). Just as novels draw negative attention to their excessively histrionic characters in order to offset by contrast their more sincere fictional creations, Fielding here presents the 'farcical' extreme of the spectrum in order to flatter by contrast the 'judicious and just Actor' who walks the same stage. The theatre, like the novel, is equally capable of artifice and sincerity. As the gentle heroine of Sarah Fielding's *History of Ophelia* remarks, when taken to see *Macbeth* performed for the first time: 'in the Acting, the whole received such an Air of Truth, that I could scarcely disbelieve a Fact in it'. A more skilful spectator than Partridge, she observes that the experience 'made my Agitations almost as strange as if I had been the Spectator of a real Tragedy'.[67]

Rather than rejecting the theatre outright, novelists reclaim and rehabilitate Shakespeare's theatricality. Celebrating the remarkable fidelity of Shakespeare's writing to life, novelists align themselves with the naturalistic forms of acting that best communicate such mimetic skill:

> after the nicest Strokes of a *Shakespear*, or a *Johnson*, of a *Wycherly* or an *Otway*, some Touches of Nature will escape the Reader, which the judicious Action of a *Garrick*, of a *Cibber*, or a *Clive*, can convey to him. (i. 493)

Novelists like Fielding style themselves and their fiction as cultural intermediaries who, like skilled actors such as Garrick, Susannah Cibber and Kitty Clive, amplify written 'Touches of Nature' through 'judicious Action'.

As Fielding observes in a footnote to this passage, these three actors have 'formed themselves on the Study of Nature only'. Garrick in particular becomes a model of the perfect communication of emotions. One fictional heroine who attends his performance of *Richard III* is described as having 'sincerely felt, and wept, the horrid uncle's cruelty';[68] while another was moved by 'the genuine operation of that variety of passions the performance naturally excited in her breast', to her companion's admiration: 'Now her lovely bosom was agitated with horror; and now her tenderness was evinced by a falling tear—now disgust was also predominant—and now astonishment, for a moment, held even feeling in suspence:—the villainies, the artifices of Richard, occasioned many beautiful changes in her aspect'.[69] Novelists satirise those characters who fail to recognise Garrick's achievement: Partridge is moved by his performance, but neglects to praise his work; while Sterne's *Tristram Shandy* invokes an audience member who, when asked 'And how did Garrick speak the soliloquy last night', could not report on his 'expression or attitude or countenance' because he had 'look'd only at the stop-watch' to time his famous pauses.[70] If the former cannot see Garrick's art, the latter is too distracted to appreciate its power. Readers are implicitly warned that to be a poor spectator of Garrick is to be a poor reader of the novel, and vice versa.

Disruptive Shakespeare

Shakespeare's reputation benefits from his novelisation: he accrues the impression of emotional authority and insight, and is associated with the most exacting and naturalistic modes of physical representation. But some novels suggest that Shakespeare's theatricality cannot be contained in this way. Quoted fragments of his plays can still bear vivid dramatic associations that disrupt their new textual home, and the novelists exploit this persistent sense of otherness. Unlike Lovelace or even Joseph Andrews, for example, Sterne's Walter Shandy is not an obviously theatrical character: he seems to stumble across Shakespeare and to quote him in surprise or consternation. It is in 'looking into *Lithopædus Senonesis de Partu difficili*' in preparation for the birth of his child that he bursts out in an exclamation from *Hamlet*:

> . . .how great was his apprehension, when he further understood, that this force, acting upon the very vertex of the head, not only injured the brain itself or cerebrum,—but that it necessarily squeez'd and propell'd the cerebrum towards the cerebellum, which was the immediate seat of the understanding.—Angels and Ministers of grace defend us! cried my father,

—can any soul withstand this shock? No wonder the intellectual web is so rent and tatter'd as we see it . . . (i. 176–7)

In Shakespeare, Hamlet's cry of 'Angels and ministers of grace defend us!' is prompted by the sight of the ghost of his late father. In Sterne, Walter's cry is prompted by a theory about the potentially damaging effects of 'the woman's efforts' on the head of the child during labour. Hamlet and Walter, for all their differences, both evoke the relationship of fathers and sons across the edges of life. The incongruity of Walter's quotation arises because he responds to his fireside reading with a cry from a scene that had electrified the London theatres, turning a book into a performance and a theoretical possibility into a present danger. He summons not so much the play, as the theatre, into the Shandy parlour.

Contemporary reports of Garrick's portrayal of Hamlet from 1742 to 1776 suggest that the ghost scene is a 'point' in the play to which audiences paid special attention, admiring the actor's representation of terror. The German natural scientist and documenter of English life Georg Christoph Lichtenberg described at length Garrick's memorable performance:

> Suddenly, as Hamlet moves towards the back of the stage slightly to the left and turns his back on the audience, Horatio starts, and saying: 'Look, my lord, it comes,' points to the right, where the ghost has already appeared and stands motionless, before anyone is aware of him. At these words Garrick turns sharply and at the same moment staggers back two or three paces with his knees giving way under him; his hat falls to the ground and both his arms, especially the left, are stretched out nearly to their full length, with the hands as high as his head, the right arm more bent and the hands lower, and the fingers apart; his mouth is open: thus he stands rooted to the spot, with legs apart, but no loss of dignity, supported by his friends, who are better acquainted with the apparition and fear lest he should collapse. His whole demeanour is so expressive of terror that it made my flesh creep even before he began to speak. The almost terror-struck silence of the audience, which preceded this appearance and filled one with a sense of insecurity, probably did much to enhance this effect. At last he speaks, not at the beginning, but at the end of a breath, with a trembling voice: 'Angels and ministers of grace defend us!' words which supply anything this scene may lack and make it one of the greatest and most terrible which will ever be played on any stage.[71]

Lichtenberg captures Garrick's postures in minute detail: 'arms. . . stretched out nearly to their full length . . . the right arm more bent and the hands lower, and the fingers apart; his mouth is open . . . he stands rooted to the spot, with legs apart'. He shows how closely Garrick adheres to the emotional language of theatrical gesture, in which terror is physically represented when 'everything is spread out, fingers, legs and feet', and when the actor 'opens wide the mouth, shortens the nose, gives the countenance an air of wildness'.[72] 'At last' (Garrick is supposed to have paused for so long before speaking that those watching thought he needed prompting[73]) come the 'trembling' words, 'Angels and ministers of grace defend us!'. Lichtenberg credits the line with making 'this scene' 'one of the greatest and most terrible which will ever be played on any stage'; it concludes, and encapsulates, this memorable gesture of terror.

So powerful is the contemporary association between these words and Garrick's performance that there would have been few readers for whom reading them would not have brought to mind Garrick's expertly delivered gestures of terror and trembling voice – not to mention the hydraulic wig that made his hairs stand on end like 'quills upon the fretful porcupine'. In his *Essay on Elocution* (first published 1774), William Enfield defied readers to

> read some dramatic speech expressive of strong passion (for example Shakespear's speech of Hamlet to the ghost) in the same unimpassioned manner in which he would read an ordinary article of intelligence. Even in silent reading, where the subject interests the passions, every one who is not destitute of feeling, whilst he understands the meaning of the words, conceives the expression that would accompany them, if they were spoken.[74]

The lines evidently retained their vivid theatricality even when excerpted: the 'expression that would accompany them' follows hard on the heels of the 'words'. A reader 'trained to conjure up the image of the actor through the words on the page'[75] would readily invoke the celebrated stage scene. The quotation, then, brings Garrick unbidden into the parlour, and the novel. It makes Walter, in the reader's imagination, involuntarily 'stagger back', throw up his arms, spread his fingers and open wide his mouth in terror when he should be quietly reading.

Other quotations conjure up stage scenes with multiple characters, to the significant disruption of the narrative. Walter becomes frustrated with Uncle Toby's relentless harping on his pet subject of 'that great mathematician and engineer' Stevinus. He snaps at Toby, only to be struck by a look from his brother of so much 'good nature;—so placid;—so fraternal;—so inexpressibly tender towards him' that he is moved to Shakespearean apology:

> it penetrated my father to his heart: He rose up hastily from his chair, and seizing hold of both my uncle *Toby*'s hands as he spoke:—Brother *Toby*,

> said he,—I beg thy pardon;—forgive, I pray thee, this rash humour which my mother gave me. (i. 133)

Toby's 'look' triggers an instant emotional response: 'it penetrated my father to his heart: He rose up hastily ... he spoke'. Walter pleads for forgiveness of 'this rash humour' in the words of Shakespeare's Cassius. This uncalculated response sounds far from the stage, yet it draws the two brothers irresistibly into a performance. Walter 'rose up' as if involuntarily, and, 'seizing' Toby's hands, pulled him to his feet too. The quotation from *Julius Caesar* pulls them both into an awkward theatrical tableau, conjuring a stage scene in the middle of the narrative. As Tristram recalls, 'At the end of the last chapter, my father and my uncle *Toby* were left both standing, like *Brutus* and *Cassius* at the close of the scene making up their accounts' (i. 134). They were 'left both standing' a chapter later, for here, as in the contemporary theatre of sensibility, 'the emotional tableau, so common in sentimental writing generally, predominated over narrative coherence'.[76] The vivid theatrical scene remains outside the linear narrative of Sterne's novel, complicating its forward progress.

The irony of this episode comes not just from 'the satirical comparison of the little characters to the great', nor the unlikelihood of Walter and Toby's being in a play,[77] but from the incongruity of the theatre in their house. Walter 'dipp'd into all kinds of books' (i. 175), and it is possible that he stumbled across the words 'this rash humour my mother gave me' in Shakespeare, or even in Dodd, and, with his 'prompt memory' (i. 428), stored it away. The line suits his preoccupations: Judith Hawley, documenting all the books, real and otherwise, that are mentioned in *Tristram Shandy*, suggests that Walter builds his library determinedly 'around the subjects which he thinks are most important in raising a perfect son: procreation, the seat of the soul, parturition, naming, noses and education'.[78] 'This rash humour my mother gave me' taps into these abiding concerns, hinting at where Walter thinks parental responsibility for the characteristics of children lies, and where, after Mrs Shandy's untimely interruption at the moment of Tristram's conception, any blame for Tristram's misfortunes should be attributed. But, as the above 'scene' suggests, it will not be calmly anthologised as an insight in Walter's mental commonplace book. Eighteenth-century novels encourage readers to store away pieces of Shakespeare for domestic use, but also reveal that they are sometimes too big for the home.

The ultimate, doomed attempt to 'novelise' Shakespeare is surely represented by Yorick in *Tristram Shandy*. In Shakespeare's *Hamlet*, Yorick is only nominally and retrospectively a character: for Hamlet, his skull, unearthed by gravediggers, functions as an impromptu memento mori. In Sterne's novel, Parson Yorick is a fully realised character with foibles and charm in equal measure, beyond Hamlet's mention of his ability to set the table in a roar. The first mention of Yorick in Sterne's novel is highly bookish, discussing not his Shakespearean namesake but his family records:

> YORICK was this parson's name, and, what is very remarkable in it, (as appears from a most antient account of the family, wrote upon strong vellum, and now in perfect preservation) it had been exactly so spelt for near,—I was within an ace of saying nine hundred years;—but I would not shake my credit in telling an improbable truth, however indisputable in itself. . . (i. 25)

In focusing on its spelling, the narrator fastens upon what is perhaps the least 'remarkable' aspect of the name 'Yorick' for the reader. He first fusses about the age ('antient account'), physical state ('strong vellum', 'perfect preservation') and accuracy ('improbable truth') of the records of Yorick's ancestry (i. 25–6), in a protracted show of concern with the reliability of documentary sources, or 'parody of historical method'.[79] It is only then that 'Yorick' is connected with his most famous manifestation: 'It has often come into my head, that this post could be no other than that of the king's chief Jester; --- and that *Hamlet's Yorick*, in our *Shakespear*, many of whose plays, you know, are founded upon authenticated facts,—was certainly the very man' (i. 26). Tristram treats Shakespeare not as an imaginative or dramatic source, but as an archive of factual information.

It is after Yorick's death that the theatricality of Shakespeare is finally restored. Yorick's gravestone reunites him with the Shakespearean lines most memorably associated with him: 'Alas, poor YORICK!' (i. 35). Yorick's 'epitaph and elegy' might be soberly engraved on a 'plain marble slabb', but neither the stone, nor the box within which they are encased in the novel, can restrain the theatricality of these three words. 'Not a passenger goes by' that can resist repeating them aloud. Did these passers-by know Yorick? One critic regards them as mourners 'paying their respects' to Yorick by 'repeating with feeling his Shakespearean epigraph', while another is more cynical about the 'endless bandying of the three unoriginal words' for 'a Yorick they never knew'.[80] Nonetheless, each of these anonymous 'passengers' is moved not just to speaking aloud, but to 'plaintive', sighing performance of Shakespeare's words. The entirely black facing page hints that this reflex of heartfelt theatrical repetition will resound into infinity or oblivion. Yorick might be novelised, and gain a tenderness of character that continues into *A Sentimental Journey*, but he cannot be contained by his new fictional home.

Some of Shakespeare's appearances in the novel, then, bring with them vivid, imaginary scenes that challenge the narrative progress of prose fiction: the black page draws a halt to narrative altogether.[81] As a narrator, however, Tristram enlists the language of the theatre to try to control the narrative. Walter Shandy said of Yorick's sermon that ''tis dramatic,— and there is something in that way of writing, skilfully managed, which catches the attention' (i. 165), and Tristram's self-conscious talk of 'stage', 'scene', 'entrance' and 'curtains' draws 'attention' to the many switches in time and point of view. He observes that 'chapters relieve the mind—that they assist—or impose upon the imagination—and that in a work of this dramatic cast they are as necessary as the shifting of scenes' (i. 337), and with declarations such as 'but this had better begin a new chapter' (i. 120) he attempts heavy-handedly to stage-manage the 'dramatic' narrative. But the theatre turns out to have a disruptive, not cohesive, effect on his narrative, and he laments the numerous interruptions that keep the story of his own birth untold for several volumes. Likewise, Tristram bids us 'look down upon the stage' and see Walter 'baffled and overthrown in all his little systems and wishes; to behold a train of events perpetually falling out against him, and in so critical and cruel a way, as if they had purposely been plann'd and pointed against him, merely to insult his speculations' (i. 63–4). Walter longs to direct the events of Tristram's birth, but he is consistently relegated to the role of vexed player.

The disruptive power of quotations lies in their ability to open up imaginary vistas in the mind of the reader. The arrival of the man-midwife, Dr Slop, at the Shandy household appeals directly to the reader's imagination. Tristram hopes that since he has managed to bring 'my uncle *Toby* from *Namur*, quite across all *Flanders*, into *England*', in the same time that Obadiah was sent a mere eight miles to fetch the midwife, this interlude will have sufficiently 'prepared the reader's imagination for the enterance of Dr. *Slop* upon the stage,—as much, at least, (I hope) as a dance, a song, or a concerto between the acts' (i. 120). Slop is introduced to the reader in theatrical terms, with all the anticipation of a musical interlude.

When Slop finally reaches the house, it is in the manner of a Shakespearean character, or actor:

> *Obadiah* had led him in as he was, *unwiped, unappointed, unanealed*, with all his stains and blotches on him.—He stood like *Hamlet*'s ghost,

> motionless and speechless, for a full minute and a half, at the parlour door, (*Obadiah* still holding his hand) with all the majesty of mud. (i. 123–4)

Sterne describes Slop's physical appearance, as if he 'stood' before an audience, 'like *Hamlet*'s ghost, motionless and speechless'. He evokes the same thrilling scene that Walter recalled with his exclamation of 'Angels and ministers of grace'. Slop, however, is '*unwiped, unappointed, unanealed,* with all his stains and blotches on him', not because, like Hamlet's father, he was untimely murdered with his sins unatoned for, 'unhous'led, disa-ppointed, unaneled,/ No reck'ning made, but sent to my account/ With all my imperfections on my head',[82] but because he fell off his 'little diminutive pony' (i. 121) on the way and is covered in mud.

This theatrical vision of Slop has bookish overtones. Sterne replaces the word 'unhouseled', which describes the spiritual state of not having had the Eucharist administered, with 'unwiped', which suggests the physical state of grubbiness; and 'disappointed', or spiritually unprepared, with the matter-of-fact 'unappointed', or not required. For all its bathos, though, the phrase '*unwiped, unappointed, unanealed*' engages with a contemporary editorial debate. It closely resembles Theobald's reading of Shakespeare's line, 'unhousel'd', 'unappointed', 'unaneal'd', which would make Sterne's 'unappointed' not a pun but a quotation. Theobald's conjecture was not, however, widely accepted. As Dodd registers in a footnote to this excerpted scene from *Hamlet*, 'This line has created the editors much trouble: both the words and the sense of them having been disputed'.[83] While all editors are agreed over the meaning of the first word,

> the second, Mr. *Theobald* alters to *unappointed*, which he explains by, '*no confession* of sins made, no reconciliation to heaven, no appointment of penance by the church.' This reading is generally disregarded, and we find *unanointed* almost universally prevail, the sense of which, as indisputably as of the first word in the line, is determined to be, *without extreme unction*.[84]

Dodd also arbitrates between Theobald, Pope and Hanmer to determine the meaning of 'unaneal'd' as '*unaknell'd*, to bear the sense Mr. *Pope* gives it' (which is to say, 'no knell rung', rather than, as in Theobald's sense, '*without extreme unction*').[85] By changing the first word of Theobald's line, Sterne engages parodically in an act of conjectural emendation, entangling this theatrical scene in a textual crux.

Slop's arrival thus requires the reader to switch rapidly back and forth between the theatre and the book. It also oscillates between 'stage' and 'parlour', and between the physical ('for a minute and a half') and the spiritual ('like Hamlet's ghost'). Slop is a 'Papist' (i. 122), and his Catholic faith is relentlessly contrasted with his ridiculous physical state: about to be knocked from his horse, 'He crossed himself', but 'he had better have kept hold of the pummel' (i. 122); as a result, he was never 'so beluted, and so transubstantiated' (i. 123). The repeated word 'presence' (i. 124) denotes at once Slop's filthy appearance and the article of his Catholic faith that fundamentally distinguishes it from Sterne's Anglican tradition: belief in the 'real presence' of Christ during the Eucharist. Dramatic quotations, Sterne suggests, force the reader to conjure up imaginative spaces that do not necessarily cohere. They are as different in shape and direction as the imaginative metaphors that see Walter flying off 'in eager pursuit of a metaphysic point into the very regions where clouds and thick darkness would soon have encompassed it about' while Toby's head was filled with 'ideas whirling round and round about in it' (i. 225).

These imaginative vistas cannot easily be controlled. The reader is asked first to 'imagine to yourself' Slop as a 'little, squat, uncourtly figure' 'with a breadth of back, and a sesquipedality of belly, which might have done honour to a Serjeant in the Horse-Guards' (i. 121); to conjure a further visual simile for this already imaginary figure when he falls from his horse 'something in the stile and manner of a pack of wool' (p. 123); and then to picture him as a muddy ghost. Keymer notes that Sterne, in urging the reader to 'imagine' Dr Slop, takes up a 'cliché of modern novelistic discourse', 'used in particular to herald set-piece exercises in the grotesque'; but that, within a short space, the relaxed convenor of collaborative meanings has mutated into a control freak', delivering a final set of 'instructions on how to view Dr Slop':[86]

> Let the reader imagine then, that Dr. *Slop* has told his tale ... Let him suppose that *Obadiah* has told his tale also ... Let him imagine that my father has stepp'd up stairs to see my mother:—And, to conclude this work of imagination,—let him imagine the Doctor wash'd—rubb'd down,—condoled with,—felicitated,—got into a pair of *Obadiah*'s pumps. (i. 126)

Keymer likens this set of instructions to the empty space in which Sterne encourages the reader to imagine the Widow Wadman in whatever way they wish: both instances 'highlight the sheer impossibility of collaboration with the reader as a mechanism for generating determinate meaning'.[87] Unlike the imaginary Widow Wadman, though, Hamlet's ghost comes with a set of familiar theatrical gestures and thus, by extension, a shared set of imaginative associations for the readers of the novel. In the bustling process by which Slop later 'wash'd—rubb'd down—condoled with—felicitated,—got into a pair of *Obadiah*'s pumps', the Shakespearean spectre raised in the rhythmically similar '*unwiped, unappointed, unanealed*' is cleaned, welcomed, and, ultimately, shut down. Slop is a liminal presence: first mentioned at the edge of a 'new chapter', his 'entrance' is heralded several times before he finally arrives at the boundaries of the Shandy house, 'entered the back parlour', and 'stood like *Hamlet*'s ghost . . . at the parlour door'. His entrance keeps the story of Tristram's birth, unfolding in the room overhead, in a state of suspension. Sterne ruefully implies that what he needs to curtail in order to progress with the narrative is the reader's vivid theatrical imagination.

Sterne's portrayal of Yorick also plays on the dramatic power of the reader's imagination. Sterne knows that, on hearing the word 'Yorick', the reader will instantly think of Shakespeare's character; and that, by detouring through ancient records, his eventual connection of Yorick with Shakespeare will lag behind the reader's by a full page. After this slow start, the novel gallops apace, in just a few pages, to Yorick's gravestone. The reader might infer that it is their own Shakespearean associations, rapidly overtaking the narrator's attempts to novelise Yorick's character, that have sped Parson Yorick to his demise.

Proleptic hints of the posthumous 'Alas, poor YORICK!' hover over Parson Yorick from the moment he appears in the novel, not least in the capitalised 'YORICK' that opens the chapter (i. 25). Yorick's dear friend Eugenius warns 'Trust me, dear *Yorick*' (i. 31); the narrator says 'alas, too late!' (i. 32), and Yorick himself returns 'alas! my friend' as the 'curtain' is drawn around his deathbed (i. 33–4). It is as if this familiar sliver of *Hamlet* tows the poor, 'unhackneyed' Yorick (i. 29) towards his end with the same 'talismanic power' that the word 'siege' has over Uncle Toby's military imagination (i. 282). These theatrical hints are entwined with other, more novelistic associations. Yorick's horse is 'full brother to *Rosinante*' (i. 18), his own character matches that of 'the peerless knight of *La Mancha*' (i. 23), and at his death, he quotes Cervantes: 'I might say with *Sancho Pança*, that should I recover, and "Mitres thereupon be suffer'd to rain down from heaven as thick as hail, not one of 'em would fit it"' (i. 34). Yorick's final words are 'utter'd with something of a *cervantick* tone;--and as he spoke it, *Eugenius* could perceive a stream of lambent fire lighted up for a moment in his eyes;----faint picture of those flashes of his spirit, which (as *Shakespear* said of his ancestor) were wont to set the table in a roar!' (i. 34). Sterne moves back and forth between novel and drama in a 'conflation of generic categories' that 'undermines unequivocal interpretation, forcing one back upon subjective conviction' – or in other words, faith.[88] This generic confusion gestures upwards to that 'superintending power' who 'directed the operations of them,—held the chain in his hand, and turned and wound it to his own purpose'.[89]

Shakespeare and the theatre of the imagination

Shakespeare, then, does not quite 'escape the stage' in the eighteenth century. Rather, that stage, as conjured in prose fiction, escapes the physical restrictions of the auditorium and expands to a previously unimaginable scale. One experimental mid-century novel, which Keymer has shown to be an important influence on Sterne, enacts this process:

> *For not at* Banquo*'s sacred Shade* Mackbeth
> *Or pious* Hamlet, *when aghast and pale*
> *The royal* Spectre *trod the conscious Lawn,*
> *Confusion felt at Heart like* Archibald.

> Forgive me, Reader, this *tragi-comical* Method of communicating to you an Idea of ineffable Surprize. If possibly you have ever seen the finest Theatrical Performer in the World appear in some of the principal Characters of *Shakespear*'s immortal Tragedy, you can easily (by the Assistance of such a Spur to Recollection,) describe in your Imagination a much livelier Picture, of a Youth under this distressful Circumstance, than I have the Vanity to pretend to.[90]

Just as Sterne would do with Walter, this novel enlists the familiar 'tragi-comical Method' of referring to the '*royal* Spectre' in *Hamlet* to convey 'an Idea of ineffable Surprize'. The narrator turns to the stage – and to 'the finest Theatrical Performer in the World' – to illuminate the analogy, as if the memory of past theatrical performance is better equipped than the novel to bring this image to life. However, that theatrical 'Recollection' is only an 'Assistance' to spur the reader to greater heights, enabling them to 'describe in your Imagination a much livelier Picture' than either the theatre or the novel can offer.

Sterne contributes to this new sense of Shakespeare's transcendence, placing the playwright not so much back on the stage as in the imagination, above both stage and novel. 'Shakespeare' himself is an imaginary world in which Yorick can roam in *A Sentimental Journey*. In France, waiting to be granted his passport, Yorick picks up *Much Ado About Nothing*, gets 'busy with Don Pedro and Benedick and Beatrice', and temporarily loses himself:

> Sweet pliability of man's spirit, that can at once surrender itself to illusions, which cheat expectation and sorrow of their weary moments! . . . when my way is too rough for my feet, or too steep for my strength, I get off it, to

> some smooth velvet path which fancy has scattered over with rose-buds of delights; and having taken a few turns in it, come back strengthen'd and refresh'd—When evils press sore upon me, and there is no retreat from them in this world, then I take a new course—I leave it—and as I have a clearer idea of the elysian fields than I have of heaven, I force myself, like Eneas, into them . . . [91]

Being 'transported' to his dramatic world is a restorative, quasi-religious experience. For Yorick, Shakespeare's plays are a place where he can 'get off' his daily path, 'leave' the world and immerse himself in 'illusions', 'fancy' and 'delights'. This place, from which he returns 'strengthen'd and refresh'd', is personal to him; visiting it, far from distracting or corrupting him, enables him to continue on his 'way'.

With this imaginary state now established, every fragment of Shakespeare's works gestures towards a greater, now immeasurable, whole:

> What the old French officer had deliver'd upon travelling, bringing Polonius's advice to his son upon the same subject into my head—and that bringing in Hamlet; and Hamlet, the rest of Shakespear's works, I stopp'd at the Quai de Conti in my return home, to purchase the whole set.[92]

Yorick's thoughts on travel bring to mind 'Polonius's advice to his son' on the same subject. Phrases like 'neither a borrower nor a lender be' and 'to thine own self be true' are now sententious: excerption in Dodd's *Beauties* under the heading that Yorick mentions here, 'Advice from a father to a son, on going to travel', has transformed Polonius's pompous proverbiality into Shakespeare's advice for all. But Yorick's imagination overcomes Shakespeare's fragmentation into moral sentiments, for Polonius's advice brings in 'Hamlet, and Hamlet, the rest of Shakespeare's works'. This single fragment conjures first a character, then a play and then all of 'Shakespeare'.

'Shakespeare', like Parson Yorick himself, is now indisputably bigger than the fragments that gesture towards him. He cannot be contained by them, just as he cannot be contained by the vellum scroll of Yorick's family history. The line resists its anthologisation, not just by restoring it to its dramatic speaker (Polonius, rather than 'a father'), but by pointing beyond words, phrases and plays to a transcendent 'Shakespeare'. As Elizabeth Wanning Harries notes, 'the fragmentary for Sterne always had Biblical overtones, overtones that suggested the importance of the fragment as a gesture toward a greater fullness and as a reminder of a more perfect communion'.[93] Shakespeare, by dramatic, disruptive quotation, acquires some of 'ungraspable fullness'[94] and unknowable completeness of Sterne's God.

Sterne and other mid-century novelists, in combining the directiveness of the novel ('imagine to yourself') with the memorably vivid gestures of the theatre, played a significant role in the establishment of Shakespeare and his words in the cultural imagination, a place that transcends any single mode of representation; his words can become the province of poetry, painting and the popular consciousness. Charles Lamb would later declare a preference for reading, rather than seeing, Shakespeare, not now out of didactic anti-theatricalism, but because the former does not hinder the imagination; William Hazlitt would say of *Hamlet* that 'There is no play that suffers so much in being transferred to the stage'.[95] Restricted by neither stage nor book, Shakespeare would 'underwrite theories of the imagination's creative power' for Romantic poets who believed that 'imagination, genius, and poetry are closely associated with each other'.[96] Admired in the eighteenth century for his truthful, mimetic representation of nature, he would be celebrated by writers such as Coleridge for his invisible 'grasp of the living principle at the heart of nature'.[97]

CHAPTER 5

Banal Shakespeare

In 1777, a visitor to England declared that 'in this island Shakespeare is not only famous, but holy; his moral maxims are heard everywhere'.[1] Georg Christoph Lichtenberg was writing more than twenty-five years after the first publication of *Clarissa*. By this point, the 'moral maxims' of Shakespeare's constructed and promoted by the mid-century novel were to be heard 'everywhere', and Shakespeare himself was widely admired as a morally authoritative, if not 'holy', figure. So much so that an 'Impartial Reader' of the *Public Advertiser* was moved to complain in the same year that:

> It has been so long the Fashion, in this Country, to '*gulp down every Drop of this immortal Man*', as Roscius has chosen to express himself in one of his Prologues, that even Shakespeare, with all his Merit, is become a public Nuisance in every Company.[2]

The Impartial Reader takes a rather more dim view of the notion that Shakespeare is 'everywhere'. For him, it is a general 'Prejudice' for Shakespeare – 'for it is impossible to call it *Taste*' – that leads all kinds of 'foolish Admirers and dumb commentators' to praise him relentlessly. As a result, 'the Press, as well as Conversation, labours under the Weight of a Subject, rendered unsufferably dull by injudicious Repetition'. Repeated ad nauseam, Shakespeare's words are now a banal 'Nuisance' in polite conversation.

To expose the banal quotation and mindless admiration of Shakespeare that characterised this period is to challenge the compelling story of Shakespeare's eighteenth-century 'accession to pre-eminence',[3] revealing a negative side to the rising trajectory assumed in studies of Shakespeare's reception. The very fact of Shakespeare's growing admiration means that some of his phrases had already become 'commonplace, common, trite; trivial, petty'.[4] Unlike the more writerly word 'hackneyed', with which 'banal' shares an otherwise similar definition, 'banal' arrives at that meaning 'From the intermediate sense of, Open to the use of all the community', and captures the effects of Shakespeare's increasing omnipresence. Similarly, the word 'commonplace', which had referred in the early modern period to important passages, often culled from Latin texts from 'authors held to be authoritative, or, at any rate, commendable in their opinions, and regarded as exemplary in terms of linguistic usage and stylistic niceties', would denote by the end of the eighteenth century the ordinary, overworn and mainstream,[5] disdained precisely because it was used by all.

Eighteenth-century novelists, I argue in this chapter, engage directly with Shakespeare's growing banality, and exploit it in their fiction. They deliberately draw comic attention to the negative implications of his growing cultural presence and fashionable status. They satirise the social compulsion at work in people's eager quotations from Shakespeare's plays. 'Banal Shakespeare' serves to nuance their characterisation: some characters' eagerness leads them into enthusiastic acts of quotation that outstrip their natural ability, while others, desperate to be *seen* to admire Shakespeare, quote with self-conscious affectation. Novelists revel in the new meanings that fragments of Shakespeare have acquired through heavy use. Far from being emptied of meaning by their detachment from their play sources, these increasingly well-worn Shakespearean tags and quotations bring to the novel an array of associations accrued in circulation in polite culture. Paying close attention to these fragments helps to challenge the received view of the novelists engaging with Shakespeare only directly, through sustained allusion or thematic reference, and reveals instead the vivid associations attached to scraps of Shakespeare's language. Yet at the same time as critiquing and creatively exploiting it, the novelists also contribute to the phenomenon of 'banal Shakespeare'. Their frequent quotations nudge some phrases, from 'patience on a monument' to 'green-eyed monster', into popularity, along with the habit of quotation. The novelists thus speeded the process by which some fragments of Shakespeare became permanently detached from their source and strongly associated with new emotional scenarios.

Most significantly still, the novelists explicitly train their readers to judge the 'injudicious repetition' performed by numerous characters. They do so not just by parading for the readers' amusement a range of desperate quotations by 'fine ladies' and 'beau-pedants'. Their methods also include emphasising the reactions of other characters to quotation; having a knowing character train the naïve hero or heroine in how to respond to literary show-offs; or contrasting an attentive female theatre-goer with the unthinking audience who chatter – and quote – around her. By suggesting how readers might respond to banal quotation, the novel recommends a more ideal critical engagement with reading, the theatre, and the habitual, polite performances of the public sphere.

As a result, the phenomenon of 'banal Shakespeare' is a major contributor to Shakespeare's growing cultural dominance in the eighteenth century. It has been suggested that for 'classic' authors such as Goethe, Schiller and Lessing, constant repetition and quotation led to a 'rather dubious banalization of the product'.[6] Shakespeare, at this point in the eighteenth century, has not yet fully achieved the status of a 'classic' author; and the commodification or repetition of his 'product' served not to undermine or cheapen his moral authority, but to contribute to it. By drawing comic attention to poor uses of his words, and encouraging the reader to judge them accordingly, they not only help the reader to navigate the social world more effectively. The novelists codify for the first time what constitutes the proper admiration of Shakespeare and other authors. In doing so, they promote prose fiction as a genre dedicated to improving, rather than undermining, the nation's cultural life.

They also promote Shakespeare. By showing their readers a Shakespeare seemingly cheapened by endless 'injudicious Repetition', the novelists ultimately elevate him. Just as, in Chapter 3, Sarah Fielding's characters' ill-fitting quotations confirmed by contrast the aptness of Shakespeare's observations, and granted him authority, the status of Shakespeare is reinforced with every colourfully misquoted, misapplied and half-understood line. (The same is true of other English authors too, but, being the most widely quoted author, and most frequently attracting this compulsive behaviour, the effects are most pronounced in his case.) 'Banal Shakespeare' finally raises the question of ownership: Shakespeare might be established as the national poet, but to whom does 'our' Shakespeare belong? The novelists' critique of aspiring quotation stratifies Shakespeare's admirers by their skill and appreciation, and promotes 'the immortal Shakespeare' above all of their attempts to adore him.

In and out of fashion

It is paradoxical to say, as the 'Impartial Reader' does, that quoting Shakespeare is 'the Fashion': it suggests at once wide recognition and thoughtless, modish admiration of Shakespeare's qualities. The Shakespeare Revival, a marked growth in the popularity of Shakespeare's plays on stage in the 1730s and early 1740s, brought Shakespeare into the centre of London's entertainments, but also linked him with other, more dubious, fashionable diversions. The 'fashion' had firmly *not* been for Shakespeare earlier in the century, and some had thought him wrongfully overlooked in favour of the more spectacular, foreign entertainments that flooded the London stage. Richard Steele complained in 1709 that 'Ladder-dancers, Rope-dancers, Juglers, and Mountebanks' had come to 'strut in the Place of *Shakespear*'s Heroes, and *Johnson*'s Humourists'[7]; and Aaron Hill knew that his own 1723 adaptation of *King Henry V*, built on the foundations of the 'inimitable, and immortal, *Shakespear*', ran against the 'taste of the *fashionable*', for whom, as experience tells him, 'the *Harlequins* are gentlemen, of better interest than the *Harrys*'.[8] Indeed, early eighteenth-century audiences, unlike these knowing critics and dramatists, might have been unaware that they were seeing 'Shakespeare' in improved or heavily adapted form.[9]

Shakespeare's re-accession to the stage was regarded as something of a moral victory. One contemporary account archly suggested that, while a desire for '*seeming* to be diverted' had had audiences flocking mindlessly to Farinelli's operas, fashion had shifted, and 'a Lady may now confess, that she prefers a good *English Play* to any *Italian Opera* without raising the Indignation of the Tea-Table'.[10] For this speaker, the increasing presence of Shakespeare on stage was a welcome development:

> The great Encouragement which has been given, for these two Winters pass'd, to the acting of *Shakespeare*'s Plays, makes me hope Fashion is at last going to side with Virtue, and if ever Publick Diversions are made Auxiliaries to Common Sense, Morality may once more have a Chance of becoming *fashionable*; and tho' from natural Amiableness of Virtue, Fashion can never be able *intirely* to banish her from the World; yet, if ever they two were to join Forces, Vice might very easily be put out of Countenance.[11]

Critics take this and other commendatory rhetoric as evidence of the significant role played by women in restoring Shakespeare to the stage, well before Garrick promoted his plays. They have attributed the success of the Shakespeare Revival not only to the availability of cheap play texts, the expansion of literacy, growing interests in antiquarianism and nationalism, and the Licensing Act of 1737, which heavily restricted the production of new plays, but also to the efforts of the Shakespeare Ladies Club – a 'fluid organisation' of female participants who 'campaigned actively for two theatrical seasons, persuading the London theatre managers to put more Shakespeare plays on the stage'.[12] Whatever the nature of their practical contribution to Shakespeare's revival, this remark suggests that women played an important *symbolic* role, for in them, 'Fashion' and 'Virtue' might, as A. Z. hopes, be combined. Women not only bring Shakespeare into fashion, but, with their 'true Taste in public Diversions',[13] connect him with a notion of taste that links aesthetic and moral qualities.[14] Now at the centre of the town's 'Public Diversions', Shakespeare might yield positive benefits to the fashionable public.

Novelists, however, reveal that the negative side of this newfound fashionable status is the unthinking admiration that it provokes. 'Shakespeare' is increasingly a name to drop, and to praise him a polite habit. The two seemingly fine ladies who visit the Vicar of Wakefield's family talk of 'nothing but high-life, and high-lived company, and other fashionable topics, such as pictures, taste, Shakespear, and the musical glasses', including Shakespeare in their voguish list of entertainments.[15] Richardson's morally upright Harriet Byron in *Sir Charles Grandison* groups Shakespeare among the 'fashionable subjects' upon which the pedantic Mr Walden 'made no great figure ... no not on that of *Plays*: For he would needs force into conversation, with a preference to our Shakespeare, his Sophocles, his Euripides, his Terence; of the merits of whose performances, except by translations, no one present but Mr. Reeves and himself could judge.' A skilled quoter of Shakespeare herself, Harriet's point is not to disparage Shakespeare so much as to promote his English value over Walden's pedantic classical preferences, which cannot be shared by the group. To do so, however, she locates Shakespeare in the potentially frivolous conversational terrain of '*Plays, Fashion, Dress*, and the *Public Entertainments*'.[16]

Novelists, I argue, are acutely engaged not just with Shakespeare himself, but with the shifting public tastes, and critical fashions, for Shakespeare. Henry Fielding remarks in 1745 that

> It is a Phrase commonly used in the Polite World, that such a Person is in Fashion; nay, I myself have known an Individual in Fashion, and then out of Fashion, and then in Fashion again. *Shakespeare* hath shared both these Fates in Poetry.[17]

'Fashion' is even the reason Fielding gives for his foray into newsprint, having been told by his bookseller '*That no Body at present reads any thing but News-Papers*'.[18] Fielding alludes here, and elsewhere, to the fickle critical attention that 'fashion' has drawn to Shakespeare. A fictional writer in his *Covent-Garden Journal* (18 April 1752) comments that, since 'there is nothing in this Age more fashionable, than to criticise on Shakespeare', he has 'employed some leisure Hours on that great Poet'. Fuelled by this critical vogue, he proudly presents his dilettante 'emendations of that most celebrated Soliloquy' from *Hamlet*: 'To be, or not. To be! That is the BASTION'.[19] Richardson's correspondent likewise laments with him the 'lumber' of criticism and commentary that has become attached to the 'divine' playwright in recent years.[20]

The novelists are highly aware of the social compulsion at work in the act of quoting Shakespeare – a practice informed not only by his changing popular status ('in and out of fashion'), but by the 'newly egalitarian practices of discussion and conversation' around which public spaces like the eighteenth-century coffee house were modelled.[21] In the light of emerging codes of conversation, quoting Shakespeare could constitute an elegant act of polite communication; a way of sharing the finest expressions of great writers in the pursuit of sociable literary criticism. Yet quoters of literature could also invite comparison with those derided consumers who 'retail' in one coffee-house the second-hand '*Scraps of Wit*', news and politics that they have purchased in another;[22] or with simpering figures whose knowledge consists only of what one contemporary commentator disdainfully calls 'Some Pieces of a whining *Romance*, some Airs of an *Opera*, or of the silliest Parts of a *Play*'.[23] In his edition of *Hamlet*, William Warburton critiques a contemporary taste for cheap quotation when he says of Polonius that the 'fine lessons of social life' that he preaches, to much admiration from contemporary readers, are not his own insights, for he is 'too weak to be the author of them'. Rather, he is 'pedant enough to have met with them in his reading' and 'fop enough to get them by heart and retail them for his own'.[24] Polite quotation holds in tension the collective discussion of admired literature, and thoughtless reliance on the 'common Set of Phrases',[25] as satirised in contemporary accounts such as Swift's *Polite Conversation*.

The ideals of polite conversation were beset with anxieties. Coffee-house culture, for example, contributed to the construction of a male public sphere, but the civilised polish of politeness, strongly associated with the French language, was increasingly characterised by eighteenth-century critics as soft, feminine and un-British. In 'newly egalitarian' social spaces such as these, people might not only be polished and improved, but undermined and unmanned.[26] Women, under the auspices of the Shakespeare Ladies Club, symbolised the moral, virtuous effects of Shakespeare's accession to the stage, but they could also represent the 'giddy' chatter about the stage and other entertainments that one commentator humorously imagines taking place in a projected female coffee house.[27] The excesses of feminisation are illustrated by the shallow conversation of the 'beau-pedant', keeping up fashionable appearances in *The Conversation of Gentlemen Considered* (1738), in the midst of the Shakespeare Revival:

> One of those Creatures enter'd lately, where I chanced to be, and was scarce well seated, when he began to lisp out something of *Desdemona*; then viewing himself in a Glass, cried out with great *Pathos, Lard! how consumedly is my Wig disorder'd with only crassing the Street.*[28]

This fashionable creature feels obliged the moment he arrives 'to lisp out something of *Desdemona*', as if he repeats a ready sentiment by rote. But he is scarcely able to sustain the thought before being distracted by that far greater source of '*Pathos*', the state of his hairpiece. A 'pleasant Gentleman' abruptly stops this 'Creature's' 'impertinent Fopperies' by sternly warning him, '*Truly, Sir, at another time we may pity* Desdemona, *and the grievous Disorder of your Wig; but at present we are upon the Grievances of the Nation*'. In this gendered reprimand, the gentleman calls a halt to the effeminate visitor's simpering conversation. With his superficial concern for a female character, and his much greater concern for himself, the fop's Shakespeare is a fashionable topic that ranks beneath serious talk of '*the Nation*' in this social space; and a threat to the rigour of public life.[29]

Another cause for concern is the ease with which those less naturally polite can assume the behaviours and speech habits of their social betters.[30] When novelists imagine scenes of polite conversation, they often reveal – to comic and moral effect – the capacity of literary discussion and quotation to deceive others. The 'fine ladies' who talk of Shakespeare and the musical glasses in *The Vicar of Wakefield* promise the polish and sophistication of town, but have really been paid to lure Dr Primrose's daughters to their ruin. Smollett's Peregrine Pickle, somewhat in the manner of Henry Higgins, trains a reluctant 'young mendicant' to 'metamorphose' into a 'fine lady': 'he culled out choice sentences from Shakespear, Otway, and Pope, and taught her to repeat them with emphasis and theatrical cadence', as well as name-dropping famous actors and humming snatches of opera. 'By means of this cultivation, she became a wonderful proficient in the polite graces of the age'.[31] Her first visitor is the parson's daughter, and, like Primrose's family, the rural neighbours are taken in: 'In short, she made a progress thro' almost all the families in the neighbourhood; and, by dint of her quotations, (which, by the bye, were not always judiciously used) she passed for a sprightly young lady, of uncommon learning and taste' (p. 600). Her quotations work in town too, until a dispute over a card game opens the 'floodgates of her own natural repartee' and reveals her true nature in a furious stream of expletives. No longer quoting

Shakespeare, she storms out, applying her hand 'to that part which was the last of her that disappeared, inviting the company to kiss it, by one of its coarsest denominations' (p. 601); My Fair Lady she is not.

Banal Shakespeare informs not only the comic set-pieces of eighteenth-century fiction, but the very fabric of quotation in the novel. Even the most conventional-looking quotations can engage with this phenomenon. Though formally presented on the page, such quotations are often tinged with the cadences of polite speech. The narrator of *Tom Jones* intones:

> So the immortal *Shakespear*.
>
> *————Life's a poor Player*
> *That struts and frets his Hour upon the Stage*
> *And then is heard no more.*
>
> For which hackneyed Quotation, I will make the Reader Amends by a very noble one, which few, I believe, have read.[32]

The narrator briskly undercuts his own grand, innocuous praise for the 'immortal Shakespeare': he dismisses his quotation as 'hackneyed', and turns instead to a lengthy quotation from Grub Street poet Samuel Boyse. For the modern reader, the writerly associations of 'hackneyed' create the first, most obvious irony in the passage: the binary of lowly hack author and immortal genius inverted for comic effect.[33] For a moment, it is as if Shakespeare is accused of dealing in familiar tropes: an impression encouraged by the narrator's casting about in this opening chapter of Book VII – 'A Comparison between the World and the Stage' – for different ways of expressing this commonplace.

Yet Fielding's abrupt change of tone can be explained more precisely by observing that this conversational narrator is switching between the formal written discourse of the admiring author and the speech habits of polite quotation. His initial praise sounds like solemn authorial esteem for a literary predecessor, but his subsequent, impatient 'hackneyed Quotation' exposes it as merely conventional admiration for Shakespeare, as 'used so frequently and indiscriminately as to have lost its freshness and interest; made trite and commonplace; stale'[34] in polite conversation. This quotation has been described by one critic as 'merely ornamental',[35] since it forms the basis of no thorough-going thematic connection with Shakespeare's play. The quotation, however, arrives in the novel not just 'in quotation marks'[36] (as Bakhtin says of a stretch of ceremonial language in *Little Dorrit* that turns out to be 'another's speech'), but in double quotation marks. Fielding's narrator is not merely quoting Shakespeare, but also mocking the polite habit of quoting Shakespeare. To engage meaningfully with this quotation, the reader does not have to be 'traditionally educated', 'used to poetic conventions and the rhetorical legerdemain of high-minded prose',[37] but alert to the sound of polite quotation.

For mid-century readers, Fielding's quotation could be a familiar truism: these lines from *Macbeth* had previously appeared in several rather different polite settings. Bickerstaff, reflecting conversationally '*From my own Apartment*' in the *Tatler* on the day of the burial of the great actor Thomas Betterton, is moved to consider 'the Emptiness of all Human Perfection and Greatness', and to quote this passage in a similarly italicised block of verse: '*Life's but a walking Shadow, a poor Player/ That struts and frets his Hour upon the Stage,/ And then is heard no more*'.[38] The lines would later be more handily excerpted under the heading 'Life' in Bysshe's *Art of English Poetry* (1702) and in Gildon's *Complete Art of Poetry* (1718) and the *Thesaurus Dramaticus* (1724).[39] Fielding's quotation suggests an ambivalence about Shakespeare's popular status, ruefully aware that the words of his admired dramatist are repeated only because he is in fashion. Bakhtin's 'heteroglossia' is, however, 'a special type of *double-voiced discourse*' that 'serves two speakers at the same time and expresses simultaneously two different intentions'.[40] The most banal quotations enable Fielding simultaneously to convey his own informed admiration for Shakespeare and to draw attention to his public misuse.

Fielding defamiliarises the most conventional praise for Shakespeare, and exposes its meaninglessness, with the satirical energy of contemporary critiques of social mores. In the ironic guide, *The Art of Conversation*, the fashionable 'Lady Air' hears that her dinner companion, Mr Rustick, comes from Stratford-upon-Avon, and exclaims 'The Birth-place of the immortal *Shakespear*, he was born there, was he not, Sir?'. Mr Rustick innocently replies that 'I can't tell that, but I suppose the People are all immortal that were born there, are they not? All Men are immortal when they are dead, at least I was always told so; and why should not they be any more immortal at *Stratford upon Avon* as well as any other Place; is it not so, Mr. Parson?'.[41] Ignorant of fashionable dinner-table discourse, Mr Rustick exposes the meaninglessness of the epithet 'immortal Shakespeare'. A word that he assumes has spiritual significance has in fact become part of that 'habit of constant emphasis' noted in polite eighteenth-century conversation. Like other fashionably 'emphatic adverbs and adjectives' such as 'Perfect, Prodigious, Vastly, Frightful, Excessively, Literally, Furious, Unique, Monstrous',[42] it cheapens the object it glorifies.

Angels and trifles: new associations

Just as polite conversation drains these admiring epithets of meaning, so too can it thoroughly detach fragments of Shakespeare's plays from their source. Richard Burt has labelled 'post-hermeneutic' those free-floating bits of Shakespeare that circulate in twentieth-century popular culture, observing that there are 'no genuinely dialectical relations between the "original" texts and their mediatised citations'.[43] Quoted in the eighteenth-century novel, however, such recycled phrases were not so much emptied of meaning as charged with the new associations they had begun to accrue in circulation. Such lines arrive in the novel laden with, in Bakhtin's phrase, the rich and contradictory 'intentions and accents' of polite conversation.[44]

Novelists, perhaps surprisingly, frequently deploy these popular meanings in their fiction. 'Trifles light as air' is one Shakespearean phrase whose meaning in the novel is inflected by its previous life in polite culture. Originally spoken by Iago in *Othello* (III. 3. 327–9), it describes the way in which the smallest things can confirm the jealous mind's suspicions – a phenomenon that Iago is keen to exploit. Several influential eighteenth-century novelists confirm, by comparison with their own jealous characters, how accurately 'Trifles light as air...' captures a well-known human emotion. Henry Fielding, in *Amelia*, observes that

> The greatest Genius the World hath ever produced, observes in one of his most excellent Plays, that
>
> ——*Trifles light as Air*
> *Are to the jealous Confirmations strong*
> *As Proofs of holy Writ.*[45]

The novel is a study of a marriage, and this quotation follows a heavy hint by Mrs James that Amelia's husband, Captain Booth, ought to be suspicious of Captain Trent. Because Booth has 'Othello's blood', he is highly susceptible to her insinuation and 'began to be possessed by this worst of Fiends'. Sarah Fielding also uses the phrase to describe jealous characters in two of her novels, *The Adventures of David Simple* (1744), in which the sensitive Camilla explains how her father was 'intoxicated by his Passion' for Livia and 'grew, like her, suspicious of every thing around him',[46] and *The History of Ophelia* (1760), as Ophelia tries, with the help of Shakespeare, to decipher Lord Dorchester's jealous behaviour. In all of these cases, it has the force of a truth.[47]

After emotional identification, however, comes overuse, and the novelists are well aware of the growing banality of a phrase that all kinds of people seem to think they can apply to their own melodramatic feelings, however inappropriately. In wider usage, the four words often stood alone to represent *Othello*, and also began to operate – with increasing separation from the play and its author – as a truism about marital jealousy and suspicion in texts ranging from poetic miscellanies to political commentaries.[48] When Henry Fielding quotes it, it follows Mrs James' hint to Booth that he ought not to trust Captain Trent: a hint bolstered with 'a very sagacious Look, a very significant Leer, and a great Flirt with her Fan'. The clichéd emotional shorthand of jealousy, combined with excessive praise for Shakespeare, now signals Mrs James' insincerity: she is a hammed-up Iago figure who should be disregarded rather than feared. It also encourages the reader to take with a pinch of salt the torments of the hero, who is more over-sensitive than tragic. The multiple quotations from *Othello* in *Amelia* have encouraged critics to see 'Trifles light as air/ Are to the jealous . . .' as part of a larger scheme of allusion to that play.[49] Since, however, the phrase had come to stand for jealousy, and jealousy for the play, in polite culture, what underpins Fielding's last novel is not so much a plot parallel with *Othello* as an extended trope of melodramatic quotation.

The abbreviated version of this quotation, 'Trifles light as air', evidently came to be a trope of insignificance. Contemporary writers might remark that 'indeed every Blessing which Fortune could confer, she should consider as Trifles light as Air, where Virtue and Honour were in the opposite Scale', or that 'temporal concerns of nations . . . are "trifles light as air" compared with the affairs of Christ's everlasting kingdom'.[50] Sterne takes up this usage in *Tristram Shandy*, borrowing the phrase to describe the 'triumph of slight incidents over the mind' in shaping opinions: 'trifles light as air, shall waft a belief into the soul, and plant it so immoveably within it. . .'.[51] Sterne, too, delivers the lines with the force of a truism: Iago's words on jealousy have become in wider circulation a more general maxim about the disproportionate power of insignificant events over people's imaginations.

Another line of Shakespeare's quoted in *Tristram Shandy* had also already accrued a fascinating set of associations in circulation. Hamlet's exclamation on seeing his father's ghost, 'Angels and Ministers of Grace defend us', was circulating not as a maxim, like 'trifles light as air', but as a theatrical 'point' made famous by Garrick. As discussed in Chapter 4, Sterne has Walter Shandy burst out with this dramatic phrase in the domestic context of the Shandy parlour, when reading a book on childbirth (see pp. 94–6). But polite culture had been appropriating the phrase for social and domestic purposes well before Sterne's novel was published. In Garrick's successful theatrical afterpiece, *Miss in her Teens*, performed at Covent Garden in 1747, the character Puff exclaims:

> *Angels, and Ministers of Grace, defend me!*
>
> It can't be! by Heav'ns, it is, that fretful Porcupine, my Wife! I can't stand it; What shall I do? I'll try to avoid her.[52]

In this farcical setting, Hamlet's phrase registers domestic terror: Puff's cry is inspired not by the sight of a ghost, but by a troublesome spouse. Garrick exploits the comic contrast with his own serious performances of *Hamlet* at Drury Lane and, in this season, at Covent Garden. Further fuelled by Sterne's borrowing in *Tristram Shandy*, the phrase would later be appropriated by polite literary characters to greet long-lost acquaintances with mild surprise: 'ANGELS and ministers of grace! cried Sir William—Fitzhenry? can it be you—Lord Fitzhenry?'[53]

In the polite conversations represented in eighteenth-century drama and fiction, 'Angels and ministers of grace!' becomes a stock expression of shock, often at the arrival of a known but slightly dreaded figure. Lady Bab cries out 'Angels and ministers of grace defend us!' in John Burgoyne's play, *The Maid of the Oaks* (1773). When Mr Dupeley asks her 'Hey-day! what is coming, Lady Bab?', she answers, 'O, that most hideous of all goblins, a country cousin—and I can neither avoid her, nor overlook her, as I should to do in town'.[54] For the eighteenth-century reader of Sterne's novel, Walter's involuntary outburst would not only bring Garrick incongruously into the Shandy parlour, hair on end, arms stretched and fingers spread in his much-discussed posture of terror. With its well-worn currency as a cry of surprise, the phrase also renders Walter a somewhat farcical player in his own drama: even his tragic exclamations fail to take him seriously.[55]

The novel not only draws on this growing cultural pool of familiar Shakespeare quotations for comic effect: it also contributes to the pool. Before the narrator of *Tom Jones* observed in 1749 that 'the whole produced that green-ey'd Monster mentioned by *Shakespear* in his Tragedy of *Othello*' (ii. 871), there are only a small handful of instances of the phrase 'green-eyed monster' in eighteenth-century publications. After Fielding's 1749 quotation, however, hundreds of writers follow suit:

> ...it is worse than *Shakespear's Green-Eyed Monster*, Jealousy, which is sometimes found to be a Weed in the noblest Natures...[56]

> For where there is love, that green eyed monster, jealousy is sure to interfere.—[57]

> Mrs. Parker reddened up; the green-eyed monster seemed to possess her, she retired in tears;. . .[58]

The first example, taken from a satire on Fielding's political career, seems from its structure most evidently mediated by that author's quotation; the second and third, without italics or quotation marks to draw attention to their borrowing, show how the phrase increasingly becomes part of idiomatic speech. Fielding appears to be responsible for popularising a metaphor for jealousy that continues to circulate independently of himself and Shakespeare.

In other cases, the promotion of a certain quotation is a collective enterprise by a number of novels. In Shakespeare's *Twelfth Night*, Viola's haunting image of a sister wasting in untold love like 'patience on a monument, smiling at grief' is really a description of her own situation. A number of narrators and fictional characters apply Viola's words to their own emotional circumstances.[59] The narrator of *Tom Jones* describes how, 'as for *Jones* himself, he "sat like Patience on a Monument smiling at Grief"', insensible to his own injuries as he awaits the recovery of his as yet untold love Sophia, after she is thrown from her horse (i. 204). Smollett's *Ferdinand Count Fathom* quotes the phrase to describe a 'beauteous mourner' writing to her 'inconstant lover'.[60] Samuel Richardson's Clementina della Porretta quotes back to Sir Charles Grandison 'those lines of your Shakespeare' which she believes he has pointedly read to her out of concern that she might be pining in secret love for him.[61] Sir Charles' eventual wife, Harriet Byron, returns to 'that admirable passage cited by her' in order to compare, in two columns in a letter, Clementina's sorry love situation with her own.[62] But Sarah Fielding's anti-heroine, the Countess of Dellwyn, fell short of these 'admirable' lines when she '*Pined in Thought*' that she could not match the 'Splendor in Dress' of her new acquaintances: 'But it could not be said, with Propriety, that, like Viola,/ *She sat, like* Patience, *on a Monument/ Smiling at* Grief'.[63] Collectively, the novelists confirm – if only, in the case of the Countess, by contrast – the aptness of Shakespeare's image as a description of patient, hopeful affection.

In the process, the novelists turn Viola's image into a trope of unrequited love. As hinted in Chapter 3, by the end of the century a comparison to 'patience on a monument' seems able to describe any sad-looking lady of quality who has not been asked to dance. The *Public Advertiser* calls it one of the 'finest Pictures that ever Shakespeare drew' when 'speaking of a Pining Beauty' and later uses the phrase to describe dejected society ladies like 'Miss B—k W—h, of C—y S—t' who 'never told her love...'.[64] In that same year, Frances Burney's fictional heroine, Evelina, is approached by 'a very fashionable, gay-looking man, who seemed about 30 years of age', and, flustered, awkwardly pretends that she is engaged to dance with someone else in order to escape his advances. He regales her with the tag from *Twelfth Night*: 'Charming creature!—and can you really bear ill usage with so much sweetness?—Can you, *like patience on a monument*, smile in the midst of disappointment?'[65] The italicised words suggest that Evelina registers his quotation, as she does '*ashopping*', '*Londonize*' and '*chat*',[66] as one of the modish, but (to her at least) unfamiliar, turns of phrase to be encountered in the new social world of London. This distancing device only confirms her ignorance of social conventions, for 'Patience on a monument' is described in 1796 as 'a line which every body knows, and which almost every body has quoted'.[67]

By the time that Jane Austen writes *Northanger Abbey*, the line is required reading for a would-be heroine. Catherine Morland previously preferred 'cricket, base ball, riding on horseback, and running about the country . . . to books', 'But from fifteen to seventeen she was in training for a heroine; she read all such works as heroines must read to supply their memories with those quotations which are so serviceable and so soothing in the vicissitudes of their eventful lives'. Her new resources include Alexander Pope, Thomas Gray and James Thomson,

> And from Shakespeare she gained a great store of information—amongst the rest, that
>
> ———"Trifles light as air,
> Are, to the jealous, confirmation strong,
> As proofs of Holy Writ." . . .
>
> And that a young woman in love always looks
>
> ———"like Patience on a monument
> Smiling at Grief."[68]

Austen's narrator wryly presents 'Trifles light as air . . . ' as a piece of 'information', and 'Patience on a monument' as an unwavering statement of fact: 'a young woman in love *always* looks' this way (italics added). These formally quoted lines do not, as has been suggested, simply replicate their appearance in the poetic anthologies marketed at women in the period.[69] Fittingly for Austen's study of the dangerous effects of romantic fiction on young women, they imitate the presentation of quotation by character in the earlier novels. It is these texts, rather than anthologies, that have turned them into tropes suitable for heroines; the repetition of 'so serviceable and so soothing' evokes the cadences of the admiring preambles of many a quoting character. Catherine, not yet schooled in Gothic fiction, appears to learn from the heroines of mid-century fiction – perhaps via novels borrowed from her mother, who has read *Sir Charles Grandison* on numerous occasions – how to apply to herself the words of authors such as Shakespeare. The irony is that, unlike Clarissa, Harriet and Clementina, Catherine earnestly commits these borrowed lines to memory before she has the real-life emotional occasions on which to deploy them. Like Charlotte Lennox's *Female Quixote*, Arabella, Catherine's reading outstrips her experience; she is unready to judge the mimetic value of these by now emotional clichés, and accepts them as fact without question.

'Without the least Judgment of poetical Beauties'

The 'Impartial Reader' of the *Public Advertiser* mentioned at the beginning of this chapter complains bitterly that:

> Every Puppy of an Apprentice and Trull of a Mantua-maker, without the least Judgment of poetical Beauties, is eternally belching out some Quotation from Shakespeare.[70]

These lowly figures repeat indiscrimately the dramatic lines they have heard. The 'Impartial Reader' presents their borrowed quotations as mindless reflexes that bypass 'judgment' and 'belch' uncontrolled from the body. The speaker's class disparagement betrays a fear that these upwardly mobile 'apprentices' and 'mantua-makers' might parrot their way into polite company by spouting what they hear, ingratiating themselves with their superiors and distracting themselves from their proper business.

The issue of 'judgment' is central to the novelists' handling of banal Shakespeare. They draw comic attention to the ways in which much-admired phrases of Shakespeare's can be repeated without thought or judgement. When Dodd gathered in his *Beauties of Shakespear* 'the finest passages of the finest poet',[71] he was guided by Longinus' principle of universal approval as a mark of literary value:

> For when persons of different humours, ages, professions, and inclinations, agree in the same joint approbation of any performance, then this union of assent, this combination of so many different judgments, stamps an high,

> and indisputable value on that performance, which meets with such general applause[72]

But such 'joint approbation', the novelists show, can lead to undiscriminating behaviour, and unthinking participation in the 'general applause'. James Noggle has recently argued that David Hume responded to the vogue for Shakespeare with 'dismay', accusing 'British culture of having a taste for Shakespeare that precedes and forecloses on the enlightened, immediate judgement he hopes a polite, modern audience would have'.[73] Noggle distinguishes in the eighteenth century between national taste and the taste shown in individual judgement. Eighteenth-century novelists, as the examples in this chapter suggest, show how, in the growing vogue for Shakespeare, people can too easily pass off clichéd admiration and quotation as their own fresh responses to the plays. They pretend to the aesthetic and moral judgement of lines whose value has already been decided for them.

Some characters strain to give the impression of their individual literary judgement. In Burney's play *The Witlings*, Lady Smatter trades in 'the names of Authors she has never read' 'with flimsy Sentences which she has the assurance to call Quotations'.[74] She exploits the author function of names such as Shakespeare, Pope and Swift, lazily attributing to them the vaguest phrases: 'A mind, indeed, cultivated and informed, as Shakespeare has it, will ever be above a mean action'.[75] Yet she will not merely join in with the general applause, and refuses to declare Shakespeare her favourite, for 'he is too common: *every* body can speak well of Shakespeare'. Her poet friend Mr Dabler agrees: 'I vow I am quite sick of his Name'.[76] But Dabler is dependent on Bysshe,[77] and asserts the superiority of his taste while recycling the derided poetic handbook of the day.

Well before Burney wrote this play, the mid-century novel had been satirising such desperate quoters. For some fictional characters, the urge to assert one's taste and judgement could be an overwhelming social compulsion. One such character makes a brief appearance in *Joseph Andrews* when Parson Adams hits an innkeeper and is drenched with the contents of 'a Pan full of Hog's-Blood' wielded by the host's vengeful wife. The ensuing kerfuffle brings other guests to the scene, and a 'Gentleman just returned from his Travels to *Italy*', seeing the 'horrible Spectacle' of the bloody Adams, told him 'he looked like the Ghost of *Othello*', and 'bid him *not shake his gory Locks at him, for he could not say he did it*'.[78] In his eagerness to parade his sketchy knowledge of Shakespeare, the gentleman confuses *Macbeth*'s Banquo with Othello. Like the faux-Italian words with which he laces his speech ('to their *Disgracia* the *English* were *accustomata* to . . .'), 'Shakespeare' is a cultivated tune this aspiring figure hums without getting the words right. He has gone abroad in search of cultural capital without mastering the tenets of his own culture. In Smollett's *Humphry Clinker*, the far less grandiose Tabitha Bramble is starstruck when she meets the celebrated actor, James Quin, in company. In an endearing attempt to replicate a refined theatrical conversation, she strains eagerly to praise his performance as the 'Ghost of Gimlet' at Drury Lane, and to recall his speech about '*quails upon the frightful porcofine*', before quizzing him about how he persuaded the cock to crow at exactly the right time.[79] Aspiring to the appearance of taste, such characters repeat what they have heard without judgement.

This is not to say that those with the best knowledge of Shakespeare (or any other author) are the most worthy people; nor that misquotation is a character flaw. There is an obvious difference between Fielding's gentleman, more concerned with appearing cosmopolitan than with helping his fellow travellers, and well-meaning Tabitha, desperate to do the right thing socially but exasperating her family in the process. In both cases, though, such literary over-reaching is comic: the reader is supposed to recognise their behaviour as ridiculous. Just as many novelists offer explicit guidance on how to read 'with the Attention which is necessary to digest, and extract Utility from Writings', rather than 'skimming over the Surface of Authors, with the View only of filling up a Chasm of Time, which is not so fortunate as to be engaged to some more entertaining Amusement',[80] so too do they train the reader to pay special attention to these acts of quotation – and to practise sensitive judgement – in several ways.

One way of promoting the reader's judgement is through the reactions of other characters. Parson Adams, unversed in English literature, looks blankly at the gentleman traveller: he deflates the man's attempt at cultured performance when he fails to recognise the act of quotation and 'very innocently answered, Sir, I am far from accusing you'. Likewise, Tabitha Bramble's nephew, Jery Melford, relating in a letter her encounter with Quin, tells how 'My uncle, frying with vexation, cried, "Good God, sister, how you talk!"', mortified (as someone who alludes with ease to *Hamlet* in his own letters) by her attempt at polite conversation.[81] In both of these instances, another character draws the reader's attention, if they had not already noticed it, to the absurdity of the botched quotation.

This practice of offsetting compulsive quotations with wry judgement by other characters is widespread in mid-century fiction. In Fielding's

Amelia, while walking in St James' Park, Captain Booth admires a fine expression of Shakespeare, and his companion, the bumptious Colonel Bath, earnestly follows suit:

> 'That *Shakespeare*,' cries the Colonel, 'was a fine Fellow. He was a very pretty Poet indeed. Was it not *Shakespeare* that wrote the Play about *Hotspur*? You must remember these Lines. I got them almost by Heart at the Play-House; for I never missed that Play whenever it was acted, if I was in Town.
>
> *By Heav'n it was an easy Leap,*
> *To pluck bright Honour into the Full Moon.*
> *Or drive into the bottomless Deep.*
>
> 'And—and—Faith I have almost forgot them; but I know it is something about saving your Honour from drowning—O it is very fine. I say, d—n me, the Man that writ those Lines was the greatest Poet the World ever produced. There is Dignity of Expression and Emphasis of thinking, d—n me.'[82]

Colonel Bath lacks any 'bookish Qualifications', but 'the Play about Hotspur' evidently appeals to his predominant interests in 'War and martial Exploits'.[83] The lines he quotes from *1 Henry IV* (1. 3. 201–5) already had an independent existence as a piece of martial pomp: in Beaumont and Fletcher's *The Knight of the Burning Pestle*, Ralph the Prentice spouts these lines of Hotspur's when called on to speak a huffing part. Bath, however, bungles his quotation, and, for all his martial vigour, spouts only some mild, clichéd epithets of admiration for Shakespeare: 'fine Fellow' and 'pretty Poet' are trilling, alliterated little phrases he must have picked up when 'in Town'. His attempt at literary criticism peters out into a repetition of 'very fine', a borrowed superlative ('the greatest Poet the World ever produced') and a meaningless combination of his own already used epithets and expletives ('Dignity of Expression and Emphasis of thinking, d—n me'). In his faltering 'And—and—Faith' and filler curses, the reader can hear Bath straining to deliver the criticism he feels the play, the company and the fashionable location demand of him. It is in Booth's tactful silence, though, that the novel incorporates a tacit judgement of this crashing act of quotation: he 'assented to the Colonel's Criticism' and quickly changed the subject.

Training the reader to judge banal quotation with proper discernment can also take the form of schooling the innocent hero. In Sarah Fielding's *David Simple*, this guidance is personified in the minor figure of Spatter, in two extended scenes. In the first, Spatter accompanies David Simple to a private home to meet a gathering of ladies and one or two gentlemen. There they find a conversation about Shakespeare already underway. Veering wildly between praising Shakespeare, scorning his interest in 'vulgar wretches' and expressing horror that the absent Lady True-Wit could even begin to pity the wife-murdering Othello, 'First Lady', 'Second Lady', 'Third Lady' et al. engage in a contradictory conversation that quickly spirals into incomprehensible noise:

> And now, Reader, if ever you have lived in the Country, and heard the Cackling of Geese, or the Gobbling of Turkeys, you may have an Idea something adequate to this Scene; but if the Town has been mostly your Place of Abode, and you are a Stranger to every rural Scene, what will give you the best Idea of this Conversation is the 'Change at Noon, where every one has a particular Business of his own, but a *Spectator* would find it a very difficult matter to comprehend anything distinctly. *Addison*, *Prior*, *Otway*, *Congreve*, *Dryden*, *Pope*, *Shakespeare*, *Tom Durfey*, &c. &c. &c. were Names all heard between whiles, tho' no one could tell who spoke them, or whether they were mention'd with Approbation or Dislike. The words *Genius*,—and *no Genius*;—*Invention*,—*Poetry*,—*fine Things*,—*bad Language*,—*no Style*,—*charming Writing*,—*Imagery*,—and *Diction*, with many more Expressions which swim on the *Surface* of *Criticism*, seem'd to have been caught by those *Fishers for the Reputation of Wit*, tho' they were intirely ignorant what Use to make of them, or how to apply them properly.[84]

The ignorant squawks of the farmyard and the aggressive trading of the Exchange – a double metaphor of city and country – evoke the crescendoing noise as these polite ladies compete to 'prove their own Judgment' in literature. Their conversation recalls the din of the coffee-house, where, as detractors complained, all stations of people are 'promiscuously' mingled together, their pet topics drowning one another out.[85] Far from being a sweetly harmonious check on the excesses of male conversation, the women's pointlessly combative discussion exhibits all its worst features. Talking without listening, their paired critical terms – '*Genius*' and '*no Genius*'; '*no Style*' and '*charming Writing*' – cancel one another out. Rather than a successful conversational exchange that creates new knowledge, this is a senseless cacophony that keeps the women far from Shakespeare. The absent Lady True-Wit's empathetic intelligence evidently enables her to engage both emotionally and intellectually with Shakespeare's plays, but the shallow, anonymous 'First Lady' and friends deal only in stock phrases, recycling tired criticism rather than quoting Shakespeare directly. Innocent in the ways of polite conversation, David leaves feeling as if he has escaped a 'Shipwreck', with 'the Bellowing of the Waves, the Cursing and Swearing of some of the Sailors' and 'the Crying and Praying of others' still ringing in his ears.[86]

Spatter afterwards explains that few of the conversants enjoyed or even read the authors they discussed, but placed 'their whole *Happiness* in the *Reputation of Wit and Sense*, and consequently all their Conversation turns on what they think will establish that *Character*'.[87] He displays another such scene for David's edification the next day when he takes David to meet a number of gentlemen in a tavern, one of whom, at the least provocation, pours out a stream of critical nonsense about Shakespeare and Jonson until his '*Breath began to fail him*'.[88] Spatter stage-manages these instructive encounters, telling David to mention 'Authors' in order to kick-start the gentleman's monologue. When he observes that their ill-fitting '*borrow'd Wit*' is soon discovered to the 'discerning Eye', Spatter urges David, and, by extension, the reader, to distinguish their superficial literary chatter from meaningful engagement.[89]

Through Spatter and other such characters, novelists promote in the reader the development of exactly such a 'discerning Eye': the ability not only to judge and admire literature, but also to see through its most self-serving uses, and recognise the lack of judgement therein, from the polite women in *David Simple* attempting furiously to 'prove their own Judgment' in literary topics, to the mantua-makers and apprentices described in the *Public Advertiser* who quote without the least 'Judgment of poetical Beauties'. They help to establish a kind of literary taste with which 'judgment' is, as twentieth-century cultural commentators have subsequently argued, closely connected. Raymond Williams described the process by which 'taste became equivalent to *discrimination*'; and Pierre Bourdieu proposed that 'The manner in which culture has been acquired lives on in the manner of using it: the importance attached to manners can be understood once it is seen that it is these imponderables of practice which distinguish the different—and ranked—modes of culture acquisition, early or late, domestic or scholastic, and the classes of individuals which they characterize (such as 'pedants' and *mondains*).'[90] The kind of judgement that novelists foster in the reader is at once literary and social, and the banal conversations they stage about Shakespeare are a significant part of that training.

One further method by which novelists encourage such careful reading of both texts and people is through the device of the innocent young female character who attends the theatre, and whose complete absorption in the action on stage, regardless of the audience around her, is a sign of her finer feeling. In *Chit-Chat* (1755), Welford and Charlotte attend 'an affecting play of Shakespear's'. 'Welford, though he doated on the amiable Charlotte, could not be inattentive to the play, while Garrick was on the stage, whose every look and gesture demanded peculiar notice.' But 'he turned, he saw, and he admired; for Charlotte gave him at that instant a fresh proof of the sensibility of her heart, by letting fall a shower of tears. He viewed her in a new light . . .'.'[91] Sarah Fielding's Ophelia's rapt attention to *Macbeth* has her companions 'taken up in observing the Passions imprest on my Countenance'.[92]

Often, the acute sensibility of the heroine is offset by the distraction of the surrounding audience, who chat, gossip or rudely gape at her. The heroine of *Ermina; or, The Fair Recluse* draws attention to such poor spectatorship when she writes to her friend 'With what lively sensations do I join in lamenting the wretched fate of poor Monimia; or in weeping at the untimely end of the two innocent princes in Richard the Third! How surprising it is to me, to see the number of beings who frequent the theatre, without any other view but that of seeing, and being seen; and can behold unmoved the most melting and pathetic scene? How incapable are such minds of receiving intellectual improvement?'.[93] One of those 'beings' might be the 'young lady' in *The History of Pompey the Little* who, before going to see '*Othellor whore of Venus*', has the play explained to her. When she hears that Othello smothers his wife, she replies

> Does he indeed? . . . well, I hate a jealous man of all things in nature; a jealous man is my particular aversion—but however, no matter what the play is, you know, ma'am, so we do but see it; for the pleasure of a play is to shew one's self in the boxes, and see the Company, and all that—Yes, ma'am, this here is the sort of ribbands I want, only if you please to let me see some of a paler blue.[94]

This young woman is evidently a fashionable creature whose priority is acquiring precisely the appropriate dress in which to 'shew one's self in the boxes', 'no matter what the play is'. Her glancing attention to the headline themes of *Othello* shows how easily 'a jealous man' becomes a banal trope for a whole play that can now be appropriated for unthinking personal use ('*I* hate a jealous man'. . . '*my* particular aversion'). Paula Backscheider argues that the set piece of female absorption should be examined as 'part of the century's project of teaching correct cultural consumption'.[95] The novel, however, is not so much presenting optimal behaviour in a didactic fashion, as training readers to judge and discriminate between multiple modes of engaging with reading and performance.

Both Shakespeare and the reader can benefit from this training, as Henry Fielding shows when he inverts the gender stereotypes of the trope of the attentive young woman at the theatre in the figure of Partridge. Shaking with fear when he watches Garrick as Hamlet respond to the appearance of the ghost, Partridge 'afforded great Mirth, not only to *Jones* and Mrs. *Miller*, but to all who sat within hearing, who were more attentive to what he said than to any Thing that passed on the Stage' (ii. 857). To the polite audience, this play is well known: they have the experience to anticipate 'the Entrance of the Ghost' (ii. 853) and 'that scene, as you called it, between him and his mother, where you told me he acted so fine' (i. 857); and Tom knowingly tells Partridge that 'he might possibly see him [the ghost] again soon, and in a Flash of Fire' (ii. 855). Partridge, by contrast, quakes in unhackneyed terror at 'Angels and ministers of grace defend us!', a line that is likely quoted by the unruffled audience in their polite conversations. While Partridge's reaction is intended to be ridiculous, the reader is also encouraged to recognise in the surrounding polite audience the dangers of the alternative: namely, that over-exposure to Shakespeare's familiar phrases might inure people to their dramatic power. It is Partridge's wildly emotional response that, through Fielding's novel, brings these familiar 'points' back to life. The novelists are well aware of the irony of a polite culture in which people repeat fragments of Shakespeare while gaining nothing from the knowledge of human nature with which they routinely credit him.[96] The novel performs the kind of attention and scrutiny, however, that can restore the force of these fragments.

To train the reader in judgement and attention is also to help them to spectate and read other fashionable people: to exert what Fielding called in his *Essay on the Knowledge of the Characters of Men* the 'Diligence and Attention in the Scrutiny' to discern men's 'real Character',[97] and to distinguish the polite hypocrisy of the 'beau-pedant', 'fine lady' and 'pseudo-critic' from the 'true *Politeness*' that is, according to Richardson, 'but another Word for *Virtue* and *Honour*'.[98] When an individual must learn to become a 'true gentleman' by spending time in company, and by imitation of other well-bred people, there is little to distinguish the acquired performance of politeness by the well-intentioned person from the pretence of those 'two Disgracers of the human Species, common called a Beau, and a fine Lady'.[99] Judgement and discernment, then, are tools not only for successful reading, but for navigating the social world.

Whose Shakespeare?

From '*Othellor whore of Venus*' to the '*fretful porcofine*', the stream of hopeless quotations by character that the novel presents to the reader for amusement and criticism might seem a sign of Shakespeare's wider devaluation. Far from detracting from Shakespeare's growing status, these instances of 'banal Shakespeare' actually contribute to it. Each instance of 'hackneyed quotation' increases, and then reinforces, the knowing reader or hearer's impression that 'Shakespeare' is above such inane conversation. Shakespeare had been called 'immortal' and 'divine' since at least the beginning of the eighteenth century; the mid-century novel laments the cheapening of these terms in polite conversation, but, in doing so, lastingly reinforces them. They contribute to the sense that he is immortal despite the overused term 'immortal', and great beyond the clichéd praise of 'greatest Genius the world ever produced'. Trained by scenes in the novel to distinguish between successful and poor quotation, the reader is left in no doubt that Shakespeare deserves more sensitive admirers than the ones paraded before them in fiction.

After the middle of the eighteenth century, Shakespeare was, thanks to the growing reservoir of quotations, technically within everyone's reach: one did not need to own a playtext nor attend the theatre to be able to repeat his phrases in public. The gathering notion that Shakespeare is a poet for all people is matched by a growing awareness that all quoters are not equal. One of the side-effects of teaching novel readers to judge and discern in this way is that Shakespeare's admirers become stratified by their respective levels of ability. A French visitor to London wrote that the company at Will's Coffee-House could be divided into two Classes, 'the first of which contains the *Wits*, justly so call'd, and the other the *Would-be-Wits*'.[100] This is a far more black-and-white distinction than would be produced by the act of quotation, in which people are judged by their idiosyncratic combinations of knowledge, modesty, performance and taste.

The hierarchising phenomenon of 'banal Shakespeare' that is explored in the novel would take physical form in 1769. The Stratford Jubilee is regarded as both 'the culmination of Shakespeare's canonization' and an event that 'encoded in itself the history to date of the Bardolatry it proclaims'.[101] One of the histories of Bardolatry that the event incorporates and amplifies is the novelistic practice of distinguishing between different kinds of bardolater. The event not only confirms the 'transcendent status' of Shakespeare,[102] but also, as is less frequently observed, underscores the distinctions that are beginning to emerge between Shakespeare's admirers. Garrick might crow that 'Our SHAKESPEARE compar'd is to no man,/ Nor *Frenchman* nor *Grecian* nor *Roman*',[103] strategically reviving anti-Gallic sentiment to assert England's ownership of 'Our SHAKESPEARE' in the face of foreign detractors, but to whom in England did 'Our SHAKESPEARE' belong? George Steevens declared to *The Gentleman's Magazine* in August that the planned pageantry and entertainments were 'solely calculated for the million, who are capable of receiving pleasure through the medium of the senses only', and sarcastically suggested that Garrick was preparing a 'dish of *Caveare*' 'for such intellectual spirits who are susceptible of more abstracted and refined indulgence'.[104] Steevens distinguishes between an intellectual and a popular or theatrical Shakespeare, claiming that 'If this Jubilee is meant to be a serious Meeting in honour of the greatest Poet ever born in any Nation, or in any Age, *why were not literary Men* placed at the Head of it?'. Shakespeare, he thinks, deserves more than 'histrionic Honours':[105] the author should be celebrated not by an actor but by scholars.

Further educational and class distinctions abounded at the Jubilee. When Garrick planted a heckler in the audience of his Jubilee Oration to criticise Shakespeare, the naïve, enraged locals were disparaged for being duped, while the 'more sophisticated London visitors'[106] recognised him as the Drury Lane comic actor, Tom King, and rolled their eyes at the tedious interruption. After the event, numerous parodic responses to the Jubilee mocked both the undeserving Stratford yokels and the inane London visitors for their lack of understanding. If mercenary motives (such as the chance to tout overpriced beds to gullible tourists) drove the former group to celebrate Shakespeare, fashionable pleasure-seeking drove the latter: 'Miss Tripsy' 'puts on her best face', 'expecting that Stratford will prove/ A delicate region of pleasure and love'; while 'Kept mistresses' and 'galant modish wives' trek to Stratford 'to ogle and flaunt', driven helplessly by 'dear fashion'; and 'smart beaux' 'haste hither to shew their fine cloaths and fine shapes': they've heard Shakespeare's name 'but his merit their shallow conception escapes'.[107] Like the novel, the Jubilee might have enabled new groups to 'sing immortal Shakespeare's praise', but it also, in the same motion, confirmed the impression that he was beyond the full comprehension of all but the most judicious readers.

It is not only the unworthiness of fops and yokels, but of the Jubilee event itself, that contributed to Shakespeare's status. Pouring rain scuppered the pageant, soaked the fireworks and caused the Avon to swell and flood the pavilion where the speeches took place; and the whole soggy affair was gleefully satirised in the press. But even without the torrential rain, the event would inevitably have failed to live up to its rhetoric of praise. The rain merely combined with the well-worn tags and clichéd criticism, the pantomimic songs and entertainments, the remoteness of muddy Stratford, the tourist-fleecing yokels and the superficial visitors, and, of course, the narcissistic actor at the centre of it, to confirm the impression that 'Shakespeare' was firmly above it all. The Stratford Jubilee is an excellent example of how 'banal Shakespeare' promotes, rather than undermines, its subject. The event should be seen as a high point in Shakespeare's eighteenth-century progress from provincial playwright to national poet, not because he was deemed worthy of such a celebration, but because of how far the celebration was seen to fall short of him, both at the time and in every retelling of the Jubilee story to the present day.[108]

Just as in the eighteenth-century novel, this simultaneous promotion of Shakespeare and division of his audiences was performed with the aid of slight fragments of Shakespeare's plays. It is frequently remarked of the Jubilee that, while fireworks, horse races, pageants and early morning serenades were planned in Shakespeare's honour, no plays were performed; some say that 'not a line of Shakespeare was spoken'.[109] On closer inspection, the Jubilee's published songs, poems and speeches, including Garrick's own Jubilee Oration and Ode, can be seen to be shot through with fragments of Shakespeare, from 'we ne'er shall look upon his like again', adapted from *Hamlet*, to 'god of our idolatry', from *Romeo and Juliet*. Like the Shakespearean tags quoted in the novel, these phrases have an independent existence. Now, though, rather than evoking theatrical points, moral maxims or knowing sayings about marital jealousy, the language of the plays is turned back upon 'Shakespeare' himself. The Jubilee celebrates not so much a body of work as a great man who hails from the English countryside; its favourite musical refrain is 'the man of all men, was a *Warwickshire* man'.[110] Yet when Garrick refers to Shakespeare, rather than Juliet to Romeo, as 'the god of our idolatry', he goes further still. He praises an abstract 'Shakespeare', greater even than the 'man of all men', not to mention the 'lad of all lads' and the 'Will of all wills', who hovers benevolently somewhere above the Jubilee. At the Jubilee, as in the novel, the slightest fragments and pieces gesture upwards towards an ever more ineffable 'Shakespeare'.

The phenomenon of 'banal Shakespeare' would ready the playwright for two important developments in the nineteenth century: first, his international exportation, and second, his adoption by the British working classes. It has been noted that the Jubilee's praise of his 'transcendent originality' prepared Shakespeare for international travel: eastwards, with every 'literate middle-class national movement' in an emergent nation, and westwards, in the name of British expansion and conquest.[111] News of the Jubilee was received with rejoicing on the Continent as a glorious folk uprising in the name of Shakespeare and Nature.[112] The oscillation at the Jubilee between small fragment and great whole, 'Warwickshire lad' and immortal genius, 'our Shakespeare' and a Shakespeare that is above all other people, repeatedly enacts this expansive movement of home and abroad. Important work remains to be done in tracing the precise role of the most familiar slivers of Shakespeare, alongside large-scale performances and publications, in taking Shakespeare to new, international audiences in Europe, America and beyond.

The social divisions visible around Shakespeare at the Jubilee would be fully realised in the class-based distinctions of the next century. Andrew Murphy attributes the growth of Shakespeare's working-class readership in the nineteenth century to the expansion of elementary education and the proliferation of cheap editions.[113] However, the banal quotation illustrated in the eighteenth-century novel suggests that pieces of Shakespeare were already becoming popularised in the eighteenth century, even among those without access to Shakespearean texts. Nineteenth-century education would crystallise the stratifications of cultural ownership that began in the eighteenth century, as the correct handling of Shakespeare becomes a matter not just of taste and judgement but of educational attainment. A poster circulated before Shakespeare's 1864 tercentenary, declaring Shakespeare 'the POET of the PEOPLE', stirred up these 'people' by demanding 'Where are the seats reserved for YOU at the coming Festival?', and telling them that their only fare at the celebrations would be cold 'wittles' '*after the swells have dined*'.[114] The working classes will be encouraged to re-appropriate not only 'Shakespeare', but also the cultural dominance and exclusivity that he comes to represent.

Banal Shakespeare, then, challenges the familiar story of Shakespeare's eighteenth-century promotion to the role of 'national poet' by exposing another, more negative dimension to his growing status. It complicates the orthodox narrative of editions and performances, and adjusts the typical unit of Shakespeare's reception from the play to the line or speech in which he circulates most widely. Yet the fragmentation of Shakespeare is a crucial constituent of his iconic status, and the novel, which borrows from, satirises, and contributes to, a growing reservoir of Shakespeare quotations, is an agent, not a mirror, in this process. In the middle of the eighteenth century, Shakespeare is not a benign authority, underwritten by centuries of admiration and compulsory schooling. He can still slip between the positive and negative connotations of fashion and morality, and of theatricality and intellect; and the mere mention of his name is not yet safely legitimating. Where twenty-first-century creative misquotation might impertinently 'reject that fidelity and decorum that govern "proper" Shakespearian interpretation',[115] the banal, misquoted, poorly applied pieces of quotation of the eighteenth century serve to construct for the first time a 'proper' Shakespeare.

In Jane Austen's *Mansfield Park*, Edward Bertram famously observes that 'we all talk Shakespeare'.[116] Chapters 6 and 7, which focus on the novels of Ann Radcliffe and Jane Austen respectively, serve as something of a coda to this book. In the late-eighteenth and early nineteenth-century fiction of these writers, the overt quotation of Shakespeare by character, so familiar from the mid-century novel, ostensibly disappears. I shall argue, however, that Shakespeare's banality, his theatricality and his achieved authority are still very much present in these later texts, but now reworked to new purposes. The quotation by character of the mid-century novel exerts an important influence on later fiction, not only powerfully mediating the way that subsequent novelists and readers engage with Shakespeare, but also informing the innovative narrative forms that continue to shape prose fiction to this day.

CHAPTER 6

Ann Radcliffe's Gothic epigraphs

I could a tale unfold[1]

Five words of Old Hamlet's ghost open Ann Radcliffe's *A Sicilian Romance* (1790). A phrase that once urged Hamlet to vengeful action now floats freely as an enigmatic epigraph for the novel. It hovers at the edge of the book like the ghost at the start of the play, evoking the fictional terrors that await the reader in this narrative of imagined hauntings, secret imprisonments and hidden passages.

The ways in which Ann Radcliffe and other 'Gothic' novelists such as Horace Walpole and Matthew Lewis deploy Shakespeare in their pseudo-medieval and early modern tales of mystery and terror can appear a drastic departure from the mid-eighteenth-century novel. These novelists cherish Shakespeare not as fodder for epistolary communication and polite conversation, but for the evocative, other-worldly power of his sublime descriptions and emotive speeches, and for a varied cast of ghosts and fairies previously rejected as 'gross improbabilities'.[2] Narratorial epigraphs, which create suspense and atmosphere, and which hint that the ghostly or murderous plots of plays such as *Macbeth* and *Hamlet* might recur in these novels, now replace self-dramatising quotations. These are not diegetic quotations, uttered by characters and embedded in the text, but paratextual devices, set apart at the head of chapters, far out of reach of the characters below.

This bold new fictional relationship with Shakespeare's words is, however, not such a great departure from the mid-century novel. Instead, as I shall argue, the quotation practices of earlier fiction are a crucial shaping influence on Gothic Shakespeare. When Clarissa scrawled the words 'I could a tale unfold/ Would harrow up thy soul' after her rape, she freighted these lines with new meaning and set them circulating independently in polite culture. She called on Shakespeare as an advisor, and the scribbled fragments of drama and poetry in Paper X at once represent the breakdown of formal quotation, and confirm Shakespeare's emotional applicability even in this most extreme situation: Clarissa clutches at his words to dramatise her wretchedness. Radcliffe thus quotes a line that, thanks to the earlier novel, is already capable of articulating the distress of an individual female protagonist. Yet while Clarissa's backward-looking quotation expressed retrospectively her horror at her physical abuse by Lovelace, Radcliffe's forward-looking narratorial epigraph, which stops before the 'laceration' of 'harrow',[3] encourages the reader to anticipate with terror the amazing 'tale' to come.

If taken to be a direct reference to the ghost of Old Hamlet, Radcliffe's opening quotation quickly establishes the possibility of supernatural elements in the subsequent story. If one acknowledges the mediating role of earlier fiction, the quotation can also construct a distinctive female voice. In Chapters 6 and 7, I argue for the mediating force of the mid-eighteenth-century novel in later fictional encounters with Shakespeare. Shakespeare has been described as a 'patron saint of imaginative freedom for the gothic, a voice from a golden age before the tyranny of neoclassicism with its rules and unities set in',[4] as if Gothic encounters with Shakespeare bypass altogether the earlier eighteenth century's relationship with the playwright and the cultural status he achieved in that period. While Radcliffe might be 'deeply read in Shakespeare, especially in the tragedies', much of her leisure time 'was spent in reading the literary productions of the day, especially poetry and novels',[5] suggesting her familiarity not only with Shakespeare's plays, but also with poems and, crucially, with the quotation practices of a literary genre not quite so far removed in time.

Radcliffe reworks the practice of quotation by character in the mid-century novel to new and influential effect. I shall reveal how, while Radcliffe's narratorial epigraphs might look very different from the quotation by character of the mid-century, they, too, are voiced. They might appear the province of the detached, authoritative narrator, but they often articulate the way that characters see the world, and themselves. Radcliffe's use of Shakespearean quotation contrasts Matthew Lewis' in this regard: where he conjures vivid horrors, she captures in her epigraphs her characters' terror of supernatural events, before they are explained away. The theatricality of Shakespearean quotation persists in Radcliffe, but now often dramatising what characters think, rather than what they say. Banal Shakespeare also persists, not only in the vivid literary pastiches of Lewis and Walpole, but also in the emotional tropes that Radcliffe's heroines repeat. The qualities that the mid-century novel found in Shakespeare – namely truth to nature, emotional insight and the capacity for self-dramatising performance – are not disbanded in favour of ghosts, fairies and the unbounded imagination. Rather, they become tools for Radcliffe's characterisation, now supporting her explorations of delusion and self-deception, the boundaries of appearance and reality, the imagination, and the unconscious. Radcliffe's use of Shakespearean quotation to represent the unspoken thoughts and fears of her characters also contributes to Shakespeare's reputation, deepening the sense of his insight into the human mind. It also gestures towards Austen's use of Shakespeare, and the narrative innovations that she will fashion from the act of quotation.

Shakespeare in quotation marks

Shakespeare arrives in the Gothic novel already in quotation marks. This is not something that has hitherto been acknowledged by critics. Scholars who have examined the role of Shakespeare in Gothic fiction of the period have described the playwright as a legitimating authority for a genre of prose fiction even more dubious than the mid-century novel, offering 'protection and aesthetic credibility' to the 'lowly turns of popular romance'; with Gray and Thomson, also quoted in epigraph, Shakespeare is one of several 'high culture authors invited like fairy godmothers to the christening of this popular culture form'.[6] Shakespeare's plays, critics suggest, are conveniently 'full of ghosts, suspense, fear-inducing moments and cultural anxieties' that can be 'emulated, adapted and appropriated'.[7] Radcliffe 'does not merely employ Shakespearean allusions in an artificial stylistic manner'; as in many studies of mid-century fiction, her direct quotations are often taken to be the outward sign of a sustained relationship with Shakespeare's plots, most typically those of *Macbeth* and *Hamlet*.[8] Richard Sickelmore's *Edgar: or, The Phantom of the Castle* (1798), 'like so many other Gothic fictions of the 1790s, derives its central narrative dynamics from *Hamlet*'[9]; Matthew Lewis 'actually reveals the secret of *The Monk* in his quotation from *Measure for Measure* at the head of Chapter I';[10] '*The Winter's Tale* provides much of the plot and the setting for *A Sicilian Romance* (1790), while the darkness, grotesquery, and triumphant female virtue of *The Italian* is reminiscent of *Cymbeline*'; and only 'the setting in north-east Scotland', 'the general theme of usurpation and revenge', and the single name 'Malcolm', are necessary to connect Radcliffe's first novel, *The Castles of Athlin and Dunbayne*, with *Macbeth*.[11] The single, five-word Shakespearean epigraph in *A Sicilian Romance* is the basis for the assertion that 'Radcliffe's plot is a non-supernatural version of *Hamlet*'.[12] The perceived debts of the Gothic novel to Shakespeare – plots, characters and ghosts – remain remarkably similar across the study of what James Watt has called a very 'heterogeneous' body of fiction.[13]

Critics of Shakespeare in Gothic fiction do not typically consider the influence of the earlier novel's relationship with the playwright. Angela Wright says of Ann Radcliffe that the 'dynamic relationship between romance writer and dramatist' evolves 'in response to the reproduction of Shakespeare's work in new editions, the production of his plays on stage, and perhaps more significantly, the changing political stage in England in the 1790s and 1800s'.[14] She notes the impression that Johnson's Preface to his edition of Shakespeare, and Sarah Siddons' performance as Lady Macbeth, made on Radcliffe; and suggests that Malone's edition provides the 'impetus' for her epigraphs. This list of intermediary figures does not include any earlier literary authors. Wright regards Radcliffe's references to Shakespeare as direct 'tributes' to the playwright, rather than as self-conscious acts of borrowing, inflected by decades of earlier quotation. Maggie Kilgour seems to bypass intermediaries when she says that Gothic chooses 'selectively from tradition' such source materials as Milton's Satan and Shakespeare's *Hamlet* and *Macbeth* in order to assuage its 'fears about its own rightful place in the English literary line'.[15] When John Drakakis explains that one of the reasons Shakespeare appealed to Gothic authors was 'because he was an indigenous poet of "Nature", a claim that had been substantially initiated by Dryden and one that had persisted throughout the Augustan period', he skips over the mid-century and the mid-century novel.[16]

Drakakis is not alone in this regard: the mid-century novel appears to play only a relatively small part in critical discussion of Gothic fiction more widely. D. L. Macdonald and Kathleen Scherf suggest that the influence of Richardson's *Clarissa* on the plot of *The Monk* is underexplored because 'until recently the academy has not been much used to thinking about a monument of the Great Tradition and a Gothic thriller at the same time'.[17] This distinction might have its origins in Gothic fiction's own declared aims: in the Preface to the second edition of *The Castle of Otranto*, Walpole opposes the 'imagination and improbability' of the ancient romance to the painstaking attempt to copy 'nature' in the modern. The latter form, he says, has suffered for its restrictions: 'Invention has not been wanting; but the great resources of fancy have been damned up, by a strict adherence to common life', for 'Nature has cramped imagination'.[18] This statement of generic contrast is quoted so frequently by critics that they have perhaps come to take Walpole at his word, seeing a rejection of the mid-century novel's restrictions in everything that makes Gothic distinctive. Walpole's aim, however, is to 'attempt to blend the two kinds of romance, the ancient and the modern', in a way that would perpetuate some of the realistic, as well as romantic, qualities of earlier fiction.

The marked distinction between mid- and late-century fiction – or, in more sweeping terms, the 'higher novel' or 'genuine novel' and the 'modern Romance'[19] – has persisted in both praise and negative criticism of the Gothic. Early reviews of *The Castles of Athlin and Dunbayne* suggested that to more mature readers not impressed by the merely 'marvellous', 'a series of events, which seem not to have their *foundation in nature*, will ever be insipid, if not disgustful' (italics added).[20] Walter Scott asserted that Radcliffe's romances bore 'nearly the same relation to the novel that the modern anomaly entitled a melodrame does to the proper drama'.[21] More recently it has been warned that to treat Gothic fiction as a mere extension of the novel of sensibility that stretches back to Richardson is to ignore the 'shifting ambiguity and many-sidedness of the Gothic'.[22] Critics have positioned Gothic fiction in a separate, 'native or distinctly "Gothick" literary genealogy that runs from Chaucer, through Spenser and Shakespeare, and into Milton and beyond'.[23] When Walpole, however, says that 'That great master of nature, Shakespeare, was the model I copied',[24] it is not only to Shakespeare that he refers, but also to the host of earlier novels that called the playwright 'That great master of nature'.

Shakespeare, by now the national poet, might indeed be a legitimating authority for the Gothic novel. More pertinent to what Gothic fiction *does* with Shakespeare, however, is the practice of quotation by character. Characters in Radcliffe's fiction do not tend, as mid-century characters did, to apply Shakespeare's words to their own situations: her quotations are technically the province of the narrator. Close reading of the epigraphs in Radcliffe's mature fiction reveals, however, that they are not removed from the characters, but amplify their feelings and their voices.

Radcliffe is praised in terms that recall the quotation practices of the mid-century novel: 'Elaborate accuracy, just discrimination, the most acute feeling, and, what is no mean praise, the happiest selection of words and significant epithets are hers'.[25] She at once perpetuates and transforms the function of Shakespeare in fiction, reworking the familiar practice of quotation by character to develop narrative techniques that represent interiority. Shakespeare's vivid theatricality is not lost in the process, for these epigraphs often hint at how characters would dramatise their plight if they could; and nor is his banality, for quotations can also represent characters' most affected emotions. Radcliffe's quotations blend the perspectives of narrator and character, and gesture towards Austen's narrative innovations.

Beyond quotation by character

Ann Radcliffe perpetuates the qualities of mid-century quotation by character in her Gothic fiction. There are only glimmers of Shakespeare in Radcliffe's early fiction: her first novel, *The Castles of Athlin and Dunbayne* (1789) alludes very indirectly in one or two instances to *Hamlet* and to *The Merchant of Venice*. Her second, *A Sicilian Romance* (1790), after its single opening epigraph from *Hamlet*, includes a scattering of verbal echoes: Louisa 'pined in silent sorrow', and Ferdinand 'pined in sorrow', just as Viola's imaginary sister 'pined in thought' (pp. 33, 96); Julia was 'unprotected—unfriended' as Hamlet's father was 'unhousel'd, unappointed, unanel'd' (p. 96); Madame de Menon describes the sorry end of her 'air-drawn schemes for futurity' (p. 32) as Lady Macbeth chastises Macbeth for his hallucinatory vision of the 'air-drawn dagger'. This handful of evocative phrases mingles with possible glancing references to plot devices from a variety of plays: Ferdinand and Julia's ship is caught in a dreadful 'tempest' (p. 152); there is talk of 'persons of consequence in disguise' (p. 82); and hints of the denouement of Shakespearean tragedies (the marquis is tricked into drinking his own poison [p. 190]) and comedies (all is happily resolved in Naples [pp. 198–99]).

It is not, however, until *The Romance of the Forest* (1791) and *The Mysteries of Udolpho* (1794) that Radcliffe begins to use epigraphs at the head of every chapter, and quotes frequently, directly, and often with attribution, from Shakespeare's plays. *The Romance of the Forest* and *The Mysteries of Udolpho* are, as their title pages declare, 'interspersed with pieces of poetry'. These 'pieces' range from poetic chapter epigraphs to the embedded fragments of verse with which the narrator enhances a description of an awe-inspiring view:

> They pursued their way for some time between high embowering banks, till they arrived at an eminence, whence
>
> 'Heaven, earth, ocean, smil'd!'
>
> They sat down on a point of rock, overshadowed by lofty palm-trees, to contemplate at leisure the magnificent scene. The sun was just emerged

from the sea, over which his rays shed a flood of light, and darted a thousand brilliant tints on the vapours that ascended the horizon . . .[26]

Quotations from authors such as James Beattie (as in this case), James Thomson and John Milton are incorporated into the body of the text. They remain, however, extra-diegetic, arising not from the conversations of characters, but from the perspective of the omniscient narrator who describes their experiences.

Sometimes, Radcliffe's quotations are delivered by characters. Whether a heroine hears them sung by a lute player, finds them etched on a tree or stone, remembers them from happier times, or even composes them in response to a beautiful sight, such quotations are diegetic, emerging from within the characters' worlds:

> Struck with the circumstances of imagery around her, she indulged the pensive tranquillity which they inspired; and while she leaned on her window, waiting till St. Aubert should descend to breakfast, her ideas arranged themselves in the following lines:
>
> THE FIRST HOUR OF MORNING
>
> How sweet to wind the forest's tangled shade,
>   When early twilight, from the eastern bound,
> Dawns on the sleeping landscape in the glade,
>   And fades as morning spreads her blush around! . . .[27]

Emily, the heroine of *Udolpho*, is inspired by her surroundings to compose this impromptu poem (in fact, Radcliffe wrote many of these pieces of poetry for the purpose). Yet that same sense of narratorial ownership is present even in poems ostensibly penned by characters, in the third-person reporting of Emily's voice ('she indulged', 'she leaned', 'her ideas arranged themselves').

Very occasionally, Shakespeare explicitly inspires Radcliffe's characters to new acts of creativity. Adeline in *The Romance of the Forest*, for example, finds solace in borrowing Shakespeare and Milton from La Luc's library:

> Adeline found that no species of writing had power so effectually to withdraw her mind from the contemplation of its own misery as the higher kinds of poetry, and in these her taste soon taught her to distinguish the superiority of the English from that of the French. The genius of the language, more perhaps than the genius of the people, if indeed the distinction may be allowed, occasioned this.
>
> She frequently took a volume of Shakespear or Milton, and, having gained some wild eminence, would seat herself beneath the pines, whose low murmurs soothed her heart, and conspired with the visions of the poet to lull her to forgetfulness of grief. (p. 261)

While both *Romance* and *Udolpho* emphasise that reading can bring comfort, this is a rare, explicit identification of the special power of Shakespeare's language to absorb the reader. Reading Shakespeare also inspires new writing: one evening Adeline 'retired to the terrace of the garden, which overlooked the sea, and as she viewed the tranquil splendour of the setting sun, and his glories reflected on the polished surface of the waves, she touched the strings of the lute in softest harmony, her voice accompanying it with words which she had one day written after having read that rich effusion of Shakespeare's genius, "A Midsummer Night's Dream"' (p. 284). The poem is called 'TITANIA TO HER LOVE', and it weaves into its lyric verses allusions to both *A Midsummer Night's Dream* and *The Tempest*.

By far the dominant way in which Shakespeare appears in Radcliffe's mature fiction, though, is in chapter epigraphs. Here he appears alongside authors such as Thomson, Beattie (both among the 'proponents of melancholy in eighteenth-century poetry'[28]) and William Collins. Out of the reach of the characters, Shakespeare helps to establish the mood of each chapter through atmospheric excerpts from plays such as *Macbeth*, *Julius Caesar* and *Hamlet*.

> Light thickens, and the crow
> Makes wing to the rooky wood:
> Good things of day begin to droop, and drowze;
> While night's black agents to their preys do rouze.
>
> MACBETH (*Udolpho*, p. 596)

This quotation seems initially to confirm the truth of two critical views: first, with its careful attribution to 'MACBETH', that Shakespeare invests an 'emerging popular and wayward genre with a degree of literary legitimacy', and second, with its mention of 'night's black agents', that 'the Shakespeare plays offering the greatest scope for allusion and imitation were predictably those that foregrounded the supernatural'.[29] Quotations like this appear to retreat from the hurly-burly of quotation by character to the crisper authority of the epigraph, and the narrator's omniscient – and extra-diegetic – overview of supernatural events.

Closer inspection, however, reveals that Shakespeare is unique in Radcliffe's fiction as an author whose words cross the boundaries between diegetic and extra-diegetic quotation, and between the narrator's vision and the personal expression of the characters. Almost all of the seemingly detached epigraphs from Shakespeare's plays are imbued with the thoughts and wishes of the characters below. It has been suggested that Radcliffe's Shakespearean epigraphs tend to cluster at 'moments of moral quandary and episodes of distress for her heroines',[30] as if Shakespeare offers emotional analogies or detached descriptions for their situations. Beyond analogy, though, these epigraphs actually give voice to Radcliffe's characters, male and female. In *The Romance of the Forest*, the Shakespearean epigraphs frequently evoke dramatic dialogue or impassioned soliloquy. The first chapter of Volume I introduces the formerly dissolute figure of Pierre La Motte and his wife, and its epigraph could easily be spoken by La Motte himself:

> I am a man,
> So weary with disasters, tugg'd with fortune,
> That I would set my life on any chance,
> To mend it, or be rid on't. (p. 1)

'I' is the first word of both chapter and book, and it renders the quotation, adapted without attribution from *Macbeth*, a clear expression of an individual voice. When, in Chapter 3, the La Mottes take their new charge, Adeline, to the safety of the forest, the epigraph captures the way they might reassure one another:

> 'Are not these woods
> More free from peril than the envious court?
> Here feel we but the penalty of Adam,
> The season's difference, as the icy fang
> And churlish chiding of the winter's wind.'
> SHAKESPEARE. (p. 32)

Here, the collective 'we' is personal to the characters, and the questioning tone conversational. Radcliffe's presentation of quotations is irregular, but in this case the inverted commas amplify the impression of direct speech, and the attribution to 'SHAKESPEARE' lends emotional credibility, suggesting that the epigraph aptly expresses what would naturally be said on such an occasion.

By quoting drama, Radcliffe can achieve quite different effects than are possible with poetry. The Shakespearean epigraph to the very next chapter is

> '——My May of life,
> Is fall'n into the sear, the yellow leaf.'
> MACBETH (p. 44)

Radcliffe, following Johnson,[31] turns 'way of life' into 'May of life', which, given the forest setting, is a natural extension of Macbeth's lament for the turning of the seasons and the passing of time. In the ensuing chapter, La Motte appears 'gloomy and reserved' and retreats to 'the most secluded parts of the forest, devoted to melancholy and secret grief'. Paired with these lines from *Macbeth* is an additional epigraph from Thomas Warton: 'Full oft, unknowing and unknown,/ He wore his endless noons alone. . . / WHARTON'. The contrast between Warton's third-person description and Shakespeare's first-person soliloquy highlights Shakespeare's peculiar capacity, as the only dramatist cited in these novels, not only to give voice to characters by articulating what they might say, but also to facilitate their self-dramatisation, by conveying how these characters see themselves. The troubled, self-pitying voice in 'My May of life', like the heightened, tragic language of 'weary with disasters', dramatises La Motte's sense of his woes, and hints that he regards himself as a tragic character.

Radcliffe exploits the self-dramatising potential of her Shakespearean epigraphs to an even greater degree in *The Mysteries of Udolpho* – even in those parts of the novel where quotations seem intended only to establish a vague atmosphere of the supernatural. There is a sudden increase in the intensity of Shakespearean quotation in a series of five chapters in Volume IV that explore the suspected haunting of the room where the Marchioness de Villeroi died. These quotations seem to imply a supernatural cause. One epigraph declares authoritatively that:

> This is no mortal business, nor no sound
> That the earth owes!
>
> SHAKESPEARE (p. 521)

This 'sound' refers to the music that has played outside the house, without discernible source, since the night the Marchioness died. In *The Tempest*, Ferdinand marvelled in these words at Ariel's song. Extracted and attributed to the knowing figure of 'SHAKESPEARE', these eerie lines now seem a confident, narratorial assertion of a supernatural presence.

Another epigraph implies that the late Marchioness haunts her former home. In the previous chapter, Dorothee the servant gave a vivid account of the 'extraordinary' and suspicious death of the Marchioness, replete with grisly details of the 'frightful blackness spread all over her face', and she and Emily resolved to visit the chambers at night. The new chapter, in which Dorothee calls for Emily with the key to the chambers, begins:

> Now it is the time of night,
> That, the graves all gaping wide
> Every one lets forth his sprite,
> In the church-way path to glide.
>
> SHAKESPEARE (p. 530)

'Now' heightens the narrative tension, connecting Shakespeare's superstitious vision of ghostly visitations with the temporal 'now' of the visit that is about to begin. The narrator echoes the language of the epigraph during their visit: 'Emily, in the partial gleam, which the lamp threw into it, thought she saw something glide along into the obscurer part of the room' (p. 535). The word 'glide' links the 'something' that Emily cannot quite make out to the 'sprites' that pour forth from the 'graves all gaping wide'. In doing so, the narrator seems to confirm that the house is haunted.

All of the supernatural hints in these quotations, however, are ultimately explained away. The 'sound' heard nightly since the Marchioness' death is thoroughly mortal: Signora Laurentini, it is revealed, jealously poisoned the Marchioness in order to win back the love of her husband the Marquis, and, driven to madness when he still did not love her, has ever after nightly escaped from the convent where she resides to haunt the surrounding area with her lute playing. More bathetically, the figures that Emily sees 'gliding' across the room are robbers who have been stockpiling their swag in the cellars of the house, and who, popping up through a secret door into the chamber, pretend to be ghosts in order to scare off unwanted visitors. These are typical examples of the 'explained supernatural' that characterises Radcliffe's work: mysterious occurrences are resolved into a rational account.

Yet if all of these rational explanations are known to the narrator at the moment of quotation, are these supernatural-sounding Shakespeare quotations merely atmospheric distractions, designed to deceive the reader into temporary terror, before being neatly cleared away? When the events of Laurentini's life are about to be revealed to Emily by the abbess, the narrator interjects:

> As the narrative of the abbess was, however, deficient in many particulars, of which the reader may wish to be informed, and the history of the nun is materially connected with the fate of the Marchioness de Villeroi, we shall omit the conversation, that passed in the parlour of the convent, and mingle with our relation a brief history of
>
> LAURENTINI DI UDOLPHO (p. 655)

The narrator takes control of the revelation, transforming it into a third-person account in which all confusions are clarified: Emily learns that the Marchioness is her aunt, and not, as she has begun to imagine, her mother. Such rare, heavy-handed intrusions confirm that the narrator has been in possession of these facts all along. When the supernatural is explained away, as Anna Letitia Barbauld notes, the reader can feel nothing but a 'sort of disappointment and shame at having felt so much, from appearances which had nothing in them beyond this "visible diurnal sphere"'.[32]

Radcliffe's Shakespeare quotations are not, however, deliberately misleading, nor heavy-handed attempts by the narrator to induce terror in the reader. Rather, they amplify the thoughts, fears and anxieties of the characters experiencing these situations for the first time – even without the explicit 'I', 'my' and 'we' of La Motte's epigraphs. The 'mortal sound' and the gaping graves, for example, evoke the anxious, superstitious chatter of the household since the Marchioness' death, but they also capture Emily's anxieties, fuelled by Dorothee – even if her staunchly anti-superstitious principles would forbid her to admit them. Examples of epigraphs that express characters' perspectives abound: 'I think it is the weakness of mine eyes,/ That shapes this monstrous apparition./ It comes upon me!/ JULIUS CAESAR' is introduced as Emily 'almost fancied she saw shapes flit past her curtains and glide into the remote obscurity of her chamber', but manages, in daylight, to dispel 'the glooms of superstition' (p. 241) (though a more real fear is confirmed towards the end of the chapter when a seeming apparition turns out to be Count Morano). The words 'Be thou a spirit of health, or goblin damn'd,/ Bring with thee airs from heaven, or blasts from hell,/ Be thy intents wicked, or charitable,/ I will speak to thee./ HAMLET' vocalise Count de Villefort's determination to clear up the mystery of Ludovico's disappearance (p. 569). Far from being dismissed, they remain valid fears even after Radcliffe's rational explanation.[33]

Radcliffe imbues her epigraphs with even more character in her subsequent novel, *The Italian*. Often shorter, more dynamic and sometimes dialogic, these epigraphs seem more obviously intended to amplify characters' perspectives: 'The bell then beating one!'; 'What, would'st thou have a serpent sting thee twice?'; 'I am settled, and bend up/ Each corporal agent to this terrible feat'; 'Is it not dead midnight?/ Cold fearful drops stand on my trembling flesh,/ What do I fear?'; 'Your's in the ranks of death'. All of these quotations are attributed to 'SHAKESPEARE'.[34] The brief epigraph, 'What if it be a poison, which the friar/ Subtly hath ministered?' (p. 54), heads the chapter in which Vivaldi visits villa Altieri after the sudden death of his beloved Ellena's guardian, Signora Bianchi. For David Salter, this epigraph represents a 'fundamental misunderstanding of the Shakespearean text'. Shakespeare's Juliet, afraid to take the sleeping draught, expresses in these words her fear of Friar Lawrence's ill intentions, but immediately dismisses this fear as groundless, 'For he hath still been tried a holy man'.

In Radcliffe, however, the out-of-context quotation is, for Salter, a 'hint to the reader', 'in the absence of any definitive proof', 'that the friar' – in this case, the menacing figure of Schedoni – 'is indeed guilty as expected' of murdering Bianchi; Radcliffe borrows Shakespeare to 'lend further credence and authority to the novel's anti-Catholic tone and outlook'.[35] If, however, we regard Radcliffe's epigraph not as a knowing narratorial 'hint', but rather as an expression of Vivaldi's uncertain suspicions, then it very closely resembles Juliet's temporary anxiety. By the end of the chapter, Vivaldi departs 'with spirits somewhat soothed by a hope, that Bianchi had not fallen prematurely' (p. 56); he is finally 'convinced' by the condemned Schedoni's avowal of innocence 'that her death was in consequence of some incident of natural decay' (p. 400). This epigraph is not (or not simply, at least) a vehicle for Radcliffe's ideological doubts about the validity of the Catholic church, but rather voices the fleeting fears of a character at a pivotal moment in the text.

Terror and horror

Matthew Lewis wrote *The Monk* (1796) in response to Radcliffe's *Udolpho*. He too quoted Shakespeare, but in order to reverse Radcliffe's technique of the explained supernatural. Both novelists quote Macbeth's cry on seeing the ghost of Banquo, Radcliffe in the following epigraph in *The Romance of the Forest*:

> Hence, horrible shadow!
> Unreal mockery, hence!
> MACBETH (p. 85)

In the ensuing chapter, a band of men, led by the Marquis, burst into La Motte's forest home. At first, it is not apparent to whom, or what, this ghostly phrase refers, beyond Adeline's fainting 'paleness of terror' (p. 88). Then suddenly, La Motte and the Marquis come face to face.

> [La Motte] advanced towards the Marquis with a complacent air, but, as he would have spoke, the words of welcome faultered on his lips, his limbs trembled, and a ghastly paleness overspread his countenance. The Marquis was a little less agitated, and, in the first moment of surprize, put his hand upon his sword, but, recollecting himself, he withdrew it, and endeavoured to regain a command of features. (p. 88)

Macbeth's words ostensibly capture the men's mutual aversion: La Motte, it is later revealed, sees in the Marquis the man he had attacked in his youth out of desperation for money. But Madame La Motte overhears her husband telling the Marquis that 'the same image has pursued me in my midnight dream, and in my daily wanderings' (pp. 89–90), as if he has seen a supernatural phenomenon. This might be explained away, but for now it intrigues.

In Lewis's *The Monk*, by contrast, the feelings of dread established by the same epigraph from *Macbeth* are not explained away, but horribly confirmed. The chapter begins without anxiety: Raymond's beloved Agnes tells him the story of the Bleeding Nun, a ghost who, centuries ago, 'made bold to seize upon the castle of Lindenberg' and, 'Having a good taste . . . took up her abode in the best room of the house'.[36] Agnes playfully explains how, every five years on the fifth of May, the 'ghostly nun' is believed to walk through the house 'with her lamp and dagger: she descends the stair-case of the eastern tower, and crosses the great hall'. The porter leaves the castle gates open for her, a courtesy Agnes thinks not 'necessary', 'since she could easily whip through the key-hole if she chose it; but merely out of politeness, and to prevent her from making her exit in a way so derogatory to the dignity of her ghostship' (p. 142). Agnes professes rational detachment from this family legend: 'I have too much reason to lament superstition's influence to be its victim myself' (p. 142). She sounds like a Radcliffean heroine, keen to distance herself from the beliefs that afflict her more credulous servants.

Raymond and Agnes plot to exploit those superstitious beliefs in order to free Agnes from Lindenberg: on the appointed day, she will dress as the bleeding nun and walk unhindered from the house. The day comes, the ghostly figure walks, and Raymond clutches Agnes to him in delight and relief. Only it is not Agnes: after a bizarre carriage accident, the figure appears to him again, and he lifts the veil to reveal:

> an animated corse. Her countenance was long and haggard; her cheeks and lips were bloodless; the paleness of death was spread over her features; and her eye-balls, fixed steadfastly upon me, were lustreless and hollow. (p. 155)

This hideous, deathly figure nightly haunts his room, its repeated cries of 'Raymond! Raymond! Thou art mine!' a disturbing misquotation of the ill-advised vows he made believing he held Agnes in his arms. In a reversal of the Radcliffean narrative of the 'explained supernatural', Raymond is surprised by the supernatural only *after* Agnes' rational explanation. (There is, however, something wonderfully rational about the scene's resolution: when the Wandering Jew intercedes with the Bleeding Nun on Raymond's behalf, she reveals that she was murdered and left unburied, and simply wants Raymond to perform a proper burial in his family vault and let precisely 'thirty masses be said for the repose of my spirit'; she departs with a distinctly unghostly 'those flames are scorching!' [p. 165]. Once this list of conditions is fulfilled, Raymond is free.)

In both Radcliffe and Lewis' novels, the same quotation from *Macbeth* dramatises the distress of key characters, to very different purposes. Where Radcliffe supplies the brief lines that describe imaginary fears – 'horrible shadow', 'unreal mockery' – Lewis fleshes them out by yoking that phrase to Macbeth's physical description of Banquo's ghost:

> Avaunt! and quit my sight! Let the earth hide thee!
> Thy bones are marrowless; thy blood is cold;
> Thou hast no speculation in those eyes
> Which thou dost glare with! Hence, horrible shadow!
> Unreal mockery, hence!
>
> MACBETH (p. 133)

Lewis' longer quotation expresses not just fearful anticipation, but also physical revulsion at a hideous sight. It is not an expression of terror, but of horror.

Radcliffe uses precisely this passage in her essay 'On the Supernatural in Poetry' to illustrate the difference between horror and terror. Whereas Shakespeare has Horatio tell his 'secret to Hamlet' in the evening, thus amplifying the feelings of terror, the appearance of Banquo at the feast affects only by 'the force of contrast': the effect, 'though sudden and strong, is also transient':

> it is the thrill of horror and surprise, which they then communicate, rather than the deep and solemn feelings excited under more accordant circumstances, and left long upon the mind. Who ever suffered for the ghost of Banquo, the gloomy and sublime kind of terror, which that of Hamlet calls forth?[37]

Radcliffe praises terror over horror: its acute sensations spring from the obscurity of the feared object, and are a source of the sublime. Neither Shakespeare nor Milton nor Burke 'looked to positive horror' for the sublime. Her quotation thus turns what is in Shakespeare an expression of horror into one of terror. Lewis, in his lurid tale, restores Macbeth's horror by connecting fragments of the same scene.

Radcliffe quotes *Macbeth* in the context of La Motte's private fears, and thus sustains suspense. Lewis, by contrast, quotes before an on-stage encounter with the horrific nun. He exaggerates the theatricality of the lines: he 'drew back the curtain' around his bed, and declaims 'what a sight presented itself to my startled eyes!'. He also emphasises Raymond's role as spectator: 'I beheld before me', 'I gazed upon the spectre before me with horror too great to be described'. Radcliffe, with her tendency towards 'narrative retrospection', ultimately 'tying up . . . loose ends by means of a narrator's report of events that could have been dramatised in the plot-order in which they occurred', seems to many critics to 'eschew dramatisation' altogether.[38] It is said that Radcliffe's 'appreciation of Shakespeare came primarily from reading him on the printed page, rather than seeing him performed on stage';[39] and that the Shakespearean fairies of her poetry emblematise the Romantic version of Shakespeare: 'the embodiment of English folk genius and imagination, increasingly a poet defined against the man of the theater'.[40]

Dramatic quotation

The heroines of Radcliffe's fiction often appear to reject the dramatic. Their poetic adaptations – Adeline's of Titania's words, and Emily's of Ariel's – 'displace[s] Shakespearean drama into lyric'.[41] Theatrical behaviour attracts criticism: when the young, eager Blanche in *Udolpho* effuses about the landscape, it is archly referred to by the narrator as an 'enthusiastic soliloquy' (p. 472), by way of contrast with the more tempered feelings of the heroine. Emily's own poetic utterances are hedged with modesty: the first time she repeats lines she has composed, it is at St. Aubert's urging, and she apologises that 'I fear they are too irregular' (p. 16). She is more likely to proffer remembered lines that assert communal ties of family and heart, than to dramatise her individual situation:

> The circumstances of the hour brought to her recollection some lines, which she had once heard St. Aubert recite on this very spot, and she had now a melancholy pleasure in repeating them (p. 96)
>
> . . . and then accompanied it with her voice, in one of the simple and affecting airs, to which, in happier days, Valancourt had often listened in rapture, and which she now adapted to the following lines (p. 665)
>
> It brought to Emily's recollection some lines of her late father, and she repeated in a low voice. . . (p. 175)

Emily's quotations are the opposite of selfish, showy performance. She abhors her aunt's 'burlesque' displays of distress, and her own quiet restraint drives that woman to reproach her for 'want of duty and feeling' (p. 281). When Emily talks of fortitude, her cruel uncle, Montoni, sneers 'You speak like a heroine' (p. 381). These ranting characters accuse Emily of sensibility as if it were she, not they, caught up in the wildness of excessive misery. Emily was trained by her father in her youth to avoid the excesses and 'dangers of sensibility' (p. 80), and now values more highly the 'strength of fortitude', and regards sensibility as 'a quality, perhaps, more to be feared, than desired' (pp. 214, 281). She studiously avoids its attention-seeking theatricality.

For all this anti-histrionic sentiment, the epigraphs of Radcliffe's fiction are powerfully dramatic. They provide an opportunity to express precisely those emotions that Emily and other virtuous characters *cannot* voice with characteristic restraint in the body of the novel. When Emily learns from the Count that Valancourt has betrayed her, the anguish that both she and Valancourt feel is dramatised in the epigraph to the chapter that describes their enforced separation:

> Is all the council that we two have shared,
> the hours that we have spent,
> When we have chid the hasty-footed time
> For parting us—Oh! and is all forgot?
>
> And will you rend our ancient love asunder?
> MIDSUMMER NIGHT'S DREAM (p. 512)

Radcliffe adapts the speech of Shakespeare's Helena, dropping the words 'sisters' vows' to transform it from a plea of female friendship to one of romantic love. Emily has struggled valiantly to rein in her emotions since speaking with the Count. On hearing the news, she tries to think, but 'her mind refused controul, and she could only feel that she was miserable' (p. 509); she battles to 'recover the command of her mind, and to teach it resignation to the event' (p. 510); on agreeing to meet Valancourt, she 'exerted herself in endeavours to attain fortitude and composure' for the encounter (p. 511), and she rallies precepts about self-command 'to enable her to act, with prudence and dignity, on this the most severe occasion of her life' (p. 518). In the midst of this silent struggle, the epigraph gives full voice to her anguish. It dramatises the betrayal in imagined, accusing dialogue. The epigraph simultaneously amplifies the voice of Valancourt, who fears that his reputed actions will lead Emily to turn away from him. Valancourt echoes the epigraph in his spoken appeals to Emily: 'I fear, indeed, I see, that you can no longer love me; else the happy hours, which we have passed together, would plead for me, and you could not look back upon them unmoved' (p. 516). For Emily, however, who strives for the appearance of dignified restraint, the epigraph represents a dialogue that takes place only in her mind.

Radcliffe adapts the self-dramatising quotation of the mid-century novel to convey interior thoughts and unarticulated emotion. Emily's outward composure masks her deep anguish, and the next epigraph captures her unspoken distress when she is left alone to come to terms with Valancourt's departure:

> Come, weep with me;–past hope, past cure, past help!
> Romeo and Juliet (p. 519)

By their very detachment from the body of the text, Radcliffe's formal epigraphs can articulate feelings that cannot be directly expressed by characters. Radcliffe has long been criticised for the 'sensibility and sameness' of her 'undiscriminated characters', but more recent twentieth-century criticism has found the primary interest of these characters in their psychology: the fear, loneliness, sorrow and anxiety that the novels most vividly realise.[42] Character-revealing epigraphs, hovering at the edges of the chapters, contribute to that impression of an internal landscape. As in the mid-century novel, Radcliffe's seeming resistance to drama is rather a rejection of theatrical sensibility and its capacity for deceit and distraction. Emily might chide the servants for throwing themselves into the drama of the ghostly figure on the battlements, but if these are stagey clichés, other Shakespeare quotations relating to her plight are truly dramatic: not just emotionally apt, but tending increasingly towards the imagination and the unconscious mind. Dramatic quotations, in this narrative form, can now express what characters think rather than what they say, and how they see themselves as much as who they really are.

Radcliffe's banal Shakespeare

Radcliffe's Shakespeare quotations not only dramatise characters' thoughts, feelings and beliefs. Because of the simultaneous presence of the narrator in each quotation, they offer scope for critique. The phenomenon of 'banal Shakespeare' is not one that many readers would naturally associate with Radcliffe's earnest fiction; it more readily describes the playfully macabre Gothic fiction of Horace Walpole and Matthew Lewis. The Shakespearean qualities of Walpole's novel are often mentioned, not least because he declaredly takes Shakespeare's writing as the 'model' for the inclusion of lowly 'domestics' alongside his aristocratic characters (p. 10). Walpole's Gothic fiction, though, is a pastiche of Shakespearean modes, as he 'pieced together his story from patches of history, folk tale, kidnapped romance, medieval superstition and Shakespearean allusions'.[43] The novel links Shakespearean character names from a range of plays that do not cohere: Hippolita (of *A Midsummer Night's Dream*) is the wife of Manfred; Isabella (of *Measure for Measure*) the daughter-in-law he desires for himself now that her husband is unfortunately 'dashed to pieces and almost buried under an enormous helmet' (p. 19). Scattered words and phrases evoke, as in Sterne, the vivid physical gestures of a familiar scene from *Hamlet*: 'Lead on! cried Manfred; I will follow thee to the gulph of perdition' (p. 26), when the image of his grandfather leaps out of his portrait and makes a sign for Manfred to follow; Diego's 'hair stood on end' as he relates the sight not of a ghost but of 'a giant, I believe' (p. 35); and Frederic recoils from the sight of 'the fleshless jaws and empty sockets of a skeleton, wrapt in a hermit's cowl', with a cry of 'Angels of grace, protect me!' (p. 106). Walpole gives Hamlet's well-known cry of terror to several characters in response to the various stimuli of a talking picture, a looming ogre and a walking skeleton.

In this fast-paced novel, allusions and even Shakespearean styles of address are jumbled together. The maid Bianca chatters to Matilda as the Nurse does to Juliet, 'As sure as I live, madam, I shall see you a bride at last' (p. 39); and Jerome's question, 'What means thy distracted rashness? . . . is this an hour for marriage?' (p. 111) recalls Friar Lawrence's warnings against too-hasty wedlock. Manfred returns to the feast after the sword falls to the ground and 'invited his silent guests to take their places', seeking to inspire 'mirth' though his heart is 'ill . . . at ease' (p. 66), as if he assumes the role of Lady Macbeth after Macbeth sees the ghost of Banquo; but later, when the sight of Theodore throws him into 'terror and amazement' and he cries 'what art thou, thou dreadful spectre', he requires, like Macbeth, the calming intervention of his wife, who urges him to 'resume your soul, command your reason. There is none here but we, your friends' (p. 83). Theodore's is a romance narrative ('I was carried at five years of age to Algiers with my mother . . . She died of grief in less than a twelvemonth' [p. 84]); and Isabella talks of Matilda, her rival for Theodore's love, in a way that others do of Isabella's namesake in *Measure for Measure*: 'She had ever appeared insensible to love; all her thoughts were set on heaven' (p. 86). The deliberate clashes of familiar, emotive moments from Shakespeare accords with a novelistic style that 'stimulates emotional effects rather than rational understanding', and focuses on 'marvellous and threatening events and the terrors they produce instead of moral resolution'.[44] Walpole's novel is fashioned out of the vivid collision of moving moments from Shakespeare.

Matthew Lewis, by contrast, tantalises readers with the possibility of a sustained plot parallel with *Measure for Measure*. His first epigraph suggests that his central figure of Ambrosio has an equivalent in

Shakespeare's Angelo, for both conceal their passionate humanity behind their public role:

> ————Lord Angelo is precise;
> Stands at a guard with envy; scarce confesses
> That his blood flows, or that his appetite
> Is more to bread than stone.
> MEASURE FOR MEASURE (p. 39)

Lewis supports this impression by borrowing a number of plot elements – a corrupt moral leader, dukes, illicit pregnancy, lusted-after nuns and anguished brothers – in a heady novelisation of the play. Ultimately, however, the links between Lewis's novel and Shakespeare's problem play are not sustained: there are only two direct references to *Measure for Measure*, and the plot tropes listed above are dispersed across numerous characters. Like Walpole, Lewis invokes a wide range of Shakespeare's plays: Matilda, disguised as the male monk Rosario, talks of a pining sister who turns out to be Matilda herself ('My sister saw him, and dared to love, though she never dared to hope', p. 77) in a deliberate echo of *Twelfth Night*. Theodore, doing his bit to find Agnes, takes on the persuasive charms of an Othello who tells compelling stories of his travels to islands inhabited 'By anthropophagi, and men whose heads/ Do grow beneath their shoulders' (p. 251) in order to win the trust of the nuns at the convent where she is thought to have died; and both Agnes and Antonia are put to sleep by an opiate, for the purposes of imprisonment and rape respectively, in terms that recall *Romeo and Juliet*: 'eight-and-forty hours after she has drank it, life will revive in her bosom' (p. 283).

These wide-ranging references not only complicate *The Monk*'s Shakespearean associations. They also confirm that Lewis, like Walpole, deals in a frenzied conflation of Shakespearean tropes made banal by their prior usage. They recall gestures or stances that are, by now, utterly familiar: pining, like patience on a monument, but also like Tom Jones, Clementina and Evelina; telling a tale, like Othello, but also like Tom Jones, to whose words Mr Dowling did 'seriously incline'; and being drugged, ultimately fatally, like Juliet, but also like Clarissa. Lewis and Walpole's Shakespeares have been heavily mediated by the mid-century novel: these Shakespearean moments are now also recognisably novelistic scenarios, and by borrowing them, Lewis and Walpole draw attention to the playful derivativeness of their plots.

By contrast, the female characters in Radcliffe's fiction resemble in their earnest quotations and compositions those mid-century heroines who scorn the banal recitation of scraps of Shakespeare. They are, however, nonetheless highly trained in responding to fragments of literature. Looking over a book that St. Aubert has left behind, Emily remembers how, on the eve of his departure from the chateau, he 'had read to her some passages from this his favourite author' (p. 95). She presents herself as a modest daughter who received gratefully the well-chosen 'passages' selected by her father for her benefit. Later, far from home, she thinks of that other important male influence, Valancourt, and 'well remembered with what discriminating judgment, with what tempered energy, he used to repeat some of the sublimest passages of their favourite authors; how often he would pause to admire with her their excellence, and with what tender delight he would listen to her remarks, and correct her taste' (p. 585). To concentrate together on the 'sublimest passages' of these texts, and admire their 'excellence', is not reductive, but educational: Valancourt's 'discriminating judgment' directs and improves Emily's 'taste', and avoids the charge that she wallows aimlessly in her reading.

The language of valuable pieces is also present in *The Romance of the Forest*:

> La Motte had several of the best English poets, a language which Adeline had learned in the convent; their beauties, therefore, she was capable of tasting, and they often inspired her with enthusiastic delight. (p. 82)

Thanks to La Motte's discriminating choice of books, Adeline reads 'the best English poets', and admires their 'beauties'. This does not necessarily mean that Adeline sampled only the best bits. 'Their beauties' could refer to the parts noted in the course of reading these poets in their entirety, but it nonetheless evokes a selective act. Adeline enjoyed little opportunity for reading, 'but the books to which she had access, operating upon a mind eager for knowledge, and upon a taste peculiarly sensible of the beautiful and the elegant, had impressed all their excellencies upon her understanding' (p. 190): again, 'their excellencies' could denote both the general quality of the works, and the serried ranks of their most admirable phrases. Emily (guided by her father and Valancourt) and Adeline (by La Motte and later La Luc's prior selections) deal in the proper admiration of the beauties of literature, learning through fragments to discern the most valuable parts of their beloved books.

These earnest accounts of the value of careful, discriminating reading can, however, obscure those important occasions when Radcliffe deals in already familiar 'beauties' of Shakespeare.

> Then, fresh tears
> Stood on her cheek, as doth the honey-dew
> Upon a gather'd lily almost wither'd
>
> SHAKESPEARE (*Udolpho*, p. 664)

Critics assume that these unattributed lines from Shakespeare's *Titus Andronicus* invoke their original source in its entirety, suggesting that readers of the novel would be 'familiar with the context of rape that precedes it' in Shakespeare's arguably 'Gothic' play.[45] To link the chapter epigraph to the play, however, requires some contortions: Craig acknowledges that, in *Udolpho*, rape is less of a threat than economic hardship; and that the sexualities of Shakespeare's Gothic have been contained by the 'amiable sensibility' of the Gothic novel (p. 57). No such contortions are required if one acknowledges the eighteenth-century anthology as a shaping influence on these lines. In *Anecdotes of Polite Literature* (1764), these lines are praised as a beautiful simile for tears, and they are quoted in Dodd's *Beauties of Shakespear* under the heading '*Tears compar'd to Dew on a Lilly*'.[46] If readers do recognise the lines, it is possible that they do so with no knowledge of Lavinia's rape and mutilation. The anthology has already shaped the lines into an independent unit of sensibility: an exportable image of beautiful tears. Perhaps the word 'fresh' recommended these lines to Radcliffe: after the abundant weeping of the final stages of the novel, in which Emily comes to terms with Valancourt's betrayal, this chapter brings a new flurry of happy tears at their reunion, and as the mysteries surrounding their family in Emily's eyes are cleared up. It permits a hint of criticism from the narrator of the emotional responses of the characters involved. It also enables us to see not just in Walpole and Lewis, but also in Radcliffe, a more self-conscious critique of the novel's emotional excesses, anticipating the complaints of wearied modern readers required to 'slog through a fair bit of lachrymose lugubriosity and lengthy descriptions of mountain views' in order to be rewarded with 'fun haunted-castle thrills'.[47]

The critique of well-worn emotional expressions can be directed at individuals. Madame La Motte wonders why her husband keeps disappearing into the forest for hours. When she hears that Adeline has also gone for a walk,

> her imagination, heated by the broodings of jealousy, suggested that they had appointed a meeting. This was confirmed to her by the entrance of Adeline, quickly followed by La Motte; and her perceptions thus jaundiced by passion, neither the presence of her son, nor her usual attention to good

manners, had been able to restrain her emotions. The behavior of Adeline, in the late scene, she considered a refined piece of art; and the indifference of La Motte as affected. So true is it, that

—'Trifles, light as air,
Are, to the jealous, confirmations strong
As proof of Holy Writ.'

And so ingenious was she 'to twist the true cause the wrong way.' (p. 79)

The narrator quotes Shakespeare to describe the common nature of Madame La Motte's misguided jealousy: 'So true it is, then' affirms the aptness of Shakespeare's description. But something of the banality of the phrase lingers, as if to suggest that the emotion that Madame La Motte experiences is well-worn. To be 'jaundiced by passion' does not suggest a fresh, immediate response, as is characteristic of the younger female figure of Adeline. This utterly familiar quotation hints that Madame La Motte is experiencing – and neglecting to question rationally – a hackneyed emotion. Even if Radcliffe's fiction is not populated by ranting quoters, the presence of 'banal Shakespeare' can still cast aspersions on those whose preoccupations the quotations amplify.

Gothic quotations of Shakespeare, then, can often be the sign not so much of thorough-going plot references, as of extended Shakespearean tropes that have accrued meaning in previous decades. This is not to say, of course, that Gothic novelists did not engage with Shakespeare; but that they also engaged with Shakespeare's role in eighteenth-century culture. Ghostly sightings – as Walpole in particular demonstrates – are one recurring trope. Dale Townshend, discussing the role of *Hamlet*'s ghost in Gothic fiction, suggests that ghosts in Radcliffe's *Udolpho* are usually misapprehensions, but that Radcliffe 'directly enlists *Hamlet* in the work of mourning' by beginning Chapter 2, which describes Madame St. Aubert's funeral, with the epigraph 'I could a tale unfold whose lightest word/ Would harrow up thy soul' (1.5.15–16). For Townshend, this quotation is an opportunity to reflect on the Protestant values of, and ultimately the secularisation of grief in, *Udolpho*, as opposed to the purgatorial overtones of the speech of old Hamlet's ghost.[48] The fragmentary use of this phrase in *A Sicilian Romance*, discussed at the start of this chapter, suggests, however, that, after multiple mid-century repetitions, the phrase 'I could a tale unfold' encapsulates in a handful of words an intense emotional response. Since its use by Clarissa, it functions as a trope of the narration of distress, rather than distress itself. It not only hints, then, at an untold story around Emily's parentage that will eventually be resolved by the end of the novel. Crucially, this ultra-familiar line gives scope for Emily St. Aubert to share the narratorial agency of the novel, and to blend into one the voices of narrator and character.

Radcliffe is the most epigraph-oriented quoter of Shakespeare in Gothic fiction, but her formal quotation practice has close resonances with the techniques of the mid-century novel. Her character-inflected epigraphs dramatise and amplify the unspoken anxieties of individuals in the text, before their fears are explained away. Where the mid-century novel captured in quotation what characters say, Radcliffe's Gothic novel uses Shakespeare to show how her characters think and feel. Familiar phrases from Shakespeare now dramatise emotions – and posturing, self-justifying delusions – that cannot be expressed outright by characters. By blurring in her quotations the perspectives of narrator and character, Radcliffe anticipates and perhaps influences the narrative developments of another late-eighteenth and early nineteenth-century author. Jane Austen's free indirect discourse silently incorporates the posturing, self-rationalising speech and characteristic thought of her characters into a third-person narrative. These authors, both called a 'prose Shakespeare',[49] build their narrative innovations on the quotation practices of mid-century fiction. The implications for our understanding of Austen's major novels are the subject of Chapter 7.

CHAPTER 7

Jane Austen and eighteenth-century Shakespeare

When Emma Woodhouse declares that 'the course of true love never did run smooth' and then smugly disputes the truism, she provides one of a small handful of quotations in Jane Austen's fiction.[1] Austen rarely quotes Shakespeare, or any other author, directly, enlisting neither poetic epigraphs, nor the 'as Shakespeare says' formula of quotation by character, in her published fiction. Some critics have taken the absence of quotation to be symptomatic of Austen's rejection of poetry in favour of prose: 'Austen did not try to associate her novels with poetry because she was a novelist, and not ashamed of being so'.[2] Austen, this chapter will argue, is not only immensely interested in the idea of poetic quotation, but also fashions some of her most radical developments in narrative representation out of the quotation practices of earlier eighteenth-century fiction.

Despite the relative absence of his words, Shakespeare is often considered to be an important presence in Austen's fiction. Shakespeare is thought to bring 'prestige' to nineteenth-century fiction; to give women 'licence to voice aspects of their lives otherwise unspoken' and 'to critique men and the society in which they lived'; and to proffer plots that Austen reduces to their emotional 'fundamentals' and reuses in her novels.[3] Critics have variously drawn plot parallels between *Sense and Sensibility* and *King Lear*[4], between *Sense and Sensibility* and *Measure for Measure*,[5] between *Mansfield Park* and *King Lear*, between *Persuasion* and *Twelfth Night*[6] and between *Emma* and *A Midsummer Night's Dream*. They have found character equivalences between Elizabeth Bennet and Beatrice; between Mr Darcy and Benedick[7]; between Fanny Price and Cordelia,[8] Katherine of Aragon and Anne Boleyn;[9] between Sir Thomas Bertram and Lear and between Henry Crawford and Henry VIII,[10] Bottom and Hal.[11]

The eighteenth-century novel – in whose pages Shakespeare's prestige is constructed, his words are often quoted by women, and his phrases, rather than whole plots, have an independent life – is not typically considered an influence on Austen's Shakespeare. Yet Austen is known to have engaged closely with the eighteenth-century novel. She read *Sir Charles Grandison* repeatedly until the 'wedding days of Lady L. and Lady G. were as well remembered as if they had been living friends',[12] and some have attributed to Austen (but others, more recently, to her young niece) a dramatic adaptation of the novel.[13] She referred in her juvenilia to 'Samuel Richardson . . . Sarah Fielding, Henry Fielding, Charlotte Lennox, Frances Brooke, Frances Burney, Laurence Sterne, Oliver Goldsmith, Henry Mackenzie's *Man of Feeling*, and Charlotte Smith's *Emmeline*', and imitated 'the idioms and tropes of popular fiction';[14] she called Burney 'the very best of English novelists'; and she parodied *The Mysteries of Udolpho*, and its credulous readers, in *Northanger Abbey*. She certainly knew its quotation style.

Shakespeare's influence on Austen is sometimes thought to go beyond echoes and parallels. Some have suggested that it lies 'much deeper, in Austen's transformation of the Shakespearean soliloquy into her mode of free indirect discourse'.[15] Austen made famous a mode of narration in which the narrator, ostensibly continuing in third-person reporting, represents unannounced the characteristic thoughts and speech habits of the characters: 'the narrative seems to float away from the novelist and take on the properties of the character, who now seems to "own" the words'.[16] If some see the origins of free indirect speech in the Shakespearean character's confiding aside, others trace it to eighteenth-century epistolary novels, and to the fictional letters that are never 'an unproblematic, uncensored transcription of thoughts on paper as they occur', but represent the tension between the letter-writer's 'past, experiencing self' and 'present, narrating self'.[17]

More recently, Daniel Pollack-Pelzner has proposed an 'alternative history of free indirect discourse'.[18] Instead of regarding Shakespeare's soliloquies as a direct model, or endorsing the more 'novel-centric' account in which free indirect speech is born of 'Austen's celebrated fusion of Henry Fielding's external mode with Samuel Richardson's internal mode',[19] Pollack-Pelzner identifies an intermediary influence. He argues that the 'interiority' of Shakespearean soliloquy and novelistic free indirect discourse are not merely a 'loose analogy', but 'actually had a strong connective link' at this point, in the form of 'earlier nineteenth-century attempts to render Shakespeare in prose': the Lambs' *Tales from Shakespeare*, which Austen might perhaps have read to her nieces.[20] Pollack-Pelzner deftly shows how the Lambs' rendering of Shakespeare into a third-person narrative that captures at once the perspectives of narrator and character is a potential source for Austen.

Pollack-Pelzner's 'Free indirect Shakespeare' could, however, have an even older prose source. Austen's technical innovation of free indirect speech might build on the multi-perspectival opportunities afforded by eighteenth-century quotation by character, a practice with which Austen was indisputably familiar. It is not often explicitly noted that free indirect speech is a kind of quotation; nor that literary quotation by character is the most visible example of the tension between the 'narrating' and the 'experiencing' self in eighteenth-century fiction. Austen's narrator often temporarily assumes the language, and outlook, of a particular character: 'How was she to bear the change?—It was true that her friend was going only half a mile from them'.[21] Sometimes, that character seems to reach for words that do not quite ring true: 'he had *almost* told her that he loved her' ... 'she *must* be a little in love with him'.[22] When mid-century characters performed in borrowed dramatic quotation, they exaggerated the inevitable gap between their feelings and their self-presentation. Radcliffe's narratorial epigraphs revealed the thoughts, wishes and sometimes delusions of her characters. Austen, in turn, develops a mode of narration that ostensibly blends first- and third-person perspectives, yet frequently expresses, in overt acts of quotation – for one can usually point to the precise words or punctuation marks with which Austen signals a temporary shift of voice – the characteristic speech, unarticulated thoughts, and even self-deceptions, of her characters. She incorporates quotation into the texture of her fiction.

The quotations that constitute Austen's free indirect speech are, as in the eighteenth-century novel, central to characterisation. As in the earlier novel, though, what is most significant is not necessarily the act of quotation itself, but the judgement that surrounds it. The quoted words are mediated by the narrator, with implicit judgement; sometimes, they are mediated by other hearing characters. Above all, it is the reader that appraises the act of quotation, noticing when the narrator assumes the partial or limited perspective of a particular character, or sensing that a character tries on language that does not fit their situation. Their sympathetic judgement is a skill in which the eighteenth-century novel had explicitly trained its readers.

Austen's intertextual engagement with Shakespeare is inflected both by the particular uses that mid-century novelists made of his words, and by their mode of quotation. I shall argue that Austen exploits the theatricality that those novelists found in Shakespeare in *Sense and Sensibility* and *Mansfield Park*, where borrowed words allow her characters, just as they allowed Lovelace et al., to perform their feelings (sometimes in the name of feminine 'sensibility', and sometimes in the guise of theatre), and deceive their least discriminating spectators. Sometimes, the injudicious spectators are the performing characters themselves: in *Emma* and *Persuasion* in particular, Austen exploits the capacity of quotation for self-deception. In free indirect speech, Austen quotes the ill-fitting language with which characters such as Emma and Anne convince themselves of their rightness, and enjoys the irony of their limited perspective, as they claim for themselves the knowing perspective of a narrator. Austen engages with banal quotation, too, from the explicit jokes of her unpublished fiction ('With all my heart Sir—apply any verses you like to it—but I want to see something applied to your leg'[23]) to the witty colloquialisms of *Pride and Prejudice*, and the rote-learning of *Northanger Abbey*'s would-be heroine.[24] Like a mid-century novelist, through banal quotation, Austen highlights the perils of poor reading and judgement. She also draws attention to the limits of novelistic experience, showing that the emotional trajectories of her heroines have already been anticipated by the eighteenth-century novel, and by Shakespeare. Though his words are liberally 'spread abroad' and often tediously repeated, Shakespeare's authority is sure. The final part of the chapter shows the implications of Austen's quotations for Shakespeare and for novelists, whose authority is increasingly entwined.

Theatre and theatricality

Shakespeare's brief presence in *Sense and Sensibility* should hint to contemporary readers familiar with the conventions of eighteenth-century fiction that characters who profess deep feelings might be acting. It is the charming and 'uncommonly handsome' John Willoughby who brings Shakespeare into the novel: 'Queen Mab' is the name of the horse he promises to Marianne Dashwood; and *Hamlet* (the reader retrospectively learns) the play they read together. After Willoughby's abrupt departure, Mrs Dashwood, 'accidentally taking up a volume of Shakespeare', thoughtlessly 'exclaimed'

> 'We have never finished Hamlet, Marianne; our dear Willoughby went away before we could get through it. We will put it by, that when he comes again ..... But it may be months, perhaps, before *that* happens.'[25]

It is tempting to ascribe proleptic significance to Austen's choice of a tragedy for family reading, and to regard Marianne as a rejected Ophelia.[26] It is more revealing, however, to see Willoughby as the catalyst for a domestic performance: a dangerously theatrical figure who encourages the Dashwoods to deliver Shakespearean speeches that are beyond their experience.

Literature forms the basis of Marianne and Willoughby's unstable relationship. When, after their initial encounter, Willoughby first returns to the Dashwoods' cottage to 'make his personal inquiries' about Marianne's health (p. 55), the pair quickly fall to talking of books:

> her favourite authors were brought forward and dwelt upon with so rapturous a delight, that any young man of five and twenty must have been insensible indeed, not to become an immediate convert to the excellence of such works, however disregarded before. Their taste was strikingly alike. The same books, the same passages were idolized by each—or if any difference appeared, any objection arose, it lasted no longer than till the force of her arguments and the brightness of her eyes could be displayed. He acquiesced in all her decisions, caught all her enthusiasm; and long before his visit concluded, they conversed with the familiarity of a long-established acquaintance. (p. 56)

This would-be Emily and Valancourt enthuse about 'the same books, the same passages', and speed towards the 'familiarity of a long-established acquaintance' that their Gothic predecessors might have remembered with a pang after years of separation. Their literary preferences are not named: Elinor's subsequent comments suggest they are for late-eighteenth and early-nineteenth-century poetry, but most important is their apparent similarity.[27] Marianne takes the instant agreement of their tastes to be evidence of their compatibility. Austen's prose allows for the possibility that Willoughby genuinely admires Marianne's favourite books and quotations, but also strongly hints that, when she displays her preferences so readily, 'any young man of five-and-twenty must have been insensible indeed' not to grasp quickly the potential rewards of enthusiasm. The narrator's declaration that 'their taste was strikingly alike' could acknowledge Willoughby's sincerity, or capture in free indirect speech the words with which Marianne willingly convinces herself of Willoughby's suitability.

Is Willoughby's display of enthusiasm the harmless, eager-to-please performance of the ardent lover, desperate only to 'engage her to talk', or a calculated deception? As the pair grow closer, 'They read, they talked, they sang together; his musical talents were considerable; and he read with all the sensibility and spirit which Edward had unfortunately wanted' (p. 58). This contrast with Edward is a mark of quality in Marianne's eyes, but to the reader it would be a warning sign: is his 'sensibility' a mark of feeling or a sustained performance? Elinor, however, 'saw nothing to censure in him but a propensity . . . of saying too much what he thought on every occasion, without attention to persons or circumstances' and of 'hastily forming and giving his opinion of other people, in sacrificing general politeness to the enjoyment of undivided attention where his heart was engaged, and in slighting too easily the forms of worldly propriety' (p. 58): a thoughtless *lack* of calculation, which likens him to Marianne. Indeed, Elinor's final conversation with a regretful Willoughby complicates the binary terms of sincerity and deceit in which the reader has been encouraged to judge his character. She realises that a 'disposition naturally open and honest, and a feeling, affectionate temper' has been ruined by early independence: 'The world had made him extravagant and vain'; a 'real attachment' to Marianne has been sacrificed as a result (p. 375).

By contrast to Willoughby, Marianne seems uncomplicated and sincere, but her 'sensibility' enmeshes her, too, in performance. After Marianne's first, rapturous conversation with Willoughby, her older sister teases her:

> 'Well, Marianne,' said Elinor, as soon as he had left them, 'for *one* morning I think you have done pretty well. You have already ascertained Mr. Willoughby's opinion in almost every matter of importance. You know what he thinks of Cowper and Scott; you are certain of his estimating their beauties as he ought, and you have received every assurance of his admiring Pope no more than is proper. . .' (pp. 56–7)

Elinor satirises Marianne not only for establishing an intimacy in the space of 'one morning', but for giving such 'importance' to literary topics, and for measuring Willoughby's quality by his declared tastes: 'estimating . . . as he ought' and 'no more than is proper'. Marianne, who regards herself as full of higher feeling, anticipates her sister's real criticisms:

> '. . .I have been too much at my ease, too happy, too frank. I have erred against every common-place notion of decorum; I have been open and sincere where I ought to have been reserved, spiritless, dull, and deceitful:—had I talked only of the weather and the roads, and had I spoken only once in ten minutes, this reproach would have been spared.' (p. 57)

Marianne believes her 'open and sincere' discussion with Willoughby to be unfettered by the tedious conventions of polite conversation. As Elinor hints, however, it is not 'the weather and the roads', but her literary delights, that are 'common-place' topics of conversation. Marianne's excitement is founded on an exchange of predictable tastes, rejecting as a matter of course the Augustan decorum of Pope for the greater emotional expressiveness of later-eighteenth-century and Romantic literature.

She unwittingly replaces the formalities of polite conversation with another set of conventional phrases, and fits Willoughby to a template of aesthetic preferences. She is not condemned, however, to remain forever the banal quoter. Marianne finds happiness in marriage with Colonel Brandon by outgrowing her own commonplaces: 'she was born to discover the falsehood of her own opinions, and to counteract, by her conduct, her most favourite maxims' (p. 429).

If Marianne's feminine 'sensibility' entangles her in self-deception, *Mansfield Park* represents a more extreme – and more masculine – kind of performance, in which the theatre threatens to disrupt domestic order. The acting-obsessed John Yates, recently disappointed in his dreams of glory in the 'private theatricals at Ecclesford, the seat of the Right Hon. Lord Ravenshaw, in Cornwall' by the inconvenient death of 'one of the nearest connections of the family', visits Mansfield Park. In the absence of the controlling Sir Thomas Bertram, Yates incites the Bertram children to put on a play of their own.[28] The determined Tom Bertram directs the preparations, and the private, domestic enterprise rapidly grows to full, theatrical scale: the carpenter's design quickly requires 'an enlargement of plan and expense' and Mrs Norris and the maids make curtains from 'an enormous roll of green baize', all before a play has even been chosen (p. 153). All the family are gripped with anticipation of the performance of Elizabeth Inchbald's *Lovers' Vows*: all, that is, except Fanny Price, who is astonished, on reading the text, that such a play 'could be proposed and accepted in a private Theatre!' (p. 161), and who resists the project when no other figure of family authority will. When Edmund, initially scandalised by the plans, agrees to join in rather than have a stranger play opposite Mary Crawford, she is deeply betrayed: 'To be acting! After all his objections—objections so just and so public!' (p. 183).

Fanny's anti-theatrical anxieties are piqued not just by the moral dubiousness of the material, but by her awareness of the capacity of acting to deceive. She is 'quiet auditor' (p. 160) to the jealous struggle that casting induces in the people around her. Julia, steered by Henry Crawford into the minor, comic role of Amelia so that her sister Maria will play opposite him, realises with great, self-dramatising anguish that she has been tricked: 'The slight had been most determined. He was, perhaps, but at treacherous play with her' (p. 159). Mr Rushworth, also edged out of the male lead role, remarks with bitter envy that Crawford and Maria Bertram rehearse their opening scene 'needlessly often' (p. 193). The reader infers that tender feelings for Maria drive Crawford's competitive behaviour. Maria infers this too, certain that the hand that continues to hold hers when their scene is interrupted by Sir Thomas's return to Mansfield Park is a sign of genuine feeling, beyond theatrical performance. Expecting a marriage proposal, Maria is mortified when Crawford airily announces his departure from Mansfield Park after the cancellation of the play; ruefully, she marries Rushworth instead. As Fanny says of Crawford's skill, 'As far as she could judge, Mr. Crawford was considerably the best actor of all; he had more confidence than Edmund, more judgment than Tom, more talent and taste than Mr. Yates.—She did not like him as a man, but she must admit him to be the best actor, and on this point there were not many who differed from her' (pp. 193–94). Crawford's acting skills are in stark contrast with his moral qualities.

Shakespeare, in *Mansfield Park*, seems to represent the moral opposite of this performance. Wordsworth observed in the Preface to *Lyrical Ballads* that 'sickly and stupid German Tragedies' such as *Lovers' Vows* and other adaptations from August von Kotzebue were forcing 'invaluable works of our elder writers, I had almost said the works of Shakespear and Milton … into neglect'.[29] The perceived contrast between the unseemly German import and home-grown Shakespeare persists into modern criticism, and affects understanding of Shakespeare's role in *Mansfield Park*, where Kotzebue's text, via Elizabeth Inchbald, is the dominant intertextual reference. Where *Lovers' Vows* is selected and rehearsed by the Bertram children and their friends to the agitation of the whole household, Shakespeare is read aloud, quietly and privately, by Fanny to her aunt. It is not quite true to say, however, that Shakespeare 'escapes the taint of transgression that Mrs Inchbald's German-derived play produced'.[30] Even in this domestic setting, Austen's Shakespeare can still furnish a dangerous performance.

Shakespeare first appears explicitly in the novel when Edmund Bertram and Henry Crawford discover Fanny reading *Henry VIII* aloud to the somnolent Lady Bertram. Or rather, they discover that Fanny *has been* reading Shakespeare aloud, for she and Lady Bertram are now 'sitting as intently and silently at work as if there were nothing else to care for', with an air of 'deep tranquillity' (p. 389). Lady Bertram reveals that a mini-performance has just taken place:

> 'Fanny has been reading to me, and only put the book down upon hearing you coming.'—And sure enough there was a book on the table which had the air of being very recently closed, a volume of Shakespeare.—'She often reads to me out of those books; and she was in the middle of a very fine speech of that man's—What's his name, Fanny?—when we heard your footsteps.' (p. 389)

Fanny, as Lady Bertram explains, is a frequent reader of Shakespeare. Putting down the familiar book (perhaps a volume of George Steevens' 1773 edition [n.3, p. 714]) on hearing people approach the room is, however, a judiciously modest gesture. The arrival of male company would instantly transform her private, domestic reading into a public performance. This is a prospect Fanny abhors, as her earlier cry of 'I really cannot act', squirming to find that 'almost every eye in the room was upon her' when she refused the role of Cottager's Wife in the play, attests (p. 171). When Crawford and Edmund appear, she reapplies herself to silent, female 'work'.

Crawford has no such scruples about Shakespeare's unruly theatricality. He wilfully disrupts the industrious 'tranquility' of the room with an impromptu performance. He first 'took the volume' that had been deliberately closed and put down, then requests, '"Let me have the pleasure of finishing that speech to your ladyship"' (p. 389). By 'carefully', and intrusively, 'giving way to the inclination of the leaves' (p. 389), he prises open the book at almost exactly the place where they had just been reading. He then proceeds to dazzle the room, not just with a 'fine speech' from Wolsey, but with a series of virtuoso performances of each of the main characters:

> The King, the Queen, Buckingham, Wolsey, Cromwell, all were given in turn; for with the happiest knack, the happiest power of jumping and guessing, he could always light, at will, on the best scene, or the best speeches of each; and whether it were dignity or pride, or tenderness or remorse, or whatever were to be expressed, he could do it with equal beauty.—It was truly dramatic. (pp. 389–90)

The dexterity with which Crawford skips between roles is astonishing. Just as quoting Shakespeare pulled Laurence Sterne's characters into involuntary dramatic postures, Crawford instantly restores the theatricality of Fanny's readerly Shakespeare, and renders his hearers helpless. Fanny is irresistibly drawn by his acting skills: 'taste was too strong in her'; 'she was forced to listen; his reading was capital, and her pleasure in good reading extreme' (p. 389). She is the unwilling audience of Crawford's performance – or even, as 'forced to listen' suggests, the victim.

Crawford's Shakespeare quotations might instantly turn the room into a theatre, but they also put Fanny on stage. For most of this scene, the narratorial perspective resides in Edmund's gaze as he scrutinises Fanny's reactions for hopeful signs that Crawford might win her over. He and the reader see as if from outside that 'All her attention was for her work.

She *seemed* determined to be interested by nothing else' (italics added; p. 389). Charting the 'progress' of the effects of Crawford's acting, Edmund 'was amused and gratified by seeing how she gradually slackened in the needle-work'; and notices how her eyes

> were turned and fixed on Crawford, fixed on him for minutes, fixed on him in short till the attraction drew Crawford's upon her, and the book was closed, and the charm was broken. Then, she was shrinking again into herself, and blushing and working as hard as ever... (p. 390)

Edmund watches her retreat from absorption to embarrassment, and draws his own conclusions: 'Edmund saw it all, and saw Fanny so determined *not* to see it...' (p. 392). In his eyes, Fanny's 'blushing' body betrays her performance of indifference. Watching her, as the reader must for several pages, without the benefit of access to her thoughts, there is a genuine sense of danger that her judgement could be eroded by Crawford's performance.

Crawford's intrusive, theatrical quotations, and Fanny's determined, anti-histrionic resistance, might remind the reader of the dynamics of Lovelace and Clarissa's quotation-filled relationship. If *Mansfield Park* is 'a reimagining of *Clarissa*', then Henry Crawford should be regarded as a response to Richardson's Lovelace.[31] Critics have observed that both men are flamboyant, Protean, actors, but not that they share a facility with quotation in general, and Shakespeare's words in particular. In *Mansfield Park*, though, the familiar trope of seduction-by-quotation is played out in dumb-show. Crawford's quotations are described only indirectly in the third person, giving him, for all his virtuosity, as little direct agency with Shakespeare's words as Sarah Fielding's Countess of Dellwyn;[32] Fanny is almost mute in response.

Crawford, like Lovelace, 'skims the surface of literature', flitting between roles in love and frustration. It is in order to counter the impression of Crawford's flippancy that Edmund praises the man's deep knowledge of the play. Hoping 'to be expressing Fanny's secret feelings too', Edmund admires the performance, avowing that this must be a favourite play of Crawford's, who read it 'as if you knew it well' (p. 390). Crawford, however, professes unfamiliarity: 'I do not think I have had a volume of Shakespeare in my hand before, since I was fifteen' (p. 390). He might have seen the play, or know someone who has, but he is not sure.

Crawford's deliberately casual stance leads him to make one of the most famous statements of Shakespeare's ubiquity in the early nineteenth century:

> But Shakespeare one gets acquainted with without knowing how. It is part of an Englishman's constitution. His thoughts and beauties are so spread

> abroad that one touches them everywhere, one is intimate with him by instinct.—No man of any brain can open at a good part of one of his plays, without falling into the flow of his meaning immediately. (pp. 391–2)

Knowledge of Shakespeare, Crawford shruggingly suggests, is something one acquires by osmosis, without 'knowing how', thanks to the omnipresence of the playwright's 'thoughts and beauties' in culture. That Shakespeare is 'part of an Englishman's constitution' is a phrase that has subsequently been frequently quoted out of this manipulative context. Despite the patriotic image, Crawford does not really believe that everyone has this instinctive familiarity with Shakespeare. One can fall 'into the flow of his meaning immediately' provided one is a 'man of any brain'. In this staged conversation, Crawford modestly aligns himself with the unremarkable Englishman, only to hint at the uniqueness of his own capabilities.

Well might Crawford shrug about his dramatic knowledge, for, like Lovelace's, it may derive from a less exalted source. Critics have been generous about Crawford's skill with Shakespeare, suggesting, for example, that in skipping between roles and catching their characteristic emotions, Crawford performs the eighteenth-century critical and editorial practice of recognising the distinctive individuality of Shakespeare's characters; or that his Protean nature is a 'talent' rather than a 'liability'.[33] Crawford, however, like Lovelace, might be a dependent retailer of borrowed quotations. To be able to light with alacrity on the best, most enlightening speeches by characters in *Henry VIII* does not guarantee deep familiarity with the play. Just as Lovelace can be seen covertly to take most of his lines from Bysshe,[34] Crawford, Austen seems to hint, has a good memory for the extract culture of the eighteenth century. That he finds the 'best' speeches, and expresses each of them with 'equal beauty', recalls Dodd's *Beauties of Shakespear*, wherein are collected the 'finest passages of the finest poet'.[35] All of the editions of the *Beauties* published in Dodd's lifetime featured twenty-six quotations from *Henry VIII*, including abstract topics such as '*ANGER*', '*Obedience to Princes*' and '*The Vicissitudes of Life*',[36] but also more character-focussed speeches, under the following headings:

> *The Duke of* Buckingham*'s Prayer for the King*
> *Queen* Catherine*'s Speech to her Husband*
> *Queen* Catherine*'s Speech to Cardinal Wolsey*
> *King* Henry*'s Character of Queen* Catherine
> *Queen* Catherine *compared to a Lilly*
> *Cardinal* Wolsey*'s Speech to Cromwell*[37]

The speeches of 'The King, the Queen, Buckingham, Wolsey, Cromwell' (p. 389) that Crawford delivers with such alacrity are all arrayed in Dodd. The 'dignity or pride, or tenderness or remorse' (p. 390) he captures in his speeches can be found in these extracts, from Catherine's comment to Wolsey that 'your heart/ Is cramm'd with arrogancy, spleen, and pride', and Wolsey's own emotional arc: 'to-day he puts forth/ The tender leaves of hope'; 'my high-blown pride/ At length broke under me'.[38] Since Dodd organises his quotations by play, and preserves the act and scene structure in which these passages originally appeared, it would be a simple task for Crawford, even if encountering the full text of *Henry VIII* for the first time, to map these beauties on to the play with only minimal 'jumping and guessing' (p. 390).

Edmund's subsequent famous statement seems implicitly to deny Crawford's dependence on this fragmentary source:

> 'No doubt, one is familiar with Shakespeare in a degree,' said Edmund, 'from one's earliest years. His celebrated passages are quoted by every body; they are in half the books we open, and we all talk Shakespeare, use his similies, and describe with his descriptions; but this is totally distinct from giving his sense as you gave it. To know him in bits and scraps, is common enough, to know him pretty thoroughly, is perhaps, not uncommon, but to read him well aloud, is no everyday talent.' (p. 391)

Edward resists any suggestion that Crawford's knowledge of Shakespeare rests on well-known fragments that are 'quoted by everybody' and in 'half the books we open' ('books' must include the novel; the speech about Wolsey's fall appears in *Tristram Shandy*). Edmund's speech here has the flattering sense of 'we all talk Shakespeare, yes, his words are everywhere and we readily borrow them, but *you*, you are something else'. Critics are distracted by Edward's ennobling praise of Crawford. Harland suggests that to 'use his similies' and 'describe with his descriptions' is to have true knowledge of the dramatic text before it has become 'common to everyone' (p. 45). But these phrases evoke an anthology culture that extracts the best 'similes' and 'descriptions' for the inspiration of aspiring poets and the admiration of readers;[39] 'use' and 'describe with his descriptions' evoke dependent copying. In a rising triplet, Edmund compares knowing Shakespeare in 'bits and scraps', to knowing him 'pretty thoroughly', and to the truest marker of deep knowledge of the text: the ability 'to read him well aloud'. A fragmentary knowledge of Shakespeare is 'totally distinct' from 'giving his sense' by good reading.

In late eighteenth- and early nineteenth-century quotation culture, however, good reading is not the opposite of knowing 'bits and scraps'. Edmund and Crawford, 'the only talkers' in this scene, continue a two-man performance for Fanny's benefit, now loudly blaming the dearth of reading skills in professional life on early education (p. 392). Ironically, though, the skill of good reading was currently being taught through the medium of bits and scraps, in collections such as Vicesimus Knox's *Elegant Extracts: or Useful and Entertaining Pieces of Poetry* (as read by Robert Martin in *Emma*[40]) and William Enfield's *The Speaker*. Edmund, who, as a child, '*to be'd* and not *to be'd*' under his father's guidance, was implicitly trained by such works 'to speak well' (p. 149). Crawford, 'in his more raffish circumstances', may not have enjoyed such training,[41] but there would be little to stop him skimming such publications in adult life. Crawford's 'truly dramatic' performance could easily be derived from books designed to help young people become better readers. The word 'dramatic' recalls the title of 'Book the Third' in Knox's *Elegant Extracts*: namely 'DRAMATIC, CHIEFLY FROM SHAKESPEARE'.[42] This section is a direct copy of Dodd's *Beauties*: in the pages devoted to 'The Life of Henry VIII' (pp. 409–411), all the same headings and extracts appear, with the explicitly educational purpose of the '*Improvement of Youth in Speaking, Reading, Thinking, Composing; and in the Conduct of Life*'. Knox also preserves the play's sequence of quotations (if not, as in Dodd, their act and scene divisions), and so it would not be difficult to locate and perform these familiar extracts on first reading the play.

Perhaps because of his fragmentary sources, Crawford is better equipped to leap with agility between roles than to inhabit any single one of them. For Fanny, this is a moral flaw that is confirmed when Crawford says that he would quite like to be a priest, but only

> '... now and then, perhaps, once or twice in the spring, after being anxiously expected for half a dozen Sundays together; but not for a constancy; it would not do for a constancy.' (p. 395)

Here, 'constancy' means 'as a permanent arrangement',[43] but for Fanny it is freighted with the sense of faithfulness to another person,[44] and it finally elicits a response from her. She involuntarily shakes her head in reproach, but immediately regrets it as Crawford leaps to question her. In a rush of dialogue, she recalls his disgraceful treatment of Maria; and he declares that he will win Fanny not by 'protestations', nor because he is her equal in merit, but because he 'sees and worships your merit the strongest' (pp. 396–97). Flustered, Fanny is only 'delivered from a grievous imprisonment of body and mind' by 'The solemn procession ... of tea-board, urn, and cake-bearers', restoring domestic ritual to a theatrical encounter that nearly cost her her 'liberty' (p. 398).

Fanny's prized 'constancy' and Crawford's theatricality seem utterly opposed until one notes that 'constancy' is a quality of performance. Brutus urges in *Julius Caesar*,

> Let not our looks put on our purposes;
> But bear it as our Roman actors do,
> With untired spirits and formal constancy. (II. I. 224–6)

With 'constancy', the decorum of part is maintained and the actor does not slip out of character. In other words, to criticise Crawford's lack of 'constancy' is not straightforwardly 'anti-theatrical', for it refers to a sustained and sincere kind of acting which Crawford does not achieve in his fragmented performance – a kind of representation that resonates with the aspirations of prose fiction.

The most dangerous aspect of this domestic performance is not Crawford's Protean 'skill ... in the fragments',[45] but Edmund's undiscerning spectatorship. Edmund watches the final, awkward exchange between Crawford and Fanny from the corner of the room where he has retreated with a newspaper, 'earnestly trying to bury every sound of the business from himself in murmurs of his own, over the various advertisements...' (p. 395); he closes the chapter with the hope, despite Fanny's 'flush of vexation', that there has been 'some profit to the speaker' (p. 398). The reader, finally given a glimpse of Fanny's desperate desire to 'get away' (p. 398), knows this is not the case. In the subsequent chapter, Fanny patiently explains to Edmund that, 'There never were two people more dissimilar. We have not one taste in common. We should be miserable' (p. 403), but Edmund is undeterred from his project of uniting his cousin with the brother of Mary Crawford:

> 'You are mistaken, Fanny. The dissimilarity is not so strong. You are quite enough alike. You *have* tastes in common. You have moral and literary tastes in common. You have both warm hearts and benevolent feelings; and Fanny, who that heard him read, and saw you listen to Shakespeare the other night, will think you unfitted as companions? ...' (p. 403)

Unwilling to register Fanny's rejection, he relies on sight instead, taking the uneasy sensory combination of 'saw you listen' for his authority. Like a poor reader lampooned in Sarah Fielding's fiction, his understanding is tainted by his own perspective; he extracts what he wishes to see, and lacks the self-awareness to recognise his own role in his cousin's agony until over a hundred pages later:

> Scarcely had he done regretting Mary Crawford, and observing to Fanny how impossible it was that he should ever meet with such another woman,

> before it began to strike him whether a very different kind of woman might not do just as well—or a great deal better; whether Fanny herself were not growing as dear, as important to him in all her smiles, and all her ways, as Mary Crawford had ever been... (p. 543–4)

Edmund will finally learn that Fanny's virtues, unlike Mary's, need no 'self deception' (p. 545) to cherish.

It is an important narrative decision to have Edmund's self-deceiving perspective dominate the Shakespeare-reading scene. Edmund's thoughts open and close the chapter, and the entire encounter is anticipated by his misreading: 'In the evening a few circumstances occurred which he thought more promising' (p. 389). A diffident heroine, Fanny's reactions to other characters are not consistently at the forefront of Austen's prose, but in this chapter they are closed off from the reader for a sustained period. Her feelings are inferred by Edmund in the third person, and mediated through his hopeful gaze, emerging towards the end of the chapter just sufficiently to reassure the reader that Fanny has not been seduced. In this scene, Austen combines omniscient, third-person narration with Edmund's limited perspective. In doing so, she transforms the mid-century's dire warnings about poor reading and turns them into a new, compelling narrative technique. The reader is placed in the role of helpless spectator, fearing for Fanny's ability to resist Crawford's performance, and frustrated by Edmund's inability to see clearly what is happening before him. If Austen's free indirect speech quotes the habitual phrases that characters use to deceive themselves, it requires the judgement of the reader, trained by the fiction of the previous century to recognise an incongruous quotation, in order to achieve its fullest effect.

Free indirect deception

The capacity of Austen's third-person narration to expose characters' self-deception will be developed to an even greater extent in *Emma*, where Austen's free indirect speech finds its fullest form. Shakespeare quotation plays an important role in that deception. In a rare direct quotation, Emma invokes *A Midsummer Night's Dream* as she muses aloud to Harriet about her own matchmaking expertise:

> There does seem to be a something in the air of Hartfield which give love exactly the right direction, and sends it into the very channel where it ought to flow.
>
> The course of true love never did run smooth—
>
> A Hartfield edition of Shakespeare would have a long note on that passage.[46]

Emma quotes 'The course of true love never did run smooth' at a moment of expansive confidence. Her plan to unite Harriet with Mr Elton seems guaranteed to succeed, and her emphatic language exudes certainty: 'gives love *exactly* the right direction', 'sends it into the *very* channel' (italics added). Like many fictional heroines before her, Emma applies an extract from Shakespeare to a new emotional setting. But unlike predecessors such as Clarissa and Portia, who tested the accuracy of Shakespeare's observations and made them maxims, Emma audaciously challenges Shakespeare's truth: to her mind, the course of true love *does* run smooth. Reaching for the higher ground of literary editing, she suggests, with not a little self-satisfaction, that Hartfield life offers an exception to the rule. Emma's act of Shakespeare quotation is a mark of her 'enchanting hubris'.[47] How long, the reader might wonder with delight, until she is proved wrong?

As in studies of the mid-century novel, critics of Austen tend quickly to bypass the character-revealing nature of this act of quotation in order to see it as a sign of a deeper connection with Shakespeare. On the strength of this single quotation, Jocelyn Harris argues that *A Midsummer Night's Dream* underpins the whole novel: 'this comedy, even more thoroughly, lies behind *Emma*'.[48] Harris collects fleeting equivalences between Austen and Shakespeare's characters: Emma is Titania, who squabbles with Mr Knightley-as-Oberon over Harriet, the Indian boy; but also Hippolyta, who is chided by Knightley's Theseus for criticising Miss Bates and encouraged to value simpleness and 'modest duty'; and Hermia, who loves Knightley's Lysander, but is pushed towards marrying Frank/Demetrius by her friends the Westons. Jane Fairfax, by contrast, is like Helena in her height and her pallor.[49] For Harris, this cascade of free associations is a sign of the increasing boldness with which Austen reworks her reading. If Austen is a 'translator' of Shakespeare who involves his 'characters, events and ideas in a new and contemporary context', she is not a slavish imitator, but 'meets him in *Emma* as an equal'.[50]

Harris envisages a direct relationship between Austen and her admired Shakespeare. In early chapters Harris shows how Austen responds to ideas from Locke in *Northanger Abbey*, and reworks characters, plots and relationships from Richardson in *Sense and Sensibility* and *Pride and Prejudice.* She chooses the word 'layering', instead of 'intertexuality', 'influence' and 'source', to describe the accumulation of connections between Austen and earlier texts.[51] Yet when Harris turns to the influence of Shakespeare, it is not through the 'layers' of those more recent sources. Because Austen's connection with Richardson is not discussed after those earlier chapters, the possibility that her handling of Shakespeare might be inflected by that of Richardson and his peers remains unexplored. When Harris observes that Clarissa quotes *Hamlet*, and Marianne and Clementina both read it with their lovers, her conclusion is that they might all have the 'lovely archetypal madwoman' of Shakespeare's Ophelia in common.[52] Layered over Clarissa and Clementina's earlier uses of *Hamlet*, though, Marianne's engagement of *Hamlet* invites consideration of what it means for fictional women to dramatise their emotional situations through Shakespeare, especially as the practice becomes more established.

Emma borrows Shakespeare's words to dramatise her confident knowledge of human nature. Despite perhaps never having read the play (Knightley observes that she has been 'meaning to read more ever since she was twelve years old' [p. 37]), she styles herself its editor, and positions herself dispassionately above the dramatic plot, as if she controls the 'true love' narrative. She will, of course, discover that she herself is both entirely enmeshed in the romantic muddle ("Mr. Elton in love with me!—What an idea!" [p. 120]) and an excellent example of long-delayed true love, who achieves the 'perfect happiness' of 'union' with Mr Knightley in the final sentence of the novel (p. 528).

The irony of Emma's limited perspective disappears, however, in a like-for-like comparison with the plot of Shakespeare's *A Midsummer Night's Dream*. Having explained that Shakespeare's play is about the love-potion-induced matching and mismatching of lovers, Harris observes:

> How like this is to *Emma*. Harriet loves Robert Martin but is made to think she loves Mr Elton and then Mr Knightley. Emma, who thinks Harriet loves Frank Churchill, is equally deceived in thinking that Jane Fairfax, who does love Frank, loves Mr Dixon. Mr Elton rebuffs the doting Harriet and makes love to the reluctant Emma, while she herself, in love with Mr Knightley, persuades herself she could love Frank and flirts with him excessively at Box Hill. Mr Knightley, in love with Emma, appears to be falling in love first with Jane Fairfax and then with Harriet. In other words Jane Austen throws everything into confusion much as Shakespeare does, so that she may have the pleasure of sorting it all out again.[53]

This 'how like' comparison suggests that *Emma* and Shakespeare's play feature an equivalent quantity of deluded lovers, blinded by love potion. The only delusion described in this passage, however, is Emma's. Almost everybody else – whether Frank Churchill, Jane Fairfax, or Mr Elton – is clear in their affections, and behaves accordingly. It is Emma who misreads their intentions; Emma who is 'equally deceived in thinking'; Emma who 'persuades herself'. It is only to Emma that Mr Knightley 'appears to be' falling in love with other people; and only because of Emma's misguided beliefs that Harriet is 'made to think' she loves where she does not.

Readers are highly attuned to judging those moments when the language in which characters reason with themselves does not fit their situation, and the 'Shakespeare says ... and that shall be my comfort' formulation of eighteenth-century quotation prepares readers for Austen's narrator's self-conscious incorporation of others' words into her own discourse. Late in the novel, Austen captures in anguished free indirect speech Emma's simultaneous realisation of who she truly loves, and how she herself might have rendered that love impossible by her interference, long before she can articulate those feelings aloud:

> Mr. Knightley to be no longer coming there for his evening comfort!—No longer walking in at all hours, as if ever willing to change his own home for their's!—How was it to be endured? And if he were to be lost to them for Harriet's sake; if he were to be thought of hereafter, as finding in Harriet's society all he wanted; if Harriet were to be the chosen, the dearest, the friend, the wife to whom he looked for all the best blessings of existence; what could be increasing Emma's wretchedness but the reflection never far distant from her mind, that it had all been her own work? (p. 460)

Fraught with the exclamation marks and question marks of direct speech, Austen's third-person narrative performs Emma's emotional epiphany with the urgent anguish of first-person narrative. Emma's pronouncement about 'the course of true love' was declared outwardly; this realisation is internal. Emma once delivered Shakespeare's line high-handedly, as if it were a narratorial epigraph that would, as in Radcliffe's fiction, be disproved in the chapter that follows: that Mr Elton's verses are intended for Harriet is, Emma says knowingly, 'a certainty', 'a sort of prologue to the play, a motto to the chapter' (p. 79). She cannot, however, escape the implications of her quotation, and the line that once signalled her charming arrogance will ultimately represent her torment as she contemplates a life without Knightley. Shakespeare was right: true love never did run smooth, and she and Harriet are respectively united with Mr Knightley and Robert Martin only after many tribulations. Emma learns that she is not the detached editor of the Hartfield Shakespeare, nor even the omniscient narrator of her own story, but a player in its midst. Like a Clarissa or Portia, Emma confirms Shakespeare's emotional authority, but unwillingly.

The heroine of Austen's *Persuasion* also reverses the trope of the quoting character who aspires to emotional situations grander than her own; she uses quotation to minimise, rather than to exaggerate, her feelings. Anne

Elliott feels obliged to walk with the chatty Musgrove sisters, but when Captain Wentworth, to whom Anne was formerly engaged, joins the party, Anne determines 'not to be in the way of anybody', and to enjoy the walk on solitary terms:

> Her *pleasure* in the walk must arise from the exercise and the day, from the view of the last smiles of the year upon the tawny leaves and withered hedges, and from repeating to herself some few of the thousand poetical descriptions extant of autumn, that season of peculiar and inexhaustible influence on the mind of taste and tenderness, that season which has drawn from every poet, worthy of being read, some attempt at description, or some lines of feeling. She occupied her mind as much as possible in such like musings and quotations . . .[54]

Austen's narrator presents Anne's decision in free indirect discourse, but where the narrator might more frequently invoke the character's typical choice of words, they here show Anne's attempt to block out personal reflection with borrowed literary words. After the forced emphasis of '*pleasure*', she doggedly builds a wall of borrowed clichés about the beauty of autumn. The long sentence enacts Anne's determined behaviour of 'repeating to herself' lines from poetry and filling her mind with 'musings and quotations'. More grimly than any Gothic heroine found solace in Shakespeare, Anne focuses on landscape descriptions to ward off real feeling.

The exquisite pain of the scene, though, is in the failure of Anne's hastily erected poetic defences. The company's trite 'praises of the day, which were continually bursting forth' (pp. 90–91) lead Wentworth to observe that his sister and the Admiral were on a long drive, and to wonder where they would be thrown from the carriage today; and Louisa to reply that 'If I loved a man, as she loves the Admiral, I would be always with him, nothing should ever separate us, and I would rather be overturned by him, than driven safely by anybody else' (p. 91). Distracted by their flirtatious conversation, Anne could not 'immediately fall into a quotation' again (p. 91). Where mid-century female characters like Fielding's Cylinda and Countess of Dellwyn would rant in dramatic words too big for their trivial emotional situations, Anne uses poetry to minimise her feelings, but cannot maintain her concentration sufficiently to defend herself completely.

There is, even in Anne's silent plight, a hint of the self-dramatisation of those mid-century quoters:

> The sweet scenes of autumn were for a while put by—unless some tender sonnet, fraught with the apt analogy of the declining year, with declining

> happiness, and the images of youth and hope, and spring, all gone together, blessed her memory. (p. 91)

There is a hint of self-pitying exaggeration in the repetition of 'declining year' and 'declining happiness'; even more so in the triplet of 'youth, and hope, and spring, all gone together'. Derailed by the painful conversation, Anne can only reach for an autumnal quotation that amplifies her emotions, representing 'declining happiness' in the 'declining year', and the loss of 'youth, and hope' in the turning of the seasons. This helpless poetic self-dramatisation is comically, and sympathetically, at odds with Anne's typical restraint. This, after all, is a woman who, on hearing Captain Benfield repeat 'impassioned descriptions of hopeless agony', and, with 'tremulous feeling, the various lines which imaged a broken heart, or a mind destroyed by wretchedness', advised him to incorporate a 'larger allowance of prose in his daily study' in order better to manage his grief (p. 108). Anne's involuntary self-dramatisation lends poignancy to her best attempts at detachment, all the more acutely because it is provoked by such quotidian conversation.

'There is no enjoyment like reading'

Books and reading furnish the basic moral contrasts in *Persuasion*. Henrietta and Louisa Musgrove have taken from school 'all the usual stock of accomplishments, and were now, like thousands of other young ladies, living to be fashionable, happy, and merry' (p. 43). Anne regards them as 'some of the happiest creatures of her acquaintance', but retains a 'comfortable feeling of superiority' that lets her value her own 'more elegant and cultivated mind' over their 'enjoyments' (p. 43). *Pride and Prejudice* (1813) appears to establish a similar contrast between bookish seriousness and sociable frivolity. When Elizabeth and Jane return to Longbourn after Jane's illness has detained them both at the Bingleys',

> They found Mary, as usual, deep in the study of thorough bass and human nature; and had some new extracts to admire, and some new observations of thread-bare morality to listen to. Catherine and Lydia had information for them of a different sort. Much had been done, and much had been said in the regiment since the preceding Wednesday; several of the officers had dined lately with their uncle, a private had been flogged, and it had actually been hinted that Colonel Forster was going to be married.[55]

It is not immediately clear whether the reader should value more highly Mary's solemnly intoned quotations of 'thread-bare morality' or Catherine and Lydia's trivial gossip. These younger sisters are repeatedly contrasted ('"Oh! Mary," said she, "I wish you had gone with us, for we had such fun!"'; 'To this, Mary very gravely replied, "Far be it from me, my dear sister, to depreciate such pleasures. They would doubtless be congenial with the generality of female minds. But I confess they would have no charms for *me*. I should infinitely prefer a book."' [p. 246]). Mary's 'pedantic air and conceited manner', proceeding from her 'vanity' (p. 27), prevents her from securing moral superiority, and locks the siblings into perpetual, farcical opposition.

In a novel whose heroine laughingly marvels that Mr Darcy knows any 'accomplished women' at all if he expects them to have dedicated themselves to improving their minds through 'extensive reading' (p. 43), books and reading have a complicated status. Darcy is a serious reader (and a responsible preserver of ancestral libraries), but his ability to communicate with other living beings is severely impaired. Miss Bingley performs for his benefit a deep enthusiasm for books – 'I declare after all there is no enjoyment like reading!' (p. 60) – but is unable to stir him from the page, and throws aside her own book, 'only chosen because it was the second volume of his' (p. 60). Mr Collins is 'much better fitted for a walker than a reader' (p. 80), but is horrified when handed a circulating library novel, and offended when Lydia interrupts his reading of Fordyce's *Sermons* (p. 77). When Lydia elopes, Mary repeats doom-laden aphorisms that offer no comfort to her sisters. Mr Bennet distracts himself from his foolish choice of a wife with his fondness for 'the country and . . . books' (p. 262). Reading can represent an escape from social and civic responsibility, and the opposite of useful knowledge.

Elizabeth Bennet, an unaccomplished reader of books but an astute observer of human interaction, is skilful, if flippant, in her handling of commonplace phrases. Asked by Charlotte Lucas to sing and play in company, she protests, and finally agrees:

> 'Very well; if it must be so, it must.' And gravely glancing at Mr. Darcy, 'There is a fine old saying, which every body here is of course familiar with—"Keep your breath to cool your porridge,"—and I shall keep mine to swell my song.' (p. 27)

The glance Lizzy gives Mr Darcy deliberately hints that the 'fine old saying' will be a serious maxim and not an alliterated piece of colloquialism. She elegantly turns it into a gesture of unaffected modesty. It is in this same, colloquial form that Shakespeare appears to make a single, glancing appearance in the novel. Visiting Pemberley with the Gardiners, Lizzy is surprised by the sudden arrival of Mr Darcy. After he has gathered himself, he meets the visitors in the grounds, and walks with them. Mrs Gardiner, 'fatigued by the exercise of the morning' (p. 283), falls behind to lean on her husband's arm, and Lizzy and Darcy stride naturally ahead.

> He then asked her to walk into the house—but she declared herself not tired, and they stood together on the lawn. At such a time, much might have been said, and silence was very awkward. She wanted to talk, but there seemed an embargo on every subject. At last she recollected that she had been travelling, and they talked of Matlock and Dove Dale with great perseverance. Yet time and her aunt moved slowly—and her patience and her ideas were nearly worn out before the tete-a-tete was over. (p. 284)

Conversational topics fail her, and Lizzy waits impatiently for the Gardiners to put an end to this agony, but 'time and her aunt moved slowly', and she and Darcy are suspended in small-talk limbo. Critics have delighted in the unlikely but 'beautiful zeugma' of 'time and her aunt', admired Austen's 'ironic philosophy, or if you prefer, her irony about philosophy', and wondered whether it captures the voice of Lizzy, or Austen, or both.[56]

It is just possible that this phrase is not conjured from nowhere. 'Time and her aunt' might deliberately recall Macbeth's familiar last-ditch philosophy, 'Time and the hour run through the roughest day'. The similar vowel sounds of 'aunt' and 'hour' even resemble the negative and positive pair, 'aren't' and 'are'. This line was, of course, memorably misquoted in the mid-century novel: Richardson's Lovelace consoles himself with the observation that 'Patience and time run through the roughest day'. The mistake can be traced (in the first instance at least) to Bysshe's *Art of English Poetry*, where Lovelace very likely found it listed under PATIENCE,[57] and, before that, to William Davenant's Restoration adaptation of *Macbeth*; and Austen invokes the terms of Lovelace's misquotation, for, in the same sentence, Lizzy's 'patience and her ideas were nearly worn out' (p. 284). In free indirect discourse, the narrator captures Lizzy's facility with proverbial, quoted language. At the same time, Lizzy appears to acknowledge the line's reworking in eighteenth-century fiction as an embodiment of 'patience'.[58] For all the novelty of her emotional experience, both Lizzy and Austen are conscious of its having been anticipated by earlier fiction.

Nowhere is this sense of mediation more prominent than in Austen's late published, but first completed, novel. The sources of *Northanger Abbey* are habitually acknowledged: critics point to *The Mysteries of Udolpho* as the focus of *Northanger*'s pastiche, and see the comedy of social confusion in Burney's *Evelina* as an influence on at least part of the novel. When Catherine Morland extracts from prior authors the requisite emotional education to become a heroine, her sources include Shakespeare, and she nods sagely at the bountiful 'information' gleaned there (see pp. 119–20). Drakakis observes that 'by late 1817, drawing attention to Shakespearean quotations – an offshoot of the editions of Rowe (1709) and Pope (1725) – had grown into a more extended practice of anthologization. . . . It is to this process of anthologizing that Austen's narrator refers'.[59] Yet between editions and late-century anthologies is something of a chronological and generic gap. Despite the repeated presence of phrases such as 'trifles light as air' and 'patience on a monument' in their pages, and despite Catherine's affection for fiction, the novel is absent from this account of the influences on her quoting behaviour. It is entirely natural that Catherine, whose mother is an avid reader of *Sir Charles Grandison* (p. 35), and who will herself learn to become a devotee of Gothic fiction, should learn, when in training for a heroine, not just the detached phrases themselves, but, by skimming novels, the ways in which other heroines have consoled themselves with quotation since the middle of the previous century. Where Clarissa et al. will turn to these comforting words in times of trial, Catherine looks to them as she imagines her trials as a future heroine. Catherine's eagerly anticipated experiences are already belated, and commonplace.

A substantial number of Austen's major characters deal in banal quotation and conversation: Marianne requires Willoughby to conform to a pre-determined standard of literary admiration; Crawford, like Lovelace, probably finds his Shakespeare quotations in an elocution manual; Emma challenges an increasingly proverbial line of Shakespeare's (and loses); Anne inwardly chants as many poetic clichés as she can to ward off the sounds of her former fiancé's flirtation with another woman; Elizabeth toys ruefully with a free-floating Shakespearean phrase and its eighteenth-century misquotation; and Catherine solemnly imbibes some of the lines of Shakespeare most often quoted in fiction. These fleeting appearances of banal fragments of Shakespeare are tools for ironic characterisation – and all the more so because, by the early nineteenth century, characters are engaging with an increasingly well-worn fictional practice of quotation, and seeing their experiences anticipated by both the novel and Shakespeare.

How do Austen and her characters go beyond it? Her burlesque of eighteenth-century fiction in her juvenilia, while 'entertaining', was ultimately 'limited and limiting'; a 'training ground rather than a lasting professional mode'.[60] Austen's technique in her published fiction is not simply to parody the act of quotation, but to inspect the phenomenon from the perspectives of both narrator and character. When Henry Crawford lights on all the 'best' speeches in *Henry VIII*, but not one is quoted directly in the text, is this judgement uttered with narratorial authority, or through the bias of Edmund's partial gaze? When the narrator only paraphrases Anne Elliot's barrage of autumn quotations, does it make Anne's desperate attempt to block out the sounds of flirtation seem futile, or excessive? When Catherine Morland 'gained a great store of information' (p. 8) from Shakespeare, her innocent enthusiasm clashes with the extreme familiarity of the quoted lines to both narrator and reader at the beginning of the nineteenth century. For all the potential banality of quotation, and, by extension, of novelistic experience, Austen fashions distinctive new characters through self-conscious reflection on the practice.

What are the implications for Shakespeare? The playwright's dramatic work has, by now, been thoroughly synthesised with the most admirable qualities of prose fiction, namely penetrating insight into human nature. His theatricality persists, but its potential to deceive has been packaged in new warning forms. His well-worn phrases remind even the most impassioned heroine that her feelings have all been felt before; and the wryly accepted truism of 'the course of true love', and the trope of 'patience on a monument', attest to his accepted emotional authority, now all the more assured because the references are so glancing. Critics have debated whether the polyvocal nature of Jane Austen's novels means that her narrator has only 'partial knowledge' of characters and events, or retains authority in a 'consistent discursive context within which shifts into figural thought or speech register as imitations'.[61] Shakespeare's words have been quoted and admired both as the omniscient wisdom of 'Shakespeare', and as an accurate representation of what his characters – and numerous novelistic ones – would say. He sounds, in other words, like Austen's narrator: at once omniscient, and capable of inhabiting the outlooks of numerous individuals. The conclusions to this book consider the long-term results of the mutual promotion of Shakespeare and fiction, which ultimately grants 'Shakespeare' the knowing authority of a narrator, or novelist, and novelists a 'Shakespearean' vision.

CHAPTER 8

Conclusions

For historians of fiction, the middle of the nineteenth century is 'arguably the great age of the novel'.[1] For historians of literary reception, the middle of the nineteenth century is arguably the great age of Shakespeare, by this point 'a living presence . . . ever available and resonating through English-language speech and writing', and a figure of 'massive cultural authority'.[2] The cultural centrality of both Shakespeare and the novel in the nineteenth century – a coincidence rarely remarked upon – is, as I have argued in this book, the direct result of their mutual cooperation in the eighteenth. By having their characters quote Shakespeare directly, overtly and admiringly in all kinds of situation, eighteenth-century novelists ascribed to the author figure of 'Shakespeare' a new emotional and moral authority. They prized in Shakespeare's dramatic language a novelistic concern with the mimetic representation of life; and trained readers to distinguish between those who admired Shakespeare in the way he deserved, and those who merely joined in the banal chorus of injudicious quotation and praise. In so doing, novelists positioned their own genre as at once emotionally authoritative, insightful and true-to-nature; a trusted cultural guide. Shakespeare and the novel legitimated each other in the eighteenth century, and the effects of that mutuality persist to this day.

Nineteenth-century novelists would benefit from the established status of both Shakespeare and prose fiction. In the decades that followed, authors from Charles Dickens to Charlotte Brontë, and from George Eliot to Thomas Hardy, would quote overtly from Shakespeare's plays. These quotations are voiced by narrators and by characters; they appear as chapter mottoes, and are thoroughly incorporated into the text. In *The Antiquary* (1816), nosy Mrs Shortcake holds a sealed letter in her hand, 'wishing, doubtless, that 'the too, too solid wax would melt and dissolve itself'.[3] In *Jane Eyre* (1847), Mr Rochester describes how he was afflicted by 'the green snake of jealousy', and remarks that it is 'passing strange' that Jane should listen 'quietly' to 'stories of his opera-mistresses'.[4] 'Take him for all in all, we ne'er shall—in short, make the acquaintance, probably, of anybody else possessing, at his time of life, the same legs for gaiters, and able to read the same description of print, without spectacles', says Mr Micawber, of his father-in-law, in *David Copperfield* (1850); 'You have no idea what obstinate hair mine is, Copperfield. I am quite a fretful porcupine', says Traddles, in the same novel.[5] The epigraph, 'They'll take suggestion as a cat laps milk', attributed to '—SHAKESPEARE: *Tempest.*' heads Chapter XXII of *Middlemarch* (1871–2).[6] Their reading in earlier fiction no doubt informed the way they included Shakespeare in their texts: the chaotic performance of *Hamlet* that Pip attends in Dickens' *Great Expectations* (1861) where, in answer to Mr Wopsle's question of whether ''twas nobler in the mind to suffer, some roared yes, and some no, and some inclining to both opinions said "toss up for it"',[7] is reminiscent of Tom Jones and Partridge's earlier visit. Yet if nineteenth-century authors' relationship with Shakespeare is partially mediated by earlier fiction, those intermediary texts also inform more broadly the ways in which they write.

First, as suggested in the chapters on Ann Radcliffe and Jane Austen, eighteenth-century quotation practices lastingly influence the narrative techniques of later fiction. Adrian Poole notes that nineteenth-century novelists have at their disposal a number of narrative devices that distinguish fiction from drama. The Victorian period's 'great two-timing first-person narrators', such as Jane Eyre, Lucy Snowe, David Copperfield and Pip, are characters able to live 'both on stage in the thick of it' and 'safely out of it, after the show is over', looking back on the events of their lives[8] – a mode of narration not available to dramatic characters. Alternatively, though,

> Third-person narration can relieve its fictional characters of the burden of reflection, but the formal difference between narrator and character creates new kinds of rivalry, co-operation, and treachery. This is where for all the relations between dramas and novels, their difference is critical.[9]

For Poole, the capacity of third-person narration to complicate the voices of character and narrator is what ultimately distinguishes the novel from the stage. For readers of the eighteenth-century novel, however, accustomed to scrutinising self-dramatising acts of quotation by character, and, in the latter part of the century, epigraphs that hover somewhere between the voice of character and narrator, this distinction between the stage and the book does not hold. Dramatic quotations are a bridge between these worlds and these voices, and the narrative developments of the nineteenth century, including two-timing and unreliable narrators, build upon this foundation.

Second, nineteenth-century novelists can now claim for themselves, rather than for their characters, some of the emotional and moral authority ascribed to Shakespeare in the eighteenth century. All of the authors mentioned above, and more, are called, or compared to, 'Shakespeare' (Eliot, notably, to Shakespeare's disadvantage), yet, as Poole observes:

> The interest and difficulty in thinking of nineteenth-century novelists as 'Shakespearean' focuses on the possibilities of a voice endowed with more patent authority than could ever be the case in a Shakespeare play. No wonder then that it was precisely the absence of Shakespeare from his own dramas that acted as such a spur, opportunity and incentive to his nineteenth-century heirs[10]

I would argue, however, that nineteenth-century novelists do not necessarily need to fill the 'absence' of Shakespeare from his own drama, since, by selective quotation, admiration and embodiment, and the repeated attribution 'as Shakespeare says', 'Shakespeare' himself had become in the eighteenth-century novel a 'voice endowed with more patent authority than could ever be the case in a Shakespeare play'. By frequent quotation, the eighteenth-century novel constructed a compelling Shakespearean voice and perspective that future writers could inhabit. Poole's book labels Scott, Dickens, Eliot and Hardy *Great Shakespeareans*, and it is unsurprising that the first use of the word 'Shakespearean', which became popular in the nineteenth century, is attributed by the *OED* to Henry Fielding, in the *Journal of a Voyage to Lisbon* (1755). It is not so much the voice of the playwright, who is, as Poole rightly observes, absent from his plays, but the voice of quoted 'Shakespeare', visible in the eighteenth-century novel, that these nineteenth-century authors would be able to emulate.

But if eighteenth-century authors gave Shakespeare the authoritative voice of a novelist, they did not fully novelise his plays. Perhaps the most significant legacy of the eighteenth-century novelists is that, by quotation, they elevated 'Shakespeare' above the genres of drama and prose fiction, and beyond the physical constraints of both book and stage, to the realm of the imagination. They did so by repeatedly asking readers to apply his words to abstract emotional situations, to picture fictional characters gesturing in his speeches, and to see him as floating somewhere above the nation's most banal attempts to praise him. Shakespeare might be 'my comfort' to numerous characters in eighteenth-century fiction, but he becomes so lofty as to be truly appreciated only by the most judicious novel reader.

Notes

Chapter 1

1 Charles Careless, *The Amours and Adventures of Charles Careless*, 2 vols. (London, 1764), ii. 109.
2 Ibid., ii. 108–9.
3 Robert Gale Noyes, *The Thespian Mirror: Shakespeare in the Eighteenth-Century Novel* (Providence, RI: Brown University, 1953), p. 31.
4 Ibid., pp. iii–iv.
5 J. Paul Hunter, 'The Novel and Social/Cultural History', in *The Cambridge Companion to the Eighteenth-Century Novel*, ed. John J. Richetti (Cambridge University Press, 1996), pp. 9–40 (p. 30).
6 Ibid.
7 Noyes, *Thespian Mirror*, pp. 13, 191.
8 Ibid., p. 14.
9 Ibid., p. 15.
10 See Chapter 2 for further discussion of the multiple ways of accessing Shakespeare in the eighteenth century, and, within this cultural landscape, the unique contribution of the novel to Shakespeare's status.
11 Patricia Meyer Spacks, *Novel Beginnings: Experiments in Eighteenth-Century Fiction* (New Haven, CT: Yale University Press, 2006), p. 8.
12 Thomas Keymer and Peter Sabor, Pamela *in the Marketplace: Literary Controversy and Print Culture in Eighteenth-Century Britain and Ireland* (Cambridge University Press, 2005), p. 5.
13 Westminster Abbey, 'History', www.westminster-abbey.org/our-history/people/william-shakespeare.
14 Michael Dobson, *The Making of the National Poet: Shakespeare, Adaptation, and Authorship, 1660–1769* (Oxford: Clarendon Press, 1992); Jonathan Bate, *The Genius of Shakespeare* (London: Picador, 1997); Jean I. Marsden, *The Re-imagined Text: Shakespeare, Adaptation, and Eighteenth-Century Literary Theory* (Lexington: The University Press of Kentucky, 1995).
15 William Shakespeare, *The Plays of William Shakespeare, in Eight Volumes, with the Corrections and Illustrations of Various Commentators; to Which Are Added Notes by Sam. Johnson* (London, 1765), i. Preface, unpaginated.

16 Peter Sabor and Paul Yachnin, 'Introduction', in *Shakespeare and the Eighteenth Century*, ed. Peter Sabor and Paul Yachnin (Aldershot: Ashgate, 2008), pp. 1–9 (p. 5). Marjorie Garber similarly bases *Shakespeare and Modern Culture* on the premise that 'Shakespeare makes modern culture and modern culture makes Shakespeare' (New York: Pantheon Books, 2008), p. xiii.
17 Sabor and Yachnin, eds., *Shakespeare and the Eighteenth Century*, back cover.
18 Garber, *Shakespeare and Modern Culture*, p. xiii.
19 'It is in fact a comparatively short step for Shakespeare's plays, once certified as fit for decent home consumption, to be thus assimilated to the tradition of didactic domestic fiction', *Making of the National Poet*, p. 211.
20 See Clifford Siskin, *The Work of Writing: Literature and Social Change in Britain, 1700–1830* (Baltimore: Johns Hopkins University Press, 1998), p. 183.
21 Janet Todd, *The Sign of Angellica: Women, Writing and Fiction, 1660–1800* (London: Virago Press, 1989), p. 2.
22 Robert D. Hume, *Reconstructing Contexts: The Aims and Principles of Archaeo-Historicism* (Oxford: Clarendon Press, 1999), p. 50.
23 Homer Obed Brown, *Institutions of the English Novel: From Defoe to Scott* (Philadelphia, PA: University of Pennsylvania Press, 1997), p. 177.
24 Dobson, *Making of the National Poet*, p. 230.
25 R. W. Babcock, *The Genesis of Shakespeare Idolatry 1766–1799: A Study in English Criticism of the Late Eighteenth Century* (Chapel Hill: University of North Carolina Press, 1931), title; Bate, *Genius of Shakespeare*, p. 169; Babcock, *Genesis of Shakespeare Idolatry*, p. 40.
26 Bate, *Genius of Shakespeare*, p. 174; Terence Hawkes, 'Bardbiz', in *Meaning by Shakespeare* (London and New York: Routledge, 1992), pp. 141–53 (p. 152); Dobson, *Making of the National Poet*, p. 223.
27 Bate, *Genius of Shakespeare*, p. 166; two phrases from Dobson, *Making of the National Poet*, p. 223; Bate, *Genius of Shakespeare*, p. 166.
28 Charlotte Lennox, *Shakespear Illustrated: or the Novels and Histories, on Which the Plays of Shakespear Are Founded, Collected and Translated from the Original Authors. With Critical Remarks*, 2 vols. (London, 1753), i. 190.
29 Jonathan Brody Kramnick, *Making the English Canon: Print-Capitalism and the Cultural Past, 1700–1770* (Cambridge University Press, 1998), p. 118.
30 Lennox, *Shakespear Illustrated*, i. xii, viii.
31 Samuel Richardson, *Clarissa, or The History of a Young Lady*, ed. Angus Ross (London: Penguin, 1985), p. 709. While most references in this book to the first edition of *Clarissa* will be to Ross, the most authoritative modern edition in existence at the time of writing, quotations will be presented in their original italics (as in Samuel Richardson, *Clarissa. Or the History of a Young Lady*, 7 vols. (London, 1748), iv. 265). Ross proposes that italicised quotations 'create an emphasis for the modern reader which is not usually required' ('A Note on the Text', p. 32), but by turning them to roman he makes them less visually distinct from the surrounding text, an important aspect of their presentation.
32 Henry Fielding, *The History of Tom Jones, a Foundling*, ed. Martin C. Battestin and Fredson Bowers, 2 vols. (Oxford: Clarendon Press, 1974), i. 271.

33 Sarah Fielding and Jane Collier, *The Cry: A New Dramatic Fable*, 3 vols. (London, 1754), ii. 115.
34 Laurence Sterne, *The Life and Opinions of Tristram Shandy: The Text* and *Notes*, ed. Melvyn New and Joan New, 3 vols. (Gainsville: University Presses of Florida, 1978–84), i. 36.
35 Nancy A. Mace, *Henry Fielding's Novels and the Classical Tradition* (Newark: University of Delaware Press; and London: Associated University Presses, 1996), p. 101.
36 See, for example, Julie Maxwell, 'How the Renaissance (Mis)Used Sources: The Art of Misquotation', in *How to Do Things with Shakespeare: New Approaches, New Essays*, ed. Laurie Maguire (Malden, MA: Blackwell Publishing, 2008), pp. 54–76. Katrin Ettenhuber examines early modern citational practices in *Donne's Augustine: Renaissance Cultures of Interpretation* (Oxford University Press, 2012).
37 Harold Bloom, *The Anxiety of Influence: A Theory of Poetry* (New York: Oxford University Press, 1973), p. 5.
38 Richardson, *Clarissa*, ed. Ross, p. 1148 (following the italic presentation of Richardson, *Clarissa*, vi. 290).
39 Valerie Grosvenor Myer, '"Well Read in Shakespeare"', in *Samuel Richardson: Passion and Prudence*, ed. Valerie Grosvenor Myer (London: Vision, 1986), pp. 126–32 (pp. 127–30).
40 John Carroll, 'Richardson at Work: Revisions, Allusions, and Quotations in *Clarissa*', in *Studies in the Eighteenth Century II*, ed. R. F. Brissenden (Canberra: Australian National University Press, 1973), pp. 53–71 (p. 70).
41 Berit R. Lindboe, '"O *Shakespear*, Had I thy Pen!": Fielding's Use of Shakespeare in *Tom Jones*', *Studies in the Novel* 14.4 (1982): 303–14 (303).
42 Jonathan Bate, *Shakespeare and the English Romantic Imagination* (Oxford: Clarendon Press, 1986), p. 30.
43 Herman Meyer, *The Poetics of Quotation in the European Novel*, trans. Theodore and Yetta Ziolkowski (Princeton University Press, 1968), pp. 49, 69. Excellent recent studies of Shakespearean intertextuality prioritise adaptation, appropriation and allusion over direct quotation, e.g. Julie Sanders, *Adaptation and Appropriation* (Abingdon: Routledge, 2006), *Novel Shakespeares: Twentieth-Century Women Novelists and Appropriation* (Manchester University Press, 2001); Christy Desmet and Robert Sawyer, eds., *Shakespeare and Appropriation* (London: Routledge, 1999).
44 Arthur H. Cash, *Laurence Sterne: The Early and Middle Years* (London: Methuen & Co Ltd, 1975), p. 200.
45 Kenneth Monkman, 'Sterne, Hamlet, and Yorick: Some New Material', in *The Winged Skull: Papers from the Laurence Sterne Bicentenary Conference*, ed. Arthur H. Cash and John M. Stedmond (London: Methuen & Co Ltd., 1971), pp. 112–23 (p. 113).
46 Julia Kristeva, 'Word, Dialogue and Novel' in *Desire in Language: A Semiotic Approach to Literature and Art*, ed. Leon S. Roudiez, trans. Thomas Gora, Alice Jardine and Leon S. Roudiez (New York: Columbia University Press, 1980), pp. 64–91 (p. 66).

47 Graham Allen, *Intertextuality* (London: Routledge, 2000), p. 36.
48 Roland Barthes, 'Theory of the Text', in *Untying the Text: A Post-Structuralist Reader*, ed. R. Young (Boston, Mass.: Routledge and Kegan Paul, 1981), pp. 59, 39.
49 Stefan Morawski, 'The Basic Functions of Quotation', in *Sign, Language, Culture*, ed. A. J. Greimas and R. Jakobson (The Hague and Paris: Mouton, 1970), pp. 690–705 (p. 691).
50 Lindboe, '"O *Shakespear*"', 305.
51 Sterne, *Tristram Shandy*, ed. New and New, iii. 28.
52 Richardson, *Clarissa*, ed. Ross, p. 532.
53 Fielding and Collier, *Cry*, iii. 302.
54 Richardson, *Clarissa*, ed. Ross, p. 1184.
55 Henry Fielding, *Amelia*, ed. Martin C. Battestin (Oxford: Clarendon Press, 1983), p. 380.
56 Fielding and Collier, *Cry*, iii. 189.
57 Samuel Richardson, *Clarissa. Or, the History of a Young Lady*, 2nd edn, 7 vols. (London, 1749), iii. 49; Sarah Fielding, *The History of the Countess of Dellwyn*, 2 vols. (London, 1759), i. 73.
58 See Deidre Shauna Lynch, *The Economy of Character: Novels, Market Culture, and the Business of Meaning* (Chicago: University of Chicago Press, 1998), p. 6; and Dror Wahrman, *The Making of the Modern Self: Identity and Culture in Eighteenth-Century England* (New Haven: Yale University Press, 2004), p. 164.
59 Fielding, *Tom Jones*, ed. Battestin and Bowers, ii. 857.
60 Fielding, *Countess of Dellwyn*, i. vii.
61 Sterne, *Tristram Shandy*, ed. New and New, i. 176, 225; Laurence Sterne, *A Sentimental Journey through France and Italy and Continuation of the Bramine's Journal: The Text and Notes*, ed. Melvyn New and W. G. Day (Gainesville: University Press of Florida, 2002), p. 65.
62 Sarah Fielding, *The History of Ophelia*, ed. Peter Sabor (Peterborough, Ont.: Broadview, 2004), pp. 184–5.
63 Samuel Richardson, *The History of Sir Charles Grandison*, ed. Jocelyn Harris, 3 vols. (London: Oxford University Press, 1972), i. 110. Austen might invoke these earlier quotations when Lady Susan remarks indignantly of her daughter that 'I had not a notion of her being such a little Devil before;—she seemed to have all the Vernon Milkiness'. Jane Austen, *Later Manuscripts*, ed. Janet Todd and Linda Bree (Cambridge University Press, 2008), p. 29.
64 Fielding and Collier, *Cry*, iii. 111.
65 Meyer, *Poetics of Quotation*, p. 18.
66 See Kate Rumbold, 'The Stratford Jubilee' in *Shakespeare in the Eighteenth Century*, ed. Fiona Ritchie and Peter Sabor (Cambridge University Press, 2012), pp. 254–76; and Dobson, *Making of the National Poet*, pp. 214–22.
67 Ann Radcliffe, *The Mysteries of Udolpho*, ed. Bonamy Dobrée (Oxford University Press, 1998), p. 102.
68 Jane Austen, *Emma*, ed. Richard Cronin and Dorothy McMillan (Cambridge University Press, 2005), p. 80.
69 Jane Austen, *Mansfield Park*, ed. John Wiltshire (Cambridge University Press, 2005), p. 391.

70 Fielding, *Countess of Dellwyn,* ii. 117–18.
71 Alan Dugald McKillop, *The Early Masters of English Fiction* (Laurence, Kansas: University of Kansas Press, 1956), p. 217.
72 Anon., *Cleanthes and Semanthe. A Dramatic History. By the Author of Leonora,* 2 vols. (London, 1764), i. 187.
73 Henry Brooke, *The Fool of Quality, or, The History of Henry Earl of Moreland,* 2nd edn, 4 vols. (London, 1767), i. 116.
74 Anon., *The Batchelor: or Speculations of Jeoffry Wagstaffe, Esq.*, 3 vols. (Dublin, 1773), iii. 159.
75 See Daniel Pollack-Pelzner, 'Dickens and Shakespeare's Household Words', *ELH* 78.3 (2011): 533–56.

Chapter 2

1 Benjamin Stillingfleet, *An Essay on Conversation* (London, 1737), p. 10.
2 Margaret Anne Doody, *The True Story of the Novel* (London: Fontana Press, 1998), pp. 144, 1.
3 Richardson, *Sir Charles Grandison*, ed. Harris, ii. 191.
4 John Cleland, *Memoirs of a Woman of Pleasure,* ed. Peter Sabor (Oxford University Press, 1985), p. 164.
5 Aphra Behn, *Love-Letters between a Noble-Man and his Sister, in Three Parts* (London, 1684), i. 91–2.
6 J. Paul Hunter, *The Reluctant Pilgrim: Defoe's Emblematic Method and the Quest for Form in* Robinson Crusoe (Baltimore: Johns Hopkins University Press, 1966), p. 159.
7 Daniel Defoe, *Moll Flanders*, ed. David Blewett (Harmondsworth: Penguin, 1989), p. 118.
8 E.g. 'I often heard the Sorrel Nag (who always loved me) crying out *Hnuy illa nyha maiah Yahoo,* Take Care of thy self, gentle Yahoo'. Jonathan Swift, *Gulliver's Travels*, ed. David Womersley (Cambridge University Press, 2012), p. 426.
9 Ibid., p. 437.
10 Gérard Genette, *Paratexts: Thresholds of Interpretation*, trans. by Jane E. Lewin (Cambridge University Press, 1997), pp. 146–7, 159.
11 Bloom, *Anxiety of Influence*, p. 10.
12 Richardson, *Clarissa,* ed. Ross, p. 1217; Sterne, *Tristram Shandy*, ed. New and New, i. 423.
13 Fielding and Collier, *Cry*, ii. 85–6.
14 Janine Barchas, *Graphic Design, Print Culture, and the Eighteenth-Century Novel* (Cambridge University Press, 2003), p. 152.
15 James McLaverty, *Pope, Print and Meaning* (Oxford University Press, 2001), p. 9.
16 Sanders, *Novel Shakespeares*, p. 4.
17 Kramnick, *Making the English Canon*, p. 2.
18 Edward Bysshe, *The Art of English Poetry: Containing, I. Rules for Making Verses. II. A Dictionary of Rhymes. III. A Collection of the Most Natural, Agreeable, and Noble Thoughts, viz. Allusions, Similes, Descriptions, and*

Characters, of Persons and Things; that Are to Be Found in the Best English Poets (London, 1702), Preface.

19 Fielding, *Tom Jones*, ed. Battestin and Bowers, ii. 541.

20 Henry Fielding, *Miscellanies*, Vol. I, ed. Henry Knight Miller, 3 vols. (Oxford: Clarendon Press, 1972–97), i. 144.

21 *Lord Chesterfield's Letters*, ed. David Roberts (Oxford University Press, 1992), p. 252–3 (Letter 73: To his Son, London, March 2, O.S., 1752).

22 Stillingfleet, *Essay on Conversation*, p. 10.

23 For discussion of the succession of editions, see, for example, Andrew Murphy, *Shakespeare in Print: A History and Chronology of Shakespeare Publishing* (Cambridge University Press, 2003); and Colin Franklin, *Shakespeare Domesticated: The Eighteenth-Century Editions* (Aldershot: Scolar Press, 1991).

24 Michael Bristol, *Big-Time Shakespeare* (London and New York: Routledge, 1996), p. 77.

25 Frederick G. Ribble and Anne G. Ribble, *Fielding's Library: An Annotated Catalogue* (Charlottesville: The Bibliographical Society of the University of Virginia, 1996), p. xvii.

26 Martin C. Battestin (with Ruthe R. Battestin) suspects that this, along with the epilogue Fielding contributed to Theobald's *Orestes* in 1731, was a move designed to court Robert Walpole's favour, *Henry Fielding: A Life* (London and New York: Routledge, 1989), p. 110.

27 Franklin, *Shakespeare Domesticated*, p. 1.

28 Robert D. Hume, 'Before the Bard: "Shakespeare" in Early Eighteenth-Century London', *ELH* 64.1 (1997): 41–75 (51).

29 Don-John Dugas and Robert D. Hume, 'The Dissemination of Shakespeare's Plays Circa 1714', *Studies in Bibliography* 56 (2003–2004): 261–79 (278).

30 William St Clair, *The Reading Nation in the Romantic Period* (Cambridge University Press, 2004), pp. 154–6.

31 William Shakespeare, *The Works of Shakespear. In Six Volumes. Collated and Corrected by the Former Editions by Mr. Pope* (London, 1725), i. xxiii.

32 The *Gentleman's Magazine* lists a price of 6s. in 1752, though cheaper editions appear to be available later in the century. 'Books publish'd in March 1752', Sylvanus Urban, Gent., *The Gentleman's Magazine, and Historical Chronicle, Vol. XXII, for the Year 1752* (London, 1752), p. 147. The *Monthly Review* for April 1752 says that Dodd has 'given his readers a greater quantity, in proportion to the price, than is usual', compared to 'most books of entertainment'. By Several Hands, *The Monthly Review, or, Literary Journal. Giving a Candid Account, with Abstracts of, or Extracts from, the New Books and Pamphlets, Published in Great-Britain, as They Come Out*, Vol. VI, 2nd edn (London, 1752), p. 317.

33 Henry Fielding, *The History of Tom Jones, a Foundling*, 4 vols. (London, 1749), iii. 61–2. Critics have traced the 'painful journey' by which Fielding banished from successive editions the 'howler', 'who steals my Cash' (Henry Fielding, *The History of Tom Jones, A Foundling*, ed. Thomas Keymer and Alice Wakely (London: Penguin, 2005), p. xlvi). A note in the errata to the first edition adds 'for Cash read Gold'; in the fourth edition, the word 'Purse'

is finally introduced. Battestin and Bowers silently emend the quotation in line with these corrections (Fielding, *Tom Jones*, ed. Battestin and Bowers, ii. 568).

34 Shakespeare, *The Works of Shakespear*, ed. Pope, vi. 531.

35 William Shakespeare, *The Works of Shakespeare: In Seven Volumes. Collated with the Oldest Copies, and Corrected; with Notes, Explanatory, and Critical: by Mr. Theobald* (London, 1733), vii. 434.

36 See St Clair on the limited circulation of quotation books between 1600 and 1774. *The Reading Nation*, pp. 66–83.

37 Ann Moss, *Printed Commonplace-Books and the Structuring of Renaissance Thought* (Oxford: Clarendon Press, 1996), pp. v, 2.

38 See also Joan Marie Lechner, *Renaissance Concepts of the Commonplaces* (Westport, Conn.: Greenwood Press, 1962); Mary Thomas Crane, *Framing Authority: Sayings, Self, and Society in Sixteenth-Century England* (Princeton University Press, 1993); and Ann M. Blair, *Too Much to Know: Managing Scholarly Information before the Modern Age* (New Haven: Yale University Press, 2010).

39 Margreta de Grazia, 'Shakespeare in Quotation Marks', in *The Appropriation of Shakespeare: Post-Renaissance Reconstructions of the Works and the Myth*, ed. Jean I. Marsden (New York: St Martin's Press, 1992), pp. 57–71 (p. 58).

40 Robert Allot, *Englands Parnassus: or, the Choysest Flowers of our Moderne Poets, with their Poetical Comparisons* (London, 1600), title page.

41 Jennifer Batt, '"It Ought Not to Be Lost to the World": The Transmission and Consumption of Eighteenth-Century Lyric Verse', *The Review of English Studies* 62.255 (2011): 414–32 (430, 416).

42 Bysshe, *Art of English Poetry*, 2nd edn (London, 1705), Preface, F5. In this edition, Bysshe also adds '*Shakespear*' to the head of the list of authors in the phrase 'I resolv'd therefore to place these, the principal Materials, under the awful Guard of the Immortal *Shakespear, Milton, Dryden*, &c.' (Bysshe, *Art of English Poetry*, 2nd edn, preface). See Stephen Jarrod Bernard, 'Edward Bysshe and *The Art of English Poetry*: Reading Writing in the Eighteenth Century', *Eighteenth-Century Studies* 46.1 (2012): 113–29 (121).

43 Leah Price, *The Anthology and the Rise of the Novel: From Richardson to George Eliot* (Cambridge University Press, 2000), p. 3.

44 Sasha Roberts, 'Reading Shakespeare's Tragedies of Love: *Romeo and Juliet, Othello*, and *Antony and Cleopatra* in Early Modern England', in *A Companion to Shakespeare's Works*, Vol. I: *The Tragedies*, ed. Richard Dutton and Jean E. Howard (Malden, MA: Blackwell Publishing, 2003), pp. 108–33 (p. 126).

45 William Dodd, *The Beauties of Shakespear*, 2 vols. (London, 1752), i. xvi–xvii.

46 Moss, *Printed Commonplace-Books*, p. v.

47 Crane, *Framing Authority*, p. 92.

48 Jeffrey Todd Knight, *Bound to Read: Compilations, Collections, and the Making of Renaissance Literature* (Philadelphia, PA: University of Pennsylvania Press, 2013), p. 9.

49 Edward Young, *Conjectures on Original Composition* (London, 1759), pp. 53–4.

50 Ibid., pp. 9, 10, 12.

51 Ibid., p. 30.
52 Bysshe, *Art of English Poetry* (1702), Preface.
53 Frances Burney, *The Witlings and The Woman-Hater*, ed. Peter Sabor and Geoffrey Sill (Peterborough, Ont.: Broadview, 2002), p. 96.
54 A. Dwight Culler, 'Edward Bysshe and the Poet's Handbook', *PMLA* 63.3 (1948): 858–85 (864–5).
55 Dodd, *Beauties of Shakespear*, ii. 209, 198.
56 Ibid., i. 222, 225, ii. 202.
57 Ibid., i. xvii.
58 Richardson, *Clarissa*, ed. Ross, pp. 146–7. Further references are given after quotations in the text.
59 Richardson, *Clarissa*, 2nd edn, i. 203.
60 Michael E. Connaughton, 'Richardson's Familiar Quotations: *Clarissa* and Bysshe's *Art of English Poetry*', *Philological Quarterly* 60.2 (1981): 183–95 (187).
61 Jocelyn Harris, 'Richardson: Original or Learned Genius?' in *Samuel Richardson: Tercentenary Essays*, ed. Margaret Anne Doody and Peter Sabor (Cambridge University Press, 1989), pp. 188–202 (pp. 188–9).
62 Price, *The Anthology and the Rise of the Novel*, p. 40.
63 Connaughton, 'Richardson's Familiar Quotations', p. 183.
64 Edward Bysshe, *The Art of English Poetry*, 8th edn, 2 vols. (London, 1737), i. 99.
65 Ibid., ii. 30.
66 Ibid., ii. 108, 160.
67 'To Miss Highmore, 4 June 1750', *The Correspondence of Samuel Richardson, Author of* Pamela, Clarissa, *and* Sir Charles Grandison. *Selected from the Original Manuscripts, Bequeathed Him to his Family, to Which Are Prefixed, a Biographical Account of that Author, and Observations on his Writings*, ed. A. L. Barbauld, 6 vols. (London: Printed for Richard Phillips, 1804), ii. 229.
68 Oliver Goldsmith, *The Beauties of Poesy*, 2 vols. (London, 1767), i. i.
69 See Chapter 3, p. 49. David Allan provides examples of real individuals who selected passages from Shakespeare in *Commonplace Books and Reading in Georgian England* (Cambridge University Press, 2010), pp. 183–95.
70 See G. A. Starr, *Defoe and Spiritual Autobiography* (Princeton University Press, 1965); Patricia Meyer Spacks, *Imagining a Self: Autobiography and Novel in Eighteenth-Century England* (Cambridge, MA: Harvard University Press, 1976); and J. Paul Hunter, *Before Novels: The Cultural Contexts of Eighteenth-Century Fiction* (New York: Norton, 1990).
71 Femke Molekamp, *Women and the Bible in Early Modern England: Religious Reading and Writing* (Oxford University Press, 2013), pp. 69, 61. See also Kate Narveson, *Bible Readers and Lay Writers in Early Modern England: Gender and Self-Definition in an Emergent Writing Culture* (Farnham: Ashgate, 2012).
72 Molekamp suggests that Beaumont's extreme use of quotation resembles the rhetorical strategies of civil war prophetesses, *Women and the Bible*, p. 69.
73 Agnes Beaumont, *The Narrative of the Persecutions of Agnes Beaumont*, ed. Vera J. Camden (East Lansing: Colleagues Press, 1992), p. 70. Further references are given after quotations in the text.

74 Samuel Richardson, *Pamela; or, Virtue Rewarded*, ed. Albert J. Rivero (Cambridge University Press, 2011), p. 193.
75 Ibid., p. 559: 'Thy servant slew both the lion and the bear: and this uncircumcised Philistine shall be as one of them, seeing he hath defied the armies of the living God. David said moreover, The LORD that delivered me out of the paw of the lion, and out of the paw of the bear, he will deliver me out of the hand of this Philistine'.
76 Ibid., p. 467. Further references are given after quotations in the text.
77 Rivero notes that '*The Spectator*, no. 44 (Friday, 20 April 1711)' is 'a possible source for Richardson other than the play itself'. Ibid., pp. 544–5.
78 Julie A. Eckerle, 'Recent Developments in Early Modern English Life Writing and Romance', *Literature Compass* 5.6 (2008): 1081–96 (1086).
79 Godfrey Frank Singer, in *The Epistolary Novel: Its Origin, Development, Decline, and Residuary Influence* (Philadelphia: University of Pennsylvania Press, 1933) found in a *Spectator* article a potential shaping influence on *Pamela* (p. 82). Hunter has documented the journalistic antecedents of the eighteenth-century novel in *Before Novels* (1990).
80 George Winchester Stone, 'Shakespeare in the Periodicals, 1700–1740: A Study of the Growth of a Knowledge of the Dramatist in the Eighteenth Century', *Shakespeare Quarterly* 2.3 (1951): 212–31 (231). While periodicals such as *The Tatler* and *The Spectator* had a significant circulation (and boasted multiple readers of each copy sold), the readership may not have been especially diverse, and the cost of periodicals rose at above the rate of inflation. See Iona Italia, *The Rise of Literary Journalism in the Eighteenth Century: Anxious Employment* (Abingdon: Routledge, 2005), pp. 1–22.
81 *The Tatler*, ed. Richmond P. Bond, 3 vols. (Oxford: Clarendon Press, 1987), ii. 169. Further references are given after quotations in the text.
82 Erin Mackie, *Market à la Mode: Fashion, Commodity and Gender in* The Tatler *and* The Spectator (Baltimore: Johns Hopkins University Press, 1997), p. 260.
83 Kramnick, *Making the English Canon*, p. 22.
84 Fielding, *Tom Jones*, ed. Battestin and Bowers, ii. 568.
85 Fielding and Collier, *Cry*, iii. 289.
86 'point', *n.*1, 24c. *OED Online*. (Oxford University Press, September 2015).
87 Sterne, *Sentimental Journey*, ed. New and Day, p. 45.
88 William Dodd, *The Sisters; or, The History of Lucy and Caroline Sanson, Entrusted to a False Friend*, 2 vols. (London, 1754), i. 238–9.
89 Ibid., p. 239.
90 Samuel Richardson, *Early Works*, ed. Alexander Pettit (Cambridge University Press, 2012), p. 19.
91 Ibid., pp. 19–21. The 'Expence of Money' was not inconsiderable: 'Admission to the patent theatres between 1660 and 1740 was normally 4*s*. for a place in a box, 2/6 for the pit, 1/6 for the first gallery, and 1*s*. for the second gallery. Around the middle of the century, prices slid up a shilling at the top price and 6*d*. at the second and third levels.' Robert D. Hume, 'The Value of Money: Incomes, Prices, Buying Power—and Some Problems in Cultural Economics', *Huntington Library Quarterly* 77.4 (2014): 373–416 (382).

92 'Letter to the Right Honourable Sir Richard Brocas, Lord Mayor of London, from an Unidentified Citizen' (London, 1730), quoted in Jonas Barish, *The Antitheatrical Prejudice* (Berkeley: University of California Press, 1981), p. 241.
93 Samuel Richardson, *Pamela in her Exalted Condition*, ed. Albert J. Rivero (Cambridge University Press, 2012), p. 341. Further references are given after quotations in the text.
94 Ian Watt, *The Rise of the Novel: Studies in Defoe, Richardson and Fielding* (London: Chatto and Windus, 1974 [1957]), p. 47.
95 Rivero suggests that this may be a quotation from Witwoud in William Congreve's *The Way of the World* (1700) rather than *Hamlet*: 'Hum, a hit, a hit, a palpable hit' (II.ii.353) (Richardson, *Pamela in her Exalted Condition*, ed. Rivero, p. 676).
96 Margaret Anne Doody, *A Natural Passion: A Study of the Novels of Samuel Richardson* (Oxford: Clarendon Press, 1974), p. 84.
97 Jenny Davidson, *Hypocrisy and the Politics of Politeness: Manners and Morals from Locke to Austen* (Cambridge University Press, 2004), pp. 46–75.
98 Fielding, *Miscellanies*, Vol. I, ed. Miller, i. 162.
99 Oliver Goldsmith, *The Vicar of Wakefield*, ed. Arthur Friedman (Oxford University Press, 1981, 2008), pp. 41, 42.
100 Ibid., pp. 43, 42.
101 Ibid., p. 44.
102 Ibid., p. 45.
103 Ibid., pp. 43, 109, 41.
104 The coffee house represented the ideals of sociable conversation, as customers were expected to take the next available seat on arrival, which meant that 'all are equal'. It could also, however, bring visitors into contact with would-be critics and retailers of scraps of learning and lewd stories (Markman Ellis, *The Coffee-House: A Cultural History* (London: Phoenix, 2004), pp. 59, 201).
105 Valerie Rumbold notes that 'many of the sayings in *Polite Conversation* that are otherwise hard to trace in the print record can be documented from plays'. Jonathan Swift, *Parodies, Hoaxes and Mock Treatises: Polite Conversation, Directions to Servants and Other Works*, ed. Valerie Rumbold (Cambridge University Press, 2013), p. lvi.
106 Eliza Haywood, *The Tea-Table: or, A Conversation between Some Polite Persons of Both Sexes, at a Lady's Visiting Day. Wherein Are Represented the Various Foibles, and Affectations, Which Form the Character of an Accomplish'd Beau, or Modern Fine Lady* (London, 1725), pp. 3–4.
107 Ibid., p. 10.
108 For example, in the year of their first publication, Richardson's *Sir Charles Grandison* (7 vols., 12m°) cost 19*s*., Henry Fielding's *Amelia* (4 vols., 12m°) 12*s*.; Sarah Fielding's *History of Ophelia* (2 vols., 12m°) 6*s*., and Sterne's *Tristram Shandy* (8v°) 5*s*. for every pair of volumes published, and 2*s*. for Vols. VI and VIII, and IX, respectively. See Antonia Forster, *Index to Book Reviews in England, 1749–1774* (Carbondale: Southern Illinois University Press, 1990), pp. 247, 108, 109, 271–2. James Raven describes the dramatic

expansion in production and increase in price between 1750 and 1820, 'Production', in *The Oxford History of the Novel in English, Vol. II: English and British Fiction 1750–1820*, ed. Peter Garside and Karen O'Brien (Oxford University Press, 2015), pp. 3–28.

109 Karen O'Brien, 'Introduction', in *Oxford History of the Novel*, ed. Garside and O'Brien, pp. xvii–xxix (p. xxi).

Chapter 3

1 William Shakespeare, *A Midsummer Night's Dream*, v. 1. 56–7.

2 See the alternative attribution of the speech, and compare 'Additional Passages', William Shakespeare, *The Oxford Shakespeare: The Complete Works*, ed. Stanley Wells and Gary Taylor (Oxford: Clarendon Press, 1988, 1998), p. 333.

3 Richardson, *Clarissa*, 2nd edn, iii. 49.

4 Marsden, *The Re-imagined Text*, p. 5.

5 The two terms were at one point almost interchangeable, when 'author' referred, in a now obsolete sense, to 'The person on whose authority a statement is made', 'author', *n.*, 5. *OED Online* (Oxford University Press, September 2015).

6 Marcus Walsh, *Shakespeare, Milton and Eighteenth-Century Literary Editing: The Beginnings of Interpretative Scholarship* (Cambridge University Press, 1997), p. 111.

7 'authority', *n.*, 5a. *OED Online* (Oxford University Press, September 2015).

8 Fiona Ritchie and Peter Sabor, 'Introduction', in *Shakespeare in the Eighteenth Century*, ed. Ritchie and Sabor, pp. 1–17 (p. 6).

9 'authority', *n.*, 5b. *OED Online* (Oxford University Press, September 2015).

10 Elizabeth Griffith, *The Morality of Shakespeare's Drama Illustrated* (London, 1775), p. 525 ('General Postscript').

11 Stephen Greenblatt, *Shakespeare's Freedom* (Chicago: University of Chicago Press, 2010); Robert Weimann and Douglas Bruster, *Shakespeare and the Power of Performance: Stage and Page in the Elizabethan Theatre* (Cambridge University Press, 2008).

12 Dobson, *Making of the National Poet*, p. 134.

13 'propriety', *n.*, 7a. *OED Online* (Oxford University Press, September 2015).

14 Samuel Johnson, *A Dictionary of the English Language; in Which the Words Are Deduced from their Originals and Illustrated in their Different Significations by Examples from the Best Writers. To Which Are Prefixed, a History of the Language, and an English Grammar*, 2 vols. (London, 1755), ii., 'PROPRIETY'.

15 'propriety', *n.*, 6. *OED Online* (Oxford University Press, September 2015).

16 Dobson, *Making of the National Poet*, pp. 134–84.

17 Ibid., p. 143.

18 Ibid., p. 134.

19 Ibid., p. 146.

20 Michel Foucault, 'What Is an Author?', trans. Donald F. Bouchard and Sherry Simon, in *Language, Counter-Memory, Practice*, ed. Donald F. Bouchard (Ithaca, New York: Cornell University Press, 1977), pp. 124–7.

21 Joseph Addison, Richard Steele et al, *The Spectator*, ed. Donald F. Bond, 5 vols. (Oxford: Clarendon Press, 1965), iv. 216–17 (No. 484, Monday September 15, 1712).

22 Thomas Hayward, *The British Muse, or, A Collection of Thoughts Moral, Natural, and Sublime, of our English Poets: Who Flourished in the Sixteenth and Seventeenth Centuries. With Several Curious Topicks, and Beautiful Passages, Never before Extracted, from Shakespear, Johnson, Beaumont, Fletcher, and above a Hundred More*, 3 vols. (London, 1738), iii. 139.

23 Richardson, *Clarissa. Or, the History of a Young Lady*, 3rd edn, 8 vols. (London, 1751), viii. 355.

24 Dodd, *Beauties of Shakespear*, i. 88; Griffith, *Morality of Shakespeare's Drama*, p. 21; *The Beauties of Shakespeare; Selected from his Plays and Poems* (London: George Kearsley, 1783), p. 51.

25 Anon., *Chit-Chat: or, Natural Characters; and the Manners of Real Life, Represented in a Series of Interesting Adventures*, 2 vols. (London, 1755), i. 12.

26 Clara Reeve, *The School for Widows. A Novel*, 3 vols. (London, 1791), iii. 250.

27 Addison, Steele, et al, *Spectator*, ed. Bond, iv. 216–17.

28 Leah Price notes how Richardson, in the third edition, has Anna observe that, while Clarissa was widely read in a range of English, French, Italian and classical texts, 'yet seldom did she quote or repeat from them'. Price describes this as an act of 'historical revisionism' that comes 'too late to be credible, for quotations riddle Clarissa's letters'; Anna is attempting to distinguish Clarissa from her sententious suitor, Rev. Brand. *The Anthology and the Rise of the Novel*, p. 28.

29 Rachel Trickett, 'Dryden's Part in *Clarissa*', in *Clarissa and her Readers: New Essays for the Clarissa Project*, ed. Carol Houlihan Flynn and Edward Copeland (New York: AMS Press, 1999), pp. 175–87 (p. 186).

30 Fielding and Collier, *Cry*, ii. 63. Further references are given after quotations in the text.

31 Richardson, *Sir Charles Grandison*, ed. Harris, ii. 153.

32 Tobias Smollett, *The Adventures of Ferdinand Count Fathom*, ed. Damian Grant (Oxford University Press, 1971), p. 183; Tobias Smollett, *The Adventures of Peregrine Pickle: In Which Are Included Memoirs of a Lady of Quality*, ed. James Clifford and rev. Paul-Gabriel Boucé (Oxford University Press, 1983), p. 275.

33 Fielding, *Amelia*, ed. Battestin, p. 430. Further references are given after quotations in the text.

34 See Watt, *Rise of the Novel*, p. 285; Henry Knight Miller, 'The Voices of Henry Fielding: Style in *Tom Jones*', in *The Augustan Milieu: Essays Presented to Louis A. Landa*, ed. Henry Knight Miller, Eric Rothstein and G. S. Rousseau (Oxford: Clarendon Press, 1970), pp. 262–88 (p. 272); and Ronald Paulson, *The Life of Henry Fielding: A Critical Biography* (Oxford: Blackwell Publishers, 2000), pp. 8–9.

35 Fielding, *Tom Jones*, ed. Battestin and Bowers, ii. 568, 792. Further references are given after quotations in the text.

36 Mace, *Henry Fielding's Novels*, p. 78.

37 John Heminges, Henry Condell, in *Comedies, Histories, Tragedies* (1623), in Shakespeare, *Complete Works*, ed. Wells and Taylor, p. xlv.

38 The meaning of 'happy' here hovers between 'fortuitous' and 'fitting': compare 'happy', *adj.*, 3, 'That happens or presents itself by chance; fortuitous; chance. *Obs. rare*'; and 'happy', *adj.*, 4b, 'Of an action, speech, etc.: pleasantly appropriate to the occasion or circumstances; felicitous, apt.'). *OED Online* (Oxford University Press, September 2015).

39 Thomas Fuller, *The History of the Worthies of England Who for Parts and Learning Have Been Eminent in the Several Counties: Together with an Historical Narrative of the Native Commodities and Rarities in Each County* (London, 1662), p. 126.

40 John Dryden, *Of Dramatick Poesie, an Essay* (London, 1668), p. 47.

41 Ben Jonson, in *Comedies, Histories, and Tragedies* (1623), in Shakespeare, *Complete Works*, ed. Wells and Taylor p. xlvi.

42 Shakespeare, *The Works of Shakespear*, ed. Pope, i. ii; Shakespeare, *The Works of Shakespear... by Mr. Pope and Mr. Warburton*, 8 vols. (London, 1747), i. xiii–xiv; Shakespeare, *The Works of Shakespeare*, ed. Theobald, i. iii.

43 Gefen Bar-On Santor, 'Looking for "Newtonian" Laws in Shakespeare: the Mystifying Case of the Character of Hamlet', in *Shakespeare and the Eighteenth Century*, ed. Sabor and Yachnin, pp. 151–64 (151–2).

44 Ibid., p. 153.

45 Marsden, *The Re-imagined Text*, p. 150.

46 Sarah Fielding, *The Adventures of David Simple*, ed. Linda Bree (London: Penguin, 2002), p. 105.

47 Ibid., p. 140.

48 Margaret Cavendish, Duchess of Newcastle, *CCXI Sociable Letters Written by the Thrice Noble, Illustrious and Excellent Princess the Lady Marchioness of Newcastle* (London: William Wilson, 1664), 'Letter CXXIII', p. 244.

49 Ibid., p. 245.

50 Gefen Bar-On Santor, 'The Culture of Newtonianism and Shakespeare's Editors: From Pope to Johnson', *Eighteenth-Century Fiction* 21.4 (2009): 593–614 (602).

51 Fielding, *Countess of Dellwyn*, i. vii. Further references are given after quotations in the text.

52 Cavendish, *Sociable Letters*, p. 246.

53 Elizabeth Montagu, *An Essay on the Writings and Genius of Shakespear, Compared with the Greek and French Dramatic Poets. With Some Remarks upon the Misrepresentations of Mons. de Voltaire* (London, 1769), p. 68.

54 David Garrick, *Shakespeare's Garland. Being a Collection of New Songs, Ballads, Roundelays, Catches, Glees, Comic-Serenatas, &c. Performed at the Jubilee at Stratford upon Avon. The Musick by Dr. Arne, Mr. Bartholomew, Mr. Ailwood, and Mr. Dibdin* (London, 1769), p. 24.

55 Dodd, *The Sisters*, ii. 171.

56 David Hume, *A Treatise of Human Nature*, ed. Ernest C. Mossner (London: Penguin, 1969, 1984).

57 Liz Bellamy, *Commerce, Morality and the Eighteenth-Century Novel* (Cambridge University Press, 1998), pp. 1–10, 39–65.

58 Ibid., pp. 115–16.
59 Clara Reeve, *The Progress of Romance, through Times, Countries and Manners, with Remarks on the Good and Bad Effects of It, on Them Respectively; in a Course of Evening Conversations*, 2 vols. (Colchester, 1785), ii. 41.
60 Fielding, *Tom Jones*, ed. Battestin and Bowers, ii. 981, quoted in Bellamy, *Commerce*, p. 64.
61 Lady Elizabeth Echlin, *An Alternative Ending to Richardson's* Clarissa, ed. Dimiter Daphinoff (Bern: Francke Verlag, 1982), p. 172.
62 Bellamy, *Commerce*, p. 93.
63 Tom Keymer, *Richardson's* Clarissa *and the Eighteenth-Century Reader* (Cambridge University Press, 1992), p. 56.
64 Women such as Lady Brilliana Harley and Lucy Hutchinson 'kept extensive religious commonplace books to record their reading and reflections upon a range of spiritual, theological, and moral topics, and to formulate statements of belief', Molekamp, *Women and the Bible*, p. 57.
65 It is tempting to infer that Fielding distinguishes typographically between those occasions where Shakespeare is invoked for a grand, preceptial statement, and those that represent an individual's experience. In *Tom Jones*, quotations that are prefixed with 'the noble Shakespeare ...' or 'the immortal Shakespear' are italicised. Where the situation of one of Fielding's characters is compared to one of Shakespeare's, the quotation appears in roman type and quotation marks.
66 Fielding, *Countess of Dellwyn*, i. xxxiii.
67 Sarah Fielding, *The Governess; or, The Little Female Academy*, ed. Candace Ward (Peterborough, Ont.: Broadview, 2005), pp. 85, 150.
68 Robert Alter, 'Fielding and the Uses of Style', *Novel: A Forum on Fiction* 1 (1967): 53–63 (62).
69 Wolfgang Iser, *The Implied Reader: Patterns of Communication in Prose Fiction from Bunyan to Beckett* (Baltimore and London: Johns Hopkins University Press, 1974), pp. 42–3
70 Adam Smith, *The Theory of Moral Sentiments*, ed. D. D. Raphael and A. L. Macfie (Oxford: Clarendon Press, 1976), p. 18. Further references are given after quotations in the text.
71 Fielding, *Countess of Dellwyn*, i. xiii.
72 John Mullan observes that it demands a 'willed uninvolvement' (*Sentiment and Sociability: The Language of Feeling in the Eighteenth Century* (Oxford: Clarendon Press, 1988), p. 46), while Terry Eagleton notes the 'paradoxical quality' of a kind of sympathy that involves 'entering into another's experience while retaining enough rational capacity of one's own to assess what one finds there' (*Trouble with Strangers: A Study of Ethics* (Chichester: Wiley-Blackwell, 2009), p. 71).
73 Adam Smith, *Lectures on Rhetoric and Belles Lettres*, ed. John M. Lothian (Edinburgh: Thomas Nelson and Sons Ltd, 1963), p. 74.
74 Eagleton, *Trouble with Strangers*, p. 75.
75 Smith, *Lectures on Rhetoric*, ed. Lothian, p. 203.
76 Ibid., p. 122.

77 Shakespeare, *Plays of William Shakespeare, in Eight Volumes . . . to Which Are Added Notes by Sam. Johnson*, i. Preface, unpaginated.
78 *Beauties of Shakespeare*, p. ii.
79 Ibid., p. i.
80 Bellamy shows how such fiction overshadows other, more communal, public-orientated or loosely structured work, e.g. *Millenium Hall, Sir Charles Grandison* and *Peregrine Pickle*, in modern criticism (*Commerce*, p. 117).
81 Francis Coventry, *The History of Pompey the Little: or, The Life and Adventures of a Lap-Dog*, 3rd edn (London, 1752), pp. iii–xii.
82 Sarah Fielding, *The Adventures of David Simple . . . The Second Edition, Revised and Corrected. With a Preface by Henry Fielding Esq.*, 2 vols. (London, 1744), i. vi, xii.

Chapter 4

1 Sterne, *Tristram Shandy*, ed. New and New, i. 35–6.
2 See Chapter 2, pp. 23–34.
3 Gary Taylor, *Reinventing Shakespeare: A Cultural History from the Restoration to the Present* (London: The Hogarth Press, 1990), pp. 81, 53.
4 Dobson, *Making of the National Poet*, pp. 214, 185.
5 Franklin, *Shakespeare Domesticated*, p. 1.
6 For example, in 1752, Drury Lane staged *Twelfth Night, Much Ado About Nothing, As You Like It, The Merchant of Venice, Richard III, Henry VIII, King Lear, Romeo and Juliet, Macbeth, Othello* and *Hamlet*; Covent Garden showed *The Merchant of Venice, Henry IV Part 1, Henry V, Richard III, Hamlet, Othello, Romeo and Juliet, Macbeth* and *King Lear*; and New Wells, Goodman's Fields, staged *Othello* and *Richard III*. See Charles Beecher Hogan, *Shakespeare in the Theatre 1701–1800, i. A Record of Performances in London 1701–1750*; *ii. London 1751–1800* (Oxford: Clarendon Press, 1952).
7 Hume, 'The Value of Money', 374–5. Hume estimates that the cheapest second gallery tickets, in the first half of the eighteenth century, would cost the equivalent of £10–15, and the most expensive box tickets £40–60, 383.
8 'theatrical', A. *adj.*, 1.a, *OED Online* (Oxford University Press, September 2015).
9 'theatrical', A. *adj.*, 2. *OED Online* (Oxford University Press, September 2015).
10 Fielding, *Tom Jones*, ed. Battestin and Bowers, ii. 853–4. Further references are given after quotations in the text.
11 Barish, *The Antitheatrical Prejudice*, pp. 236–55.
12 Herbert Lawrence, *The Contemplative Man; or, The History of Christopher Crab, Esq.; of North-Wales*, 2 vols. (London, 1771), i. 135–7.
13 Anon., *The Adventures of Jack Wander. Written by Himself. Interspers'd with Some Humorous Anecdotes, and Original Memoirs* (London, [1766?]), p. 17.
14 Ibid., pp. 17–18.
15 Ibid., p. 18.
16 Smollett, *The Expedition of Humphry Clinker*, ed. Lewis M. Knapp and rev. Paul-Gabriel Boucé (Oxford University Press, 1966, 1988), p. 13.

17 Anon., *Jack Wander*, p. 21.
18 Ibid., pp. 18–19.
19 Janet Todd, *Sensibility: An Introduction* (London and New York: Methuen, 1986), p. 4.
20 *Monthly Review*, LI (1774), 486, quoted in a typed annotation by Robert Gale Noyes inserted in his author copy of *The Thespian Mirror*, p. 89n.
21 Anon., *The Life, Travels, and Adventures of Christopher Wagstaff, Gentleman, Grandfather to Tristram Shandy*, 2 vols. (London, 1762), ii. 174–81.
22 Ibid., pp. 177–80.
23 Ibid., p. 180.
24 Fielding, *David Simple*, ed. Bree, p. 234.
25 Sarah Fielding, *Familiar Letters between the Principal Characters in David Simple, and Some Others*, 2 vols. (London, 1747), i. 213.
26 Fielding and Collier, *Cry*, iii. 84, 74.
27 Ibid., iii. 279.
28 Ibid., iii. 279.
29 Paul Yachnin and Myrna Wyatt Selkirk, 'Metatheater and the Performance of Character in *The Winter's Tale*', in *Shakespeare and Character: Theory, History, Performance, and Theatrical Persons*, ed. Paul Yachnin and Jessica Slights (Basingstoke: Palgrave Macmillan, 2009), pp. 139–57 (p. 151).
30 The Right Honourable Anthony, Earl of Shaftesbury, *Characteristicks of Men, Manners, Opinions, Times. The Sixth Edition, with the Addition of a Letter Concerning Design*, 3 vols. (London, 1737), iii. 368.
31 T. S. Eliot, 'Shakespeare and the Stoicism of Seneca', in *Selected Essays* (London: Faber and Faber, 1999), pp. 129–30.
32 Richardson, *Pamela*, ed. Rivero, p. 9.
33 Henry Fielding, *The Journal of a Voyage to Lisbon, Shamela, and Occasional Writings*, ed. Martin C. Battestin, with the late Sheridan W. Baker, Jr., and Hugh Amory (Oxford: Clarendon Press, 2008), p. 165.
34 Henry Mackenzie, *The Man of Feeling*, ed. Brian Vickers (Oxford University Press, 1967), p. 84.
35 Henry Fielding, *Joseph Andrews*, ed. Martin C. Battestin (Oxford: Clarendon Press, 1967), p. 267.
36 Ibid., p. 27.
37 Jill Campbell, *Natural Masques: Gender and Identity in Fielding's Plays and Novels* (Stanford, Calif.: Stanford University Press, 1995), p. 130.
38 Fielding, *Joseph Andrews*, ed. Battestin, p. 270.
39 Richardson, *Clarissa*, 2nd edn, i. vii.
40 Richardson, *Clarissa*, ed. Ross, p. 146. Further references are given after quotations in the text.
41 Richardson, *Clarissa*, 2nd edn, i. 202.
42 Clarissa and Lovelace invert the gendered quoting conventions of the female 'tragedy rant', as discussed in Richardson, *Sir Charles Grandison*, ed. Harris, ii. 397.
43 Lovelace's Shakespeare quotations average a verbose 6.25 lines in length compared to Clarissa's pithy 2.5.

44 J. Paul Hunter, 'The World as Stage and Closet', in *British Theatre and the Other Arts, 1660–1800*, ed. Shirley Strum Kenny (London and Toronto: Associated University Presses, 1984), pp. 271–87 (p. 279).
45 John J. Richetti, 'Richardson's Dramatic Art in *Clarissa*', in *British Theatre and the Other Arts, 1660–1800*, ed. Shirley Strum Kenny (London and Toronto: Associated University Presses, 1984), pp. 288–308 (p. 296).
46 Doody, *A Natural Passion*, p. 118.
47 Ira Konigsberg, *Narrative Technique in the English Novel: Defoe to Austen* (Hamden, Connecticut: Archon Books, 1985), p. 71.
48 Richardson's letters create a 'dramatic present-tense experience', and are written in a dramatic multi-perspective epistolary form, with dialogue, stage directions and heightened, stagey language that likens Lovelace and Clarissa to the heroes and heroines of Restoration drama. Mark Kinkead-Weekes, *Samuel Richardson: Dramatic Novelist* (London: Methuen and Co. Ltd., 1973), p. 1; Ira Konigsberg, *Samuel Richardson and the Dramatic Novel* (Lexington: University of Kentucky Press, 1968).
49 Todd, *Sensibility*, p. 79.
50 Dr Peter Shaw, *The Reflector: Representing Human Affairs as They Are, and as They May Be Improved* (London, 1750), in a passage taken without acknowledgment from Holberg, *Moral Thoughts* (1744); discussed in Alan Dugald McKillop, *Samuel Richardson: Printer and Novelist* (Hamden, Conn.: Shoestring Press, 1960), pp. 101–2.
51 Kinkead-Weekes, *Samuel Richardson: Dramatic Novelist*, p. 9.
52 Davidson, *Hypocrisy and the Politics of Politeness*, p. 109.
53 From Richardson's response to Lady Bradshaigh's comment in the margins of *Clarissa*: Anna] I had been inquiring privately, how to procure you a conveyance from Harlowe-Place, and yet not appear in it.../ LB] This conveyance should have been procur'd & no appointment made with Lovelace, then wou'd she have been blameless./ R] I did not want her to be wholly blameless. Janine Barchas and Gordon D. Fulton, *The Annotations in Lady Bradshaigh's Copy of Clarissa* (Victoria, BC: University of Victoria 1998), p. 55.
54 Watt, *The Rise of the Novel*, pp. 13, 32.
55 Ibid., p. 272.
56 Lynch, *Economy of Character*, pp. 23–79.
57 Wahrman, *Making of the Modern Self*, pp. 166–8.
58 See Lionel Trilling, *Sincerity and Authenticity* (London: Oxford University Press, 1972); Bernard Williams, *Truth and Truthfulness: An Essay in Genealogy* (Princeton University Press, 2002); and Davidson, *Hypocrisy and the Politics of Politeness*.
59 Trilling, *Sincerity and Authenticity*, pp. 10–11. Bernard Williams notes that the association of sincerity with personal authenticity 'first came into distinct existence in the eighteenth century', *Truth and Truthfulness*, p. 172.
60 Fielding, *Amelia*, ed. Battestin, p. 203. Further references are given after quotations in the text.

61 Lisa A. Freeman, *Character's Theater: Genre and Identity on the Eighteenth-Century English Stage* (Philadelphia: University of Pennsylvania Press, 2002), p. 45.

62 Freeman (p. 18) quotes as evidence *Remarks on Clarissa*: '*Clarissa* is not intended as a Dramatic, but as a real Picture of human Life, where Story can move but slowly, where the Characters must open by degrees, and the Reader's own Judgment form them from different Parts, as they display themselves according to the Incidents that arise' (Sarah Fielding, *Remarks on Clarissa, Addressed to the Author. Occasioned by Some Critical Conversations on the Characters and Conduct of that Work* (London, 1749), p. 35). Richardson, however, does declare *Clarissa* a Christian tragedy, with many letters written 'in the Dialogue or Dramatic way' (p. 35).

63 Nora Nachumi, *Acting Like a Lady: British Women Novelists and the Eighteenth-Century Theater* (New York: AMS Press, Inc., 2008), pp. 174–5.

64 Emily Hodgson Anderson, *Eighteenth-Century Authorship and the Play of Fiction: Novels and the Theater, Haywood to Austen* (New York and Abingdon: Routledge, 2009), p. 1.

65 Fielding, *Miscellanies*, Vol. I, ed. Miller, i. 155.

66 Ibid., i. 161–2.

67 Fielding, *History of Ophelia*, ed. Sabor, p. 112.

68 Anon., *Almira. Being the History of a Young Lady of Good Birth and Fortune, but More Distinguish'd Merit*, 2 vols. (London, 1762), i. 17.

69 Anon., *The History of Miss Pittborough. In a Series of Letters. By a Lady*, 2 vols. (London, 1767), i. 22–3.

70 Sterne, *Tristram Shandy*, ed. New and New, i. 213. Further references are given after quotations in the text.

71 *Lichtenberg's Visits to England, as Described in his Letters and Diaries*, trans. Margaret L. Mare and W. H. Quarrell (Oxford: Clarendon Press, 1938), p. 10.

72 Dene Barnett, *The Art of Gesture: The Practices and Principles of Eighteenth-Century Acting* (Heidelberg: C. Winter, 1987), p. 11.

73 Joseph R. Roach, *The Player's Passion: Studies in the Science of Acting* (Cranbury, NJ: Associated University Presses, 1985), p. 87.

74 William Enfield, *The Speaker: or, Miscellaneous Pieces, Selected from the Best English Writers, and Disposed under Proper Heads, with a View to Facilitate the Improvement of Youth in Reading and Speaking. A New Edition, Corrected and Enlarged. To Which Are Prefixed Two Essays: I. On Elocution. II. On Reading Works of Taste* (London, 1790), pp. xxx–xxxi.

75 Alexis Tadié, *Sterne's Whimsical Theatres of Language: Orality, Gesture, Literacy* (Aldershot: Ashgate, 2003), p. 81.

76 Todd, *Sensibility*, p. 3–4.

77 Tadié, *Sterne's Whimsical Theatres*, p. 83.

78 Judith Hawley, '"Hints and Documents" 2: A Bibliography for *Tristram Shandy*', *The Shandean* 4 (1992): 48–64 (51).

79 Everett Zimmerman, '*Tristram Shandy* and Narrative Representation', *The Eighteenth Century* 28.2 (1987): 127–47 (131).

80 John M. Stedmond, *The Comic Art of Laurence Sterne: Convention and Innovation in* Tristram Shandy *and* A Sentimental Journey (Toronto: University of Toronto Press, 1967), p. 70; Jonathan Lamb, *Sterne's Fiction and the Double Principle* (Cambridge University Press, 1989), p. 18.
81 This two-chapter 'sketch of his life and conversation' is ostensibly outside the plot: 'When this is done, if nothing stops us in our way, we will go on with the midwife' (i. 24).
82 *Hamlet,* I. 5. 77–8.
83 Dodd, *Beauties of Shakespear*, i. 228.
84 Ibid., i. 229.
85 Ibid.
86 Tom Keymer, *Sterne, the Moderns, and the Novel* (Oxford University Press, 2002), pp. 29, 35.
87 Ibid., p. 48.
88 Donald Wehrs, 'Sterne, Cervantes, Montaigne: Fideistic Skepticism and the Rhetoric of Desire', *Comparative Literature Studies* 25.2 (1988): 127–51 (139).
89 Laurence Sterne, *The Sermons of Laurence Sterne*, ed. Melvyn New (Gainesville: University Press of Florida, 1996), p. 79.
90 John Kidgell, *The Card*, 2 vols. (London, 1755), i. 154–5.
91 Sterne, *Sentimental Journey*, ed. New and Day, p. 114.
92 Ibid., p. 87.
93 Elizabeth Wanning Harries, *The Unfinished Manner: Essays on the Fragment in the Later Eighteenth Century* (Charlottesville and London: University Press of Virginia, 1994), p. 55.
94 Ibid.
95 William Hazlitt, *Characters of Shakespeare's Plays* (London: Oxford University Press, 1966), p. 87, quoted in Joseph M. Ortiz, 'Introduction', *Shakespeare and the Culture of Romanticism*, ed. Joseph M. Ortiz (Farnham: Ashgate, 2013), pp. 1–10 (p. 4).
96 Bate, *Shakespeare and the English Romantic Imagination*, pp. 241, 6. Ortiz usefully notes that other writers retained a sense of Shakespeare's theatricality in, for example, their drama and criticism, *Shakespeare and the Culture of Romanticism*, pp. 3–5.
97 Bate, *Shakespeare and the English Romantic Imagination*, p. 9.

Chapter 5

1 *Lichtenberg's Visits to England*, trans. Mare and Quarrell, p. 16.
2 Impartial Reader, '*To the Printer of the* Public Advertiser', *Public Advertiser*, Friday, 31 January, 1777.
3 Dobson, *Making of the National Poet*, p. 223.
4 'banal', *adj*., 2, *OED Online* (Oxford University Press, September 2015).
5 Moss, *Printed Commonplace-Books*, pp. v, 1–2. Moss notes that the 'degradation of the word since the eighteenth century is not peculiar to the English language': 'lieux communs' 'takes the same downward path' in French,

from 'arguments, développements et preuves applicables à tous les sujets' to 'banalités', p. 1.

6 Meyer, *Poetics of Quotation*, p. 18.

7 *The Tatler*, ed. Bond, i. 107.

8 Aaron Hill, *The Dramatic Works of Aaron Hill, Esq.*, 2 vols. (London, 1760), i. 221.

9 Hume, 'Before the Bard', 41–75.

10 A. Z., 'To the Author of Common Sense', Saturday, 24 June, 1738. *Common Sense: or, the Englishman's Journal. Being a Collection of Letters, Political, Humorous, and Moral; Publish'd Weekly under that Title*, 2 vols. (London, 1739), ii. 123–8 (124).

11 Ibid., ii. 125.

12 Fiona Ritchie, *Women and Shakespeare in the Eighteenth Century* (Cambridge University Press, 2014), p. 143.

13 James Ralph, *The Case of our Present Theatrical Disputes, Fairly Stated* (London, 1743), p. 44.

14 Walter Jackson Bate, *From Classic to Romantic: Premises of Taste in Eighteenth-Century England* (New York: Harper & Brothers, 1946), p. 114.

15 Goldsmith, *Vicar of Wakefield*, ed. Friedman, p. 46.

16 Richardson, *Sir Charles Grandison*, ed. Harris, i. 59.

17 Henry Fielding, *The True Patriot and Related Writings*, ed. W. B. Coley, (Oxford: Clarendon Press, 1987), p. 104.

18 Ibid., p. 106.

19 Fielding, *The Covent-Garden Journal and A Plan of the Universal Register-Office*, ed. Bertrand A. Goldgar (Oxford: Clarendon Press, 1988), pp. 192–3.

20 Richardson, *Correspondence*, ed. Barbauld, iii. 44.

21 Markman Ellis, ed., *Eighteenth-Century Coffee-House Culture*, 4 vols. (London: Pickering & Chatto, 2006), i. xi.

22 'Letter III. The Same to the Same. Containing an Account of *Will*'s Coffee-house, and of the *Toasting* and *Kit-Kat-Clubs*. Made English', in *Letters of Wit, Politicks, and Morality. Written Originally in Italian, by the Famous Cardinal Bentivoglio* . . ., ed. Abel Boyer (London, 1701), p. 222.

23 John Constable, *The Conversation of Gentlemen Considered in Most of the Ways, that Make their Mutual Company Agreeable, or Disagreeable. In Six Dialogues* (London, 1738), p. 97.

24 Shakespeare, *The Works of Shakespear in Eight Volumes . . . by Mr. Pope and Mr. Warburton*, viii. 160–1.

25 Nobleman of Distinguished Abilities, *The Art of Conversation; or, The Polite Entertainer: Calculated for the Improvement of Both Sexes* (London, 1757)', p. 43.

26 See e.g. Philip Carter, *Men and the Emergence of Polite Society, Britain 1660–1800* (Harlow: Longman, 2001), and Michèle Cohen, *Fashioning Masculinity: National Identity and Language in the Eighteenth Century* (London: Routledge, 1996).

27 'Lady *Last-stakes*, came according to Appointment, to meet Lady *Betty Modish*; is gone to hear *Shuter* give the *London Cries*; will be here again after the Play;

when she will be glad to have a Party of *Picquet* with Lady *Betty*, and spend the Remainder of the Evening.' Arthur Murphy, *The Gray's-Inn Journal*, 2 vols. (Dublin, 1756), ii. 48–9.

28 Constable, *Conversation of Gentlemen*, pp. 97–8.

29 Coffee houses had different conversational orientations depending on their location in the city: in the Bedford Coffee House, located in the theatre district, '*dramatic affairs* are here the *affairs of state*'. Anon., *Memoirs of the Bedford Coffee-House. By a Genius*, 2nd edn (London, 1763), p. 5.

30 On politeness and social mobility (or lack of it), see Paul Langford, 'The Uses of Eighteenth-Century Politeness', *Transactions of the Royal Historical Society* 12 (2002): 311–31, and Helen Berry, 'Rethinking Politeness in Eighteenth-Century England: Moll King's Coffee House and the Significance of "Flash Talk"' (The Alexander Prize Lecture), *Transactions of the Royal Historical Society* 11 (2001): 65–81.

31 Smollett, *Peregrine Pickle*, ed. Clifford and rev. Boucé, pp. 596–600. Further references are given after quotations in the text.

32 Fielding, *Tom Jones*, ed. Battestin and Bowers, i. 324. Further references are given after quotations in the text. The Wesleyan edition follows Fielding's fourth edition; earlier editions have '*storms and struts his hour*'.

33 This contrast is not as pronounced as it seems: Fielding had positively reviewed Boyse's poem, 'The Deity', in the *Champion* (12 February 1740). Fielding, *Tom Jones*, ed. Keymer and Wakely, p. 915, n.5.

34 'hackneyed', *adj*., 2. *OED Online* (Oxford University Press, September 2015).

35 Lindboe, '"O *Shakespear*"', 303.

36 Michael Holquist, ed., *The Dialogic Imagination: Four Essays by M. M. Bakhtin*, trans. Caryl Emerson and Michael Holquist (Austin: University of Texas Press, 1981), p. 303.

37 Hunter, *Before Novels*, p. 19.

38 *The Tatler*, ed. Bond, ii. 425.

39 *The Art of English Poetry* (p. 202) and the *Thesaurus* (i. 219) have 'Life's but a walking Shadow; a Poor Player/ That frets, and struts his Hour upon a Stage/ And then is heard no more'; *The Complete Art of Poetry* has 'the Stage' (p. 357).

40 Holquist, ed., *Dialogic Imagination*, p. 324.

41 Nobleman, *Art of Conversation*, p. 26.

42 William Matthews, 'Polite Speech in the Eighteenth Century', *English* 1 (1937): 493–511 (500).

43 Richard Burt, *Unspeakable ShaXXXpeares: Queer Theory and American Kiddie Culture* (New York: St Martin's, 1998), p. 243.

44 Holquist, ed., *Dialogic Imagination*, p. 293.

45 Fielding, *Amelia*, ed. Battestin, p. 246, n. 1.

46 Fielding, *David Simple*, ed. Bree, p. 134. The quotation is absent from the second edition.

47 Fielding, *History of Ophelia*, ed. Sabor, p. 128.

48 Dodd heads this short passage '*JEALOUSY*' (*Beauties of Shakespear*, ii. 166), and an admirer of this 'noble, but irregular' play notes 'how finely has *Shakespear*

expressed the Nature of Jealousie in those Lines', *The Guardian*, 2 vols. (London, 1714), No. 37 (Thursday, 23 Apr.), p. 149. William Bruce, in *Some Facts and Observations Relative to the Fate of the Late Linen Bill, Last Session of Parliament in This Kingdom* (London, 1753), observes, without mentioning *Othello* or Shakespeare, that, while it would be hard for people to suspect that the country had been 'brought into Danger, by a Trick; in order, that Deliverance may be afterwards conferred on us as a Favour', still, '*to the Jealous, Trifles light as Air, turn Confirmations strong, as Proofs from Holy Writ*' (p. 17).

49 See e.g. Fielding, *Amelia*, ed. Battestin, p. 246.

50 Dudley Bradstreet, *Bradstreet's Lives: Being a Genuine History of Several Gentlemen and Ladies, All Living within These Ten Years Past, Remarkable for their Virtues* (Dublin, 1757), p. 67; *The Evangelical Magazine for 1796*, 8 vols. (London, 1793–1800), iv. 505.

51 Sterne, *Tristram Shandy*, ed. New and New, i. 383.

52 David Garrick, *Miss in her Teens: or, the Medley of Lovers. A Farce. In Two Acts. As It Is Perform'd at the Theatre-Royal in Covent-Garden* (London, 1747), p. 6.

53 Elizabeth Gunning, *The Packet: A Novel*, 4 vols. (London, 1794), iv. 177.

54 John Burgoyne, *The Maid of the Oaks: A New Dramatic Entertainment. As It Is Performed at the Theatre-Royal, in Drury-Lane* (London, 1774), p. 63. Garrick provided a prologue.

55 See also Arthur Sherbo, 'Some Not-So-Hidden Allusions in *Tristram Shandy*', in *Studies in the Eighteenth Century English Novel* (Michigan: Michigan State University Press, 1969), pp. 128–35 (p. 132).

56 Anon., *A Journey through the Head of a Modern Poet, Being the Substance of a Dream, Occasioned by Reading the Sixth Book of Virgil* (London, 1750), p. 30.

57 Anon., *The History of Miss Dorinda Catsby, and Miss Emilia Faulkner: In a Series of Letters*, 2 vols. (London, 1772), i. 34.

58 Anon., *Amusements in High Life; or, Conjugal Infidelities in 1786. In a Series of Confidential Letters, between Ladies Who Have Distinguished Themselves by the Multiplicity and Singularity of their Amours* (London, 1786), p. 142.

59 See Chapter 3, p. 64.

60 Smollett, *Ferdinand Count Fathom*, ed. Grant, p. 231.

61 Richardson, *Sir Charles Grandison*, ed. Harris, ii. 153.

62 Ibid., ii. 157.

63 Fielding, *Countess of Dellwyn*, i. 41.

64 R. D., 'To the Printer of the Public Advertiser', *Public Advertiser*, Saturday, March 21, 1767; '*Applications* to MODERN CHARACTERS from Shakespeare', *Public Advertiser*, Wednesday, April 8, 1778.

65 Frances Burney, *Evelina*, ed. Margaret Anne Doody (London: Penguin, 1994), pp. 44–5.

66 Ibid., pp. 29, 28, 43.

67 Anon., *Elegant Extracts in Miniature, Selected from New Publications, Monthly Magazines, Reviews, &c. Embellished with Elegant Engravings* (Edinburgh, 1796), p. 205.

68 Jane Austen, *Northanger Abbey*, ed. Barbara M. Benedict and Deirdre Le Faye (Cambridge University Press, 2006), pp. 7–8.
69 Barbara Benedict, 'Reading by the Book in *Northanger Abbey*'. *Persuasions*, 20.1 (1999), www.jasna.org/persuasions/on-line/vol20no1/benedict.html.
70 Impartial Reader, '*To the Printer*'.
71 Dodd, *Beauties of Shakespear*, i. xiii.
72 Ibid., i. xvii.
73 James Noggle, *The Temporality of Taste in Eighteenth-Century British Writing* (Oxford University Press, 2012), p. 115.
74 Burney, *The Witlings*, ed. Sabor and Sill, p. 92.
75 Ibid., p. 85.
76 Ibid., p. 118.
77 See Chapter 2, p. 30.
78 Fielding, *Joseph Andrews*, ed. Battestin, p. 121.
79 Smollett, *Humphry Clinker*, ed. Knapp and rev. Boucé, p. 53.
80 Fielding, *Countess of Dellwyn*, ii. 118.
81 Smollett, *Humphry Clinker*, ed. Knapp and rev. Boucé, p. 53.
82 Fielding, *Amelia*, ed. Battestin, p. 430.
83 Ibid., p. 126.
84 Fielding, *David Simple*, ed. Bree, p. 77.
85 Ellis, ed., *Coffee-House Culture*, ii. 360.
86 Fielding, *David Simple*, ed. Bree, p. 77.
87 Ibid., p. 78.
88 Ibid., p. 81.
89 Ibid., p. 79.
90 Raymond Williams, *Keywords: A Vocabulary of Culture and Society* (London: Flamingo, 1976, 1981), p. 313; Pierre Bourdieu, *Distinction: A Social Critique of the Judgement of Taste*, trans. Richard Nice (London: Routledge, 1996), p. 2.
91 Anon., *Chit-Chat*, i. 19–20.
92 Fielding, *History of Ophelia*, ed. Sabor, p. 112.
93 Anon., *Ermina; or, The Fair Recluse. A Novel. In a Series of Letters by a Lady, Author of Dorinda Calsby [sic] &c*, 2 vols. (London, 1772), ii. 7.
94 Francis Coventry, *The History of Pompey the Little: or, The Life and Adventures of a Lap-Dog*, 4th edn (London, 1761), pp. 198–9. This conversation first appears in this edition of the novel.
95 Paula Backscheider, 'Shadowing Theatrical Change', in *Players, Playwrights, Playhouses: Investigating Performance, 1660–1800*, ed. Michael Cordner and Peter Holland (Basingstoke: Palgrave Macmillan, 2007), pp. 78–100 (p. 79).
96 See Richardson, *Sir Charles Grandison*, ed. Harris, iii. 245; Fielding, *Miscellanies*, Vol. I, ed. Miller, p. 159; Fielding, *Countess of Dellwyn*, i. vii.
97 Fielding, *Miscellanies*, Vol. I, ed. Miller, i. 155.
98 Richardson, *Pamela in her Exalted Condition*, ed. Rivero, p. 599.
99 Fielding, *Miscellanies*, Vol. I, ed. Miller, i. 140. Miller connects Fielding's attitude with Bellegarde's *Reflexions upon Ridicule* which proposes that politeness is gained by 'the frequent Sight of polite Persons, and copying from their

Plan'. *Essays on Fielding's* Miscellanies*: A Commentary on Volume One* (Princeton University Press, 1961), p. 186.

100 'Letter from a French Gentleman in London to his Friend in Paris', in *Letters of Wit . . . by the Famous Cardinal Bentivoglio. . .*, ed. Abel Boyer, pp. 215–24 (p. 216) (see Ellis, ed., *Coffee-House Culture*, i. 247–60 [250]).

101 Dobson, *Making of the National Poet*, pp. 214, 15.

102 Ibid., p. 186.

103 Garrick, *Shakespeare's Garland*, p. 3.

104 Christian Deelman, *The Great Shakespeare Jubilee* (London: Michael Joseph, 1964), p. 142.

105 Martha Winburn England, *Garrick's Jubilee* (Columbus, OH: Ohio State University Press, 1964), p. 21.

106 Deelman, *Great Shakespeare Jubilee*, p. 228.

107 Francis Gentleman, *The Stratford Jubilee* (London, 1769), p. 5.

108 Rumbold, 'The Stratford Jubilee', pp. 254–76.

109 Jack Lynch, *Becoming Shakespeare: The Unlikely Afterlife that Turned a Provincial Playwright into the Bard* (New York: Walker, 2007), p. 9.

110 Garrick, *Shakespeare's Garland*, pp. 2–4.

111 Dobson, *Making of the National Poet*, p. 227.

112 See Martha Winburn England, 'Garrick's Stratford Jubilee: Reactions in France and Germany', *Shakespeare Survey* 9 (1956): 90–100.

113 Andrew Murphy, *Shakespeare for the People: Working-Class Readers, 1800–1900* (Cambridge University Press, 2008), pp. 28–94.

114 Poster in Stratford Records Office, quoted in ibid., p. 1.

115 Douglas Lanier, *Shakespeare and Modern Popular Culture* (Oxford University Press, 2002), p. 53.

116 Jane Austen, *Mansfield Park*, ed. John Wiltshire (Cambridge University Press, 2005), p. 391.

Chapter 6

1 Ann Radcliffe, *A Sicilian Romance*, ed. Alison Milbank (Oxford University Press, 1993, 1998), title-page epigraph. Further references are given after quotations in the text.

2 E. J. Clery, *The Rise of Supernatural Fiction, 1762–1800* (Cambridge University Press, 1995), p. 64.

3 'To lacerate or wound the feelings of; to vex, pain, or distress greatly. (Rarely with *up*.)', 'harrow', v^{1}, 4a, *OED Online* (Oxford University Press, September 2015).

4 Maggie Kilgour, *The Rise of the Gothic Novel* (London: Routledge, 1995), p. 21.

5 Edith Birkhead, *The Tale of Terror: A Study of the Gothic Romance* (London: Constable, 1921), pp. 38–62.

6 Dale Townsend, 'Gothic and the Ghost of *Hamlet*', in *Gothic Shakespeares*, ed. John Drakakis and Dale Townshend (Abingdon: Routledge, 2008), pp. 60–97 (pp. 72–3); Clery, *Rise of Supernatural Fiction*, p. 113.

7 Drakakis and Townshend, eds., *Gothic Shakespeares*, p. i.
8 Rictor Norton, 'Ann Radcliffe, "The Shakespeare of Romance Writers"', in *Shakespearean Gothic*, ed. Christy Desmet and Anne Williams (Cardiff: University of Wales Press, 2009), pp. 37–59 (p. 54).
9 Townshend, 'Gothic and the Ghost of *Hamlet*', p. 86.
10 Coral Ann Howells, *Love, Mystery and Misery: Feeling in Gothic Fiction* (London: Bloomsbury, 2013), p. 18.
11 Ann Radcliffe, *The Castles of Athlin and Dunbayne*, ed. Alison Milbank (Oxford University Press, 1995), p. x.
12 Radcliffe, *Sicilian Romance*, ed. Milbank, p. 200.
13 James Watt, *Contesting the Gothic: Fiction, Genre and Cultural Conflict, 1764–1832* (Cambridge University Press, 1999), p. 1.
14 Angela Wright, 'In Search of Arden: Ann Radcliffe's William Shakespeare', in *Gothic Shakespeares*, ed. Drakakis and Townshend, pp. 111–30 (p. 113).
15 Kilgour, *Rise of the Gothic Novel*, p. 40.
16 John Drakakis, 'Introduction', in *Gothic Shakespeares*, ed. Drakakis and Townshend, pp. 1–20 (p. 8).
17 Matthew Gregory Lewis, *The Monk: A Romance*, ed. D. L. Macdonald and Kathleen Scherf (Peterborough, Ont.: Broadview, 2004), p. 13.
18 Horace Walpole, *The Castle of Otranto*, ed. W. S. Lewis (Oxford University Press, 1982, 1988), p. 9.
19 *Monthly Review*, March 1797.
20 *Critical Review*, September 1789.
21 Sir Walter Scott, *The Lives of the Novelists*, ed. H. Frowde (Oxford University Press, 1906), p. 320.
22 Jacqueline Howard, *Reading Gothic Fiction: A Bakhtinian Approach* (Oxford: Clarendon Press, 1994), p. 99.
23 Townshend, 'Gothic and the Ghost of *Hamlet*', p. 73.
24 Walpole, *Castle of Otranto*, ed. Lewis, pp. 10–11.
25 *Critical Review* 14 (1795): 241–55.
26 Ann Radcliffe, *The Romance of the Forest*, ed. Chloe Chard (Oxford University Press, 1986, 1999), pp. 281–2. Further references are given after quotations in the text.
27 Radcliffe, *Mysteries of Udolpho*, ed. Dobrée, pp. 74–5. Further references are given after quotations in the text.
28 Radcliffe, *Castles*, ed. Milbank, p. xvi.
29 Catherine Belsey, '*Shakespearean Gothic* (review)', *Shakespeare Quarterly* 62.2 (2011): 298–300 (298).
30 Wright, 'In Search of Arden', p. 116.
31 Norton, 'Ann Radcliffe', p. 44.
32 Anna Laetitia Barbauld, *The British Novelists; With an Essay and Prefaces, Biographical and Critical*, 50 vols. (London, 1810), xliii. iv.
33 James Watt notes that instead of presenting Emily as a 'female Quixote' whose romance-fuelled fears are all groundless, the 'sensitive description' of Emily's frightening situations at Udolpho actually 'authorizes Emily's experience of "nameless terrors"', *Contesting the Gothic*, p. 105.

34 Ann Radcliffe, *The Italian; or The Confessional of the Black Penitents: A Romance*, ed. Frederick Garber (Oxford University Press, 1968, 1981, 1998), pp. 70, 109, 225, 325, 389. Further references follow quotations in the text.
35 David Salter, '"This Demon in the Garb of a Monk": Shakespeare, the Gothic and the Discourse of Anti-Catholicism', *Shakespeare* 5.1 (2009): 52–67 (55).
36 Lewis, *The Monk*, ed. Macdonald and Scherf, p. 141. Further references follow quotations in the text.
37 Ann Radcliffe, 'On the Supernatural in Poetry', *New Monthly Magazine* 16.1 (1826): 145–52.
38 Marcie Frank, 'Fairy Time from Shakespeare to Scott', in *Shakespeare and the Eighteenth Century*, ed. Sabor and Yachnin, pp. 103–17 (p. 114–15).
39 Norton, 'Ann Radcliffe', p. 50.
40 Frank, 'Fairy Time', p. 115.
41 Ibid., p. 112.
42 Deborah D. Rogers, ed., *The Critical Response to Ann Radcliffe* (Westport, CT: Greenwood Press, 1994), pp. xxxvii, xxxv.
43 Anne Williams, 'Reading Walpole Reading Shakespeare', in *Shakespearean Gothic*, ed. Desmet and Williams, pp. 13–36 (p. 13).
44 Fred Botting, *Gothic* (Abingdon: Routledge, 1996), p. 51.
45 Steven Craig, 'Shakespeare among the Goths', in *Gothic Shakespeares*, ed. Drakakis and Townshend, pp. 42–59 (p. 56).
46 Anon., *Anecdotes of Polite Literature*, 5 vols. (London, 1764), v. 176; Dodd, *Beauties of Shakespear*, ii. 239.
47 Amazon.com customer review of *The Mysteries of Udolpho*, 28 October 2012.
48 Townshend, 'Gothic and the Ghost of Hamlet', p. 89.
49 George Henry Lewes, 'Recent Novels: French and English', *Fraser's Magazine* 36 (1847): 686–95 (687).

Chapter 7

1 Austen, *Emma*, ed. Cronin and McMillan, p. 80.
2 Ibid., p. xliii.
3 Gail Marshall, 'Shakespeare and Fiction', in *Shakespeare in the Nineteenth Century*, ed. Gail Marshall (Cambridge University Press, 2012), pp. 96–112 (pp. 99, 101).
4 Park Honan, *Jane Austen: Her Life* (London: Weidenfeld & Nicolson, 1987), pp. 277–8.
5 Stephen Derry, 'Jane Austen's Use of *Measure for Measure* in *Sense and Sensibility*', *Persuasions* 15 (1993): 37–46.
6 John K. Hale, '*Persuasion*, Vol. IV, Chapter XI', *Persuasions* 16 (1994): 34–35.
7 Marcia Leveson, 'Comedy and Courtship: *Much Ado About Nothing* and *Pride and Prejudice*', *Johannesburg Shakespeare Quarterly* 1.2 (1994): 15–27.
8 Clara Calvo, 'Rewriting Lear's Untender Daughter: Fanny Price as a Regency Cordelia in Jane Austen's *Mansfield Park*', *Shakespeare Survey* 58 (2005): 83–94.

9 Elaine Bander, 'The Other Play in *Mansfield Park*: Shakespeare's *Henry VIII*', *Persuasions* 17 (1995): 111–20.
10 Ibid., 111–20.
11 David Selwyn, *Jane Austen and Leisure* (London: The Hambledon Press, 1999), pp. 234–5.
12 James Edward Austen-Leigh, *A Memoir of Jane Austen and Other Family Recollections*, ed. Kathryn Sutherland (Oxford University Press, 2002), p. 71.
13 Austen, *Later Manuscripts*, ed. Todd and Bree, pp. cxi–cxviii.
14 Vivien Jones, 'Jane Austen's Domestic Realism', in *Oxford History of the Novel*, ed. Garside and O'Brien, pp. 273–95 (p. 280).
15 Austen, *Mansfield Park*, ed. Wiltshire, p. lvii.
16 James Wood, *How Fiction Works* (London: Vintage Books, 2009), p. 9.
17 Joe Bray, *The Epistolary Novel: Representations of Consciousness* (London and New York: Routledge, 2003), pp. 20, 23.
18 Daniel Pollack-Pelzner, 'Jane Austen, the Prose Shakespeare', *Studies in English Literature, 1500–1900* 53.4 (2013): 763–92 (764).
19 Ibid., 765–6.
20 Ibid., 766.
21 Austen, *Emma*, ed. Cronin and McMillan, p. 5.
22 Ibid., pp. 282–3.
23 Austen, *Later Manuscripts*, ed. Todd and Bree, p. 145.
24 Megan Taylor has recently applied the notion of 'banal Shakespeare' to Austen, suggesting that she reinvigorates quotations through her understanding of their original sources, and their continued relevance. 'Jane Austen and "Banal Shakespeare"', *Eighteenth-Century Fiction* 27.1 (2014): 105–25.
25 Jane Austen, *Sense and Sensibility*, ed. Edward Copeland (Cambridge University Press, 2006), p. 98. Further references are given after quotations in the text.
26 See ibid., p. 457; Jocelyn Harris, *Jane Austen's Art of Memory* (Cambridge University Press, 1989), p. 59; Isobel Armstrong, *Jane Austen: Sense and Sensibility* (London: Penguin, 2000), pp. 16, 65.
27 In the 1995 film version of *Sense and Sensibility*, this literary conversation is exclusively focussed on Shakespeare, whose sonnets Marianne is discovered to be reading. Willoughby (Greg Wise) asks Marianne (Kate Winslet) to declare a favourite: when she ventures Sonnet 116, he quotes it back to her, and, taking out a volume of poems, professes, to her delight, to 'carry it with me always'. They piece together the poem from memory, the words 'Let me not to the marriage of true minds/ Admit impediment' suggesting their instant intimacy. When Marianne next quotes the poem, though, it is not in blushing dialogue but in hopeless soliloquy. She laments 'Love is not love/ That alters when it alteration finds' as (in a conflation of scenes) she gazes over the horizon to Combe Magna, in a rain storm that proves almost fatal to her health. *Sense and Sensibility*, dir. Ang Lee (Columbia Pictures Corporation, 1995).
28 Austen, *Mansfield Park*, ed. Wiltshire, p. 142. Further references are given after quotations in the text.

29 William Wordsworth, 'Preface to Lyrical Ballads', in *William Wordsworth, Lyrical Ballads, and Other Poems, 1797–1800*, ed. James Butler and Karen Green (Ithaca: Cornell University Press, 1992, 1996), p. 747.
30 Penny Gay, *Jane Austen and the Theatre* (Cambridge University Press, 2002), p. 102.
31 Kathleen E. Urda, 'Going from Extremes: *Mansfield Park* as a Revision of *Clarissa*', *Persuasions On-Line* 30.1 (2009), unpaginated, www.jasna.org/persuasions/on-line/vol30no1/urda.html. Sir Edward in *Sanditon*, another lover of quotation, 'felt that he was formed to be a dangerous man—quite in the line of the Lovelaces', *Later Manuscripts*, ed. Todd and Bree, p. 184.
32 See Chapter 3, pp. 65–6.
33 Susan Harland, '"Talking" and Reading Shakespeare in Jane Austen's *Mansfield Park*', *Wordsworth Circle*, 39.1/2 (2008): 43–6 (44–5).
34 See Chapter 2 and Chapter 3, pp. 33–4, 57, 69–70.
35 Dodd, *Beauties of Shakespear*, i. xiii.
36 Ibid., ii. 58, ii. 62, ii. 64.
37 Ibid., ii. 59, ii. 60, ii. 61 (ii. 71, added in 2nd edn of 1757), ii. 65.
38 Ibid., ii. 61, ii. 64.
39 For example, Dodd selects from *Measure for Measure* '*A Simile on the Presence of the belov'd Object*', and from *Love's Labour's Lost* '*A comical Description of* Cupid, *or Love*', i. 47, 33.
40 Susan Allen Ford, 'Reading *Elegant Extracts* in *Emma*: Very Entertaining!', *Persuasions On-Line* 28.1 (2007): unpaginated, www.jasna.org/persuasions/on-line/vol28no1/ford.htm. Ford notes that Austen gave a copy of the prose *Elegant Extracts* to her niece; and that a copy of the poetry version, signed 'Edward Austen, 1808', resides at Chawton House library.
41 Marshall, 'Shakespeare and Fiction', p. 102.
42 Vicesimus Knox, *Elegant Extracts: or Useful and Entertaining Pieces of Poetry, Selected for the Improvement of Youth, in Speaking, Reading, Thinking, Composing; and in the Conduct of Life; Being Similar in Design to Elegant Extracts in Prose* (London, 1784), p. 337.
43 'constancy', *n.*, 4. (with *a*) Something permanent, a permanency. *for a constancy*: as a permanent arrangement. *OED Online* (Oxford University Press, September 2015).
44 'constancy', *n.*, 2. 'Steadfastness of attachment to a person or cause; faithfulness, fidelity'. *OED Online* (Oxford University Press, September 2015).
45 Sterne, *Tristram Shandy*, ed. New and New, i. 423.
46 Austen, *Emma*, ed. Cronin and McMillan, pp. 79–80. Further references are given after quotations in the text.
47 Harris, *Jane Austen's Art of Memory*, p. 169.
48 Ibid.
49 Ibid., pp. 177–83.
50 Ibid., p. 187.
51 Ibid., p. 220.
52 Ibid., p. 59.

53 Ibid., pp. 175–6.
54 Jane Austen, *Persuasion*, ed. Janet Todd and Antje Blank (Cambridge University Press, 2006), p. 90. Further references are given after quotations in the text.
55 Jane Austen, *Pride and Prejudice*, ed. Pat Rogers (Cambridge University Press, 2006, 2013), p. 67. Further references are given after quotations in the text.
56 Michael Wood, 'Time and her Aunt', in *A Companion to Jane Austen*, ed. Claudia L. Johnson and Clara Tuite (Malden, MA: Blackwell Publishing, 2012), pp. 195–205 (p. 198); Norman Page, *The Language of Jane Austen* (Abingdon: Routledge, 1972, 2001), p. 29; Carole Moses, 'Jane Austen and Elizabeth Bennet: The Limits of Irony', *Persuasions* 25 (2003): 155–64 (159).
57 Bysshe, *Art of English Poetry*, 8th edn, 2 vols. (London, 1737), ii. 108. See also William D'Avenant, *Macbeth. A Tragedy. With All the Alterations, Amendments, Additions, and New Songs. As It Is Now Acted at the Queen's Theatre* (London, 1710).
58 The misquoted phrase could still be found in stories and books of excerpts for young people in the late eighteenth century, e.g., Anon., *A Short Story: Interspersed with Poetry. By a Young Lady*, 2 vols. (London, 1800), i. 176; and Anon., *The Instructor: or Young Man's Best Companion. Containing, Spelling, Reading, Writing, and Arithmetic. . .New Edn* (London, 1800), p. 31.
59 John Drakakis, 'Introduction', in *Gothic Shakespeares*, ed. John Drakakis and Dale Townshend (Abingdon: Routledge, 2008), pp. 1–20 (p. 2). Benedict and Le Faye note that these three quoted phrases 'appear in *Elegant Extracts*', Austen, *Northanger Abbey*, ed. Benedict and Le Faye, p. 296.
60 Vivien Jones, 'Jane Austen's Domestic Realism', in *Oxford History of the Novel in English*, ed. Garside and O'Brien, pp. 273–95 (p. 281).
61 Tara Ghoshal Wallace, *Jane Austen and Narrative Authority* (Basingstoke: Macmillan, 1995), p. 14; Daniel P. Gunn, 'Free Indirect Discourse and Narrative Authority in *Emma*', *Narrative* 12 (2004): 35–54.

Chapter 8

1 John Kucich and Jenny Bourne Taylor, eds., 'Introduction', *The Oxford History of the Novel in English: Vol. III: The Nineteenth-Century Novel, 1820–1880* (Oxford University Press, 2012), p. xviii.
2 Marshall, ed., 'Introduction', *Shakespeare in the Nineteenth Century*, p. 1; Adrian Poole, 'Introduction', *Victorian Shakespeare: Volume 2: Literature and Culture* (Basingstoke: Palgrave Macmillan, 2003), p. 12.
3 Walter Scott, *The Antiquary*, ed. David Hewitt (Edinburgh University Press, 1995), p. 113.
4 Charlotte Brontë, *Jane Eyre*, ed. Jane Jack and Margaret Smith (Oxford: Clarendon Press, 1969), p. 176.
5 Charles Dickens, *David Copperfield*, ed. Nina Burgis (Oxford: Clarendon Press, 1981), pp. 149–50, 505.
6 George Eliot, *Middlemarch*, ed. David Carroll (Oxford: Clarendon Press, 1986), p. 296.

7 Charles Dickens, *Great Expectations*, ed. Margaret Cardwell (Oxford: Clarendon Press, 1993), p. 254.
8 Adrian Poole, ed., *Great Shakespeareans, Vol V: Scott, Dickens, Eliot, Hardy* (London: Continuum, 2011), p. 3.
9 Ibid., p. 3.
10 Ibid., pp. 3–4.

Bibliography

Primary works

A. Z., 'To the Author of Common Sense', Saturday, 24 June, 1738. *Common Sense: or, the Englishman's Journal. Being a Collection of Letters, Political, Humorous, and Moral; Publish'd Weekly under that Title*, 2 vols. (London, 1739), ii. 123–8

Allot, Robert, *Englands Parnassus: or, the Choysest Flowers of our Moderne Poets, with their Poetical Comparisons* (London, 1600)

Amory, Thomas, *The Life of John Buncle, Esq*. (London, 1756)

Anon., *The Adventures of Jack Wander. Written by Himself. Interspers'd with Some Humorous Anecdotes, and Original Memoirs* (London, [1766?])

The Adventures of Oxymel Classic, Esq; Once an Oxford Scholar (London, 1768)

A Journey through the Head of a Modern Poet, Being the Substance of a Dream, Occasioned by Reading the Sixth Book of Virgil (London, 1750)

A Short Story: Interspersed with Poetry. By a Young Lady, 2 vols. (London, 1800)

Almira. Being the History of a Young Lady of Good Birth and Fortune, but More Distinguished Merit (London, 1762)

Amusements in High Life; or, Conjugal Infidelities in 1786. In a Series of Confidential Letters, between Ladies Who Have Distinguished Themselves by the Multiplicity and Singularity of their Amours (London, 1786)

Anecdotes of Polite Literature, 5 vols. (London, 1764)

Chit-Chat: or, Natural Characters; and the Manners of Real Life, Represented in a Series of Interesting Adventures, 2 vols. (London, 1755)

Cleanthes and Semanthe. A Dramatic History. By the Author of Leonora, 2 vols. (London, 1764)

Elegant Extracts in Miniature, Selected from New Publications, Monthly Magazines, Reviews, &c. Embellished with Elegant Engravings (Edinburgh, 1796)

Ermina; or, The Fair Recluse. In a Series of Letters. By a Lady, Author of Dorinda Calsby [sic] &c, 2 vols. (London, 1772)

Memoirs and Interesting Adventures of an Embroidered Waistcoat (London, 1751)

Memoirs of the Bedford Coffee-House. By a Genius, 2nd edn (London, 1763)

The Batchelor: or Speculations of Jeoffry Wagstaffe, Esq., 3 vols. (Dublin, 1773)

The Beauties of Shakespeare; Selected from his Plays and Poems (London: George Kearsley, 1783)
The History of Lavinia Rawlins, 2 vols. (London, 1756)
The History of Miss Dorinda Catsby, and Miss Emilia Faulkner: In a Series of Letters, 2 vols. (London, 1772)
The History of Miss Pittborough. In a Series of Letters. By a Lady, 2 vols. (London, 1767)
The History of Sophia Shakespear (London, 1753)
The Instructor: or Young Man's Best Companion. Containing, Spelling, Reading, Writing, and Arithmetic...New Edn (London, 1800)
The Life and Memoirs of Mr. Ephraim Tristram Bates (London, 1756)
The Life, Travels, and Adventures of Christopher Wagstaff, Gentleman, Grandfather to Tristram Shandy, 2 vols. (London, 1762)
The Unfortunate Beauty: or Memoirs of Miss Anna Maria Soames, and Several Others; a Narrative Founded on Known Facts (London, 1757)
The Younger Brother, a Tale, 2 vols. (London, 1770–2)
Critical Remarks on Sir Charles Grandison, Clarissa *and* Pamela (London, 1754) (Los Angeles: University of California, 1950)
Pamela Censured (London, 1741) (Los Angeles: University of California, 1976)
Austen, Jane, *Emma*, ed. Richard Cronin and Dorothy McMillan (Cambridge University Press, 2005)
Juvenilia, ed. Peter Sabor (Cambridge University Press, 2006)
Later Manuscripts, ed. Janet Todd and Linda Bree (Cambridge University Press, 2008)
Mansfield Park, ed. John Wiltshire (Cambridge University Press, 2005)
Northanger Abbey, ed. Barbara M. Benedict and Deirdre Le Faye (Cambridge University Press, 2006)
Persuasion, ed. Janet Todd and Antje Blank (Cambridge University Press, 2006)
Pride and Prejudice, ed. Pat Rogers (Cambridge University Press, 2006, 2013)
Sense and Sensibility, ed. Edward Copeland (Cambridge University Press, 2006)
Barbauld, A. L., *The British Novelists; With an Essay and Prefaces, Biographical and Critical*, 50 vols. (London, 1810)
Barker, Jane, *Amours of Bosvil and Galesia* (London, 1715)
Beaumont, Agnes, *The Narrative of the Persecutions of Agnes Beaumont*, ed. Vera Camden (East Lansing: Colleagues Press, 1992)
Behn, Aphra, *Love-Letters between a Noble-Man and his Sister, in Three Parts* (London, 1684)
Bellamy, George Anne, *An Apology for the Life of George Anne Bellamy. Late of Covent Garden Theatre. Written by Herself*, 5 vols. (London, 1785)
Bentivoglio, Cardinal, *Letters of Wit, Politicks, and Morality. Written Originally in Italian, by the Famous Cardinal Bentivoglio ...*, ed. Abel Boyer (London, 1701)

Bradstreet, Dudley, *Bradstreet's Lives: Being a Genuine History of Several Gentlemen and Ladies, All Living within These Ten Years Past, Remarkable for their Virtues* (Dublin, 1757)

Brontë, Charlotte, *Jane Eyre*, ed. Jane Jack and Margaret Smith (Oxford: Clarendon Press, 1969)

Brooke, Henry, *The Fool of Quality, or, The History of Henry Earl of Moreland*, 2nd edn, 4 vols. (London, 1767)

Brooke, Frances, *The Excursion*, ed. Paula R. Backscheider and Hope D. Cotton (Lexington: University Press of Kentucky, 1997)

Bruce, William, *Some Facts and Observations Relative to the Fate of the Late Linen Bill, Last Session of Parliament in This Kingdom* (London, 1753)

Burgoyne, John, *The Maid of the Oaks: A New Dramatic Entertainment. As It Is Performed at the Theatre-Royal, in Drury-Lane* (London, 1774)

Burney, Frances, *Evelina*, ed. Margaret Anne Doody (London: Penguin, 1994)

The Witlings and The Woman-Hater, ed. Peter Sabor and Geoffrey Sill (Peterborough, Ont.: Broadview, 2002)

Bysshe, Edward, *The Art of English Poetry: Containing, I. Rules for Making Verses. II. A Dictionary of Rhymes. III. A Collection of the Most Natural, Agreeable, and Noble Thoughts, viz. Allusions, Similes, Descriptions, and Characters, of Persons and Things; that Are to Be Found in the Best English Poets* (London, 1702)

The Art of English Poetry, 2nd edn (London, 1705)

The Art of English Poetry, 3rd edn (London, 1708)

The Art of English Poetry, 8th edn, 2 vols. (London, 1737)

Careless, Charles, *The Amours and Adventures of Charles Careless*, 2 vols. (London, 1764)

Cavendish, Margaret, Duchess of Newcastle, *CCXI Sociable Letters Written by the Thrice Noble, Illustrious and Excellent Princess the Lady Marchioness of Newcastle* (London: William Wilson, 1664)

Cervantes Saavedra, Miguel de, *The Adventures of Don Quixote*, trans. J. M. Cohen (London: Penguin, 1950)

Charke, Charlotte, *The History of Henry Dumont, Esq, and Miss Charlotte Evelyn: Consisting of a Variety of Entertaining Characters and Very Interesting Subjects: with Some Critical Remarks on Comic Actors* (London, 1756)

Cleland, John, *Memoirs of a Woman of Pleasure*, 2 vols. (London, 1748–9)

Memoirs of a Woman of Pleasure, ed. Peter Sabor (Oxford University Press, 1985)

Cogan, Thomas, *John Buncle, Junior, Gentleman* (London, 1776–8)

Constable, John, *The Conversation of Gentlemen Considered in Most of the Ways, that Make their Mutual Company Agreeable, or Disagreeable. In Six Dialogues* (London, 1738)

Coventry, Francis, *The History of Pompey the Little: or, The Life and Adventures of a Lap-Dog*, 3rd edn (London 1752)

The History of Pompey the Little . . ., 4th edn (London, 1761)

Critical Review (Edinburgh, 1756–1818)

D'Avenant, William, *Macbeth. A Tragedy. With All the Alterations, Amendments, Additions, and New Songs. As It Is Now Acted at the Queen's Theatre* (London, 1710)

Davys, Mary, *The Accomplish'd Rake; or, Modern Fine Gentleman. Being an Exact Description of the Conduct and Behaviour of a Person of Distinction* (London, 1727)

Defoe, Daniel, *Moll Flanders*, ed. David Blewett (Harmondsworth: Penguin, 1989)

Dickens, Charles, *David Copperfield*, ed. Nina Burgis (Oxford: Clarendon Press, 1981)

Great Expectations, ed. Margaret Cardwell (Oxford: Clarendon Press, 1993)

Dodd, William, *The Beauties of Shakespear*, 2 vols. (London, 1752)

The Beauties of Shakespear, 2nd edn (London, 1757)

The Beauties of Shakespear, 3rd edn (Dublin, 1773)

The Sisters; or, The History of Lucy and Caroline Sanson, Entrusted to a False Friend (London, 1754)

Dryden, John, *Of Dramatick Poesie, an Essay* (London, 1668)

Echlin, Lady Elizabeth, *An Alternative Ending to Richardson's* Clarissa, ed. Dimiter Daphinoff (Bern: Francke Verlag, 1982)

Eliot, George, *Middlemarch*, ed. David Carroll (Oxford: Clarendon Press, 1986)

Enfield, William, *The Speaker: or, Miscellaneous Pieces, Selected from the Best English Writers, and Disposed under Proper Heads, with a View to Facilitate the Improvement of Youth in Reading and Speaking. A New Edition, Corrected and Enlarged. To which Are Prefixed Two Essays: I. On Elocution. II. On Reading Works of Taste* (London, 1790)

Evangelical Magazine (London, 1793–1800)

Fielding, Henry, *Amelia*, 4 vols. (London, 1752)

Amelia, ed. Martin C. Battestin (Oxford: Clarendon Press, 1983)

Don Quixote in England. A Comedy. As It Is Acted at the New Theatre in the Hay-Market (London, 1734)

The Author's Farce (London, 1730)

The Covent-Garden Journal and A Plan of the Universal Register-Office, ed. Bertrand A. Goldgar (Oxford: Clarendon Press, 1988)

The Fathers (London, 1778)

The Historical Register for 1736 (London, 1737)

The History of the Adventures of Joseph Andrews, 2 vols. (London, 1742)

The History of Tom Jones, a Foundling, 4 vols. (London, 1749)

The History of Tom Jones, a Foundling, ed. Martin C. Battestin and Fredson Bowers, 2 vols. (Oxford: Clarendon Press, 1974)

The Tragedy of Tragedies, or, the Life and Death of Tom Thumb the Great: As It Is Acted at the Theatre in the Hay-market. With Annotations of H. Scriblerus Secundus (London, 1731)

The True Patriot and Related Writings, ed. W. B. Coley (Oxford: Clarendon Press, 1987)

An Enquiry into the Causes of the Late Increase in Robbers and Related Writings, ed. Malvin R. Zirker (Oxford: Clarendon Press, 1988)

and Sarah Fielding, *The Correspondence of Henry and Sarah Fielding*, ed. Martin C. Battestin and Clive T. Probyn (Oxford: Clarendon Press, 1993)
Joseph Andrews, ed. Martin C. Battestin (Oxford: Clarendon Press, 1967)
Miscellanies by Henry Fielding, Esq., Vol. I, ed. Henry Knight Miller, 3 vols. (Oxford: Clarendon Press, 1972–97)
Plays, ed. Thomas Lockwood (Oxford: Clarendon Press, 2004–11)
The History of the Adventures of Joseph Andrews, and of his Friend Mr. Abraham Adams, and An Apology for the Life of Mrs. Shamela Andrews, ed. Douglas Brooks-Davies and rev. Thomas Keymer (Oxford University Press, 1999)
The History of Tom Jones, a Foundling, ed. Thomas Keymer and Alice Wakely (London: Penguin, 2005)
The Journal of a Voyage to Lisbon, Shamela, and Occasional Writings, ed. Martin C. Battestin, with the late Sheridan W. Baker, Jr., and Hugh Amory (Oxford: Clarendon Press, 2008)
Tom Jones, ed. John Bender and Simon Stern (Oxford University Press, 1996, 1998)
Fielding, Sarah, *The Adventures of David Simple*, 2 vols. (London, 1744)
The Adventures of David Simple, 2nd edn, 2 vols. (London, 1744)
The Adventures of David Simple, ed. Linda Bree (London: Penguin, 2002)
The Adventures of David Simple: Volume the Last (London, 1753)
The Adventures of David Simple and Volume the Last, ed. Peter Sabor (Lexington: University Press of Kentucky, 1998)
Familiar Letters between the Principal Characters in David Simple, and Some Others, 2 vols. (London, 1747)
The Governess; or, Little Female Academy (London, 1749)
The Governess; or, The Little Female Academy, ed. Candace Ward (Peterborough, Ont.: Broadview, 2005)
The Governess; or, Little Female Academy: A Facsimile Reproduction of the First Edition of 1749, with an Introduction and Bibliography by Jill E. Grey (London: Oxford University Press, 1968)
The History of the Countess of Dellwyn, 2 vols. (London, 1759)
The History of Ophelia, 2 vols. (London, 1760)
The History of Ophelia, ed. Peter Sabor (Peterborough, Ont.: Broadview, 2004)
Remarks on Clarissa, *Addressed to the Author, Occasioned by Some Critical Conversations on the Characters and Conduct of that Work. With Some Reflections on the Character and Behaviour of Prior's Emma* (London, 1749)
and Jane Collier, *The Cry: A New Dramatic Fable*, 3 vols. (London, 1754)
Fuller, Thomas, *The History of the Worthies of England Who for Parts and Learning Have Been Eminent in the Several Counties: Together with an Historical Narrative of the Native Commodities and Rarities in Each County* (London, 1662)
Garrick, David, *Shakespeare's Garland. Being a Collection of New Songs, Ballads, Roundelays, Catches, Glees, Comic-Serenatas, &c. Performed at the Jubilee at Stratford upon Avon. The Musick by Dr. Arne, Mr. Bartholomew, Mr. Ailwood, and Mr. Dibdin* (London, 1769)

Miss in her Teens: or, The Medley of Lovers. A Farce in Two Acts. As It Is Performed at the Theatre-Royal in Covent-Garden (London, 1747)

Gentleman, Francis, *The Stratford Jubilee* (London, 1769)

The Gentleman's Magazine, or, Monthly Intelligencer [afterw.] and Historical Chronicle, Collected Chiefly from the Public Papers by Sylvanus Urban (London, 1731–1868)

Goldsmith, Oliver, *The Beauties of Poesy*, 2 vols. (London, 1767)

'Of the Stage', in *An Enquiry into the Present State of Polite Learning in Europe* (London, 1759)

The Vicar of Wakefield (London, 1766)

The Vicar of Wakefield, ed. Arthur Friedman (Oxford University Press, 1981, 2008)

Goodall, William, *The Adventures of Capt. Greenland. Written in Imitation of All Those Wise, Learned, Witty and Humorous Authors, Who Either Have, or Hereafter May Write in the Same Stile and Manner* (London, 1752)

Griffith, Elizabeth, *The Morality of Shakespeare's Drama Illustrated* (London, 1775)

Guardian, The, 2 vols. (London, 1714)

Gunning, Elizabeth, *The Packet: A Novel*, 4 vols. (London, 1794)

Hayward, Thomas, *The British Muse, or, A Collection of Thoughts Moral, Natural, and Sublime, of our English Poets: Who Flourished in the Sixteenth and Seventeenth Centuries. With Several Curious Topicks, and Beautiful Passages, Never before Extracted, from Shakespear, Johnson, Beaumont, Fletcher, and above a Hundred More*, 3 vols. (London, 1738)

Haywood, Eliza, *The Tea-Table: or, A Conversation between Some Polite Persons of Both Sexes, at a Lady's Visiting Day. Wherein Are Represented the Various Foibles, and Affectations, Which Form the Character of an Accomplish'd Beau, or Modern Fine Lady* (London, 1725)

Hill, Aaron, *The Dramatic Works of Aaron Hill, Esq.*, 2 vols. (London, 1760)

Hume, David, *A Treatise of Human Nature*, ed. Ernest C. Mossner (London: Penguin, 1969, 1984)

Johnson, Samuel, *A Dictionary of the English Language; in Which the Words Are Deduced from their Originals and Illustrated in their Different Significations by Examples from the Best Writers. To Which Are Prefixed, a History of the Language, and an English Grammar*, 2 vols. (London, 1755)

The Yale Edition of the Works of Samuel Johnson, ed. Arthur Sherbo (Yale University Press: New Haven and London, 1968)

Kidgell, John, *The Card*, 2 vols. (London, 1755)

Kimber, Edward, *The Juvenile Adventures of David Ranger, Esq; from an Original Manuscript Found in the Collections of a Late Noble Lord*, 2 vols. (London, 1757)

Knox, Vicesimus, *Elegant Extracts: or Useful and Entertaining Pieces of Poetry, Selected for the Improvement of Youth, in Speaking, Reading, Thinking, Composing; and in the Conduct of Life; Being Similar in Design to Elegant Extracts in Prose* (London, 1784)

'Lady Bradshaigh to Samuel Richardson, 2–22 March 1754', Forster Collection reel 15, F.48.E.5.28, National Art Library, London

Lawrence, Herbert, *The Contemplative Man; or, The History of Christopher Crab, Esq.; of North-Wales,* 2 vols. (London, 1771)
Lee, Ang, dir., *Sense and Sensibility* (Columbia Pictures Corporation, 1995)
Le Faucheur, Michel, *An Essay upon Pronunciation and Gesture, Founded upon the Best Rules and Authorities of the Ancients, Ecclesiastical and Civil, and Adorned with the Finest Rules of Elocution* (London, 1750)
Lennox, Charlotte, *Shakespear Illustrated: or the Novels and Histories, on Which the Plays of Shakespear Are Founded, Collected and Translated from the Original Authors. With Critical Remarks,* 2 vols. (London, 1753)
Lewes, George Henry, 'Recent Novels: French and English', *Fraser's Magazine* 36 (1847): 686–95
Lewis, Matthew Gregory, *The Monk: A Romance,* ed. D. L. Macdonald and Kathleen Scherf (Peterborough, Ont.: Broadview, 2004)
Lichtenberg, Georg Christoph, *Lichtenberg's Visits to England, as Described in his Letters and Diaries,* trans. Margaret L. Mare and W. H. Quarrell (Oxford: Clarendon Press, 1938)
Mackenzie, Henry, *The Man of Feeling,* ed. Brian Vickers (Oxford University Press, 1967)
Molloy, Charles, *The Coquet: or, The English Chevalier. A Comedy. As It Is Acted by His Majesty's Servants* (London, 1718)
Montagu, Elizabeth, *An Essay on the Writings and Genius of Shakespear, Compared with the Greek and French Dramatic Poets. With Some Remarks upon the Misrepresentations of Mons. de Voltaire* (London, 1769)
Monthly Review, The (London: 1749–1828)
Morgann, Maurice, *An Essay on the Dramatic Character of Sir John Falstaff* (London, 1777)
Morvan de Bellegarde, Jean Baptiste, *Reflexions upon Ridicule; or, What It Is that Makes a Man Ridiculous; and the Means to Avoid It* (London, 1707)
Murphy, Arthur, *The Gray's-Inn Journal,* 2 vols. (Dublin, 1756)
Nobleman of Distinguished Abilities, *The Art of Conversation; or, The Polite Entertainer: Calculated for the Improvement of Both Sexes* (London, 1757)
Poole, Josua, *The English Parnassus: or, A Helpe to English Poesie* (London, 1657)
Public Advertiser (London 1752–94)
Radcliffe, Ann, *The Castles of Athlin and Dunbayne,* ed. Alison Milbank (Oxford University Press, 1995)
The Italian; or The Confessional of the Black Penitents: A Romance, ed. Frederick Garber (Oxford University Press, 1968, 1981, 1998)
'On the Supernatural in Poetry', *New Monthly Magazine* 16.1 (1826): 145–52
A Sicilian Romance, ed. Alison Milbank (Oxford University Press, 1993, 1998)
The Mysteries of Udolpho, ed. Bonamy Dobrée (Oxford University Press, 1998)
The Romance of the Forest, ed. Chloe Chard (Oxford University Press, 1986, 1999)
Ralph, James, *The Case of our Present Theatrical Disputes, Fairly Stated* (London, 1743)

Reeve, Clara, *The Progress of Romance, through Times, Countries and Manners, with Remarks on the Good and Bad Effects of It, on Them Respectively; in a Course of Evening Conversations*, 2 vols. (Colchester, 1785)

The School for Widows. A Novel, 3 vols. (London, 1791)

Richardson, Samuel, *Clarissa. Or, the History of a Young Lady: Comprehending the Most Important Concerns of Private Life. And Particularly Shewing, the Distresses that May Attend the Misconduct Both of Parents and Children, in Relation to Marriage. Published by the Editor of Pamela*, 7 vols. (London, 1748)

Clarissa. Or, the History of a Young Lady, 2nd edn, 7 vols. (London, 1749)

Clarissa. Or, the History of a Young Lady, 3rd edn, 8 vols. (London, 1751)

Clarissa, 4 vols. (London: Everyman, 1932)

Clarissa, or, The History of a Young Lady, ed. Angus Ross (Harmondsworth: Penguin, 1985)

A Collection of the Moral and Instructive Sentiments, Maxims, Cautions, and Reflexions, Contained in the Histories of Pamela, Clarissa, and Sir Charles Grandison. Digested under Proper Heads (London, 1755)

The Correspondence of Samuel Richardson, Author of Pamela, Clarissa, *and* Sir Charles Grandison. *Selected from the Original Manuscripts, Bequeathed Him to his Family, to Which Are Prefixed, a Biographical Account of that Author, and Observations on his Writings*, ed. A. L. Barbauld, 6 vols. (London: Printed for Richard Phillips, 1804)

Early Works, ed. Alexander Pettit (Cambridge University Press, 2012)

The History of Sir Charles Grandison, 2nd edn, 6 vols. (London, 1753–4)

The History of Sir Charles Grandison, ed. Jocelyn Harris, 3 vols. (London: Oxford University Press, 1972)

Letters Written to and for Particular Friends, on the Most Important Occasions. Directing Not Only the Requisite Style and Forms to be Observed in Writing Familiar Letters; but How to Think and Act Justly and Prudently, in the Common Concerns of Human Life (London, 1741)

Pamela: or, Virtue Rewarded. In a Series of Familiar Letters from a Beautiful Young Damsel to her Parents (London, 1742)

Pamela: Or, Virtue Rewarded. In a Series of Familiar Letters from a Beautiful Young Damsel to her Parents: and Afterwards, in her Exalted Condition, between Her, and Persons of Figure and Quality, upon the Most Important and Entertaining Subjects in Genteel Life. The Third and Fourth Volumes. Publish'd in Order to Cultivate the Principles of Virtue and Religion in the Minds of the Youth of Both Sexes. By the Editor of the Two First (London, 1742)

Pamela in her Exalted Condition, ed. Albert J. Rivero (Cambridge University Press, 2012)

Pamela; or, Virtue Rewarded, ed. Albert J. Rivero (Cambridge University Press, 2011)

Pamela; or, Virtue Rewarded, ed. Thomas Keymer and Alice Wakely (Oxford University Press, 2001)

The Paths of Virtue Delineated; or, The History in Miniature of the Celebrated Clarissa Harlowe, Familiarised and Adapted to the Capacities of Youth (London, 1756)

Selected Letters of Samuel Richardson, ed. John Carroll (Oxford: Clarendon Press, 1964)

Richardson, William, *A Philosophical Analysis and Illustration of Some of Shakespeare's Remarkable Characters* (London, 1774)

Scott, Sir Walter, *The Antiquary*, ed. David Hewitt (Edinburgh University Press, 1995)

The Lives of the Novelists, ed. H. Frowde (Oxford University Press, 1906)

Several Hands, *The Monthly Review, or, Literary Journal. Giving a Candid Account, with Abstracts of, or Extracts from, the New Books and Pamphlets, Published in Great-Britain, as They Come Out*, Vol. VI, 2nd edn (London, 1752)

Shaftesbury, Anthony Ashley Cooper, 3rd Earl of, *Characteristicks of Men, Manners, Opinions, Times.*, 6th edn, 3 vols. (London, 1737)

Shakespeare, William, *The Works of William Shakespear. In Six Volumes, Collated and Corrected by the Former Editions by Mr. Pope* (London, 1725)

The Works of Shakespeare: In Seven Volumes. Collated with the Oldest Copies, and Corrected; with Notes, Explanatory, and Critical: by Mr. Theobald (London, 1733)

The Works of Shakespear in Eight Volumes . . . by Mr. Pope and Mr. Warburton, 8 vols. (London, 1747)

The Plays of William Shakespeare, in Eight Volumes, with the Corrections and Illustrations of Various Commentators; to Which Are Added Notes by Sam. Johnson (London, 1765)

The Oxford Shakespeare: The Complete Works, ed. Stanley Wells and Gary Taylor (Oxford University Press, 1988)

Shaw, Dr Peter, *The Reflector: Representing Human Affairs as They Are, and as They May Be Improved* (London, 1750)

Smith, Adam, *Lectures on Rhetoric and Belles Lettres*, ed. John M. Lothian (Edinburgh: Thomas Nelson and Sons Ltd, 1963)

The Theory of Moral Sentiments, ed. D. D. Raphael and A. L. Macfie (Oxford: Clarendon Press, 1976)

Smollett, Tobias, *The Adventures of Ferdinand Count Fathom*, ed. Damian Grant (Oxford University Press, 1971)

The Adventures of Peregrine Pickle: In Which Are Included Memoirs of a Lady of Quality, ed. James Clifford and rev. Paul-Gabriel Boucé (Oxford University Press, 1983)

The Expedition of Humphry Clinker, ed. Lewis M. Knapp and rev. Paul-Gabriel Boucé (Oxford University Press, 1966, 1988)

Stanhope, Philip, 4th Earl of Chesterfield. *Lord Chesterfield's Letters*, ed. David Roberts (Oxford University Press, 1992)

Steele, Richard, *The Lucubrations of Isaac Bickerstaff, Esq.: Revised and Corrected by the Author*, 4 vols. (London 1710)

Sterne, Laurence, *Letters of Laurence Sterne*, ed. Lewis Perry Curtis (Oxford: Clarendon Press, 1935)

The Life and Opinions of Tristram Shandy, Gentleman, 9 vols. (London, 1760–67)
The Life and Opinions of Tristram Shandy: The Text and Notes, ed. Melvyn New and Joan New, 3 vols. (Gainsville: University Presses of Florida, 1978–84)
The Life and Opinions of Tristram Shandy, Gentleman, ed. Ian Campbell Ross (Oxford University Press, 1983, 1999)
A Sentimental Journey through France and Italy, 2 vols. (London, 1768)
A Sentimental Journey through France and Italy, by Mr. Yorick, including A Journal to Eliza, ed. Ian Jack (Oxford University Press, 1998)
A Sentimental Journey through France and Italy and Continuation of the Bramine's Journal: The Text and Notes, ed. Melvyn New and W. G. Day (Gainesville: University Press of Florida, 2002)
The Sermons of Laurence Sterne, ed. Melvyn New (Gainesville: University Press of Florida, 1996)
Stillingfleet, Benjamin, *An Essay on Conversation* (London, 1737)
Swift, Jonathan, *Gulliver's Travels*, ed. David Womersley (Cambridge University Press, 2012)
Parodies, Hoaxes and Mock Treatises: Polite Conversation, Directions to Servants and Other Works, ed. Valerie Rumbold (Cambridge University Press, 2013)
The Tatler, ed. Richmond P. Bond, 3 vols. (Oxford: Clarendon Press, 1987)
Urban, Sylvanus, Gent., *The Gentleman's Magazine, and Historical Chronicle, Vol. XXII, for the Year 1752* (London, 1752)
Walpole, Horace, *The Castle of Otranto*, ed. W. S. Lewis (Oxford University Press, 1982, 1988)
Whately, Thomas, *Remarks on Some of the Characters of Shakespeare* (London, 1770)
Young, Edward, *Conjectures on Original Composition* (London, 1759)

Secondary works

Aikins, Janet E., 'A Plot Discover'd; or, The Uses of *Venice Preserv'd* within *Clarissa*', *University of Toronto Quarterly* 55 (1986): 219–34
Alexander, Catherine M. S., 'Shakespeare and the Eighteenth Century: Criticism and Research', *Shakespeare Survey* 51 (1998): 1–15
Allan, David, *Commonplace Books and Reading in Georgian England* (Cambridge University Press, 2010)
Allen, Graham, *Intertextuality* (London: Routledge, 2000)
Alter, Robert, 'Fielding and the Uses of Style', *Novel: A Forum on Fiction* 1 (1967): 53–63
Altick, Richard D., *The English Common Reader: A Social History of the Mass Reading Public, 1800–1900*, 2nd edn (Columbus: Ohio State University Press, 1957)
Anderson, Emily Hodgson, *Eighteenth-Century Authorship and the Play of Fiction: Novels and the Theater, Haywood to Austen* (New York and Abingdon: Routledge, 2009)

Armstrong, Isobel, *Jane Austen: Sense and Sensibility* (London: Penguin, 2000)
Armstrong, Nancy, *Desire and Domestic Fiction: A Political History of the Novel* (New York: Oxford University Press, 1987)
How Novels Think: The Limits of British Individualism from 1719–1900 (New York: Columbia University Press, 2006)
Austen-Leigh, James Edward, *A Memoir of Jane Austen and Other Family Recollections*, ed. Kathryn Sutherland (Oxford University Press, 2002)
Babcock, R. W., *The Genesis of Shakespeare Idolatry 1766–1799: A Study in English Criticism of the Late Eighteenth Century* (Chapel Hill: University of North Carolina Press, 1931)
Backscheider, Paula R., 'Shadowing Theatrical Change', in *Players, Playwrights, Playhouses: Investigating Performance, 1660-1800*, ed. Michael Cordner and Peter Holland (Basingstoke: Palgrave Macmillan, 2007), pp. 78–100
Ballaster, Ros, *Seductive Forms: Women's Amatory Fiction from 1684–1740* (Oxford: Clarendon Press, 1992)
Bander, Elaine, 'The Other Play in *Mansfield Park*: Shakespeare's *Henry VIII*', *Persuasions* 17 (1995): 111–20
Barchas, Janine, *Graphic Design, Print Culture, and the Eighteenth-Century Novel* (Cambridge University Press, 2003)
'Sarah Fielding's Dashing Style and Eighteenth-Century Print Culture', *ELH* 63.3 (1996): 633–56
and Gordon D. Fulton, *The Annotations in Lady Bradshaigh's Copy of* Clarissa, (Victoria, BC: University of Victoria, 1998)
Barish, Jonas, *The Antitheatrical Prejudice* (Berkeley: University of California Press, 1981)
Barker-Benfield, G. J., *The Culture of Sensibility: Sex and Society in Eighteenth-Century Britain* (Chicago and London: University of Chicago Press, 1992)
Barnett, Dene, *The Art of Gesture: The Practices and Principles of Eighteenth-Century Acting* (Heidelberg: C. Winter, 1987)
Barthes, Roland, 'Theory of the Text', in *Untying the Text: A Post-Structuralist Reader*, ed. R. Young (Boston, Mass.: Routledge & Kegan Paul, 1981)
Bate, Jonathan, *Shakespeare and the English Romantic Imagination* (Oxford: Clarendon Press, 1986)
Shakespearean Constitutions: Politics, Theatre, Criticism 1730–1830 (Oxford: Clarendon Press, 1989)
The Genius of Shakespeare (London: Picador, 1997)
Bate, Walter Jackson, *From Classic to Romantic: Premises of Taste in Eighteenth-Century England* (New York: Harper & Brothers, 1946)
Batt, Jennifer '"It Ought Not to Be Lost to the World": The Transmission and Consumption of Eighteenth-Century Lyric Verse', *The Review of English Studies*, 62.255 (2011): 414–32
Battestin, Martin C., *The Moral Basis of Fielding's Art: A Study of* Joseph Andrews (Middletown, Connecticut: Wesleyan University Press, 1959)

with Ruthe R. Battestin, *Henry Fielding: A Life* (London and New York: Routledge, 1989)

Beer, Gillian, *Arguing with the Past: Essays in Narrative from Woolf to Sidney* (London and New York: Routledge, 1989)

Bell, Ian A., *Henry Fielding: Authorship and Authority* (London and New York: Longman, 1994)

Bellamy, Liz, *Commerce, Morality and the Eighteenth-Century Novel* (Cambridge University Press, 1998)

Belsey, Catherine 'Shakespearean Gothic (review)', *Shakespeare Quarterly* 62.2 (2011): 298–300

Benedetti, Jean, *David Garrick and the Birth of Modern Theatre* (London: Methuen, 2001)

Benedict, Barbara, *Making the Modern Reader: Cultural Mediation in Early Modern Anthologies* (Princeton University Press, 1996)

Bernard, Stephen Jarrod, 'Edward Bysshe and *The Art of English Poetry*: Reading Writing in the Eighteenth Century', *Eighteenth-Century Studies* 46.1 (2012): 113–29

Berry, Helen, 'Rethinking Politeness in Eighteenth-Century England: Moll King's Coffee House and the Significance of "Flash Talk"' (The Alexander Prize Lecture), *Transactions of the Royal Historical Society* 11 (2001): 65–81 (68)

Birkhead, Edith, *The Tale of Terror: A Study of the Gothic Romance* (London: Constable, 1921)

Blackwell, Mark, ed., *The Secret Life of Things: Animals, Objects and It-Narratives in Eighteenth-Century England* (Lewisburg, PA: Bucknell University Press, 2007)

Blair, Ann M., *Too Much to Know: Managing Scholarly Information before the Modern Age* (New Haven: Yale University Press, 2010)

Blewett, David, ed., *Reconsidering the Rise of the Novel, Eighteenth-Century Fiction* 12.2–3 (1999–2000)

Bloom, Harold, *The Anxiety of Influence: A Theory of Poetry* (New York: Oxford University Press, 1973)

Bloomfield, Morton W., 'Quoting and Alluding: Shakespeare in the English Language', in *Shakespeare: Aspects of Influence*, ed. G. B. Evans (Cambridge, Mass.: Harvard University Press, 1976), pp. 1–20

Bond, Richmond P., The Tatler*: The Making of a Literary Journal* (Cambridge, Mass.: Harvard University Press, 1971)

Booth, Wayne C., *The Rhetoric of Fiction* (Chicago: University of Chicago Press, 1961)

Borsay, Peter, 'The Culture of Improvement', in *The Eighteenth Century, 1688–1815*, ed. Paul Langford (Oxford University Press, 2002), pp. 183–210

Botting, Fred, *Gothic* (Abingdon: Routledge, 1996)

Bourdieu, Pierre, *Distinction: A Social Critique of the Judgement of Taste*, trans. Richard Nice (London: Routledge, 1996)

Bray, Joe, *The Epistolary Novel: Representations of Consciousness* (London and New York: Routledge, 2003)

Bree, Linda, *Sarah Fielding* (New York: Twayne, 1996)

Brewer, John, *The Pleasures of the Imagination: English Culture in the Eighteenth Century* (London: HarperCollins, 1997)

Bristol, Michael, *Big-Time Shakespeare* (London and New York: Routledge, 1996)

Brooks-Davies, Douglas, *Fielding, Dickens, Gosse, Iris Murdoch and Oedipal* Hamlet (Basingstoke: Macmillan, 1989)

Brown, Homer Obed, *Institutions of the English Novel: From Defoe to Scott* (Philadelphia, PA: University of Pennsylvania Press, 1997)

Bruster, Douglas, *Quoting Shakespeare: Form and Culture in Early Modern Drama* (Lincoln and London: University of Nebraska Press, 2000)

Burt, Richard, *Unspeakable ShaXXXpeares: Queer Theory and American Kiddie Culture* (New York: St Martin's, 1998)

Calvo, Clara, 'Rewriting Lear's Untender Daughter: Fanny Price as a Regency Cordelia in Jane Austen's *Mansfield Park*', *Shakespeare Survey* 58 (2005): 83–94

Campbell, Jill, 'Fielding's Style', *ELH* 72.2 (2005): 407–28

Natural Masques: Gender and Identity in Fielding's Plays and Novels (Stanford, Calif.: Stanford University Press, 1995)

Carroll, John, 'Richardson at Work: Revisions, Allusions, and Quotations in *Clarissa*', in *Studies in the Eighteenth Century II*, ed. R. F. Brissenden (Canberra: Australian National University Press, 1973), pp. 53–71

Carter, Philip, *Men and the Emergence of Polite Society, Britain 1660-1800* (Harlow: Longman, 2001)

Cash, Arthur H., *Laurence Sterne: The Early and Middle Years* (London: Methuen & Co Ltd, 1975)

Laurence Sterne: The Later Years (London: Routledge, 1992)

Chibka, Robert L., 'The Hobby-Horse's Epitaph: *Tristram Shandy*, *Hamlet*, and the Vehicles of Memory', *Eighteenth-Century Fiction* 3.2 (1991): 125–51

Clery, E. J., *The Rise of Supernatural Fiction, 1762-1800* (Cambridge University Press, 1995)

Cohen, Michèle, *Fashioning Masculinity: National Identity and Language in the Eighteenth Century* (London: Routledge, 1996)

Cohen, Richard, *Literary References and their Effect upon Characterization in the Novels of Samuel Richardson* (Bangor, Me.: Judson College Press, 1970)

Connaughton, Michael E., 'Richardson's Familiar Quotations: *Clarissa* and Bysshe's *Art of English Poetry*', *Philological Quarterly* 60.2 (1981): 183–95

Connely, William, *Laurence Sterne as Yorick* (London: Bodley Head, 1958)

Craig, Steven, 'Shakespeare among the Goths', in *Gothic Shakespeares,* ed. John Drakakis and Dale Townshend (Abingdon: Routledge, 2008), pp. 42–59

Crane, Mary Thomas, *Framing Authority: Sayings, Self, and Society in Sixteenth-Century England* (Princeton University Press, 1993)

Culler, A. Dwight, 'Edward Bysshe and the Poet's Handbook', *PMLA* 63.3 (1948): 858–85

Davidson, Jenny, *Hypocrisy and the Politics of Politeness: Manners and Morals from Locke to Austen* (Cambridge University Press, 2004)

Deelman, Christian, *The Great Shakespeare Jubilee* (London: Michael Joseph, 1964)

De Grazia, Margreta, 'Shakespeare in Quotation Marks', in *The Appropriation of Shakespeare: Post-Renaissance Reconstructions of the Works and the Myth*, ed. Jean I. Marsden (New York: St Martin's Press, 1992), pp. 57–71

Shakespeare Verbatim: The Reproduction of Authenticity and the 1790 Apparatus (Oxford: Clarendon Press, 1991)

Derry, Stephen, 'Jane Austen's Use of *Measure for Measure* in *Sense and Sensibility*', *Persuasions* 15 (1993): 37–46

Desmet, Christy, and Robert Sawyer, eds., *Shakespeare and Appropriation* (London: Routledge, 1999)

Dobson, Michael, *The Making of the National Poet: Shakespeare, Adaptation, and Authorship, 1660–1769* (Oxford: Clarendon Press, 1992)

Doody, Margaret Anne, *A Natural Passion: A Study of the Novels of Samuel Richardson* (Oxford: Clarendon Press, 1974)

The True Story of the Novel (London: Fontana Press, 1998)

'Shakespeare's Novels: Charlotte Lennox Illustrated', *Studies in the Novel* 19.3 (1987): 296–310

and Peter Sabor, eds., *Samuel Richardson: Tercentenary Essays* (Cambridge University Press, 1989)

Drakakis, John and Dale Townshend, eds., *Gothic Shakespeares* (Abingdon: Routledge, 2008)

Dussinger, John A., 'Richardson's Tragic Muse', *Philological Quarterly* 46 (1967): 18–33

Dugas, Don-John and Robert D. Hume, 'The Dissemination of Shakespeare's Plays Circa 1714', *Studies in Bibliography* 56 (2003–2004): 261–79

Eagleton, Terry, *Trouble with Strangers: A Study of Ethics* (Chichester: Wiley-Blackwell, 2009)

Eckerle, Julie A., 'Recent Developments in Early Modern English Life Writing and Romance', *Literature Compass* 5.6 (2008): 1081–96

Eliot, T. S., 'Shakespeare and the Stoicism of Seneca', *Selected Essays* (London: Faber & Faber, 1999)

Ellis, Markman, ed., *Eighteenth-Century Coffee-House Culture*, 4 vols. (London: Pickering & Chatto, 2006)

The Coffee-House: A Cultural History (London: Phoenix, 2004)

England, Martha Winburn, *Garrick's Jubilee* (Columbus, OH: Ohio State University Press, 1964)

'Garrick's Stratford Jubilee: Reactions in France and Germany', *Shakespeare Survey* 9 (1956): 90–100

Ettenhuber, Katrin, *Donne's Augustine: Renaissance Cultures of Interpretation* (Oxford University Press, 2012)

Felperin, Howard, 'Bardolatry Then and Now', in *The Appropriation of Shakespeare*, ed. Marsden, pp. 129–44

Flynn, Carol Houlihan, and Edward Copeland, eds., *Clarissa and her Readers: New Essays for the Clarissa Project* (New York: AMS Press, 1999)

Ford, Susan Allen, 'Reading *Elegant Extracts* in *Emma*: Very Entertaining!', *Persuasions On-Line* 28.1 (2007): unpaginated

Forster, Antonia, *Index to Book Reviews in England, 1749-1774* (Carbondale: Southern Illinois University Press, 1990)

Foucault, Michel, 'What Is an Author?', *in Language, Counter-Memory, Practice*, ed. Donald F. Bouchard, trans. Donald F. Bouchard and Sherry Simon (Ithaca, New York: Cornell University Press, 1977), pp. 124–27

Frank, Marcie, 'Fairy Time from Shakespeare to Scott', in *Shakespeare and the Eighteenth Century*, ed. Peter Sabor and Paul Yachnin (Aldershot: Ashgate, 2008), pp. 103–17

Franklin, Colin, *Shakespeare Domesticated: The Eighteenth-Century Editions* (Aldershot: Scolar Press, 1991)

Freeman, Lisa A., *Character's Theater: Genre and Identity on the Eighteenth-Century English Stage* (Philadelphia: University of Pennsylvania Press, 2002)

Garber, Marjorie, *Shakespeare and Modern Culture* (New York: Pantheon Books, 2008)

Quotation Marks (New York: Routledge, 2003)

Garside, Peter, and Karen O'Brien, eds., *The Oxford History of the Novel in English, Vol. II: English and British Fiction 1750-1820* (Oxford University Press, 2015)

Gay, Penny, *Jane Austen and the Theatre* (Cambridge University Press, 2002)

Genette, Gérard, *Paratexts: Thresholds of Interpretation*, trans. Jane E. Lewin (Cambridge University Press, 1997)

Gerard, W. B., *Laurence Sterne and the Visual Imagination* (Aldershot: Ashgate, 2006)

Golden, Morris, *Fielding's Moral Psychology* (Amherst: University of Massachusetts Press, 1966)

Greenblatt, Stephen, *Shakespeare's Freedom* (Chicago: University of Chicago Press, 2010)

Griffin, Dustin, *Regaining Paradise: Milton and the Eighteenth Century* (Cambridge University Press, 1986)

Gunn, Daniel P., 'Free Indirect Discourse and Narrative Authority in *Emma*', *Narrative* 12 (2004): 35–54

Hale, John K., '*Persuasion*, Vol. IV, Chapter XI', *Persuasions* 16 (1994): 34–5

Harland, Susan, '"Talking" and Reading Shakespeare in Jane Austen's *Mansfield Park*', *Wordsworth Circle*, 39.1/2 (2008): 43–6

Harries, Elizabeth Wanning, *The Unfinished Manner: Essays on the Fragment in the Later Eighteenth Century* (Charlottesville and London: University Press of Virginia, 1994)

Harris, Jocelyn, *Jane Austen's Art of Memory* (Cambridge University Press, 1989)

'Learning and Genius in *Sir Charles Grandison*', in *Studies in the Eighteenth Century IV*, ed. R. F. Brissenden and J. C. Eade (Canberra: Australian National University Press, 1979), pp. 167–98

'Richardson: Original or Learned Genius?' in *Samuel Richardson: Tercentenary Essays*, ed. Doody and Sabor, pp. 188–202

Hawkes, Terence, 'Bardbiz', in *Meaning by Shakespeare* (London and New York: Routledge, 1992), pp. 141–53

Hawley, Judith, 'Shakespearean Sensibilities: Women Writers Reading Shakespeare, 1753–1808', in *Shakespearean Continuities: Essays in Honour of E. A. J. Honigmann*, ed. John Batchelor, Tom Cain and Claire Lamont (Basingstoke: Macmillan, 1997)

'"Hints and Documents" 1: Tristram Shandy's Library', and '"Hints and Documents" 2: A Bibliography for *Tristram Shandy*', *The Shandean* 1.3 (1991): 9–36; 2.4 (1992): 49–65

'Laurence Sterne and the Circle of Sciences: A Study of *Tristram Shandy* and its Relation to Encyclopedias' (University of Oxford: unpublished D.Phil. thesis, 1990)

Hogan, Charles Beecher, *Shakespeare in the Theatre 1701–1800*, i. *A Record of Performances in London 1701–1750*; ii. *London 1751–1800* (Oxford: Clarendon Press, 1952)

Hollander, John, *The Figure of Echo: A Mode of Allusion in Milton and after* (Berkeley and Los Angeles: University of California Press, 1984)

Holquist, Michael, ed., *The Dialogic Imagination: Four Essays by M. M. Bakhtin*, trans. Caryl Emerson and Michael Holquist (Austin: University of Texas Press, 1981)

Honan, Park, *Jane Austen: Her Life* (London: Weidenfeld & Nicolson, 1987)

Howard, Jacqueline, *Reading Gothic Fiction: A Bakhtinian Approach* (Oxford: Clarendon Press, 1994)

Howells, Coral Ann, *Love, Mystery and Misery: Feeling in Gothic Fiction* (London: Bloomsbury, 2013)

Hudson, Nicholas, 'Social Rank, "The Rise of the Novel," and Whig Histories of Eighteenth-Century Fiction', *Eighteenth-Century Fiction* 17.4 (2005): 563–98

Hume, Robert D., 'The Value of Money: Incomes, Prices, Buying Power—and Some Problems in Cultural Economics', *Huntington Library Quarterly* 77.4 (2014): 373–416

'The Aims and Limits of Historical Scholarship', *The Review of English Studies* 53.211 (2002): 399–422

Reconstructing Contexts: The Aims and Principles of Archaeo-Historicism (Oxford: Clarendon Press, 1999)

'Before the Bard: "Shakespeare" in Early Eighteenth-Century London', *ELH* 64.1 (1997): 41-75

Henry Fielding and the London Theatre, 1728–1737 (Oxford: Clarendon Press, 1988)

The London Theatre World, 1600–1800 (Carbondale: Southern Illinois University Press, 1980)

Hunter, J. Paul, *Before Novels: The Cultural Contexts of Eighteenth-Century Fiction* (New York: Norton, 1990)

'The Novel and Social/Cultural History', in *The Cambridge Companion to the Eighteenth-Century Novel*, ed. John J. Richetti (Cambridge University Press, 1996), pp. 9–40
The Reluctant Pilgrim: Defoe's Emblem Method and the Quest for Form in Robinson Crusoe (Baltimore: Johns Hopkins University Press, 1966)
'The World as Stage and Closet', in *British Theatre and the Other Arts, 1660–1800*, ed. Shirley Strum Kenny (London and Toronto: Associated University Presses, 1984), pp. 271–87
Iser, Wolfgang, *The Implied Reader: Patterns of Communication in Prose Fiction from Bunyan to Beckett* (Baltimore: Johns Hopkins University Press, 1978)
Italia, Iona, *The Rise of Literary Journalism in the Eighteenth Century: Anxious Employment* (Abingdon: Routledge, 2005)
Jarvis, Simon, *Scholars and Gentlemen: Shakespearian Textual Criticism and Representations of Scholarly Labour* (Oxford: Clarendon Press, 1996)
Jefferson, D. W., '*Tristram Shandy* and the Tradition of Learned Wit', *Essays in Criticism* 1 (1951): 225–48
Jones, Vivien, 'Jane Austen's Domestic Realism', in *The Oxford History of the Novel in English, Vol. II*, ed. Garside and O'Brien, pp. 273–95
Kellett, E. E., *Literary Quotation and Allusion* (Cambridge: W. Heffer & Sons, 1933)
Kenny, Shirley Strum, ed., *British Theatre and the Other Arts, 1660–1800* (London and Toronto: Associated University Presses, 1984)
Keymer, Tom, *Richardson's* Clarissa *and the Eighteenth-Century Reader* (Cambridge University Press, 1992)
Sterne, the Moderns, and the Novel (Oxford University Press, 2002)
and Peter Sabor, Pamela *in the Marketplace: Literary Controversy and Print Culture in Eighteenth-Century Britain and Ireland* (Cambridge University Press, 2005)
Kilgour, Maggie, *The Rise of the Gothic Novel* (London: Routledge, 1995)
Kinkead-Weekes, Mark, *Samuel Richardson: Dramatic Novelist* (London: Methuen & Co. Ltd., 1973)
Klein, Lawrence E., *Shaftesbury and the Culture of Politeness: Moral Discourse and Cultural Politics in Early Eighteenth-Century England* (Cambridge University Press, 1994)
Knight, Jeffrey Todd, *Bound to Read: Compilations, Collections, and the Making of Renaissance Literature* (Philadelphia, PA: University of Pennsylvania Press, 2013)
Konigsberg, Ira, *Narrative Technique in the English Novel: Defoe to Austen* (Hamden, Connecticut: Archon Books, 1985)
Samuel Richardson and the Dramatic Novel (Lexington: University of Kentucky Press, 1968)
Kraft, Elizabeth, *Character and Consciousness in Eighteenth-Century Comic Fiction* (University of Georgia Press, 1992)

Kramnick, Jonathan Brody, *Making the English Canon: Print-Capitalism and the Cultural Past, 1700–1770* (Cambridge University Press, 1998)

'Reading Shakespeare's Novels: Literary History and Cultural Politics in the Lennox-Johnson Debate', *Modern Language Quarterly* 55.4 (1994): 429–53

Kristeva, Julia, 'Word, Dialogue, Novel', in *Desire in Language: A Semiotic Approach to Literature and Art*, ed. Leon S. Roudiez, trans. Thomas Gora, Alice Jardine and Leon S. Roudiez (New York: Columbia University Press, 1980)

Kucich, John and Jenny Bourne Taylor, eds., *The Oxford History of the Novel in English: Vol. III: The Nineteenth-Century Novel, 1820-1880* (Oxford University Press, 2012)

Lamb, Jonathan, *Sterne's Fiction and the Double Principle* (Cambridge University Press, 1989)

'Sterne's System of Imitation', *The Modern Language Review* 76.4 (1981): 794–810

Langford, Paul, 'The Uses of Eighteenth-Century Politeness', *Transactions of the Royal Historical Society* 12 (2002): 311–31

A Polite and Commercial People: England 1727–1783 (Oxford: Clarendon Press, 1989, 1998)

Lanier, Douglas, *Shakespeare and Modern Popular Culture* (Oxford University Press, 2002)

Lechner, Joan Marie, *Renaissance Concepts of the Commonplaces* (Westport, Conn.: Greenwood Press, 1962)

Leveson, Marcia, 'Comedy and Courtship: *Much Ado About Nothing* and *Pride and Prejudice*', *Johannesburg Shakespeare Quarterly* 1.2 (1994): 15–27

Lindboe, Berit R., '"O *Shakespear*, Had I thy Pen!": Fielding's Use of Shakespeare in *Tom Jones*', *Studies in the Novel* 14.4 (1982): 303–14

Lynch, Deidre Shauna, *The Economy of Character: Novels, Market Culture, and the Business of Inner Meaning* (Chicago: University of Chicago Press, 1998)

Lynch, Jack, *Becoming Shakespeare: the Unlikely Afterlife that Turned a Provincial Playwright into the Bard* (New York: Walker, 2007)

The Age of Elizabeth in the Age of Johnson (Cambridge University Press, 2003)

Mace, Nancy A., *Henry Fielding's Novels and the Classical Tradition* (Newark: University of Delaware Press; London: Associated University Presses, 1996)

MacKenzie, Scott R., 'Homunculus Economicus: Laurence Sterne's Labour Theory of Literary Value', *Eighteenth-Century Fiction* 18.1 (2005), 49–66

Mackie, Erin, *Market à la Mode: Fashion, Commodity and Gender in* The Tatler *and* The Spectator (Baltimore: Johns Hopkins University Press, 1997)

von Maltzahn, Nick, 'The Whig Milton, 1667–1700', in *Milton and Republicanism*, ed. David Armitage, Armand Himy and Quentin Skinner (Cambridge University Press, 1995)

Marsden, Jean I., ed., *The Appropriation of Shakespeare: Post-Renaissance Reconstructions of the Works and the Myth* (Hemel Hempstead: Harvester Wheatsheaf, 1991)

The Re-imagined Text: Shakespeare, Adaptation, and Eighteenth-Century Literary Theory (Lexington: The University Press of Kentucky, 1995)

Marshall, Gail, 'Shakespeare and Fiction', in *Shakespeare in the Nineteenth Century*, ed. Gail Marshall (Cambridge University Press, 2012), pp. 96–112

ed., *Shakespeare in the Nineteenth Century* (Cambridge University Press, 2012)

Marshall, Gail, and Adrian Poole, eds., *Victorian Shakespeare*, 2 vols. (Basingstoke: Palgrave Macmillan, 2003)

Matthews, William, 'Polite Speech in the Eighteenth Century', *English* 1 (1937): 493–511

Maxwell, Julie, 'How the Renaissance (Mis)Used Sources: The Art of Misquotation', in *How to Do Things with Shakespeare: New Approaches, New Essays,* ed. Laurie Maguire (Malden, MA: Blackwell Publishing, 2008), pp. 54–76

'The Part of Allusion: Religious Controversy on the English Renaissance Stage' (University of Oxford: unpublished D.Phil. thesis, 2004)

McKeon, Michael, *The Origins of the English Novel, 1600–1740* (Baltimore: Johns Hopkins University Press, 1987)

McKillop, Alan Dugald, *The Early Masters of English Fiction* (Laurence, Kansas: University of Kansas Press, 1956)

Samuel Richardson: Printer and Novelist (Hamden, Conn.: Shoe String Press, 1960)

McLaverty, James, *Pope, Print and Meaning* (Oxford University Press, 2001)

Meyer, Herman, *The Poetics of Quotation in the European Novel*, trans. Theodore and Yetta Ziolkowski (Princeton University Press, 1968)

Miller, Henry Knight, *Essays on Fielding's* Miscellanies*: A Commentary on Volume One* (Princeton University Press, 1961)

'The Voices of Henry Fielding: Style in *Tom Jones*', in *The Augustan Milieu: Essays Presented to Louis A. Landa*, ed. Henry Knight Miller, Eric Rothstein and G. S. Rousseau (Oxford: Clarendon Press, 1970), pp. 262–88

Molekamp, Femke, *Women and the Bible in Early Modern England: Religious Reading and Writing* (Oxford University Press, 2013)

Monkman, Kenneth, 'Sterne, Hamlet, and Yorick: Some New Material', in *The Winged Skull: Papers from the Laurence Sterne Bicentenary Conference*, ed. Arthur H. Cash and John M. Stedmond (London: Methuen & Co. Ltd., 1971), pp. 112–23

Morawski, Stefan, 'The Basic Functions of Quotation', in *Sign, Language, Culture*, ed. A. J. Greimas and R. Jakobson (The Hague and Paris: Mouton, 1970)

Moses, Carole, 'Jane Austen and Elizabeth Bennet: The Limits of Irony', *Persuasions* 25 (2003): 155–64

Moss, Ann, *Printed Commonplace-Books and the Structuring of Renaissance Thought* (Oxford: Clarendon Press, 1996)

Mullan, John, *Sentiment and Sociability: The Language of Feeling in the Eighteenth Century* (Oxford: Clarendon Press, 1988)

Murphy, Andrew, *Shakespeare for the People: Working-Class Readers, 1800-1900* (Cambridge University Press, 2008)

Shakespeare in Print: A History and Chronology of Shakespeare Publishing (Cambridge University Press, 2003)

Myer, Valerie Grosvenor, '"Well Read in Shakespeare"', in *Samuel Richardson: Passion and Prudence*, ed. Valerie Grosvenor Myer (London: Vision, 1986), pp. 126–32

Nachumi, Nora, *Acting Like a Lady: British Women Novelists and the Eighteenth-Century Theater* (New York: AMS Press, Inc., 2008)

Narveson, Kate, *Bible Readers and Lay Writers in Early Modern England: Gender and Self-Definition in an Emergent Writing Culture* (Farnham: Ashgate, 2012)

Noggle, James, *The Temporality of Taste in Eighteenth-Century British Writing* (Oxford University Press, 2012)

Norton, Rictor, 'Ann Radcliffe, "The Shakespeare of Romance Writers"', in *Shakespearean Gothic*, ed. Christy Desmet and Anne Williams (Cardiff: University of Wales Press, 2009), pp. 37–59

Novy, Marianne L., *Women's Re-visions of Shakespeare: On the Responses of Dickinson, Woolf, Rich, H.D., George Eliot, and Others* (Urbana: University of Illinois Press, 1990)

Noyes, Robert Gale, *The Thespian Mirror: Shakespeare in the Eighteenth-Century Novel* (Providence, RI: Brown University, 1953)

Ortiz, Joseph M., ed., *Shakespeare and the Culture of Romanticism* (Farnham: Ashgate, 2013)

Page, Norman, *The Language of Jane Austen* (Abingdon: Routledge, 1972, 2001)

Parrinder, Patrick, *Nation and Novel: The English Novel from its Origins to the Present Day* (Oxford University Press, 2006)

Pascal, Roy, *The Dual Voice: Free Indirect Speech and its Functioning in the Nineteenth-Century European Novel* (Manchester University Press, 1977)

Paulson, Ronald, *The Life of Henry Fielding: A Critical Biography* (Oxford: Blackwell Publishers, 2000)

Pierce, John B., 'Pamela's Textual Authority', in *Passion and Virtue: Essays on the Novels of Samuel Richardson*, ed. David Blewitt (Toronto: University of Toronto Press, 2001), pp. 8–26

Pollack-Pelzner, Daniel, 'Dickens and Shakespeare's Household Words', *ELH* 78.3 (2011): 533–56

'Jane Austen, the Prose Shakespeare', *Studies in English Literature, 1500-1900* 53.4 (2013): 763–92

Poole, Adrian, ed., *Great Shakespeareans, Vol V: Scott, Dickens, Eliot, Hardy* (London: Continuum, 2011)

Victorian Shakespeare: Volume 2: Literature and Culture (Basingstoke: Palgrave Macmillan, 2003)

Preston, John, *The Created Self: The Reader's Role in Eighteenth-Century Fiction* (London: Heinemann, 1970)

Price, Leah, *The Anthology and the Rise of the Novel: From Richardson to George Eliot* (Cambridge University Press, 2000)
Pucci, Joseph, *The Full-Knowing Reader: Allusion and the Power of the Reader in the Western Literary Tradition* (New Haven: Yale University Press, 1998)
Raven, James, 'Production', in *The Oxford History of the Novel in English, Vol. II*, ed. Garside and O'Brien, pp. 3–28
Reid, Christopher, '"Community of Mind": Quotation and Persuasion in the Eighteenth-Century House of Commons', *The Age of Johnson* 17 (2006): 317–40
Ribble, Frederick G., and Anne G. Ribble, *Fielding's Library: An Annotated Catalogue* (Charlottesville: The Bibliographical Society of the University of Virginia, 1996)
Richetti, John J., *The Cambridge Companion to the Eighteenth-Century Novel* (Cambridge University Press, 1996)
Popular Fiction before Richardson: Narrative Patterns 1700–1739 (Oxford University Press, 1969, 1992)
'Richardson's Dramatic Art in *Clarissa*', in *British Theatre and the Other Arts, 1660–1800*, ed. Kenny, pp. 288–308
Ricks, Christopher, *Allusion to the Poets* (Oxford University Press, 2002)
Ritchie, Fiona, *Women and Shakespeare in the Eighteenth Century* (Cambridge University Press, 2014)
and Peter Sabor, eds., *Shakespeare in the Eighteenth Century* (Cambridge University Press, 2012)
Rivero, Albert, *The Plays of Henry Fielding: A Critical Study of his Dramatic Career* (Charlottesville: University Press of Virginia, 1989)
Roach, Joseph, *The Player's Passion: Studies in the Science of Acting* (Cranbury, NJ: Associated University Presses, 1985)
Roberts, Sasha, 'Reading Shakespeare's Tragedies of Love: *Romeo and Juliet*, *Othello*, and *Antony and Cleopatra* in Early Modern England', in *A Companion to Shakespeare's Works*, Vol I: *The Tragedies*, ed. Richard Dutton and Jean E. Howard (Malden, MA: Blackwell Publishing, 2003), pp. 108–33
Rogers, Deborah D., ed., *The Critical Response to Ann Radcliffe* (Westport, CT: Greenwood Press, 1994)
Rogers, Pat, 'Tristram Shandy's Polite Conversation', *Essays in Criticism* 32 (1982): 305–20
Rumbold, Kate, 'The Stratford Jubilee', in *Shakespeare in the Eighteenth Century*, ed. Ritchie and Sabor, pp. 254–76
'"So Common-Hackneyed in the Eyes of Men": Banal Shakespeare and the Eighteenth-Century Novel', *Literature Compass* 4.3 (May 2007): 610–21
Sabor, Peter, 'Richardson, Henry Fielding, and Sarah Fielding', in *The Cambridge Companion to English Literature 1740–1830*, ed. Tom Keymer and Jon Mee (Cambridge University Press, 2004), pp. 139–56

and Paul Yachnin, eds., *Shakespeare and the Eighteenth Century* (Aldershot: Ashgate, 2008)

Salter, David, '"This Demon in the Garb of a Monk": Shakespeare, the Gothic and the Discourse of Anti-Catholicism', *Shakespeare* 5.1 (2009): 52–67

Sanders, Julie, *Adaptation and Appropriation* (Abingdon: Routledge, 2006)

Novel Shakespeares: Twentieth-Century Women Novelists and Appropriation (Manchester University Press, 2001)

Santor, Gefen Bar-On, 'Looking for "Newtonian" Laws in Shakespeare: the Mystifying Case of the Character of Hamlet', in *Shakespeare and the Eighteenth Century*, ed. Sabor and Yachnin, pp. 151–64

'The Culture of Newtonianism and Shakespeare's Editors: From Pope to Johnson', *Eighteenth-Century Fiction* 21.4 (2009): 593–614

Schellenberg, Betty, *The Professionalization of Women Writers in Eighteenth-Century Britain* (Cambridge University Press, 2005)

Scofield, Martin, 'Shakespeare and *Clarissa*: "General Nature", Genre and Sexuality', *Shakespeare Survey* 51 (1998): 27–43

Seary, Peter, *Lewis Theobald and the Editing of Shakespeare* (Oxford: Clarendon Press, 1990)

Selwyn, David, *Jane Austen and Leisure* (London: The Hambledon Press, 1999)

Sherbo, Arthur, 'Some Not-So-Hidden Allusions in *Tristram Shandy*' in *Studies in the Eighteenth Century English Novel* (East Lansing: Michigan State University Press, 1969), pp. 128–35

Singer, Godfrey Frank, *The Epistolary Novel: Its Origin, Development, Decline, and Residuary Influence* (Philadelphia: University of Pennsylvania Press, 1933)

Siskin, Clifford, *The Work of Writing: Literature and Social Change in Britain, 1700-1830* (Baltimore: Johns Hopkins University Press, 1998)

Smith, David Nichol, *Shakespeare in the Eighteenth Century* (Oxford: Clarendon Press, 1928)

Smith, Margaret M. and Alexander Lindsay, *Index of English Literary Manuscripts, iii. 1700–1800* (London: Mansell, 1992)

Smyth, Orla, 'Books Within Books: What Did Clarissa Harlowe Read? A Note on the History of Reading Practices', *Bulletin de la Société d'Études Anglo-Américaines des XVIIe et XVIIIe Siècles* 48 (1999): 103–21

Spacks, Patricia Meyer, *Novel Beginnings: Experiments in Eighteenth-Century Fiction* (New Haven, CT: Yale University Press, 2006)

Imagining a Self: Autobiography and Novel in Eighteenth-Century England (Cambridge, MA: Harvard University Press, 1976)

Spender, Dale, ed., *Living by the Pen: Early British Women Writers* (New York: Teacher's College Press, 1992)

St Clair, William, *The Reading Nation in the Romantic Period* (Cambridge University Press, 2004)

Starr, G. A., *Defoe and Spiritual Autobiography* (Princeton University Press, 1965)

Starr, G. Gabrielle, *Lyric Generations: Poetry and the Novel in the Long Eighteenth Century* (Baltimore: Johns Hopkins University Press, 2004)

Stedmond, John M., *The Comic Art of Laurence Sterne: Convention and Innovation in* Tristram Shandy *and* A Sentimental Journey (Toronto: University of Toronto Press, 1967)

Stone Jr., George Winchester, 'Shakespeare in the Periodicals, 1700–1740: A Study of the Growth of a Knowledge of the Dramatist in the Eighteenth Century' (2 parts), *Shakespeare Quarterly* 2 (1951): 212–31, and 3 (1952): 313–28

Tadié, Alexis, *Sterne's Whimsical Theatres of Language: Orality, Gesture, Literacy* (Aldershot: Ashgate, 2003)

Taylor, Gary, *Reinventing Shakespeare: A Cultural History from the Restoration to the Present* (London: The Hogarth Press, 1990)

Taylor, Megan, 'Jane Austen and "Banal Shakespeare"', *Eighteenth-Century Fiction* 27.1 (2014): 105–25

Thompson, Ann, and Sasha Roberts, eds., *Women Reading Shakespeare 1660–1900: An Anthology of Criticism* (Manchester University Press, 1997)

Todd, Janet, *The Sign of Angellica: Women, Writing and Fiction, 1660-1800* (London: Virago Press, 1989)

Sensibility: An Introduction (London and New York: Methuen, 1986)

Townshend, Dale, 'Gothic and the Ghost of *Hamlet*', in *Gothic Shakespeares,* ed. Drakakis and Townshend, pp. 60–97

Trickett, Rachel, 'Dryden's Part in *Clarissa*', in *Clarissa and her Readers*, ed. Flynn and Copeland, pp. 175–87

Trilling, Lionel, *Sincerity and Authenticity* (London: Oxford University Press, 1972)

Tweg, Sue, 'Readers, Audiences, Players and *The Beauties of Shakespeare*', in *Shakespeare: Readers, Audiences, Players,* ed. R. S. White, Charles Edelman and Christopher Wortham (Nedlands: University of Western Australia Press, 1998), pp. 29–46

Urda, Kathleen E., 'Going from Extremes: *Mansfield Park* as a Revision of *Clarissa*', *Persuasions On-Line* 30.1 (2009), unpaginated

Wahrman, Dror, *The Making of the Modern Self: Identity and Culture in Eighteenth-Century England* (New Haven: Yale University Press, 2004)

Walsh, Marcus, *Shakespeare, Milton and Eighteenth-Century Literary Editing: The Beginnings of Interpretative Scholarship* (Cambridge University Press, 1997)

Warner, William Beatty, *Licensing Entertainment: The Elevation of Novel Reading in Britain, 1684–1750* (Berkeley: University of California Press, 1998)

Wasserman, Earl R., 'Shakespeare and the English Romantic Movement', in *The Persistence of Shakespeare Idolatry: Essays in Honor of Robert W. Babcock,* ed. Herbert M. Schueller (Detroit: Wayne State University Press, 1964), pp. 77–103

Watt, Ian, *The Rise of the Novel: Studies in Defoe, Richardson and Fielding* (London: Chatto and Windus, 1974 [1957])

Watt, James, *Contesting the Gothic: Fiction, Genre and Cultural Conflict, 1764-1832* (Cambridge University Press, 1999)

Wehrs, Donald R., 'Sterne, Cervantes, Montaigne: Fideistic Skepticism and the Rhetoric of Desire', in *Comparative Literature Studies* 25.2 (1988): 127–51

Weimann, Robert and Douglas Bruster, *Shakespeare and the Power of Performance: Stage and Page in the Elizabethan Theatre* (Cambridge University Press, 2008)

Williams, Anne, 'Reading Walpole Reading Shakespeare', in *Shakespearean Gothic,* ed. Christy Desmet and Anne Williams (Cardiff: University of Wales Press, 2009), pp. 13–36

Williams, Bernard, *Truth and Truthfulness: An Essay in Genealogy* (Princeton University Press, 2002)

Williams, Raymond, *Keywords: A Vocabulary of Culture and Society* (London: Flamingo, 1976, 1981)

Wood, James, *How Fiction Works* (London: Vintage Books, 2009)

Wood, Michael, 'Time and her Aunt', in *A Companion to Jane Austen*, ed. Claudia L. Johnson and Clara Tuite (Malden, MA: Blackwell Publishing, 2012), pp. 195–205

Wright, Angela, 'In Search of Arden: Ann Radcliffe's William Shakespeare', in *Gothic Shakespeares*, ed. Drakakis and Townshend, pp. 111–30

Yachnin, Paul and Myrna Wyatt Selkirk, 'Metatheater and the Performance of Character in *The Winter's Tale*', in *Shakespeare and Character: Theory, History, Performance, and Theatrical Persons,* ed. Paul Yachnin and Jessica Slights (Basingstoke: Palgrave Macmillan, 2009)

Zimmerman, Everett, '*Tristram Shandy* and Narrative Representation', *The Eighteenth Century* 28.2 (1987): 127–47

Index

Lightning Source UK Ltd.
Milton Keynes UK
UKHW020920250819
348529UK00019B/272/P

9 781107 584891